INTERNATIONAL RETAILING

Nicholas Alexander

First published 1997

2 4 6 8 10 9 7 5 3 1

Blackwell Publishers Ltd
108 Cowley Road
Oxford OX4 1JF
UK

Blackwell Publishers Inc.
350 Main Street
Malden, MA 02148
USA

British Library Cataloguing in Publication Data

A CIP catalogue record for this book is available from the British Library.

Library of Congress Cataloging in Publication Data
Alexander, Nicholas, 1962–
    International retailing/Nicholas Alexander.
      p. cm.
    Includes bibliographical references and index.
    ISBN 0-631-19722-2 (alk. paper)
    1. Retail trade.   2. International trade.   I. Title.
  HF5429.A55   1997
  382 – dc20   96-41659
                                    CIP

ISBN 0-631-197222

Commissioning Editor: Catriona King
Development Editor: Clare Fisher
Desk Editor: Linda Auld
Production Manager/Controller: Lisa Parker
Text Designer: Lisa Parker

Typeset in 10 on 12 pt Caslon
by Best-set Typesetter Ltd., Hong Kong
Printed in Great Britain by T.J. International, Padstow, Cornwall

This book is printed on acid-free paper

Brief Contents

Contents

Tables

Figures

Exhibits

Boxed Illustrations

About This Book

PHILOSOPHY BEHIND THE BOOK

This book has been written specifically with the final year student of retail management or marketing studies in mind. It is also appropriate to final year students completing dissertations on international retailing and students beginning higher degrees where an initial reading in international retailing is required. The contents of the book, while chosen to provide as interesting a discussion as possible, also maintain a rigorous approach toward the subject area.

The approach taken by this book is one which assumes that final year students are capable of understanding and addressing the complexities, ironies, inconsistencies and idiosyncrasies of international business and that students welcome the opportunity to apply intelligent and critical thought.

This book is offered for those students who wish to engage with the issues which international retailing raises, and for those academics seeking a text for a final year course on international retailing.

Essentially, the philosophy of this book is that the so-called answers to questions are only the precursors to other questions.

STRUCTURE OF THE BOOK

Part I introduces the main topics to be discussed in the text. The three chapters in this section provide a conceptual framework for the other sections of the book. This part may be read in isolation by students on other courses in international business who require a relatively brief introduction to issues and aspects of international retail activity. For the student of international retailing, it provides the foundations of further knowledge.

Chapter 1 provides a review of the literature and the main themes which have emerged in the study of internationalization in recent years. The chapter provides a comprehensive list of references for students who wish to develop a fuller understanding of the literature and its development.

Chapter 2 discusses the problems of definition which surround the issue of international retailing and hence what internationalization involves. The chapter thereby provides a framework for the further consideration of international boundaries which is developed in part IV.

Chapter 3 describes various classification systems which may be used to analyse the international retail environment. The systems discussed raise important issues associated with the internationalization process thereby providing a framework in which other aspects of international may be set. The chapter provides a basis upon which further conceptualizations are discussed later.

Part II brings together the themes discussed in other parts to provide a discussion of retailing from the national to the global level. This part focuses on the dynamic of change and process within internationalization.

Chapter 4 addresses the issue of channel development within the national and trans-national context. It also considers the transfer of retail innovation across national boundaries through direct and indirect means.

Chapter 5 chronologically considers the development of modern international retail activity and places institutional and corporate development within that context.

Part III considers the theoretical context in which international retailing should be considered. This part includes a consideration of trade theory, retail development theories and the motivational structure of international retail development.

Chapter 6 describes and discusses trade theory and retail development theory. It covers a wide academic area and must therefore be considered an introduction to the concepts considered rather than a full presentation of them. An appreciation of the wider theoretical material is important to an understanding of international retail development.

Chapter 7 considers the reasons behind the development of international retail operations and the motivations which stimulate the process of internationalization. Again, as in chapter 6, a theoretical approach is taken. Frameworks into which different retailer responses to the internationalization process may be placed are described and discussed.

Part IV is concerned with patterns of international expansion and those factors which determine market choice. Retailers are constrained by a complex interplay of market and organizational factors; this part considers these factors in some depth.

Chapter 8 places the other chapters in part IV in context. Patterns of international expansion are described and discussed. Determining factors behind patterns of international retail development are identified.

Chapter 9 considers political environments and the means by which they may be assessed as a market opportunity. Consideration is given to the regulatory issues which retailers face in different markets around the world.

Chapter 10 considers the economic trading environment in which retailers operate. It considers international retailers' place within that environment. The importance of the economic conditions within which retailers choose to operate is considered along with those factors which create such environments.

Chapter 11 is concerned with the social environment in which retailers operate. It is concerned with those issues which are the context for shopper behaviour and purchasing patterns and those characteristics of the market which contribute to the social context in which retailers recruit their workforce.

Chapter 12 considers the issue of culture. It does not attempt to didactically characterize or define elements of culture, but rather to raise questions. The most important attribute with which any international marketer should be equipped is the ability to keep asking questions and learning.

Chapter 13 considers retail structure. The retail structure which exists in any market is the product of regulation, economic activity, society and culture within that market. It is also a reflection of retailers' indigenous ability to create competitive retail forms. Retail structures vary considerably both within and between markets.

Part V considers various operational aspects of the internationalization process.

Chapter 14 addresses issues raised by the different growth strategies used by international retail operations. Methods of market entry are described and discussed. Retailers use a wide variety of entry methods in the international environment, some are better suited than others to specific market objectives.

Chapter 15 addresses the issue of marketing in the international retail environment. Retailers who internationalize their operation may have to address issues they have not fully explored with respect to their domestic operation. Positioning a retail operation in a new market may prove to be a particularly daunting organizational experience.

Part VI is the concluding part.

Chapter 16 provides some concluding remarks on retail internationalization and looks to the future of international retailing.

DEDICATION

This book is dedicated to:
   Myfanwy, Myfanwy, Eleanor, Amelia, Lucia and, of course, Henrietta.

Acknowledgements

No matter how much work an author puts into a book, a book will not happen unless there is someone prepared to liaise with the author on behalf of the publisher. Therefore, I would like to thank Clare Fisher for her invaluable support.

There are many individuals who influence an author during the writing of a book; however, there are clearly a few who either provide inspiration, moral support, a listening ear, practical suggestions or simply the right word at the right moment. Sometimes the support provides the basis on which future activity occurs and sometimes it is detailed consideration of a statement or objective. I will refrain from attributing specific types of support to individuals because to mention one type of support would tend to understate rather than fully express my gratitude. Instead, I would simply like to thank those members of my family, close colleagues and close friends who have provided one, some or all of the above, for their invaluable contribution. I hope I shall soon find myself in a position to offer similar support.

I would also like to express my sincere gratitude to those reviewers who provided extremely useful comments. I would like to thank those who recommended changes should be made, but especially those who suggested that the changes once made should be changed back again.

Also, I would like to thank my students at the University of Edinburgh, the University of Surrey and the University of Ulster for their responses to this material over the years.

Finally, I am responsible for any errors and all imperfections.

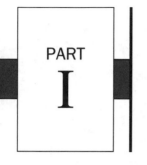

PART

I

Introduction: The Concept of International Retailing

Introduction

▌ OBJECTIVES ▌

This chapter considers the development of international retailing as a subject area and delineates the important issues which have defined, and are defining, this area of study. Research material referred to in the text provides students with an opportunity for further reading and to develop their studies to the advanced level of their choice. It also provides an initial discussion of issues which are considered later in the book.

INTRODUCTION

International retail operations are fundamentally changing the methods by which consumer goods are distributed and marketed globally. Retail operations have been traditionally perceived as localized operations, with limited market power and limited managerial skills and sophistication. In the past, this has been a valid perception as far as most retailers and most markets were concerned. Small retail operations with limited horizons have been the outlets for goods produced by large manufacturing organizations with national or international markets. Consequently, these large suppliers have dominated national marketing and international marketing efforts within the distribution channel, so that retailers, for the most part, have merely acted as the conduits through which goods reached the market.

The emerging channel power of large retail operations has been altering this situation for some time, but the relative market power, international presence, and strong brand identification of large suppliers has often overshadowed the growing influence of large retail operations. On the national level, and in those economies around the world which have been able to support the growth of large retail operations, individual retail organizations such as Sears Roebuck in the US, Coles Myer in Australia, Marks & Spencer in the UK, have exerted considerable power within the distribution channel for decades. These organizations have built an impressive market presence which has enabled them to control and manage the distribution function of which they have been a part. As distribution systems have developed within advanced economies, these organizations have been joined by other organizations who have also built a significant share of the national market. Such organizations, through the market concentration which they have created by virtue of their operational growth, have shifted the balance of channel power from the supplier to the retailer.

The increased size of retail operations has stimulated and supported international expansion. Revenue earned within the domestic market has been invested in operations in new markets in an attempt to sustain financial growth targets. Large organizations, faced with limited opportunities domestically, have sought expansion in non-domestic markets. An important part of the logic of international retail development has been the pressures exerted by restrictions within the domestic market. However, growth has also been achieved through the development of sophisticated operations within the context of a developed economy and retail structure. The growth of large retail organizations has stimulated functional development within the organizational structure. Large retailers have been able to develop specialized managerial functions. For example, the formalized marketing function developed relatively late within the retail sector. In turn, this has allowed retailers to consider expansion outside the national market. However, this general development of the retail structure and the market oriented role which retailers have adopted has also facilitated the growth of international retail operations, who are not so much forced out into the international arena but pulled into other markets through the international relevance of the product and service which they offer. Internationally, organizations such as Benetton and The Body Shop have projected distinct images to customers who respond to that message as much as they would to manufacturer brand names such as Coca-Cola and Sony.

International retailing for many retailers is no longer a regrettable logic precipitated by limited growth potential domestically, but an opportunity to expand their operating base into markets where their products will be valued by a hitherto unreached customer base.

CONCEPTUAL DEVELOPMENTS

Before the issues raised above may be considered in further detail, it is necessary to establish the course of development of international retail studies in order to understand the way in which certain issues have been addressed. Changes in the international retail environment have had, and continue to have, an impact on academic perceptions and understanding. International retailing is a subject area which has attracted considerable attention in recent years. It is important to remember that many of the concepts put forward today will be challenged in future years as a greater understanding of the retail internationalization process is achieved. Therefore, this chapter considers the development of international retailing as a subject area and delineates the important issues which have defined and are defining this area of study. It also provides an initial discussion of various issues which are considered later in the book.

Comparatively recent developments in international retail activity (those of the last ten to twenty years) have led to a dramatic increase in the number of publications on international retail activity. Recent interest in international retailing has mirrored the most recent wave of international retail activity. In the 1980s and 1990s, the literature on international retailing grew considerably. Conference papers and journal articles began to describe and define the nature of international activity in the light of new initiatives by retailers based in markets with developed retail structures. The activities of European retailers in Europe and North America in particular encouraged consideration of this interesting phenomenon. The literature published before the mid-1980s was comparatively limited, although the literature of this earlier period should not be dismissed as unimportant. The early literature has had a major influence on more recent research activity, defining the research directions and structuring intellectual perceptions.

A litany of international retail examples remains nothing more than a set of isolated facts unless a cognitive structure is first established. Before a full understanding of international retailing may be achieved, it is necessary to understand how the subject area has developed, the influences which have acted upon its development which, in turn, have focused research efforts. Only then is it possible to understand the nature of various questions which remain to be fully answered and to understand the significance of individual company examples within the context of the interpretive structures which have been adopted.

AMERICAN PERSPECTIVE

Texts such as Hollander's (1970), Waldman's (1978), and Kacker's (1985) have helped define international retailing as a subject area. These texts are evidence of how thinking has evolved in the area of international retailing, but they also show how earlier interpretations retain a validity and how important they were in identifying fundamental issues. Hollander's (1970) work, in particular, continues to impress new generations of students. Its lucid style and rigorous approach, ensures that it remains an important milestone in the development of international retail studies and it is a reminder of the breadth of issues which are involved in the internationalization process.

Hollander, Kacker and Waldman wrote and carried out their research within the US University environment and from the perspective of the US commercial context, as indeed did many of the early writers on this subject.[1] Therefore, the early literature is heavily influenced by US ideas, perspectives and concerns. There were two main reasons for this.

- US retailers were amongst the earliest retailers to establish large international retail operations.

- Heavy investment in US retailing by European companies in the late 1970s attracted interest and comment.

Woolworths and Sears Roebuck are two early examples of US retailers who have had an important impact on markets outside the US (Fritsch, 1962; Truitt, 1984; Wood and Keyser, 1953; Woolworth, 1954). Woolworths undertook operations in the Canadian market in 1897, in the UK by the end of 1909, and Germany by the end of 1926 (Woolworth, 1954). Woolworth was to become a household name around the world in the first half of the twentieth century. 'Woolies' represented an early example of the potency of the large retail operation's ability to achieve an important role in the distribution of goods in a society where the consumption of manufactured goods was increasing rapidly. While Woolworth was to achieve a particularly wide geographical development, other US retailers were to have a major impact on distribution structures in the countries which they entered as trading operations. In the 1940s, Sears Roebuck began operating in less developed markets contiguous to the US: Cuba in 1942 and Mexico in 1947 (Sun, 1992). In these markets, Sears Roebuck was to play an important role in the development of distribution channels. Faced with a retail structure, and hence distribution system, vastly different to that of the US, Sears Roebuck became involved with technology transfer to suppliers and the development of the suppliers operation.

The innovative nature of the retail structure in the US provided US companies with transferable retail concepts. The rapidly expanding economy of the US during the second industrial revolution of the late nineteenth century, and the opportunity to establish a new distribution system without having to dismantle an old established system, provided US retailers with an ideal opportunity to create innovative concepts. Unencumbered with preconceptions, and supported by a buoyant economy, retailers such as Frank Woolworth were able to develop systems suited to the new logic of industrial production and distribution. As other economies developed along similar lines, US innovation was readily adopted where regulation and social mores permitted.

In the US, early academic interest in the phenomenon of international retailing was stimulated by the recognition of international commercial opportunities for US companies (Yoshino, 1966). In the 1940s and 1950s, retailers in Europe and Japan borrowed heavily from US retail experience. The chain store operation in the US with its efficient operational systems, had an important impact on Japanese retailing; likewise, the US self-service approach to grocery retailing had an important impact on the thinking of European retailers. US retailers and academics came to recognize the comparative vitality of US operations and hence the potential opportunities for US retail operational expansion in the post-war world which this suggested.

It was, however, not only US operations which looked covetously on underdeveloped retail structures in economically developed parts of the world such as Europe. As European retailers developed sufficiently to invest in non-domestic markets, they saw the US as an attractive market with excellent investment and growth potential. It has been estimated that, 10 per cent of the US grocery market was owned by European companies by the end of the 1970s (Ball, 1980). The 1970s witnessed a significant shift in the direction of investment activity. There were only 'six foreign owned retailers in 1975' in the US food sector, by 1980 there were twenty-three grocery operations of which over half had been 'acquired since 1978' (Seigle and Handy, 1981, p. 14). Therefore, US interest in international retailing was again stimulated, but on this occasion it was inward investment and the perceived threat to US retailing which this posed, rather than the lure of non-domestic opportunities for US entrepreneurs, which encouraged academic interest, comment and research. The US market was at that time an attractive operating environment, in many ways preferable to the European market. European retailers saw opportunities in North America which they did not perceive in Europe. Concern was generated in the US by the acquisition by European operators of sizeable chunks of US retailing.

It is important to appreciate that this was not the first time non-US companies had invested in the US market. The UK company Lipton's established a small retail operation in the US in the 1890s (Mathias, 1967); while the Canadian company Lobaw acquired the US's National Tea operation in 1956 and by virtue of this acquisition became the first 'significant foreign' investor 'in US food retailing prior to 1970' (Seigle and Handy, 1981, p. 14). However, these investments did not occur on anything like the scale achieved in the 1970s.

The early literature is, therefore, strongly influenced by the observations and standpoint of US writers. The twin themes of US retail expansion around the world and the threat to the US domestic retail interests by retailers attracted to the US market were important to the development of the subject of international retailing in a country which had already accepted the validity of retailing as a subject for academic study.

INTERNATIONAL RESPONSE

As observed above, the US has been seen as a source of retail innovation throughout the twentieth century. The biographies of prominent European retailers are punctuated with incidents of visits to the US or periods of working in the US, when the innovations of that market were observed and consequently introduced to the retailer's home market. Simon Marks, the son of Michael Marks, the founder of the UK retail operation Marks & Spencer, travelled across the US in the 1920s, in order to gain an understanding of modern retailing techniques. From his visit to the US, he gained a better understanding of the importance of the visual impact of retail premises, the advantages of unimpeded customer movement within the store, efficient administrative techniques, the usefulness of ratios in controlling stock in respect of sales, the significance of square footage calculations in assessing contributions to profit, and the desirability of the swift transfer of information within the retail organization (Sieff, 1970). There was much to learn from the marketing activities of US retailers.

Within the European retail environment, the US was synonymous with innovative retailing in the early and mid twentieth century. By the late 1970s, such perceptions of the US stimulated an interest in the acquisition of US retailing operations and the expansion into the US. In consequence, there developed a body of research which assessed the opportunities available in the US market and the impact of European retailers on that market (Seigle and Handy, 1981; Tordjman, 1988; Hildebrand, 1989; Wrigley, 1989; Hallsworth, 1990; Hamill and Crosbie, 1990; Lane and Hildebrand, 1990; Alexander, 1993b). Academic study recognized the fascination which North American operating opportunities had for many European retailers and the considerable advantages those retailers anticipated from their transatlantic investments. It was particularly noticeable that while considerable French and German investments were made in the North American market, retailers from countries such as the Netherlands and the UK were especially active in that market.

However, by the 1980s, this interest in US retailing had to be placed in a wider international context as cross-border activity increased elsewhere in the world, not least within Europe and at the Pacific Rim. From the early 1960s, the pre-eminence of US retailing was eroded as European retailers not only developed large and efficient operations in their domestic markets, but were increasingly capable of investing in, and bringing managerial expertise to, US markets. European retailing has had a particularly important part to play in the new wave of international activity which began to develop in the late 1970s but which began to have a considerable impact on host markets by the mid 1980s.

EUROPE

Environmental changes within European domestic markets in the post-war period, and the effects of those changes on the retail structures within those European markets, fundamentally altered the opportunities available to European retailers and their capacity to respond to those opportunities. For example, the attainment of the Wohlstandsgesellschaft (affluent society) in Germany and the Trente Glorieuses (thirty years of growth) in France provided conditions conducive to the development of large and efficient retail operations in the context of buoyant and expanding economies. European retail structures developed to a point where those structures could support more than incidental international operations.

European retail systems in the early post-war period were less developed than those of the US. As late as the early 1970s, it was possible for Langeard (1974) to observe of the European retail environment: 'the current market resembles that of the United States of America in the late nineteen-fifties' (p. 125). US academics have concurred with such conclusions. Commenting on the changes in European retailing in the 1950s, and hence retail development in the early years of the Common Market, Gomez remarked:

> In Europe even more than America, small-scale retailing is a 'way of life'; it attracts shopkeepers whose limited horizons reflect their inability to adapt to change ... [and] ... progress made in European retailing in the 1950s appears to offer more grounds for skepticism than for comfort in assessing the extent to which consumers will realize the potential benefit of higher living standards promised through a Common Market (Gomez, 1963, p. 8).

Kacker echoed such sentiments in the 1980s when he suggested, 'The retailing industry in Europe stands today at a crossroads' (Kacker, 1986, p. 15). However, his discussion of the structural changes within European retailing, coming as it did after a period of considerable development in European retailing, ended on a more positive note, suggesting that 'Europe has undergone several structural changes during the past two decades, especially since the formation of the EEC' (p. 21).

The European Union, or in its various stages of development, the European Community, the European Economic Community, or, more colloquially, the Common Market, has had a role to play in these developments, but how direct this role has been is open to debate. It has been suggested that the Single European Market (SEM): 'can be seen as a contingent factor in retail internationalization while the enduring pressures for growth and for new markets can be seen as contextual' (Hallsworth, 1992). Essentially, integration within Europe may be seen either as an additional factor which has encouraged cross-border activity in Europe or a fundamental prerequisite of the internationalization process.

Retailers are often reluctant to admit that integration has had a direct effect on their plans to expand within Europe and certainly important moments in European integration, such as the establishment of the SEM, are not seen as the primary factor behind internationalization. Many retailers would suggest that the SEM has only aided internationalization and not stimulated it (Alexander and Morlock, 1992). That is, retailing in the EU has become, as a consequence of the SEM, a more attractive option, but that cross-border EU retail activity must be placed in a wider context. However, survey results show that, in the run-up to the SEM, there was a belief amongst major UK retailers that the SEM would create a more attractive environment in which to operate (Alexander, 1990a). The size of the new market and the level of economic prosperity within the market were seen as key attractions of the SEM, while different consumer tastes and issues surrounding site acquisition were seen as the main problems.

Within the European context, it would be contentious to suggest that the SEM has been the most important stimulus toward internationalization; there have been important contextual factors. Underlying socio-economic factors have been fundamental to the changes witnessed in European retailing. The 'consumption and the behavioral processes associated with consumption' have stimulated retail development (Burt, 1989, p. 5). The frequency of international retail actions are the product of economic conditions. When economic growth has been slow, international retailing has been curtailed. Burt (1993, p. 396) suggests that economic factors 'particularly the effect of the oil crises in the mid 1970s' help to explain the decline in activity after the late 1960s and early 1970s wave of European retailers' international expansion. Likewise, international activity in this period is mirrored by domestic acquisition and merger activity within the UK during the same period (Alexander, 1993a) and indicates that a lack of confidence amongst UK retail operations, as a result of economic factors, curtailed activity in the wider EU context.

Certainly, European retailing has become more concentrated, sophisticated and international during the period of European economic and political integration, but the relationship between the two processes remains comparatively unexplored, and, as the example of UK retailers' involvement in Europe shows, the contingent or contextual argument is difficult to prove either way. To understand the relevance of the SEM to international retailers, it is necessary, as it is with so many other factors pertaining to international retailing, to understand the global activities of retailers, and in turn, it is necessary to appreciate the wider literature on the internationalization of business operations and place the SEM within that framework.

RECENT LITERATURE

A strong theme in the literature has been the identification of international activity (Mitton, 1987; Treadgold, 1988), examples of cross-border influence on retail structures in given markets (Exstein and Weitzman, 1991; Goldman, 1974a, 1974b, 1981; Kaynak, 1980, 1985) and the experience of individual companies (Bunce, 1989; Laulajainen, 1991, 1992; Lord et al., 1988; Martenson, 1981; Treadgold, 1991). This has led to the identification of certain key aspects of retail internationalization such as retailers' orientation to markets which are geographically proximate, culturally proximate and economically similar. Treadgold (1988, 1991) has identified the reluctant and cautious nature of early international moves. In this context, markets close to the domestic market are preferred. This choice in itself will tend to suggest cultural proximity and similar levels of economic development.

It has not been until comparatively recently that research has focused on specific issues of internationalization, and different research methodologies have been employed. This has been the case as far as the motivations behind internationalization are concerned (Alexander, 1990a, 1990b; Williams, 1992a, 1992b) and the organizational cultural issues (McGoldrick and Fryer, 1993) associated with internationalization. Indeed, in recent years, much of the ground work of international retail studies undertaken by such as Sanghavi and Treadgold (1989), OXIRM (1989a, 1989b, 1990), and White's (1984) culling of information from directories such as Newman's (1984), has been superseded by the efforts of commercial operations, such as the CIG (1988, 1991, 1992), and by official bodies, such as Eurostat (1993). Information on international activity is far more readily available than it once was; although, as the research of Burt (1993) and Davies (1993) indicates, if fundamental questions concerning the development of international activity are to be asked, there remains the need for academic study to undertake painstaking and structured analysis and data collection.

DIRECTION OF ACTIVITY

An important theme of the literature is the direction of international retail activity. This has grown out of early concern to identify international opportunities, and the influx of non-domestic retailers in home markets. The literature recognizes the importance of geographical proximity, psychological or cultural proximity, and the attractions of large prosperous markets as well as the opportunities in under-developed markets which show signs of developing retail structures.

These trends are common to all global regions. The Australian retailer Coles Myer's first international action took place in New Zealand. In 1988, with the acquisition of Progressive Enterprises Limited, Coles Myer gained control of a chain of Foodtown supermarkets, the 3 Guys discount food operation and Georgie Pie family restaurants. In the same year as Coles grew through acquisition in the New Zealand market, the company also chose to develop organically through the introduction of its Kmart format (Roberts, 1992).

Japanese stores have taken an interest in opportunities in markets close to Japan. However, Japan's physical location means that Japanese companies face the problem of developing countries' reluctance to provide access to their markets (Davies, 1993). Therefore, Japanese retailers have taken a particular interest in Hong Kong and Singapore markets.

Within the EU, retailers have also followed these patterns. UK retailers have expanded into the Republic of Ireland, the Netherlands and France, all geographically proximate markets, and into Canada and North America, markets which are perceived to be culturally proximate. German operators have expanded into Austria taking advantage of geographic and cultural proximity. French Hypermarket operations have exploited Spanish opportunities and contributed to the development of the retail structure of that country.

Robinson and Clarke-Hill (1990) provide a useful analysis of major German, Belgian, Dutch, Danish, French and UK retailers, using Knee and Walters (1985) paradigm to explore the 'directional growth' of European retailers. Robinson and

Clarke-Hill (1990, p. 13) note that: 'Many of the European retailers studied have expanded into countries within what is now the European Community'. This has led retailers into the markets of their European neighbours, within the EU, but as they also acknowledge, this has not always led to expansion from one EU member state to another, but has frequently involved expansion into markets, such as Spain, before that country joined the EU. Retailers are often attracted to expand into geographically proximate markets where the markets of destination, while showing signs of economic development, possess a retail structure which is not as developed as the retail structure in the internationalizing retailer's domestic market. Therefore, as Robinson and Clarke-Hill (1990) observe, retailers may expand across Free Trade Area boundaries to access new opportunities in developing environments and, as Hollander (1970) has observed, pre-empt moves by other retailers and by moving into the market to gain market share.

As a logical progression from their analysis Robinson and Clarke-Hill (1990, p. 13) suggest that: 'Events in late 1989 in the GDR, Poland, Hungary and Czechoslovakia may well bring considerable opportunities for Western retailers'. While enthusiasm for development into east Europe has been dampened by the realization of the immensity of the task which faces retailers operating in those markets, the logic of the statement remains. European retailers have readily expanded into adjacent European markets, perhaps in anticipation that the state into which they have moved would eventually join the EU. In the decade or more preceding Spain's entry into the EU, French hypermarket retailers were able to make a considerable impact on the Spanish market and capture a substantial share of the market. A similar process may well occur in those markets such as Hungary and the Czech Lands, which are considered likely, in time, to join the EU. Fulop (1991) has observed of the Hungarian market, that there are opportunities for development despite the problems associated with supply, different customer perceptions and appreciations of brand names, and the ongoing issue of liberalization and general economic development. However, those retailers who will access these market are likely to be from those markets which stand in geographical proximity to the Hungarian market. Already, geographical and psychological proximity has again proved significant.

> To a large extent, it has been Austrian and German retailers who have been most willing to enter the Hungarian market. (Fulop, 1991, pp. 394–5)

The direction of international retail activity is determined, in great part, by the geographical proximity of markets, their cultural proximity and the stage in the new markets economic development. Particularly where an imbalance exists between the economic development of a market and the development of the retail structure of that market, expansion will occur. However, expansion is often precluded by the political environment and the regulations to be found in such markets. While some markets in East Europe have encouraged inward investment, the sensitivity of this issue will inevitably remain a theme within the area and become particularly poignant in periods of unemployment and poor economic conditions. In the Far East, countries such as Cambodia and Laos remain closed opportunities, while other countries, such as Vietnam and the Republic of China, have seen moves toward liberalization (Davies, 1993). However, countries, such as the Philippines, which might be expected to value and hence be open to inward investment, retain tight control over retail expansion and do not allow for foreign ownership of retail operations.

INTERNATIONAL STRATEGIES

Interest in the direction and nature of international retail activity has prompted some academics to suggest taxonomies which group international retail operations activities on identifiable criteria. Treadgold (1988) has suggested four operational strategies employed by international retail operations: 'the cautious international-ists', 'emboldened internationalists', 'aggressive internationalists' and 'world powers'. Treadgold's categories are defined by entry and operating strategies; they are also defined by the geographical expansion that individual retailers have achieved. Thus to some extent, these categories refer to stages in the development of international retail operations. In a later publication, following further research and observation, Treadgold (1991) develops this theme by suggesting a typology of international activity based on geographic presence and time. He suggests that it is possible to understand the development of an international operation in terms of reluctant, cautious and ambitious stages. On the basis of the companies development at the end of the 1980s, he placed Tesco in the first group, Sainsbury in the second and Aldi in the third, and described international retailing in general as falling into the second category.

This approach fits into the conclusions drawn about the direction of international expansion. In the European environment, he records, this cautious attitude has led to 'French hypermarket groups in Spain, Dutch retailers in Belgium, German groups in Denmark, and Swedish retailers moving first into other Scandinavian countries' (Treadgold, 1991, p. 21).

It would, however, be incorrect to suggest that all retailers have followed similar expansion routes and considerable diversity is also observable. Salmon and Tordjman (1989) have suggested three categories of international action: investment, multinational and global. The first is self explanatory and involves the transfer of funds for the partial or full acquisition of a retail operation in another market. The other two categories are imbued with specific meaning which are not necessarily the same as that implied by the common usage of the words. Salmon and Tordjman (1989) use these terms in order to describe the degree of similarity international operations have to the parent companies operation in the home market. Therefore, their global category describes retailers who 'replicate the same formula worldwide' and multinational operations where the formula is adapted to local conditions (p. 12).

RETAIL COMPANIES

The study of individual company experiences in the international environment has been adopted as a means of understanding the retailer's experience of internationalization (Woolworth, 1954; Kaynak, 1980; Truitt, 1984; Arbose, 1985; Martenson, 1981, 1987, 1988; Lord et al., 1988; Hildebrand, 1989; Whitehead, 1992; Fernie, 1992; Clarke-Hill and Robinson, 1992; Sparks, 1996).

Some early examples in the literature, such as Woolworth and Sears Roebuck, remain interesting and valid examples today (Woolworth, 1954; Truitt, 1984) and provide useful contrasts and comparisons with the more recent international development of companies such as Ikea (Arbose, 1985; Martenson, 1981, 1988) and Carrefour (Burt, 1986) by way of illustrating the motives behind internationalization and the process of international development.

These case studies may all be considered in the light of Treadgold's (1988) analysis of the level of international development reached by a retail organization. Treadgold's (1988) classification system is a useful means by which to categorize international activity and, although, he later qualifies this analysis by describing it as 'a relatively crude classification of retailers trading internationally' (Treadgold, 1990, p. 9), it remains a useful framework for examining the development of retail companies and the overall trends in international activity.

While, ultimately, the literature on business development, through its underlying absorbtion of social science assumptions, may seek to identify what may at times appear to be laws of corporate or operational development, there is considerable advantage in the consideration of individual company experiences. Individual examples may mislead the reader who wishes to establish such rigorous laws, but they also provide useful insights into the reality of operational development.

Where such experiences are related by corporate-sponsored historians or high-profile entrepreneurs, they may be somewhat fixed in their purpose and assumptions, but they nonetheless provide a reminder of the less than scientific nature of the international commercial environment.

NATIONAL MARKETS

Research has also concentrated on the conditions in different markets or the effect of change or innovation in specific markets (Dunn, 1962; Jefferys, 1968; Arndt, 1972; Goldman, 1974a, 1974b; Dawson, 1976; Dickson, 1979; Goldman, 1981; Kaynak and Cavusgil, 1982; Burt, 1984; Truitt, 1984; Kaynak, 1985; Ho and Sin, 1987; Tordjman, 1988; Hildebrand, 1989; Lane and Hildebrand, 1990; Fulop, 1991; Burns and Rayman, 1996). This research has provided both detailed studies of the markets concerned, and insights into the effects of specific developments emphasized in other research. The work of Goldman (1974a,b, 1981) and others (Conners et al., 1985; Kaynak, 1985; Alawi 1986) represents the interest shown in the transfer and development of the supermarket and self-service operations.

Arndt's (1972) consideration of temporal lags in retailing is an example of the type of research that remains relatively unexplored. Arndt took an environmental approach in respect of the fundamental dynamic which lies behind retail innovation (Brown, 1987). Arndt compared the development of retail structures in the Swedish and Norwegian markets and the lag between the development of retailing forms in these markets. While the approach appears appropriate to the markets chosen, the approach has not been so successfully employed where greater geographical distances have existed between markets. The predictive power of such analysis did not develop sufficiently to allow confidence to be placed in such analysis, 'the sheer variety of social, political, cultural, legal and historical forces at work within individual countries, indicates that institutional diversity rather than uniformity is the hallmark of retail innovation' (Brown, 1987, p. 7). Brown (1987) notes the problems of transferring the supermarket into Spain, Sears Roebuck's problems in Belgium and Spain and Marks & Spencer's initial problems in France.

However, despite the drawbacks of this analytical approach, the fundamental assumption is frequently made in the literature that markets will experience common patterns of retail structural development. This is particularly true in the European context where the 'under-developed markets' of 'Spain and Italy but also Portugal and Greece' are seen as providing 'growth opportunities' for European companies constrained in North European markets (Treadgold, 1991, p. 11). These statements are not unqualified. The differences in consumer tastes and trading conditions are recognized, but where, as in the EU, 'convergence of national markets, or at least the blurring of boundaries between them' (p. 26) is perceived, the logic of temporal lags in development remains a fundamental premise.

SATURATION

International activity is sometimes explained as primarily a response to restricted market opportunities in the domestic environment. This may take the form of limited market opportunities but it may also take the form of regulation within the home market. Large retailers, faced with increasingly limited expansion opportunities in the domestic market, are faced with the options of either vertical integration, product diversification or international expansion. Retailers may consider that international expansion is the logical next step in a situation of market saturation. Such a move, however, may be precipitous, as retailers will ignore some of the challenges of cross-border activity. Saturation is an issue that all expanding retailers have to face. However, retailers should not plan for international activity when limited opportunities are experienced within the domestic market, but in advance of those experiences.

Limited market opportunities may force retailers into the international arena but regulation in the domestic market may also encourage retailers to seek international market alternatives. The Loi Royer in France and the Loi Cadenas in Belgium have both sought to restrict the growth of retail operations. Both regulatory frameworks have been examined in the literature and form an interesting example of the impact of regulation on domestic as well as international growth (Dawson, 1976, 1982; Fries, 1978; Burt, 1984, 1986; Leunis and Francois, 1988; Francois and Leunis, 1991).

Opinions as to the effects of these regulations differ, but the existence of such restrictions on development will inevitably encourage some retailers to internationalize in an attempt to access opportunities in less regulated markets while other retailers may be discouraged from entering some markets because of the restricted opportunities available to them. Davies and Whitehead (1993) have considered the effect of the legislative environment on retail structures. Their findings indicate a relationship between economic and retail development and a situation 'where countries with the highest divergence from the correlation tend to have either relatively liberal or relatively restricted planning environments' (p. 1). Davies and Whitehead's (1993) research findings support Leunis and Francois (1988), who suggested that the Belgian Loi Cadenas or Padlock Law 'has had a major impact upon the evolution of the number of supermarkets and of the number of hypermarkets' (p. 151). However, this contrasts with Burt's (1984) contention 'that the Loi Royer may not have had the restrictive effect on growth that was expected' (p. 19).

Market saturation has played a fundamental part in the development of the discussion on the motivations which lie behind internationalization. Literature on this issue deserves particular consideration. Retail saturation may be understood, however, on a number of levels. For example, it may be considered to be saturation of the format such as the superstore or the fascia such as Sainsbury. In the UK, a crucial level of saturation in the superstore sector was reached sometime between 1992 and the end of 1994. However, the Sainsbury fascia did not reach saturation until after that date.

The UK grocery sector has received considerable attention in respect of this issue (Killen and Lees, 1988a, 1988b; Treadgold and Reynolds, 1989; Duke, 1991; Guy, 1993) and is an example, not only of the problems raised in defining saturation, but also the strategic response that retailers will need to consider (Alexander and Morlock, 1992). Saturation also raises the issue of how the entry of non-domestic operators into the market alters an understanding of saturation and how formats and format saturation may be described.

MOTIVES

Saturation lies at the heart of the debate behind the reasons for internationalization. If internationalization is principally the result of 'limited opportunities for sustained domestic growth' (Treadgold, 1988, p. 8) then, clearly, an appreciation of the issue of saturation is fundamental to the understanding of internationalization. However, what is meant by saturation, both within the academic and commercial world appears at times to be something of a matter of personal choice (Guy, 1993). Even if an opposing view is taken that the major motive behind internationalization is predicated on an 'internationally appealing and innovative offering and growth oriented and proactive motives' (Williams, 1992a), the issue of saturation remains important in terms of recognizing such a proactive rather than reactive response.

Two schools of thought have emerged. The first makes the assumption that saturation is the primary reason for international activity, while the other sees internationalization as fundamentally a response to opportunities in the international market-place. The importance of reactive or proactive responses to the international market may, in part, be the product of the macro and micro stages of industry and company development.

International retailing in the late 1960s and early 1970s went through a period of growth. Large retailers based in the European market sought expansion opportunities in international markets. This may largely have been a reaction to the effects of market saturation in the domestic market and a product of general economic developments which saw a sizeable number of retailers reach national coverage for the first time. It may also be a product of retailers' lack of sophisticated response to the opportunities in the international environment and ability to cope with the new challenges which this entailed. Thus both macro and micro factors may have led to an essentially reactive rather than proactive period of internationalization. However, by the late 1980s, it is possible that a more proactive period of international had arrived, as international retail structures began to emerge, and retailers internal organizational development and, in some cases, experience of international activity sustained a more sophisticated, proactive response to the international environment. If these interpretations are accepted, or at the very least seen to contain elements of a viable interpretive framework, then the literature on this subject must be interpreted within the context of its own time, rather than as a timeless indicator of motivational structures.

FUTURE

The role that Europe has played in the development of international retailing has changed from being one where Europe was a recipient of American innovation to one where Europe has become an exporter of retail operations. Likewise, other markets such as those at the Pacific Rim are playing an international role. That is, as Europe has previously seen, they have attracted inward investment but also are now playing a role in the transfer of know-how and operations across state boundaries. Therefore, the changes recently witnessed in Europe may find a parallel in the Far East. Japan's economic sphere of influence may see similar retail developments and structures as Europe has achieved by the mid 1990s. In response to this, the literature on international retailing is reflecting this increasingly important collection of markets and the role these markets will play in the development of international retailing (Davies, 1993, 1994; Davies and Jones, 1993; Cheung, 1994; Chen and Sternquist, 1994, 1996; Sternquist and Runyan, 1993; Davies and Fergusson, 1996) as indeed it is increasingly exploring the opportunities and problems of retail expansion in Eastern Europe (Fulop, 1991; Spannagel, 1993; Loker et al., 1994).

CONCLUSION

The international dimension of retailing continues to attract considerable attention, as recent conferences on retailing have shown (Boutsouki et al., 1995; Clarke-Hill et al., 1995; Dupuis, 1995; Helfferich and Hinfelaar, 1995; McGoldrick, 1995; Myers and Alexander, 1995a, 1995b; Sanghavi, 1995; Topoland Sherman, 1995; Treadgold, 1995; Vida and Fairhurst, 1995). It is a dynamic area of research, which will develop rapidly in the next few years. Many of the assumptions which have already been made will have to be overturned or radically modified in the light of further internationalization, theoretical developments and empirical studies. Not least, consideration must be given to the fundamental characteristics of the internationalization process itself and the management of the problems which emerge.

NOTES

1   Charles Waldman, at the time of the publication of his book was Associate Professor at the Ecole Superieure des Sciences Economiques et Commerciales (ESSEC) in France. However, the text had its origins in his doctoral thesis presented at Harvard University.

QUESTIONS – DISCUSSION POINTS

1   What fundamental changes in the retail environment have led to the internationalization of retailing?

2   Why has international retailing become an important area of study?

3   Why has the US been so important in the development of international retail thought?

4   Why has European retailing become an important force in international retailing?

5   What are the main questions that have been asked about the development of international retailing?

6   Why will the Pacific Rim be important to our understanding of international retailing in the future?

REFERENCES

Alawi, H., (1986) Saudi Arabia; Making Sense of Self-Service, *International Marketing Review*, Spring: pp. 21–38.

Alexander, N. (1990a) Retailing Post-1992, *Service Industries Journal*, Vol. 10, No. 2, pp. 172–187.

Alexander, N., (1990b) Retailers and International Markets: Motives for Expansion, *International Marketing Review*, Vol. 7, No. 4, pp. 75–85.

Alexander, N., (1993a) UK Retailers' Changing Attitude to European Expansion, *7th International Conference on Research in the Distributive Trades*, Institute for Retail Studies, University of Stirling, 6–8 September.

Alexander, N., (1993b) Internationalisation: Interpreting the Motives, *International Issues in Retailing, ESRC Seminars: Research Themes in Retailing*, Manchester Business School/Manchester School of Management, 15 March.

Alexander, N., and Morlock, W., (1992) Saturation and Internationalization: The Future of Grocery Retailing in the UK, *International Journal of Retail & Distribution Management*, Vol. 20, No. 3, pp. 33–9.

Arbose, J., (1985) The Folksy Theories that Inspire Lifestyle Merchant IKEA, *International Management (UK)*, Vol. 40, No. 11, November, pp. 51–4.

Arndt, J., (1972) Temporal Lags in Comparative Retailing, *Journal of Marketing*, Vol., 36, October, pp. 40–5.

Ball, R., (1980) Europe's US Shopping Spree, *Fortune*, 1 December, p. 82–8.

Boutsouki, C., Bennison, D., and Bourlakis, C., (1995) The Impact of Retail Internationalisation on the Host Country: A Case Study of Greece, *8th International Conference on the Distributive Trades*, Università Bocconi, Milan, 1–2 September, pp. A7.11–18.

Brown, S., (1987) Institutional Change in Retailing: A Review and Synthesis, *European Journal of Marketing*, Vol. 21, No. 6, pp. 5–36.

Bunce, M., (1989) The International Approach of Laura Ashley, in ESOMAR Proceedings, *Adding Value to Retail Offerings*, Edinburgh, 24–6 April 1989, pp. 101–16.

Burns, D., and Rayman, D., (1996) Retailing in Canada and the United States: Historical Comparisons, G. Akehurst, N. Alexander (eds) *The Internationalisation of Retailing*, Cass, London, pp. 164–76.

Burt, S., (1984) Hypermarkets in France: Has The Loi Royer had any Effect?, *Retail and Distribution Management*, January/February, Vol. 12, No. 1, pp. 16–19.

Burt, S., (1986) The Carrefour Group – the first 25 years, *International Journal of Retailing*, Vol. 1, No. 3, pp. 54–78.

Burt, S., (1989) Trends and Management Issues in European Retailing, *International Journal of Retailing*, Vol. 4, No. 4, monograph.

Burt, S., (1993) Temporal Trends in the Internationalisation of British Retailing, *International Review of Retail, Distribution and Consumer Research*, Vol. 3, No. 4, pp. 391–410.

Chen, Y., and Sternquist, B., (1994) Japanese Multinational Retailers: Are they Different from those Who Stay at Home?, *Retailing: Theories and Practices for Today and Tomorrow*, Proceedings of the Fourth Triennial National Retailing Conference, R. King (ed.), The Academy of Marketing Science and The American Collegiate Retailing Association, Special Conference Series Vol. VII, Richmond Virginia, October 22–4, pp. 158.

Chen, Y., and Sternquist, B., (1996) Differences between International and Domestic Japanese Retailers, G. Akehurst, N. Alexander (eds) *The Internationalisation of Retailing*, Cass, London, pp. 118–33.

Cheung, C., (1994) Globalization of Japanese Major Retailers and Stages of thier Global Strategic Management, *Recent Advances in Retailing & Services Science Conference*, Banff – Alberta, 7–10 May.

CIG, (1988) *Retailing and 1992 – The Impact and Opportunities*, The Corporate Intelligence Group, London.

CIG, (1991) *Cross-Border Retailing in Europe*, The Corporate Intelligence Group, London.

CIG, (1992) *European Retail Alliances*, The Corporate Intelligence Group, London.

Clarke-Hill, C., and Robinson, T., (1992) Co-operation as a Competitive Strategy in European Retailing, *European Business and Economic Development*, Vol. 1, No. 2, pp. 1–6.

Clarke-Hill, C., Robinson, T., and Bailey, J., (1995) European Retail Alliances – Competencies Transfer and Competitive Advantage, *8th International Conference on the Distributive Trades*, Università Bocconi, Milan, 1–2 September, pp. A7.29–37.

Conners, S., Samli, A., and Kaynak, E., (1985) Transfer of Food Retail Technology into Less Developed Countries, in A. Samli (ed.) *Technology Transfer*, Westport; Quorum, pp. 27–44.

Davies, B., and Jones, P., (1993) The International Activity of Japanese Department Stores, *The Service Industries Journal*, Vol. 13, No. 1, pp. 126–32.

Davies, G., and Whitehead, M., (1993) The Legislative Environment as a Measure of Attractiveness for Internationalisation, *International Issues in Retailing, ESRC Seminars: Research Themes in Retailing*, Manchester Business School/Manchester School of Management, 15 March.

Davies, K., (1993) Trade Barriers in East and South East Asia: The Implications for Retailers, *The International Review of Retail, Distribution and Consumer Research*, Vol. 3, No. 4, pp. 345–66.

Davies, K., (1994) Internationalization of Retailing: The Examples of East and South-East Asia, *Recent Advances in Retailing & Services Science Conference*, Banff – Alberta, 7–10 May.

Davies, K., and Fergusson, F., (1996) The International Activities of Japanese Retailers, G. Akehurst, N. Alexander (eds) *The Internationalisation of Retailing*, Cass, London, pp. 97–117.

Dawson, J., (1976) Control Over Larger Units in France The Loi Royer and its Effects, *Retail and Distribution Management*, July/August, Vol. 4, No. 4, pp. 14–18.

Dawson, J., (1982) *Distribution in Europe*, Croom Helm, London.

de Somogyi, J., (1986) Retail Planning for the Next Ten Years, *Retail and Distribution Management*, Vol. 14, No. 5, pp. 9–13.

Dickson, M., (1979) West German Retailing in Perspective, *European Journal of Marketing*, Vol. 13, No. 7, pp. 246–58.

Drtina, T., (1996), The Internationalisation of Retailing in the Czech and Slovak Republics, G. Akehurst, N. Alexander (eds) *The Internationalisation of Retailing*, Cass, London, pp. 191–203.

Duke, R., (1991) Post-saturation Competition in UK Grocery Retailing, *Journal of Marketing Management*, Vol. 7, No. 1, pp. 63–75.

Dunn, S., (1962) French Retailing and the Common Market, *Journal of Marketing*, January, p. 20.

Dupuis, M., (1995) The World Challenge of Discount, *8th International Conference on the Distributive Trades*, Università Bocconi, Milan, 1–2 September.

Eurostat, (1993) *Retailing in the Single European Market 1993*, Commission of the European Communities, Brussels.

Exstein, M., and Weitzman, F., (1991) Foreign Investment in US Retailing: An Optimistic Overview, *Retail Control*, January, pp. 9–14.

Fernie, J., (1992) Distribution Strategies of European Retailers, *European Journal of Marketing*, Vol. 26, No. 8/9, pp. 269–85.

Francois, P., and Leunis, J., (1991) Public Policy and the Establishment of Large Stores in Belgium, *The International Review of Retail, Distribution and Consumer Research*, Vol. 1, No. 4, pp. 469–86.

Fries, J., (1978) Government Intervention in France – How has it affected development? *Retail and Distribution Management*, March/April, Vol. 6, No. 2, pp. 41–5.

Fritsch, W., (1962) *Progress and Profits: The Sears Roebuck Story in Peru*, Washington DC: Action Committee for International Development.

Fulop, C., (1991) The Changing Structure of Hungarian Retailing: Prospects for Foreign Retailers, *Journal of Marketing Management*, Vol. 7, No. 4, pp. 383–96.

Goldman, A., (1974a) Growth of Large Food Stores in Developing Countries, *Journal of Retailing*, Vol. 50, No. 2, pp. 139–89.

Goldman, A., (1974b) Outreach of Consumers and the Modernization of Urban Food Retailing in Developing Countries, *Journal of Marketing*, Vol. 38, No. 4, pp. 8–16.

Goldman, A., (1981) Transfer of a Retailing Technology into Less Developed Countries: the Supermarket Case, *Journal of Retailing*, Vol. 57, No. 2, pp. 5–29.

Gomez, H., (1963) Common Market Benefits: Will the European Retailer Utilize Them?, *Journal of Retailing*, Vol. 39, No. 4, pp. 1–8, 56.

Guy, C., (1993) Grocery Store Saturation: An Empirical Analysis, *7th International Conference on Research in the Distributive Trades*, Institute for Retail Studies, University of Stirling, 6–8 September.

Hallsworth, A., (1990) The Lure of the USA: Some Further Reflections, *Environment and Planning*, A22, pp. 551–8.

Hallsworth, A., (1992) Retail Internationalisation: Contingency and Context? *European Journal of Marketing*, Vol. 26, No. 8/9, pp. 25–34.

Hamill, J., and Crosbie, J., (1990) British Retail Acquisitions in the US, *International Journal of Retail and Distribution Management*, Vol. 18, No. 5, pp. 15–20.

Helfferich, E., and Hinfelaar, M., (1995) The Export of Retail Formats, *8th International Conference on the Distributive Trades*, Università Bocconi, Milan, 1–2 September, pp. A7.19–28.

Hildebrand, T., (1989) *An Investigation of Retailers Entering and Adapting to the US Market*, Ph.D. Thesis, London: University of Western Ontario.

Ho, S., and Sin, Y., (1987) International Transfer of Retail Technology: The Successful Case of Convenience Stores in Hong Kong, *International Journal of Retailing*, Vol. 2, No. 3, pp. 36–48.

Hollander, S., (1970) *Multinational Retailing*, Michigan State University, East Lancing, MI.

Jefferys, J., (1968) Large Scale Retail Firms in Europe: their characteristics, relative importance and future developments, *British Journal of Marketing*, Vol. 2, No. 4, pp. 268–72.

Kacker, M., (1985) *Transatlantic Trends in Retailing*, Quorum, Connecticut.

Kacker, M., (1986) The Metamorphosis of European Retailing, *European Journal of Marketing*, Vol. 20, No. 8, pp. 15–22.

Kaynak, E., (1980) Transfer of Supermarket Technology from Developed to Less Developed Countries: The Case of Migros-Turk, *Finnish Journal of Business Economics*, Vol. 29, No. 1.

Kaynak, E., (1985) Global Spread of Supermarkets: some experiences from Turkey, in E. Kaynak (ed.) *Global Perspectives in Marketing*, Praeger, New York.

Kaynak, E., and Cavusgil, S., (1982) The Evolution of Food Retailing Systems: Contrasting the Experience of Developed and Developing Countries, *Journal of the Academy of Marketing Science*, Vol. 10, No. 3.

Killen, V., and Lees, R., (1988a) The Future of Grocery Retailing in the UK: Part I, *Retail and Distribution Management*, July–August, pp. 8–12.

Killen, V., and Lees, R., (1988b) The Future of Grocery Retailing in the UK: Part II, *Retail and Distribution Management*, November–December, pp. 27–9.

Knee, D., and Walters, D., (1985) *Strategies in Retailing: Theory and Application*, Philip Allen, Oxford.

Lane, H., and Hildebrand, T., (1990) How to Survive in US Retail Markets, *Business Quarterly*, Vol. 54, No. 3, pp. 62–6.

Langeard, E., (1974) Corporate Strategy of Mass Distribution Firms within the European Environment, in D. Thorpe (ed.) *Research into Retailing and Distribution*, Farnborough: Saxon House, pp. 125–47.

Laulajainen, R., (1991) Two Retailers Go Global: The Geographical Dimension, *International Review of Retail Distribution and Consumer Research*, Vol. 1, No. 5, pp. 607–26.

Laulajainen, R., (1992) Louis Vuitton Malletier: A Truly Global Retailer, *Annals of the Japan Association of Economic Geographers*, Vol. 38, No. 2, pp. 55–70.

Leunis, J., and Francois, P., (1988) The Impact of Belgian Public Policy upon Retailing: The Case of the Second Padlock Law, E. Kaynak (ed.) *Transnational Retailing*, Walter de Gruyter, New York, pp. 135–53.

Loker, S., Good, L., and Huddleston, P., (1994) Entering Eastern European Markets: Lessons from Kmart, *Recent Advances in Retailing & Services Science Conference*, Banff – Alberta, 7–10 May.

Lord, D., Moran, W., Parker, T., and Sparks, L., (1988) Retailing on Three Continents: The Discount Food Operations of Albert Gubay, *International Journal of Retailing*, Vol. 3, No. 3, pp. 1–54.

McGoldrick, P., (1995) International Retailing: Market Appraisal and Positioning, *2nd Recent Advances in Retailing & Services Science Conference*, Brisbane – Australia, 11–14 July.

McGoldrick, P., and Fryer, E., (1993) Organisational Culture and the Internationalisation of Retailers, *7th International Conference on Research in the Distributive Trades*, Institute for Retail Studies, University of Stirling, 6–8 September.

Martenson, R., (1981) *Innovations in Multinational Retailing: IKEA on the Swedish, Swiss, German and Austrian Furniture Markets*, Gotenburg, University of Gotenburg.

Martenson, R., (1987) Culture Bound Industries? A European Case Study, *International Marketing Review*, Vol. 4, No. 3, pp. 7–17.

Martenson, R., (1988) Cross-cultural Similarities and Differences in Multinational Retailing, in E. Kaynak (ed.) *Transnational Retailing*, New York, Walter de Gruyter.

Mathias, P., (1967) *Retailing Revolution*, Longmans, London.

Mitton, A., (1987) Foreign Retail Companies Operating in the UK: strategy and performance, *Retail and Distribution Management*, Jan/Feb, pp. 29–31.

Myers, H., and Alexander, N., (1995a) European Food Retailers' Global Expansion: An Empirical Consideration of the Direction of Growth, *2nd Recent Advances in Retailing & Services Science Conference*, Brisbane – Australia, 11–14 July.

Myers, H., and Alexander, N., (1995b) Direction of International Food Retail Expansion: An Empirical Study of European Retailers, *8th International Conference on the Distributive Trades*, Università Bocconi, Milan, 1–2 September.

Newman, (1984) *Stores of the World Directory*, Vol. 1 Europe, 1984–5 edition, Newman Books Ltd., London.

OXIRM, (1989a) Foreign Retailers in the USA, *OXIRM Fact Sheet*, September.

OXIRM, (1989b) Europe's International Retailers, *OXIRM Fact Sheet*, December.

OXIRM, (1990) International Retailers in Europe, *OXIRM Fact Sheet*, September.

Roberts, J., (1992) Coles Myer Ltd., A. Hast, D. Pascal, P. Barbour, J. Griffin (eds) *International Directory of Company Histories*, Vol. V, St James Press, Detroit, pp. 33–5.

Robinson, T., and Clarke-Hill, C., (1990) Directional Growth by European Retailers, *International Journal of Retail and Distribution Management*, Vol. 18, No. 5, pp. 3–14.

Sanghavi, N., (1995) Internationalisation of Retailing – A Study of Retailing in Developing Economies of South East Asia, India and China, *2nd Recent Advances in Retailing & Services Science Conference*, Brisbane – Australia, 11–14 July.

Sanghavi, N., and Treadgold, A., eds (1989) *Developments in European Retailing*, Dower House, Yeovil.

Salmon, W., and Tordjman, A., (1989) The Internationalisation of Retailing, *International Journal of Retailing*, Vol. 4, No. 2, pp. 3–16.

Sieff, I., (1970) *Memoirs*, Weidenfeld & Nicholson, London.

Seigle, N., and Handy, C., (1981) Foreign Ownership in Food Retailing, *National Food Review*, Winter, pp. 14–16.

Spannagel, R., (1993) Small and Medium Enterprises in Retailing in Germany – Strong in West, Weak in East, *7th International Conference on Research in the Distributive Trades*, Institute for Retail Studies, University of Stirling, 6–8 September.

Sparks, L., (1996) Reciprocal Retail Internationalisation: The Southland Corporation, Ito-Yokado and 7-Eleven Convenience Stores, G. Akehurst, N. Alexander (eds) *The Internationalisation of Retailing*, Cass, London, pp. 57–96.

Sternquist, B., and Runyan, R., (1993) Coercion and Reciprocal Actions in Distribution Systems: A Comparison of Japan and the United States, *7th International Conference on Research in the Distributive Trades*, University of Stirling, 6–8 September, pp. 554–62.

Sun, D., (1992) Sears, Roebuck and Co., A. Hast, D. Pascal, P. Barbour, J. Griffin (eds) *International Directory of Company Histories*, Vol. V, St James Press, Detroit, pp. 33–5.

Topol, T., and Sherman, E., (1995) International Interactive Retailing: Opportunities and Obstacles, *8th International Conference on the Distributive Trades*, Università Bocconi, Milan, 1–2 September.

Tordjman, A., (1988) The French Hypermarket Could it be Developed in the States?, *Retail and Distribution Management*, Vol. 4, No. 2, pp. 3–16.

Treadgold, A., (1988) Retailing Without Frontiers, *Retail and Distribution Management*, Vol. 16, No. 6, pp. 8–12.

Treadgold, A., (1990) The Developing Internationalisation of Retailing, *International Journal of Retail and Distribution Management*, Vol. 18, No. 2, pp. 4–11.

Treadgold, A., (1991) The Emerging Internationalisation of Retailing: Present Status and Future Challenges, *Irish Marketing Review*, Vol. 5, No. 2, pp. 11–27.

Treadgold, A., (1995) Structural Trends and Developments in Food Retailing and Distribution in South East Asia, *2nd Recent Advances in Retailing & Services Science Conference*, Brisbane – Australia, 11–14 July.

Treadgold, A., and Reynolds, J., (1989) *Retail Saturation: Examining the Evidence*, Oxford Institute of Retail Management, Longman, London.

Truitt, N., (1984) Mass Merchandising and Economic Development: Sears Roebuck & Co in Mexico and Peru, in S. Shelp et al. (eds) *Service Industries and Economic Development*, Praeger, New York.

Vida, I., and Fairhurst, A., (1995) A Model of Factors Influencing the Internationalization Process of A Firm: Application to the US Retailing Industry, *8th International Conference on the Distributive Trades*, Università Bocconi, Milan, 1–2 September.

Waldman, C., (1978) *Strategies of International Mass Retailers*, Praeger, New York.

White, R., (1984) Multinational Retailing: A Slow Advance?, *Retail & Distribution Management*, Vol. 12, No. 2, pp. 8–13.

Whitehead, M., (1992) Internationalisation of Retailing: Developing New Perspectives, *European Journal of Marketing*, Vol. 26, No. 8/9, pp. 74–9.

Williams, D., (1992a) Motives for Retailer Internationalization: Their Impact, Structure, and Implications, *Journal of Marketing Management*, Vol. 8, pp. 269–85.

Williams, D., (1992b) Retailer Internationalization: An Empirical Inquiry, *European Journal of Marketing*, Vol. 26, No. 8/9, pp. 269–85.

Wood, R., and Keyser, V., (1953) *United States Business Performance Abroad; The Case Study of Sears, Roebuck de Mexico, S.A.*, Washington DC: National Planning Association.

Woolworth, (1954) *Woolworth's First 75 Years: The Story of Everybody's Store*, New York, Woolworth.

Wrigley, N., (1989) The Lure of The USA: Further Reflections on the Internationalisation of British Grocery Retailing Capital, *Environment and Planning*, A21, pp. 283–8.

Yoshino, S., (1966) International Opportunities for American Retailers, *Journal of Retailing*, Vol. 43, No. 3, pp. 1–10, 76.

Defining International Activity

▌ OBJECTIVES ▌

This chapter addresses the following questions: what is international retailing and what constitutes internationalization? While the literature available on this subject uses the term freely, and a particular activity is assumed to be understood by it, the term is often used loosely. Here the internationalization process is discussed in the context of the various boundaries which international retailers face. This provides an initial discussion, and hence framework, within which a discussion of the internationalization process is further developed in part III.

INTRODUCTION

When, on 9 November 1989, Günter Schabowski announced that East German citizens would be allowed greater freedom to cross East Germany's border into

West Germany, and that, in effect, a major barrier to the movement of individuals was to be discarded, the information was delivered almost as an aside. Schabowski was a member of the East German Politburo; he was responsible for propaganda.

The DDR's International Press Centre in East Berlin was not an inspiring location; to say that it lacked character might be considered an understatement. At 6.55 p.m. on 9 November 1989, a group of Western journalists were listening, or, in many cases, not listening, to the announcements made by the member of the Politburo with responsibility for information. As the meeting drew to its, as yet uneventful, conclusion, Schabowski began to talk about the new regulations governing movement across East and West Germany's shared border. East Germans would be allowed greater access to the West. Although the events of the past two years should have prepared his audience for the news, Schabowski's down-beat presentation and the psychological significance of the news stunned the now attentive group of journalists. Finally, after Schabowski signalled that he would take only one more question, the question was asked (Johnson, 1989):

What will become of the Berlin Wall?

The answer when it came was as unemotional as the original announcement but the words were by then unimportant: events would answer that question.

> Berlin still held power as a symbol of the Cold War at Checkpoint Charlie on a cold night in January 1990. But the ease with which the border crossing was accomplished – a simple wave of the guard's hand once he had given passports the merest of glances – proved that if the Wall was not yet removed, then the bricks, mortar, and barbed wire had at least been stripped of much of their ominous meaning. (Horsman and Marshall, 1994, p. 41)

International retailers confront many barriers to international trade. The division between East and West Europe was one of the most clearly defined of such barriers: it was a political barrier of major significance. The international manager, however, is faced with other, more subtle, barriers which restrict international trade. As the citizens of former East and West Germany have come to appreciate, political boundaries are only the first of many boundaries they must cross if they are going to establish national coherence. While the Wall may have disappeared in substance, its existence has bequeathed to the new German state social tensions which will have to be addressed over a considerable period of time. Likewise, international retailers must appreciate that it is not only the obvious boundaries, such as political boundaries that they must cross if they are to successfully build global operations. Important boundaries exist not only on planning charts but in the minds of those who operate in unfamiliar markets.

While psychologically significant, the Berlin Wall, by the time of Schabowski's announcement, was only a poignant physical manifestation of an international boundary that had already been breached. Two years earlier, the relaxation of controls along Hungary's border with 'the West' had begun the process that was to be so vividly recorded in Berlin in November 1989. However, by 1994, when the President of the United States and the Chancellor of a united Germany walked together through the Brandenburg Gate, the physical barrier had been removed but the integration of East and West Germany was still somewhere in the future and important differences still separated the Lander of Brandenburg, Mecklenburg-Vorpommern, Sachsen, Sachsen-Ahalt, Thuringen and Berlin from the ten Lander in the rest of the FDR.

A DEFINITION

This chapter addresses the problem of defining international retailing. While the literature available on this subject uses the term freely, and a particular activity is assumed to be understood by it, the term has essentially been used loosely. Consequently, the word 'internationalization' is as poorly defined and as it is understood.

> as soon as one starts thinking about it, it becomes elusive. Does the word identify a clear area of firms' strategies, does it draw a clear border between a given set of actions and the remaining alternatives open to the firm? The answer is probably no. (Pellegrini, 1994, p. 121)

This is not satisfactory. Any subject area must have a clearly defined vocabulary on which to draw. Failure to establish a sufficiently robust lexicon will result in confusion and the subject will atrophy.

This chapter proposes a definition of international retailing and of internationalization and discusses these definitions on the basis of the boundaries which themselves define the process. Other chapters in the book will address international retailing and retailers from this perspective and within the framework described.

International retailing

International retailing is commonly assumed to concern retail operations, owned by a single company, in more than one country. For example, Dawson (1993, p. 11) has commented:

> International retail operations may be defined as the operation, by a single firm, of shops, or other forms of retail distribution, in more than one country.

While a useful rule of thumb definition, such a definition is insufficient to describe the multi-faceted nature of international retailing and the global retail environment. Irrespective of the baldness of such a definition, each of the key words used above demand qualification and explanation.

In this context, what is retailing?

> Retailers are the final commercial link in the distribution chain. They sell to the
> final consumers or to customers who may not themselves consume the final prod-
> uct but who will not offer the product for resale.

This draws on the standard definition of retailing, such as that offered by Lewison
(1989). Therefore, international retailing is not the transfer of concepts to new
environments but it is the establishment of operations in new markets. Internationalization of a concept may occur without an international transferring organization
but international retailing suggests physical presence.

If this is so, what is meant by 'operations'? If international retailing, as opposed
to the process of internationalization, demands the physical presence of a retailer,
much that is associated with the international relationships of retailers is excluded.
Thus, Strategic Retail Alliances, as exemplified by the European Retail Alliance
(ERA) involving primarily Ahold (Netherlands), Casino (France), and Safeway
(UK) should not be included in a definition of international retailing. Buying
associations which facilitate the exchange of information, the export of retail
branded goods, and the infrastructure of international moves, such as property
development and distribution arrangements, are not implied by, and therefore
included in, a definition of international retailing, except where such concerns
impinge on the operational aspects of the retail facility and the strategic and
marketing of the retail operation.

Similarly, it is necessary to ask what is meant by more than one country? What
defines a country which makes it different from a retail perspective? International,
as a word, literally means between or among nations (Partridge, 1966). The word
'nation', deriving as it does from natio (Latin birth), indicates common descent of
a people. In the nineteenth and twentieth centuries, the nation came to be associated with the area contained within a state. This is how countries are commonly
recognized, that is the national state with sovereign rights. The internationalization
of a company therefore is taken to mean the movement of goods or services from
one nation-state to another. The word nation or the word national is useful short-
hand version of what is intended, but is potentially confusing when the essential
elements of the process are considered. The word nation infers common ancestry,
which in turn implies shared values and culture. However, the trappings of
statehood are regulatory and political in nature. Therefore, by simply using the
word 'international', a wealth of associations are thereby implied, which might
not always be intended or useful in understanding the process described as
internationalization.

While inter-state boundaries are an important element in the definition of 'international retailing' given above, they do not alone represent or describe the complex
nature of the international retailer's task and the barriers which the international
retailer has to address.

State boundaries do not describe the cultural differences which exist between
countries, or conversely, they do not indicate that there are many countries
which share important cultural characteristics which make international expansion across state boundaries relatively easy. Likewise, different cultural

groups are often contained within state boundaries, as are different economic and social groups which may or may not correspond with internal administrative boundaries.

Some markets will be culturally heterogeneous in nature, while others will display a degree of homogeneity. The latter may have many common cultural characteristics which they share with the population of another state. Perceptions of the nation-state are often close to the situation which exists in Japan. That is, there is a strong degree of homogeneity within the state and that the state boundary registers an important cultural divide. This perception may also exist where important cultural differences exist but the majority culture is accepted as dominant. Canada and the US are examples of states which have been seen in the recent past as culturally homogenous societies, yet increasingly French and Spanish speakers are now perceived as distinct and influential groups within these societies. In Europe, historical events have separated and reunited culturally similar populations. Before the unification of East and West German the expression 'the two Germanies' was commonly used. To a considerable extent there are still two Germanies in Europe, in the sense that Austria and Germany share many common cultural features.

Although international retailers should recognize state boundaries as a fundamental determinant of operating conditions, they should also be aware that fundamental differences exist within states and in some instances, there may be important similarities across political frontiers as well as within them.

INTERNATIONAL BOUNDARIES

To achieve a better understanding of what international retail activity encompasses and therefore is, and the barriers which international operations face, it is convenient to think of internationalization in terms of retailers crossing political, economic, social, cultural, and retail boundaries.

Political boundaries

These boundaries are determined by geo-politics and geo-political divisions and are represented by both the regulatory contexts that face retailers in the international environment, and also the political environment that leads to the formulation of the regulatory environment.

Regulation
Usually, state boundaries are used to describe the extent of international activity. On this basis a German retailer operating in the US may be said to operate in one international market and will be considered to have less of an international profile than a Japanese retailer operating in France, Germany, and the UK. This, however, is far too simplistic a method of describing the differences which these retailers will face in terms of the political, and hence regulatory, environment.

The German retailer, in this example, may have operations in California, New York and Texas, and while subject to the Federal regulations of the United States government, will also be subject to the regulations of the individual states of California, New York and Texas. Local taxes will need to be considered, and the effect they will have on retailers' pricing structure. Also, a retailer will have to be aware of the agreements that the United States government has signed with Canada and Mexico in establishing a Free Trade Area. A retailer may find that this agreement will allow products to be sourced more easily from these markets than had at first been assumed.

The Japanese retailer operating in Europe will have to conform to Belgian, British and German government regulations but will be subject to local regulations. Germany has a federal political structure and, from a business perspective, federal states that are prepared to intervene in business activities (Randlesome, 1993). The CDU government in Lower Saxony was reluctant in the 1980s to see the car manufacturer Volkswagen returned to private ownership. The company was the largest single source of employment in the Land, or federal state. The state government retained a fifth of the company's shares when privatization occurred in 1988. In the UK, local planning requirements may restrict development of retail outlets in certain locations, while the different legal code in England and Wales to that in Scotland will be one further detail that the incoming retailer will need to appreciate. In Belgium, the Japanese retailer will find that local regulations concerning the use of language will be important. The Japanese retailer will also have to be aware of the supra-national regulations of the European Union. While national regulations are expected to conform to European law, national governments are not always as eager to implement these regulations as their treaty obligations imply they should be. Incoming retailers should be aware, therefore, of the final authority vested in European Union institutions.

The regulatory environment is directly relevant to international retailers in a number of ways, not least in terms of employment and planning laws. Retailers moving into mainland Europe – conditions in the UK are somewhat different in respect of employment conditions – may find that they had not anticipated the training schemes and payments they will be required to make, nor the planning regulations which they must observe. The difference which had already grown up between the UK and continental European markets was emphasized when the UK declined the opportunity to subscribe to the Social Chapter of the Maastricht Treaty. Social issues and working conditions may surprise some retailers moving into Germany. Unionization within the retail workforce, and hence the influence of shop staff, has contributed to restricted store opening times. The Ladenschlußgesetz (Shop Opening Hours Act) of 1956, which established opening hours as 7 a.m. to 6.30 p.m. weekdays and 7 a.m. to 2 p.m. Saturday – except for one Saturday in the month when a closing time of 6.30 is permitted – remains the basis for opening hours, although the system was relaxed in 1989 to allow Thursday opening until 9 p.m.

Local practices also affect other areas of retail activity. While in France shops open for much longer than they do in Germany, French retailers have been restricted by the Loi Royer which came into force in 1973. This law established local commissions to regulate the development of large scale retail operations such as hypermarkets. The Loi Cadenas or the Padlock Law, which was introduced around the same time as the Loi Royer, has controlled the growth of similar operations in Belgium.

Therefore, regulatory boundaries may be considered on three levels:

- intra-state boundaries:
  - in Australia where individual states from New South Wales to Western Australia form the federal structure
  - in US where individual states from Maine to New Mexico form the federal structure
  - in Germany individual Lander from Schleswig-Holstein to Bayern form the federal structure
- state boundaries:
  - in Asia: Japan, Malaysia, Singapore
  - in North America: Canada, Mexico, the US
  - in Europe: France, Germany, Spain
- supra-state boundaries:
  - Association of Southeast Asian Nations
  - North American Free Trade Area
  - European Union

The regulatory environment, therefore, while appearing to provide the clearest division as far as international retail activity is concerned, is in itself a complex structure of interrelated regulatory environments which define the international challenge faced by the individual retail operation. Retailers will find that while some markets may at times appear conducive to expansion, regulations or changes in regulations will make it difficult for them to operate. This may occur in markets which appear psychologically proximate. Surprisingly, W. H. Smith the UK retailer, found itself in this position in the Canadian market in the 1980s. With a history of nearly four decades in the Canadian market behind it, the company was finally prompted to withdraw from the market when the Canadian government's regulations on non-domestic ownership in the book sector required W. H. Smith to part with 49 per cent of its subsidiary to Canadian investors (Brass, 1992).

Politics

Political uncertainty is an important issue for any retailer considering international activity. Retailers are particularly susceptible to changes in the political climate as they may have considerable property investments in non-domestic markets which are not easily realized in times of political crises.

Political boundaries are not as fixed as they may sometimes appear. The political uncertainty in Canada and the uncertain future of the Canadian Federation in the context of the Quebec nationalism and the volatility of the electorate as witnessed by the Federal elections of 1993, in a state that would be classified as politically stable, emphasizes the need to avoid complaisant assessments of political conditions in international markets. Western Europe between 1945 and 1990 saw not only considerable economic growth but also a somewhat uncharacteristic stability in national boundaries. The 1990s, particularly in Central and Eastern Europe, have witnessed a rapid changes in boundaries, the stability of which had so recently seemed assured.

The importance of changing political boundaries is exemplified by the experience of Julius Meinl, an Austrian food retailer. When Julius Meinl considered the problems of retail operations in Prague and Budapest in the first decade of the twentieth century, the retailer was not considering moving outside the country of which Vienna was the capital. Until the peace treaties which followed the First World War, the Austro-Hungarian Empire encompassed the area that was to become Austria, Czechoslovakia and Hungary as well as much of Yugoslavia and Rumania. Today, Julius Meinl is again operating in Prague and Budapest after a period when the political boundaries of central Europe have undergone considerable change and a period when, even should they have wanted to, the company would not have been able to operate in the cities concerned, because of the command economies of the states in which they were located and the political dominance of the Soviet Union.

Retailers may therefore experience inadvertent internationalisation (Hollander, 1970) where changing political boundaries set new regulatory agendas for retailers. The potential problems facing a retailer in Eastern Europe and post-federated Canada, should substantial political reorganization occur, may be very different in form and substance, but the need to assess the consequences remain, and define the nature of the retailer's international operations.

The case of Julius Meinl may appear an extreme one, but similar changes have occurred, and are occurring, in other parts of the world where change, if less dramatic, has certainly been as profound. UK retailers, when considering international expansion in the 1950s would have seen markets such as Australia, Canada or South Africa as a natural choice because of the common origin of the legal systems which governed the regulation of commerce and shared political inheritance. In the 1990s, the common regulatory environment of the Single European Market has in this respect made Europe the natural choice for international expansion.

Economic boundaries

As Hollander (1970, p. 109) has noted:

> There is no point in going abroad, no matter how attractive the tax, the antitrust, or customs exemption privileges may appear to be, unless potential customers are available.

International retailers often reduce risk by avoiding operating in significantly different economic conditions. Retailers based in developed economies will favour moving into markets that have reached similar levels of economic development where they will be able to operate the type of retail outlets they have developed in their domestic market and, in consequence, serve a similar set of customers. Likewise, the more economically advanced a country, the more movement there will be into that country and from that country.

In economic, as well as political terms, retailers must also be aware of the fundamental differences which exist within national markets in the global environment. These differences help to explain different growth patterns of international operations. Luxury goods retailers such as Gucci and Cerruti will often be dispersed around the globe in cosmopolitan centres such as London, Montreal, New York, Paris, Sidney and Tokyo, but not develop national chains within the countries in which they operate. Other retailers may enter markets and develop operations in relatively restricted regional markets rather than expand into less attractive economic regions.

A German retailer, for example, considering expansion in the US, will have various issues to address on the economic as well as the political side. While the US has the highest GDP in the world, there are considerable variations between the States of the Union. In the late 1980s, when there was considerable interest in the US market, particularly from UK companies, US personal income per capita of the state at the bottom of the scale was half of the state at the top of the scale. In 1988, in Mississippi, personal income per capita was $11,116 while in Connecticut it was $23,059 (Bureau of Census, 1990). The US average was $16,489. Between 1987 and 1988 personal income in New Hampshire and Delaware rose by 6.2 per cent. In North Dakota it fell by 4.3 per cent. The German retailer would, therefore, find areas of the United states which fell below German levels of personal income as well as those which were above the German average.

Retailers must be aware of the evolving global environment. Even in a relatively short time, relative market positions may change substantially. In 1988, German GDP per capita was 81 per cent of the US figure, by 1991 it had risen to 88 per cent (Eurostat, 1993a). Other changes may be of a longer term nature but of fundamental significance. A non-domestic retailer considering the Belgian market in 1950 would have faced a market devastated by war and of less than 10 million people. With the establishment of the SEM and continued integration in the EU, a very different prospect would confront a potential investor. In the 1990s, Belgium at the administrative and geographical centre of a Europe of more than 350 million people, would appear far more attractive option than a relatively small state of 10 million people.

In Germany, old industrial centres, such as Bremen and Hamburg, have not seen the growth rates experienced in other parts of the country. Bavaria, together with Baden-Württemberg, Lower Saxony and Hesse, have seen higher growth rates in recent decades than many areas of the FDR. While the new Lander in the East may not appear economically attractive in some respects, they may attract retailers who provide appropriate retail formats and suitably priced merchandise. The same retailer may, however, not wish to move into similar markets in Slovakia because, unlike the Eastern Lander of Germany, Slovakia is not at present part of the EU and the Japanese retailer, referred to above, may reasonably conclude that economic development will therefore be swifter in the Eastern Lander.

The same Japanese retailer may for economic reasons feel that the UK is not necessarily the best economic option for expansion in Europe. The South East of England and East Anglia, with a combined population of 19 million, are the only UK regions with a standard of living above the EU average. In France, there are nine such regions with a combined population of 30 million. In Italy, there are eleven regions with a combined population of 36 million. These French and Italian regions have the advantage of being in close proximity and comparatively easy travelling distance of other prosperous European regions (Eurostat, 1993b).

When assessing the international expansion of international retailers, it is important to understand the economic conditions within a company's domestic market. This will have a fundamental effect on the nature of the process. Different answers to the following questions will describe very different international retail operations. Has the retailer only accessed wealthy cosmopolitan centres? Has the retailer entered a national market with similar levels of GDP per capita to be found in the retailer's domestic market? Has the retailer targeted the most economically developed markets suitable for expansion or less developed markets?

Social boundaries

International retailers cross social boundaries. Social conditions will be linked to economic development but not inextricably so. Social conditions will also be affected by culture but again, different markets may be influenced by similar cultural traditions but exhibit very different social conditions. The different contexts in which customers live, work and consume the products they purchase will play an important part in the international retailer's role within different societies.

Social factors are defined here as those factors such as demographic factors and the consumer artefacts of everyday life. The size of households and the ownership of specific goods are important indicators for retailers of a society's readiness for retail structural change and the introduction of retail operations into a market. In the 1960s, UK electrical goods retailers, such as Granada and Thorn, moved into other European markets in anticipation or in response to similar levels of interest in the new consumer products that their domestic market had found so attractive.

The hypothetical Japanese retailer discussed above will need to consider demographic factors when entering European markets. From an economic perspective, the German market or regions within it may appear the most attractive option. However, if the Japanese retailer's products are targeted at a particular demographic segment there may be conditions in the German market which would make that market less attractive. Germany has a rapidly aging population, and a decreasing number of consumers in the younger age range. It is projected that in the year 2010 there will be only 12 per cent of a population of 58.2 million under the age of fifteen in the western Lander in Germany. In the UK the figure is projected to be

19 per cent of 59.9 million (Eurostat, 1990). In the long term this may make the UK more attractive. However, with smaller family sizes in Germany, high levels of spending on children may more than compensate for the comparatively limited size of the market.

In Europe, such variations in social conditions may be expected. However, in other societies, such as the US, a considerable degree of heterogeneity also exists. A retailer operating in the US will find considerable differences in the social conditions across the United States. The US, it has been suggested, is not formed by fifty states, rather North America as a whole constitutes nine broader social environments or 'nations' (Garreau, 1981) which do not recognize what are often arbitrary state boundaries. Garreau would suggest that there were nine such environments, but many more might be inferred on the basis of the consideration of local conditions.

Cultural boundaries

Culture will be considered in some detail in chapter 12 later in the book, but it is important at this stage to raise the issue and its importance in determining the nature of international retailing. Retailers, when internationalizing their operation, will often seek to expand into markets which they believe their operations will have an immediate relevance and with which they will feel familiar. Therefore, German retailers may find themselves considering expansion in Austria before other markets because of the lack of language barriers and the existence of cultural empathy. The same may be said of UK retailers expansion in the Republic of Ireland, the US and in markets of the 'old' Commonwealth; Australia, Canada and New Zealand.

However, cultural differences may appear where they are least expected. UK retailers have expanded into the US, only to find the market encompasses greater differences than they had imagined and is far from being one market. Therefore, the German retailer referred to above, considering expansion in California and Texas, may find the Hispanic culture contrasts with the New York cultural environment where it may already have operations. The Japanese retailer may be more inclined to anticipate cultural diversity in Europe but may find that diversity is of a greater complexity than expected. As Hollander (1970, p. 112) has observed, although:

> Ardent nationalists may want to disagree . . . the market and economic differences between say, Germany and Austria or between the United States and Canada are certainly no greater than the differences within any of those countries.

Retailers may, therefore, seek in the first instance to move into markets which are not culturally distant. In time, the same retailer may look to less culturally similar but economically more attractive markets. Therefore, international retail activity may be considered at different levels of cultural penetration. However, it should be remembered that just because a retailer operates in markets which may ostensibly appear to be culturally distinct it does not necessarily follow that the retailer has addressed cultural differences. The retailer may be serving customers who have accepted the cultural agenda of the retailer or may be serving the needs of expatriates of the retailer's domestic market in new markets.

Retail structural boundaries

A retail structure defines the competitive environment in which the international retailer will have to operate on entering a new market. The retail structure will be determined by the factors discussed above but they are also a product of the historical experience of retailers in specific markets.

National retail structures are themselves a product of regional and local development which has led to differences within the countries as well as between countries. In 1985, in Baden-Württemberg and Bayern, there were less than two retail outlets per square kilometre. However, in Baden-Württemberg there are fifty-seven retail outlets per 10,000 inhabitants and in Bayern there are seventy-one (Eurostat, 1993b). These Lander with a similar geographic density of retail outlets had notably different numbers of inhabitants per outlet. In the same year, in Bremen, there were seventy-three inhabitants per retail outlet, similar to the figure for Bayern, while the density of outlets was very different at over 12 per square kilometre. These differences are in part a product of regulatory, economic, social and cultural differences but also the historical competitive environment.

During the last ten years, the UK grocery market has attracted mainland European operators such as Aldi and Netto. Wide margins in the food sector has been one reason why retailers have been attracted to the market. UK grocery retailers' attractive profit figures compared favourably with those of other European countries. Food retailers earning margins of 1–2 per cent in mainland Europe have been attracted by the margins of 7–8 per cent achieved by UK grocery retailers. UK grocery retailers had focused on a limited retail offering, the superstore. Mainland European markets, conversely, have seen a greater variety of format development: 'format choice has not developed in Britain to the extent observed elsewhere in Europe' (Burt and Sparks, 1994, p. 141). UK grocery retailers had therefore left gaps in the market which non-domestic retailers sought to fill. That is, the UK grocery retail structure had not developed in such a way as to provide the consumer with alternative shopping opportunities and hence was vulnerable to incursions from outside by retailers which had developed appropriate formats within other retail structures.

Retailers will sometimes be attracted to a market where the retail structure lags behind economic development, but where the opportunity exists for providing the developing market with its current and future needs. The development of hypermarkets by French retailers in Spain may be considered an example of this. Carrefour's early history shows an interest in other economically developed markets in Europe such as Belgium, Germany, Switzerland and the UK, and yet it was ultimately to be Spain where the company developed its strongest European presence outside France. Carrefour has since developed its operation in South America, where again it has filled a gap in the developing retail structure.

Problems are encountered when comparisons are made between the retail structures in one country and another. The terms used are not always compatible and this often leads to confusion and misinterpretations. Thus, retail structures in different markets have to be described in local terms or through the use of general operational, organizational, format or conceptual descriptions which are difficult to measure and will at times blur one into another. Perhaps because of this, it is particularly important to understand the nuances of different retail structures when market entry is considered as retail structures have an important impact on the success or failure of retailers entering new markets.

CONCLUSION

When considering international expansion retailers should be aware of the different boundaries which they propose crossing and the degree of unfamiliarity they will encounter. Likewise, in discussing international activity it is important to draw distinctions between international activities, the international activity of one company in different markets or a number of companies around the world.

As the preceding discussion shows, a detailed definition of international retailing is required.

International Retailing is:

the management of retail operations in markets which are different from each other in their regulation, economic development, social conditions, cultural environment, and retail structures.

The internationalization of retailing may therefore be defined.

The Internationalization of Retailing is:

the transfer of retail management technology or the establishment of international trading relationships which bring to a retail organization a level of international integration which establishes the retailer within the international environment in such a way as to transcend regulatory, economic, social, cultural, and retail structural boundaries.

However, as the previous discussion suggests, in order to reduce risks, retailers will often confine their operations to a relatively limited and comparatively safe collection of markets. Retail techniques, however, may well spread beyond the markets in which the key proponents of operational approaches expand. Internationalization must therefore be seen to include the spread of know-how independently of retailers.

QUESTIONS – DISCUSSION POINTS

1 In his definition of international retailing, Dawson (1993) uses the term country. What is a 'country', and on which of the five boundaries discussed in this chapter does the term place particular emphasis?

2 How many regulatory levels do retailers have to consider when internationalizing? You may wish to consider this issue with reference to:

   (a) a Japanese retailer considering the Chinese market
   (b) a Danish retailer considering the Italian market
   (c) a US retailer considering the German market.

3 With reference to the definition of international retailing given at the end of this chapter, consider Hollander's (1970) comment on cultural differences between Germany and Austria, the US and Canada. Is it possible to talk about 'internationalization' within a state?

REFERENCES

Brass, (1992) W H Smith Group PLC, A. Hast, D. Pascal, P. Barbour, J. Griffin (eds) *International Directory of Company Histories*, Vol. V, St James Press, Detroit, pp. 211–13.

Bureau of Census, (1990) *Statistical Abstract of the United States 1990*, US Department of Commerce.

Burt, S., and Sparks, L., (1994) Understanding Retail Grocery Store Format Change in Great Britain: The Continental European Dimension, *Retailing: Theories and Practices for Today and Tomorrow*, Proceedings of the Fourth Triennial National Retailing Conference, R. King (ed.), The Academy of Marketing Science and The American Collegiate Retailing Association, Special Conference Series Vol. VII, Richmond Virginia, 22–24 October, pp. 139–42.

Dawson, J., (1993) The Internationalisation of Retailing, *Department of Business Studies, University of Edinburgh, Working Paper*, 93/2.

Eurostat, (1990) *Demographic Statistics*, Theme 3 Series C, Population and Social Conditions, Commission of the European Communities, Brussels.

Eurostat, (1993a) *Basic Statistics of the European Community*, Commission of the European Communities, Brussels.

Eurostat, (1993b) *Retailing in the Single European Market 1993*, Commission of the European Communities, Brussels.

Garreau, J., (1981) *The Nine Nations of North America*, Houghton Mifflen, Boston.

Hollander, S., (1970) *Multinational Retailing*, Michigan State University, East Lancing, MI.

Horsman, M., and Marshall, A., (1994) *After the Nation-State*, Harper Collins, 1994.

Johnson, D., (1989) 'Last Question', *The Spectator*, 2 December, p. 12.

Lewison, D., (1989) *Essentials of Retailing*, Merrill, Columbus Ohio.

Partridge, E., (1966) Origins; *An Etymological Dictionary of Modern English*, 4th edition, Routledge, London.

Pellegrini, L., (1994) Alternatives for Growth and Internationalization in Retailing, *The International Review of Retail, Distribution and Consumer Research*, Vol. 4, No. 2, pp. 121–48.

Randlesome, C., (1993) The Business Culture in Germany, C. Randlesome (ed.) *Business Cultures in Europe*, Butterworth-Heinnemann, Oxford.

International Retailers

▌ OBJECTIVES ▌

This chapter considers the means by which international retail activity may be classified. This allows for the identification of those fundamental differences which distinguish retail strategies used within the international environment. Various approaches to this issue are presented and discussed. These analytical frameworks form the basis for further discussion of conceptual developments which are presented in subsequent sections.

INTRODUCTION

The international retail sector encompasses a wide collection of retail types. International retail operations may take the form of large warehouse style operations with limited service provision; they may take the form of concessions with limited operating space but high service levels. To refer to international retailing, and to include all forms of retailing within that description, will inevitably lead to generalizations. At times, these generalizations may be misleading. Therefore, it is essential that some understanding is achieved of the different types of retail operation which make up the international retailing community. Only then, on that basis, an evaluation of the different opportunities and problems which such retailers face may be attempted.

Different types of retail operation have been influential in the development of retailing in markets around the world during different stages of international development. At different stages in the development of international retailing, some retail formats have been at a dynamic stage of their development while other retail forms have been less significant than they once were. In the 1990s, the category killer, represented by such fascias as Toys R Us and Ikea, has become an important player in the development of world markets, whereas the variety store has lost its international appeal. The relevance of different retail forms is determined by levels of economic and social development in global markets. In order to understand the different trends within international retailing, it is necessary to categorize the various retail operations that have developed and are continuing to develop international activity.

The categorization process, however, is not a straightforward one, not least because retailing itself does not have a robust taxonomy. There is not an 'off the shelf' classification system that is universally acceptable. This chapter, therefore, discusses international retailing on the basis of fundamental retail classification criteria, merchandise and format, and, subsequently, on the basis of academic analysis of the international retail environment.

ANALYTICAL FRAMEWORKS

Merchandise

One important means by which international retailers may be classified and hence analysed is by merchandise category. Food and non-food may be used as a basis by which to categorize stores. These two categories may be further subdivided. In the UK, for example, food retailers have often been categorized as grocery retailers, bakers, butchers, greengrocers, and fishmongers. Non-food retailers have been categorized as clothing retailers, footwear retailers, other non-food retailers such as electrical goods retailers and jewellers. Other retailers have been classified as mixed retailers and CTNs (Confectioners, Tobacconists and Newsagents). However, these categories do not remain stable over time. The number of retailers in such categories will change as a result of the utility of different merchandise ranges.

Food retailers
In the UK, since the 1950s, the number of specialists food retailers has declined in the face of competition from retailers in the grocery retail category. In this period, successful grocery operators expanded their range of goods to the extent that the largest grocery retailers' merchandise range encompassed the merchandise

carried by bakers, butchers, greengrocers and fishmongers. This fulfilled the requirements of customers who required products of enhanced quality, suitably packaged, sold through outlets which conveniently provided a range of household requirements.

The role of the large food retailers who had emerged from the traditional grocery sector in the late 1950s and through the 1960s, increased dramatically in the late 1970s and early 1980s as the impact of the superstore and hypermarket format were felt in the market-place. As table 3.1 illustrates, in these early years of superstore and hypermarket development, the grocery retailers not only increasingly came to dominate the distribution of grocery items, which had traditionally been retailed in other retail outlets, but also distribute food items traditionally sold through specialist retail stores.

Thus, the traditional demarcation lines between food retailers has been eroded in recent decades. This process of change has not been limited to the UK. In France, the hypermarket came to epitomize changing social requirements and the

Table 3.1 Respective food market shares of large grocery retailers and specialist outlets: Great Britain 1976–82

		Year			
Product		*1976*	*1978*	*1980*	*1982*
Grocery products	A	68.7	72.4	88.6	88.0
Fresh fruit and vegetables	A	27.5	36.0	44.1	47.2
	B1	54.8	47.0	45.8	43.2
Fresh milk and cream	A	12.5	12.1	32.4	34.4
	B2	67.3	65.8	65.3	63.0
Carcass meat etc.	A	15.8	21.2	30.1	32.8
	B3	73.8	68.9	67.2	64.8
Fresh fish, poultry and game	A	22.1	33.6	36.6	41.6
	B4	47.6	30.6	29.4	25.8
Bakery products	A	32.5	40.0	45.5	48.9
	B5	41.4	36.2	37.2	35.6
Alcoholic beverages	A	25.9	30.7	41.7	44.0
	B6	58.2	51.8	48.4	45.9

A   Grocery retailers   B4   Fishmongers and poulterers
B1   Greengrocers and fruiterers   B5   Bread and flour confectioners
B2   Dairymen   B6   Off-Licences
B3   Butchers

Source: Retail Inquiry, 1976, 1978, 1980, 1982.

scrambling of merchandise lines. Thus, in the development of international food retailing operations, those retailers who revolutionized the domestic retail environment have been most prominent in the development of international food retailing. Operations such as Auchan, Carrefour, Casino and Promodès have achieved a high international profile. They are examples of retailers who challenged traditional assumptions of merchandise range. In consequence, there are relatively few specialized international food retailers. However, examples do exist, and changing social and economic factors may see an increasing number of international retailers of this type. The Brioche Dorèe, which is based in France, is a chain of bakeries and coffee shops, which has franchised operations in European markets (Ireland, Italy, Spain and the UK), North America (Canada, USA) and Japan (CIG, 1994). Likewise, Thorntons, the UK based confectionery retailer, has entered the international market. It franchises Thorntons' outlets in Ireland and entered the French market in 1989 where, along with production facilities, the company acquired a chain of stores operating under the Martial fascia (CIG, 1994).

Non-food retailers

International non-food retailers have become familiar on high streets and in shopping centres in developed markets around the world. Many of these retailers are specialized operations with well-defined product ranges. The German retail market has attracted a large number of retailers from Europe, North America and Japan. These include specialist clothing retailers such as the Jeans Shop, which is partly owned by the Woolworths operation in the US, High & Mighty, the UK based clothing operation for outsize men, Pronuptia, the French bridal wear retailer (CIG, 1994). In other product areas retailers, such as Books R Us, the US based and Toys R Us owned operation, Yves Rocher, the French beauty product company, and Komet, the Swiss electrical goods retail chain provide customers with well defined product ranges (CIG, 1994).

The situation in the non-food sector has been almost diametrically opposed to the position in the food sector. While in the food sector it is the wide merchandise retailer who has made the greatest impact in the last twenty years, in the non-food sector the specialist merchandise retailer has not only been particularly prominent but also had the greatest impact. Not only have specialist non-food retailers expanded into a dispersed collection of markets, they have also seen the development of substantial chains in individual markets. In the German market, Benetton has over 450 stores, Photo Porst (Switzerland, photograph processing) nearly 3,000 stores, Mr Minit (Belgium, services) over 800 stores (CIG, 1994).

In the non-food sector, the development of wide merchandise range operations has not been eclipsed in the same way as the specialist stores in the food sector, but the vitality of such stores has certainly been less noticeable in recent years. Well known international wide merchandise retailers which operate in European markets today are often the product of international actions taken at a relatively early date. In the German market, the Woolworth operation, which is still owned by the US parent and currently has 316 stores, was established in 1927 (CIG, 1994; Woolworth, 1954). C&A began developing an international operation in 1911

(Siewart, 1992). Originally based in the Netherlands, the company now has strong German associations; the company expanded into the UK in 1922. In 1962–3, C&A entered the US market with the purchase of Nathan Ohrbach stores in New York (Siewart, 1992; Ball, 1980).

The development of category killer operations with specialized, yet extensive merchandise ranges, is an innovative new force in the international market place in the non-food sector. The Toys R Us operation has attracted considerable attention in recent years with its rapid international expansion. The company's rapid internationalization in the mid and late 1980s (Laulajainen, 1991) saw the international division making profits for the first time in 1987 (Monke, 1992). Between 1989 and 1993, Toys R Us saw turnover grow from £94.5m to £219.2m on the bases of developments in markets in Europe, North America and on the Pacific Rim (EIU, 1994). The success of Toys R Us may be equated with the development of Ikea (Laulajainen, 1991). While Ikea has a longer international history than Toys R Us, (its first non-Swedish store was established in Norway in 1963), the development of the Ikea operations illustrates the vitality of this type of non-food retailer and the considerable impact which such retailers are capable of having on the competitive structure within a retail market (Martenson, 1981), as illustrated by the fact that in 1990 the company estimated that 78 million people passed through the company's stores worldwide (Jefferys, 1992).

Comparisons

Non-food retailers have achieved an international status that food retailers have not achieved. Some retailers, such as the Body Shop and Benetton have succeeded in developing operations in a considerable number of markets around the world. This geographical spread has not been achieved by food retailers, unless, that is, catering operations such as McDonalds are included within the definition of retailing. Many grocery retailers have either remained within their national markets or internationalized into a relatively limited number of markets. Only some, such as Carrefour, have established a dispersed international operation.

However, where non-food retailers have developed a world presence they have often operated only a limited number of outlets in the markets they serve, whereas food retailers have been forced, by the very nature of their business, to develop a considerable presence in order to compete effectively. Large food retail operations such as superstores and hypermarkets will depend on a distribution system to supply them which is fundamentally different to distribution systems which supply non-food operations. This requires them to build sufficient market presence to support the sourcing and distribution of merchandise on the scale which their operation demands.

In 1991, the Corporate Intelligence Group (1991) identified twenty-five fashion retailers operating 251 outlets in the Netherlands, an average of around ten stores per chain. The largest chain was operated by Benetton with fifty-five outlets, while a number of retailers such as Chipie and Fil à Fil (France) operated only one store. In comparison, the German food retailer Aldi operated 210 outlets in the market. Tengelmann (Germany) was the only other operator in the Dutch supermarket sector with a chain of 114 outlets. Likewise, in 1994, the Corporate Intelligence Group (1994) identified (if C&A are excluded because they were differently classified in 1991) 31 fashion outlets, with 308 outlets, an average of around ten outlets per chain. Aldi's store numbers had risen to 270 and Tengelmann's to 125.

Merchandise is a determinant of international retail strategy. It will affect not only the decision to internationalize but also the method which is adopted to build a non-domestic market presence. The merchandise range may be a primary reason why retailers internationalize. Some retailers like Dunhill (UK) have a distinct product range of luxury goods. They are represented in major centres around the world. While Dunhill has used franchise operations, it has tended to retain in-house control of most of its international operations. The international chain is not large; Japan is host to the largest number of international Dunhill stores with a chain of thirty. Even the US only has eleven stores. Dunhill appeals to an affluent customer group and therefore is able to retain in-house control over seventy-one stores while having sixteen managed by third parties. In comparison, Benetton, which while possessing a distinct merchandise range, has a global network of more than 7,000 stores, has followed the franchise route to global expansion. In France and Germany combined, the company has more than 1,000 stores. This level of market penetration and hence mass market product appeal has been met through and realized by the use of methods other than organic in-house expansion.

Format

As merchandise has been a factor which has encouraged retailers to expand internationally so innovative formats, developed in the domestic market, have been viewed as an asset from which the company will benefit in the non-domestic market. Formats, unlike merchandise, which may to some extent be protected through patents, are not easily protected. Thus formats, such as the variety store and the supermarket, have often been internationalized through the transfer of know how and not simply through the operational expansion of one retail operation.

Within format groups, internationalization has occurred at a different rate. The department store and variety store sector have not been prime determinants of international retailing in the latter years of the twentieth century, although both sectors had been an important element of the internationalization process in the earlier years of the century. Operations such as C&A, which built up a European operation from 1911, when it opened a store in Berlin (Siewart, 1992), while still an important player in international market, are not typical of more recent European international activities. Nevertheless, while this sector has proved to be less important in the European environment, the internationalization of Japanese retailing in the last few decades has seen the expansion of department store operations such as Daimura and Yaohan, retailers who have a long history of internationalization behind them (Chen and Sternquist, 1995).

The innovative format does, of course, have considerable advantage in a new market environment. The new form may fill an as yet unfilled gap in the distribution system and thereby prove a competitive force within the environment. However, retailers may have difficulty developing the innovative format because of planning regulations and other associated constraints. CostCo's entry into the UK was affected by legal issues concerning the nature of the business: was it a retailer or a wholesaler? Likewise, stores such as Toys R Us were faced with considerable problems when they attempted to enter the Japanese market because they challenged the restrictive regulations which governed Japanese retail development. The innovative format therefore has many advantages, but its operators may also have many problems to overcome.

One response to the problems of introducing innovative retail formats into developed markets is to target markets with less developed retail structures. This has certainly been the case with French superstore operators in their development of the Spanish and Portuguese markets, and the markets of Argentina, Brazil, Malaysia and Taiwan. The advantages of underdeveloped markets has not been lost on food retailers throughout Europe who have increasingly come to recognize the opportunities that such markets offer (Myers and Alexander, 1995a,b).

Retailers who employ distinctive but essentially traditional shop formats, may internationalize their operation more quickly than those that rely on the market absorbing a fundamentally new retail approach. Retailers that are able to fit into traditional high street locations or standardized units within shopping centres or malls will be able to build a market presence without over turning preconceptions and altering shopping patterns. The style of their store may be individual and the merchandise defining, but the format will be essentially the shop-in-a-box style. Laura Ashley describe their distinctive store layout as the 'green box', a form which while enhanced by a suitably characteristically English setting in the domestic market, may also be fitted into the predefined dimensions of a US mall.

Hollander

When discussing international retailers, Hollander (1970) suggested the categories and subcategories given in exhibit 3.1. His categorization system provides an insight into the fundamentals of internationalization (see figure 3.1).

Some of these categories while applicable to the environment of the late 1960s may be considered in need of re-evaluation today. For example, supermarkets or the superstores and hypermarkets, are more appropriate in the general merchandise category, if this category is to infer a wider range of merchandise, as well as a variety of merchandise.

Trading companies, direct selling and automatic vending meanwhile may not appear to be important categories. However, such categories should not be totally ignored. While they may not constitute a major element of international retail activity, or as important an element as they may have done, they remain an area where such activity may develop in the future. Direct selling companies such as Tupperware and Encyclopedia Britannica have been household names for a number of decades and continue to represent a feasible retail channel for the appropriate products. Vending machines, while not every European shopper's first stop retail option, are an important element of retailing in Japan.

Exhibit 3.1 Hollander's taxonomy of international retailers

Dealers in luxury goods. The cultural origins of such retailers are often important in conveying the elite luxurious qualities of such retailers. They are to be found in the cosmopolitan centres of retail activity typified by such cities as London, Paris and New York.

General merchandise dealers. They have frequently offered non-domestic environments an innovative format.

* department stores
* variety and discount stores
* mail order
* supermarkets

Trading companies. These operations are associated with developing markets. They have other main business activities from which retailing developed.

Specialized chains. These operations have relatively narrow product ranges. Their development in the international environment has varied between product groups.

* food and supermarkets
* clothing and related items
* shoes
* other specialist
* service trades

Direct selling and automatic vending. Direct selling operations have been used to distribute products in global markets for many years. The products of the Singer organization is a well known example. Automatic vending while widely used has not seen large scale internationalization by operators.

Source: Hollander, 1970.

The most intriguing category that Hollander (1970) suggested was that of the trading company. This category is intriguing for two reasons. First, it seems highly irrelevant to contemporary retailing and secondly it is associated with retail trade with the third world. These two factors are connected.

If ever the statement that international retailing is not a new phenomenon were appropriately applied, it is in this context. The Hudson Bay Company was incorporated in 1670; 320 years later it accounted for 7 per cent of non-food Canadian retail sales, with nearly 500 stores trading under the Bay, Zellers and Fields fascias and an

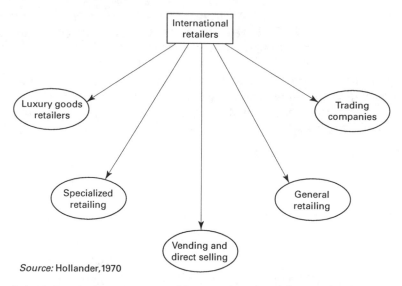

Source: Hollander,1970

Figure 3.1 Hollander's taxonomy of international retail organizations

annual retail revenue of C\$4.5 billion (Badaracco, 1992). While it may be argued that the activities of the Hudson Bay Company have evolved somewhat over the years and their involvement with retailing has passed through many metamorphoses, the place of the trading company in the development of international retailing is assured.

Booker McConnell was an important trading company in Africa before it began to reinvest in its home market as its third world operations became more precarious in the 1960s. Companies such as Booker McConnell served third world markets but their outlets were not necessarily rudimentary. These companies operated stores that reflected the operating techniques of their domestic market and were therefore engaged in a process of technology transfer, although, perhaps not always a totally successful transfer in the long run. The activity was also big business. By 1954, the United Africa Companies store in Lagos was turning over £1.5 million per annum (Hollander, 1970).

Some merchants found themselves increasingly involved in retailing, although, their original trading intentions had been very different. Booker McConnell was a sugar merchant. Its retail operation developed as the markets with which it traded sought more merchandise but also as a means by which to utilize the cargo space of its shipping facilities on the outward stage of the journey to the Caribbean (Hollander, 1970).

These trading company retailers exploited market opportunities for the same reasons as other retailers have moved into markets. Japanese retailers in the 1980s moved into non-domestic markets to better serve the expatriate Japanese community in those markets and the Irish retailer Dunnes has moved into the Spanish market to serve expatriate communities. Other retailers such as Sears Roebuck (US) and Carrefour (France) have moved into less developed retail markets. The trading companies entered non-domestic markets for reasons which are still fundamental motivating factors behind international retail activity.

Treadgold

Hollander's (1970) classification of international retailers was influenced by the merchandise, format and operational characteristics of the retailers included in his survey. While this approach provides a taxonomy which may be used to compare the retailers within any one category, there remains the problem that the categories themselves may change over time as new merchandise groupings, format innovations and operational techniques are exploited. It may therefore be more appropriate to attempt to classify retailers on the basis of other factors which characterize their international operations.

Treadgold's (1988) typology of trans-national retailing is based on entry and operating strategy and geographical presence of international retailers. Figure 3.2 provides a diagrammatic representation of Treadgold's classification system. It is Treadgold's observation that high cost entry strategies allow retailers to retain high control over their non-domestic operation while low cost entry strategies will demand the loss of some control. Thus high cost, high control, strategies such as acquisition stand at one end of the spectrum and franchising stands at the other end of the spectrum representing low cost, low control, strategies. In between these extremes, Treadgold would classify 50/50 joint venture agreements.

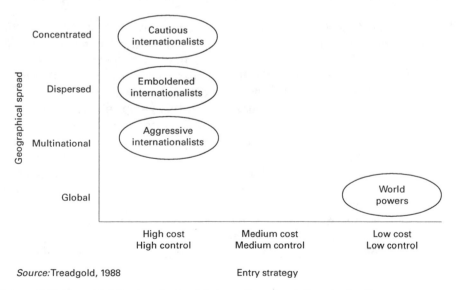

Source: Treadgold, 1988

Figure 3.2 Treadgold's typology of international retail organizations

The geographical presence of retailers in the international arena is also seen by Treadgold as representing differences between international retail operations. He observes that retailers' activities range from concentrated internationalization, where retailers are involved in border-hopping expansion to global internationalization, where retailers 'have succeeded in developing a truly "Global" presence yet who often have ambitions to trade in still more countries' (Treadgold, 1988, p. 10). Between these two polarities, Treadgold identifies dispersed international retailers and the more adventurous multinational retailers. Dispersed international retailers are those who have established 'a presence in a number of markets geographically remote and culturally diverse from their domestic market place' (Treadgold, 1988, p. 9). Multinational retailers are described as retailers who 'have developed a presence in a large number of overseas markets' (Treadgold, 1988, p. 9). Like the dispersed international retailers, these retailers will operate in remote and culturally diverse markets.

Treadgold's observations, which were made in the mid 1980s, suggested that retailers fell into four clusters (see exhibit 3.2). Treadgold's clusters reflect Hollander's classification system. If trading companies and vending operations are excluded, as they did not represent a significant part of 1980s international retailing or Treadgold's analysis, the clusters which emerge in Treadgold's typological analysis bear some resemblance to Hollander's specialist, general and luxury retailer categories. Figure 3.3 shows that cautious and emboldened internationalists are often general or wide merchandise range retailers, luxury goods retailers are

Exhibit 3.2 Treadgold's typology of international retailers

Cluster one, cautious internationalists. This group were distinguished by their retention of high control in the international market and a limited international market presence. The higher control and thus the higher costs of market entry were self defining in this respect. The companies in this cluster operate in markets which are either geographically or culturally proximate.

Cluster two, emboldened internationalists. In this group retailers continue to exercise high control and therefore incur high entry costs but have through the longevity of their international expansion begun to move into markets which are remote both culturally and geographically.

Cluster three, aggressive internationalists. Again this group has retained high levels of control over its operations but has expanded into a wider variety of markets.

Cluster four, world powers. Unlike the other three clusters, retailers in this group have used low control methods of market entry and have therefore established a presence in a very high number of markets around the world.

Source: Treadgold, 1988.

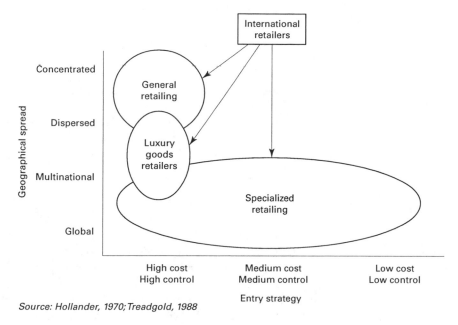

Source: Hollander, 1970; Treadgold, 1988

Figure 3.3 Comparison of Hollander's and Treadgold's typology of international retail organizations

emboldened internationalists, while specialist retailers are either aggressive inter-nationalists or world powers. This would suggest that the entry strategy axis, while it may identify the most international of retailers in the mid 1980s, does so only because it is the entry strategy itself which has facilitated this, rather than funda-mental characteristics of the company such as an internationally appealing offering. There is a danger that the argument becomes circular here, particularly when it is considered that these clusters are the product of a particular point in time.

Treadgold's clusters represent the position of corporate entities. However, in-creasingly, retail companies, through the use of different fascias and operating strategies in the international market place, are not easily defined as operating low of high control and cost strategies. In some markets, they will use one approach, in another market they will utilize a different entry strategy. One fascia owned by the company may be placed in the border hopping category, another in the global category. Marks & Spencer's Brooks Brothers operation resembles the strategies adopted by other luxury retailers. It had expanded out of the US market into the Japanese market, where a sufficiently affluent and aspiring social group was acces-sible but the fascia has not been used in other markets. Marks & Spencer, however, has passed through various phases of development by expanding into culturally similar but geographically distant markets, such as Canada, and consequently ostensibly culturally different but geographically proximate markets in Europe. Marks & Spencer has also acquired other fascias in Canada and the US, which conforms to another form of internationalization. While Marks & Spencer's international experience may not be the norm, it is shared by an increasing number of retailers as different formats and approaches to internationalization are utilized within one organizational structure.

The entry strategy classification used by Treadgold (1988) distinguishes the most global of operations from those retailers with a comparatively limited market presence. Thus, it effectively identifies those retailers with a globally relevant operation, unit-format or focused merchandise range from those with internationally limited relevance, broader merchandise ranges or large formats. To some extent, therefore, it distinguishes along merchandise and format lines, that is, food retailers from fashion retailers, large store retailers from shop-in-a-box retailers.

Salmon and Tordjman

While Treadgold focused on entry strategy and geographical presence, the fundamental issue considered in Salmon and Tordjman's (1989) analysis was the problem of reconciling the need to adapt to local conditions and the operational advantages of maintaining a common approach in all markets. They note that there are three fundamental retail strategies: global, multinational and investment. However, they are primarily concerned with the global and multinational approach (see exhibit 3.3).

Salmon and Tordjman's classification system is accessible and identifies an important dichotomy within international retailing. There is a fundamental difference between retailers who replicate their retail operations globally, with only modest adaptations in the local environment, and those retailers who seek to operate distinct operations in different markets adapting to local needs to a significant degree. In some respects, the investment and multinational strategies described by Salmon and Tordjman have much in common, in that they represent a fundamental orientation to the market of destination rather than a global segment. However, the multinational strategy recognizes the fact that some retailers, while maintaining distinct operations, operate in similar markets, and encourage the transfer of information across national boundaries. However, the investment strategy may, over time, lead to many of the benefits of, and in many respects become indistinct from, the multinational strategic approach. Marks & Spencer's acquisitions in the US may be classified as investments on one level, yet there is a regular transfer of skills between the company's US operations and its European stores.

Salmon and Tordjman's classification system may be usefully compared with Treadgold's typology. These two systems were both developed in the mid 1980s and therefore considered individual companies at the same stage in their development. The companies which Salmon and Tordjman place in their global classification are, in great part, those classified by Treadgold as aggressive internationalists and world powers, while Salmon and Tordjman's multinational retailers are classified as cautious or emboldened internationalists, as exhibit 3.3 indicates.

Many of the retailers considered by Treadgold (1988) were also considered by Salmon and Tordjman (1989) and, perhaps partly in consequence of this, a considerable degree of agreement emerges from these two studies (see exhibit 3.4). However, the categorization of Marks & Spencer stands out. Salmon and Tordjman's consideration of Marks & Spencer as a 'specialised' (Salmon and Tordjman, 1989, p. 4) store may have encouraged them to classify Marks & Spencer in a manner which to some extent begs to be challenged. It might be more appropriate to liken Marks & Spencer to C&A rather than Benetton in terms of the store's level of specialization. The classification of Marks & Spencer in this way also raises the problem noted above with reference to Treadgold's classification system that some companies have adopted a variety of strategies in the international environment. Therefore, it is more precise to say that the international development of the Marks & Spencer fascia in Canada and some European markets resembles a global approach to internationalization, whereas its development of the Marks & Spencer fascia has, in some markets, seen considerable product range changes akin to a multinational strategy, and in Canada and the US a modified investment strategy has been followed.

This problem of classification and indeed dilemma of strategic planning was addressed by Treadgold (1990) in later work in this area. He recognized the

---

Exhibit 3.3 Salmon and Tordjman's classification of international retail strategies

Global. The retail formula is replicated in all markets around the world in which the company has a presence. The formula appeals to a global segment and is correspondingly positioned. There is a standardization of marketing mix strategy. There is vertical integration in distribution, production and design. Management is centralized and depends on the rapid exchange of information. There exists a capacity to grow quickly taking advantages of considerable economies of scale. There is limited transfer of know-how as the companies outlets are all following the same marketing strategy.

Multinational. The retail formula is adapted to local conditions, as is the marketing mix strategy, but the retailer continues to operate within a broad sector maintaining similarities across markets. Management is decentralized although there exists regular communication between markets. There is restricted growth capacity with few economies of scale, but an important transfer of know-how.

Investment. An existing company is purchased in the non-domestic market. This forms part of a portfolio of non-domestic investment. Development is isolated with little communication between markets. This facilitates the swift development of an international presence. Risk is low and the transfer of skills is not considered an important factor.

Source: Salmon and Tordjman, 1989.

Exhibit 3.4 Corresponding retailer positions in Treadgold's and Salmon and Tordjman's classification system

	Aggressive internationalists/ world powers: Treadgold	Cautious and emboldened internationalists: Treadgold
Global: Salmon and Tordjman	Benetton, Laura Ashley, Ikea, McDonalds	Marks & Spencer
Multinational: Salmon and Tordjman		C&A, Printemps, Carrefour, Auchan, Promodes, Docks de France

Source: Salmon and Tordjman, 1989; Treadgold, 1988.

---

problem of adopting a localized marketing offering where a global offering was inappropriate. The problem of localization reduces the benefits of trading internationally, through the reduction of cross-border exchange of knowledge and operating experience. However, he also recognized that it is only a relatively limited number of retailers who may aspire to a truly global positioning. Thus, he suggests that 'international retailers should strive to be not multinational but trans-national organisations' (Treadgold, 1990). In this, Treadgold suggests there is a reconciliation of the conflicting objectives of responsiveness to local needs and the organizational efficiency which is achieved through global integration. As Treadgold (1990) notes, Bartlett and Ghoshal (1989) have recognized the dilemma inherent within international organizations of reconciling the three factors of global efficiency, local responsiveness and the development and exploitation of knowledge. Thus Treadgold (1990) suggests that C&A, Carrefour and Marks & Spencer may all be considered to adopt transnational positions, because they respond to local needs while maintaining an integration across international boundaries which utilizes knowledge and achieves efficiencies.

Both Treadgold (1988) and Salmon and Tordjman's (1989) classification systems identify those retailers who have a considerable international relevance, market in a similar form around the globe and are inclined to use rapid expansion strategies in order to reach markets with their merchandise concept and own brand products quickly. To a considerable extent these are a synthesis of Hollander's luxury goods retailers and his specialist retailers in 1980s guise. They appeal to a global market segment and operate in the cosmopolitan centres of the world but through the use of franchising have also been able to establish market coverage in provincial markets at a rapid rate. Other global retailers mentioned by Salmon and Tordjman but not considered by Treadgold – Conran and Yves Rocher – could certainly find a place under Hollander's (1970) definition of a luxury goods retailer.

Bailey, Clarke-Hill and Robinson

The preceding classification systems of international retail activity focused on the international retailers themselves and the characteristics of their international

---

Exhibit 3.5 Bailey, Clarke-Hill and Robinson hierarchy of alliance types

Loose affiliations. Trade bodies which are interested in disseminating information, political lobbying and shared distribution in certain contexts. Conseil National du Commerce (France), Hauptgeminschaft des Deutschen Einzelhandels (Germany), Institute of Grocery Distributors and Retail Consortium (UK), Confédération Européene du Commerce de Detail (Europe).

National buying clubs. Established for the sourcing of merchandise within the national context. These groups while inherently national in nature may have international associations. Nisa (UK) is a member of the European Marketing Distribution (Europe).

Co-market agreements. Working partnerships which recognize the mutual advantages of cooperation in the marketing of products. This may lead to joint ventures. Concessions and licensing agreements are included in the definition. Monsoon (UK) has licence agreements in Norway, Malaysia and New Zealand. Olympus (UK) has a concession in Galerias Preciades (Spain).

International alliances with central secretariats. Coordination of operational activities includes buying, branding, information and skills exchange, and marketing. The role of these organizations is developing as the development of retail brands develop. Association Commerciale Internationale, Intercoop, SEDD (Europe).

Equity participation alliances. This type alliance has a strategic role. Participants equity stakes in the other members. ERA is formed by Casino (France), Ahold (Netherlands), Argyll Group (UK).

Joint ventures. Where at least two companies form a separate enterprise. This may be due to product and market knowledge: Sainsbury (UK) and GIB (Belgium) have formed Homebase (UK).

Partial acquisition and equity participation. Where a retailer acquires a part interest in another retailer.

Controlling interest or full merger with retained identity of subsidiary. Where a full relationship has developed.

Source: Bailey, Clarke-Hill and Robinson, 1995.

---

activities. This does not include the full range of international involvement that an individual company may have. Particularly in the European environment, international strategic alliances have become an important aspect of cross-border involvement.

Bailey, Clarke-Hill and Robinson (1995) have developed a model, hereafter referred to as the BCR model, which seeks to develop a taxonomy of retail alliances. The BCR model, accepting Stafford's (1994) assertion that there is a continuum of inter-company relationships, includes features of international activity discussed above but places such relationships in a framework which seeks to integrate them within the context of the looser associations currently developing in the international market-place. The model identifies an eight stage continuum from loose affiliations through to full merger (see exhibit 3.5).

These different types of alliance are a means by which retailers may reduce risk when expand into unfamiliar markets. They may be useful to large retailers but may be far more useful to retailers that are not in the first rank of size, assets and management expertise. Such alliances may provide retailers with an ability to negotiate with suppliers on a pan-European rather than national basis, but they also provide an opportunity for the international flow of ideas and technical knowledge. Through such networking of retail organizations, retailers are better placed to understand the environment in which they operate and thereby facilitate competitive advantage, as Kanter (1989) has suggested such allied firms should aim to do. They will arguably form an important aspect of international activity as the international agenda is increasingly recognized as an important element in the retail environment.

CONCLUSION

These classification systems provide a means by which the more significant variables which differentiate international retail operations may be recognized and acknowledged. Trends in the internationalization process are more easily identified when the fundamental divisions within the retail structure are understood. Food retailers will experience similar problems to non-food retailers in the international environment but the emphasis they will need to give to certain problems will differ by virtue of their merchandise range.

Classification systems are useful management tools where they provide an indication of the issues which retailers face in commercial environments. Treadgold's matrix discussed above, provides a structure on the basis of which international retail managers may place their operations and the growth potential of the company while it pursues given objectives. 'Cautious internationalists' will not see the same growth rates as retailers in the 'world powers' group. However, they may achieve sustained long term growth and market presence which the 'world powers' will not. Salmon and Tordjman's classification system identifies a fundamental difference in approaches to retail internationalization. Some retailers will not be able to adopt a global strategy, they will be forced through the nature of their business to adopt either an investment or multinational approach. It is important that retailers should be aware of the strengths of the type of operation they have the opportunity to develop in the international market-place, and the fundamental problems and threats which must be faced. It is important because, otherwise, there is a danger that they will pursue strategies which are based on models which do not conform to the same fundamental characteristics as the retail operation they seek to develop.

QUESTIONS – DISCUSSION POINTS

1 Are there fundamental differences between food retailers and non-food retailers which require them to be categorized entirely separately when international retailing is considered?

2 Hollander's (1970) use of terms such as 'dealer in luxury goods' and 'general merchandise dealers' may sound old fashioned to the contemporary ear. Nevertheless, how useful are such terms in developing a fundamental understanding of the factors which categorize international retailers?

3 What are the underlying assumptions which determine Treadgold's (1988) and Salmon and Tordjman's (1989) classification systems, and how do the two systems differ?

4 Are alliances a temporary phenomenon in the international environment brought about through the defensive actions of retailers who feel threatened by the changing global environment?

REFERENCES

Badaracco, C., (1992) Hudson's Bay Company, A. Hast, D. Pascal, P. Barbour, J. Griffin (eds) *International Directory of Company Histories*, Vol. V, St James Press, Detroit, pp. 79–81.

Bartlett, C., Ghosal, S., (1989) *Managing Across Borders: The Transnational Solution*, Hutchinson, Boston, Mass.

Bailey, J., Clarke-Hill, C., and Robinson, T., (1995) International Retail Alliances – Toward a Taxonomy, *The Service Industries Journal*, Vol. 15, No. 4, pp. 25–41.

Ball, R., (1980) Europe's US Shopping Spree, *Fortune*, 1 December, pp. 82–8.

Chen, Y., and Sternquist, B., (1995) Differences Between International and Domestic Japanese Retailers, *The Service Industries Journal*, Vol. 15, No. 4, pp. 118–33.

CIG (Corporate Intelligence Group), (1991) *Cross-Border Retailing in Europe*, The Corporate Intelligence Group, London.

CIG, (1994) *Cross-Border Retailing in Europe*, The Corporate Intelligence Group, London.

EIU, (1994) Toys R Us, *Retail Trade Review*, No. 30, June, Economist Intelligence Unit, London.

Hollander, S., (1970) *Multinational Retailing*, Michigan State University, East Lancing, MI.

Jefferys, J., (1992) The Ikea Group, A. Hast, D. Pascal, P. Barbour, J. Griffin (eds) *International Directory of Company Histories*, Vol. V, St James Press, Detroit, pp. 82–4.

Kanter, R., (1989) Becoming PALS: Pooling, Allying and Linking Across Companies, *Academy of Management Executive*, Vol. 3, pp. 183–93.

Laulajainen, R., (1991) Two Retailers Go Global: The Geographical Dimension, *International Review of Retail Distribution and Consumer Research*, Vol. 1, No. 5, pp. 607–26.

Martenson, R., (1981) *Innovations in Multinational Retailing: IKEA on the Swedish, Swiss, German and Austrian Furniture Markets*, Gothenburg, University of Gothenburg.

Monke, M., (1992) Toys R Us, Inc., A. Hast, D. Pascal, P. Barbour, J. Griffin (eds) *International Directory of Company Histories*, Vol. V, St James Press, Detroit, pp. 203–6.

Myers, H., and Alexander, N., (1995a) European Food Retailers' Global Expansion: An Empirical Consideration of the Direction of Growth, *2nd Recent Advances in Retailing & Services Science Conference*, Brisbane – Australia, 11–14 July.

Myers, H., and Alexander, N., (1995b) Direction of International Food Retail Expansion: An Empirical Study of European Retailers, *8th International Conference on the Distributive Trades*, Università Bocconi, Milan, 1–2 September.

Retail Inquiry, 1976, HMSO: London.

Retail Inquiry, 1978, HMSO: London.

Retail Inquiry, 1980, HMSO: London.

Retail Inquiry, 1982, HMSO: London.

Salmon, W., and Tordjman, A., (1989) The Internationalisation of Retailing, *International Journal of Retailing*, Vol. 4, No. 2, pp. 3–16.

Siewart, C., (1992) C&A Brenninkmeyer KG, A. Hast, D. Pascal, P. Barbour, J. Griffin (eds) *International Directory of Company Histories*, Vol. V, St James Press, Detroit, pp. 79–81.

Stafford, E., (1994) Using Co-operative Strategies to Make Alliances Work, *Long Range Planning*, Vol. 27, No. 3, pp. 67–74.

Treadgold, A., (1988) Retailing Without Frontiers, *Retail and Distribution Management*, Vol. 16, No. 6, pp. 8–12.

Treadgold, A., (1990) The Emerging Internationalisation of Retailing: Present Status and Future Challenges *Irish Marketing Review*, Vol. 5, No. 2, pp. 11–27.

Woolworth, (1954) *Woolworth's First 75 Years: The Story of Everybody's Store*, New York, Woolworth.

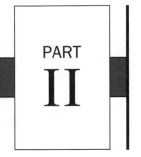

PART II

Development of International Retailing

National to International Retailing

▌ OBJECTIVES ▌

This chapter addresses the issue of channel development within the national and trans-national context. It also considers the transfer of retail innovation across national boundaries through direct and indirect means.

INTRODUCTION

The development of international retail activity is inextricably linked to the fundamental dynamics of retail development on a national level. Fundamental to an understanding of the process of internationalization is the identification of the catalysts of institutional and retail structural change.

THE DISTRIBUTION SYSTEM

Until comparatively recently, retailing has been localized in nature. In many parts of the world, it remains so today. Large retail companies have developed in the context of an urbanized and industrialized society. The trading environment of such societies, and the social context in which the populations of such societies live, has facilitated the growth of large retail organizations. Nevertheless, developments have not been even. Public policy and cultural environments have influenced the development of large retail organizations so that, in markets with similar economic and social conditions, retail structures will differ considerably. While in some markets the large retail organization will have attained a dominant market share, in other markets the small, local, single-unit retailer will retain considerable market share, influence within society, and consequently place within the retail structure.

As large manufacturing companies have grown and sought improved distribution facilities for their goods, retailers have developed larger operations and central buying points to ease the flow of goods. The development of large manufacturing operations has preceded the development of large retail operations within the industrial context. That is, the growth of large manufacturing operations and hence the production and availability of consumer goods has in turn stimulated the development of distribution systems and the growth of large organizations within retailing.

This has had considerable implications for those retailers who have chosen to expand in markets where this industrial infrastructure does not exist. International retailing often takes place between markets where there are comparable or similar socio-economic conditions. However, expansion into less developed markets is also a feature of international retailing. This has taken the form of companies expanding into colonial or former colonial territories but it has also taken the form of expansion by retailers into geographically proximate markets which have not seen the same level of retail structural development as the country in which the retailer is based. In such markets, the international retailer is faced with the problem of introducing concepts and formats which do not have the same distribution support systems to supply them, nor the socio-cultural reference points to explain them. It is, therefore, important that the international retailer should understand the dynamics of change within the domestic market, so that the retailer may more easily interpret the problems and face the challenges of non-domestic markets.

STAGES OF DEVELOPMENT

In the 1950s, in North America and Western Europe, manufacturing operations dominated distribution channels. Large manufacturing corporations sold their products to intermediaries – wholesalers – who would in turn sell the manufactured products on to the retailer. This may be described as a traditional distribution channel (Walters, 1979). With the emergence of large retail companies, this traditional pattern of distribution broke down, as the newly empowered retail operations bought directly from the manufacturer and removed the costs of the middle-man from the system. Therefore, by the 1980s, the retailer, in many instances, had asserted control over the distribution system and hence was in a strong position to influence the actions of the manufacturer. This development is illustrated in figures 4.1 to 4.6 and described in the section below.

Stylized representation of channel development

In the situation illustrated in figure 4.1, the manufacturers, with relatively small market shares, sell to wholesalers, who in turn sell on to retailers with relatively small market shares. This is a traditional channel structure. The wholesaler, in this situation, fulfils the important function of bringing the small manufacturer and retailer together in an efficient system. If, in the situation depicted in figure 4.1, the wholesaler did not exist, the retailers would have to source directly from all six manufacturers, rather than the single wholesaler. Hence, the number of

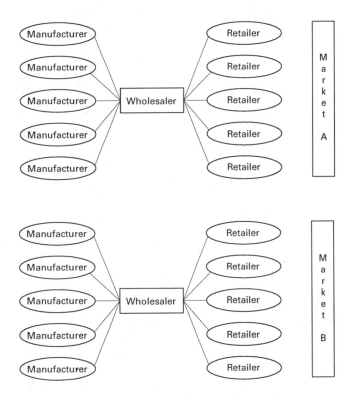

Figure 4.1 Distribution channel development – traditional structure

transactions would multiply. In practice, of course, the retailer would not be able to deal directly with each manufacturer nor the manufacturer directly with each retailer, so that the manufacturers' products would not reach some parts of the market. The principle of transactional efficiency (Alderson, 1954; Gist, 1968) suggests that the situation illustrated in figure 4.1 will develop.

In figure 4.1, the two markets would not share the same distribution and retail structure, although, the distribution structures are similar in terms of the number of channel levels. In both markets A and B, there are two levels between the manufacturer and the consumer: the wholesaler and retailer. Because of the relatively small size of the manufacturing organizations, an international marketing effort would not be feasible, although agents may buy from manufacturers and wholesalers in one market and sell to wholesalers or retailers in the other market, thereby adding another level to the distribution channel. In figure 4.2, the role of some manufacturers is enhanced as their greater market share allows them to exercise control over the distribution channel. This may include determining the price of goods at the point of sale. While international trade will occur the distribution channel will be characterized by national distribution facilities and relationships.

In figure 4.3, the growth of large retail organizations, in part, a response to the

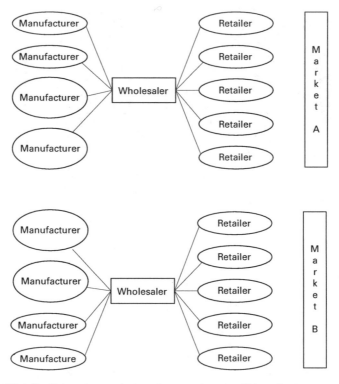

Figure 4.2 Distribution channel development – traditional structure: manufacturer development

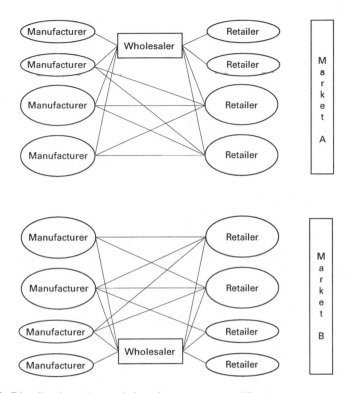

Figure 4.3 Distribution channel development – modified structure: countervailing retail development

power of large manufacturers in the channel, has radically altered relationships within the channel. In this situation, retailers, because of their size, are able to buy in sufficient bulk from the manufacturer, thereby achieving discounts. These discounts are passed on to the consumer in the form of lower prices as well as being retained by the retailer to support expansion. This will in turn enable retailers to increase their market share.

In figure 4.4, the manufacturers, in part responding to the growth of retail operations, but also responding to demand for export goods, have expanded to the point where they may be considered international operations. The distribution systems of the two markets are thereby increasingly linked. The manufacturer supplies both wholesalers and retailers directly in both markets. The large retailers have, in this illustration, begun to dominate some of the smaller manufacturers, to the extent that these smaller manufacturers are fundamentally dependent on sales to a single large retailer. The manufacturer may be providing retail own brand goods.

In figure 4.5, in response to the international marketing power of the international manufacturing operation, retailers based in different markets have joined

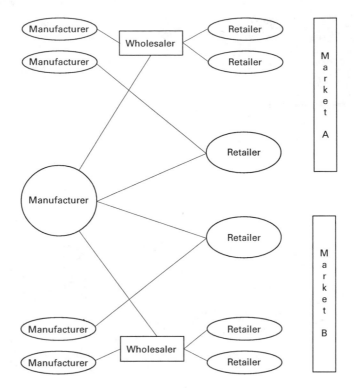

Figure 4.4 Distribution channel development – modified structure: manufacturer internationalization

together in buying groups in order to balance the power of the large manufacturer. These retailers will continue to source from smaller manufacturers and may even exchange own brand products.

In figure 4.6, an alternative or subsequent development from the situation illustrated in figure 4.5 is given. Here, the retailer commands greater market power than the manufacturer, operating, as it does, on an international basis. In this situation, while distinct market structures exist, linking the smaller retailers with the smaller manufacturers as well as the international manufacturers, an international retail structure has also emerged which is shared by both markets.

Periodization of distribution channel development

This is essentially a stylized depiction of the development of national and international distribution structures but it is one that may be recognized as reflecting the position in different markets at different times. Pommering (1979) has described this process in terms of three periods, in which, in turn the manufacturer, consumer and trade have been pre-eminent.

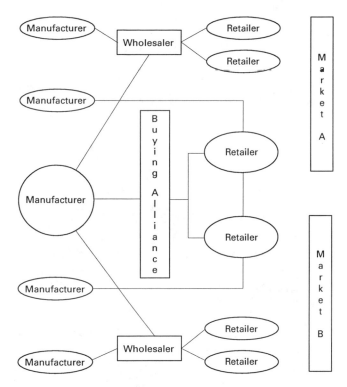

Figure 4.5 Distribution channel development – modified structure: international retail buying alliance

First stage

After the Second World War the manufacturer, in the context of unsophisticated distribution systems, emerged as the dominant force, within channel relationships. The decade of the 1950s is seen as the period of manufacturing dominance.

Second stage

With the increase in wealth within Western society and thereby an increasing supply of goods available to the consumer, the consumer become empowered and hence there emerged the need for a marketing rather than sales-based approach to product development and distribution. The decade of the 1960s is seen as the period when the consumer's role was paramount.

Third stage

With the emergence of large retail enterprises and the concentration of market power within the retail sector, the retail trade began to assume functions which hitherto had been the domain of the manufacturing sector. The decade of the 1970s is seen as the period of trade – that is, retail – dominance.

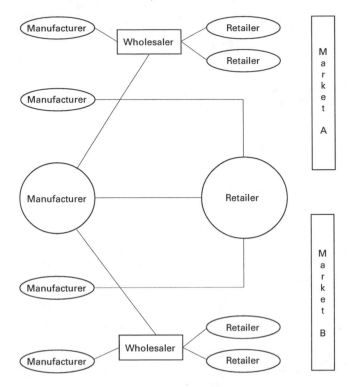

Figure 4.6 Distribution channel development – modified structure: retailer internationalization

As with all exercises in periodization, it is possible to criticize the dates which are intended to divide one period from another and point to examples which show that certain companies or distribution systems do not conform to the patterns described. However, there is much to be said for Pommering's (1979) assertions. His periodization usefully characterizes the post-war experience within Western consumer society within the *trente glorieuse* (1945–75).

The emergence of the retailer as a powerful force within the distribution channel has led to changes in the functions carried out at different levels within the channel of distribution. Walters (1979) has suggested that, traditionally, manufacturers, wholesalers and retailers carried out fundamentally different functions. The manufacturer would be responsible for production, hence the branding of the product the manufacturer had designed and made. The manufacturer would seek to manage the promotion of the product, its price and of course the selling function. The wholesaler would buy from the manufacturer, display the product at locations away from the point of manufacture, deliver products to the retailer, provide finance within the channel. Like the manufacturer, but at a different level within the channel, the wholesaler would promote and sell the product. Retailers would buy, stock, finance, display, promote, sell and often deliver the product. Again, the retailer would carry out similar tasks to other channel members but at a particular level and within a distinct framework.

This may be seen to represent a description of a conventional channel. However, with the breakdown in the traditional structure of distribution, these roles have changed, so that it is possible to suggest that manufacturers, wholesalers and retailers may carry out any of these functions. Therefore, by the 1980s, retailer's functions had come to include product development and branding in a way, and on a scale, not previously seen within distribution channels in the second half of the present century.

THE RETAILERS' NEW ROLE

The growth of retail marketing departments is evidence of the changing influence of suppliers and retailers. Increasingly, large retail companies have developed their own marketing approach and thereby taken on functions which previously would have been carried out by the manufacturer or wholesaler. In the early 1980s, there was a rapid growth in the number of marketing departments within UK retail operations (Piercy and Alexander, 1988). By the mid 1980s, many large retail organizations in the UK considered they had primary control over a number of key marketing functions. The retailer had, therefore, become involved in own brand products as a means of building loyalty, providing attractive margins and allow retailers greater competitive flexibility.

These changes are certainly characteristic of the second half of the twentieth century: however, individual companies and distribution systems have been established in earlier periods which indicate that this distribution process is not new. Marks & Spencer's St Michael label has a long history, as does Sainsbury's use of own label products. The early history of F. W. Woolworth illustrates the important role and influence that some retailers have long had and the need to recognize the importance of, and manage, the buying or sourcing function which lies at the heart of the retailers' relationship with other channel members.

NATIONAL TO INTERNATIONAL RETAILING

International retailers have emerged in significant numbers from markets which have developed sophisticated and efficient distribution systems within the context of an urbanized and industrialized society. Many of the retailers who today operate in markets other than their domestic market have already developed a large chain operation at home. They operate in a retail environment where retail concentration levels are relatively high.

International retailers' domestic markets have provided them with a basis on which to develop operations elsewhere. In turn, their domestic markets have attracted international operators based in other markets. Their home market will have attracted retailers eager to access and learn from the experience of operating in an advanced and competitive market or fill niches that domestic operators do not adequately fill. Much of the world's international retail activity is based in, and directed at, a relatively limited number of markets. Therefore, by the 1990s, international retailing had become primarily focused on the markets of Australasia, the European Union, Japan and North America. That is not to say that other markets do not play host to international retailers or that international retailers are not be based outside these markets, but that the vast majority of activity is contained within, and an overwhelming majority of retailers are based within, these markets. In this, retailing reflects wider trading patterns.

INTERNATIONAL FLOW OF KNOWLEDGE

International retailing as noted in chapter 2 has essentially two forms:

- international flow of knowledge
- international operational development

Therefore, retailers may influence developments in another country without operating outside their domestic market through the international flow of ideas or know-how. Conversely, they may help to influence the development of non-domestic markets through the formats they use and the merchandise they sell in host markets around the world.

Kacker (1988) has suggested that the nature of the flow of know-how may be described as diffusion and transfer. The diffusion of know-how is unplanned or incidental, whereas the transfer of know-how is planned or purposive. Diffusion occurs, he suggests, through such as observation, which might take the form of seminars or conventions. Foreign direct investment and franchising are other forms. These are the vehicles of flow, which take the form of foreign direct investment, joint ventures, management contracts, and franchising where transfer is concerned. Clearly, the same vehicles may contribute to different types of flow.

The know-how envisaged here is, by Kacker's (1988) definition, either of a managerial dimension or a technical dimension. The managerial dimension concerns concepts, policies, systems and control. The technical dimension concerns matters such as site selection, atmospherics and communication with the market. However, as Kacker observes, the flow of know-how will be constrained by consumer and trade resistance, which will lead to compromises in innovative introductions. Price levels may change, merchandise mixes may be altered and patronage patterns may be distinct in the new market.

The diffusion and transfer of know-how is well illustrated by the example of the variety store format.

The variety store concept

The variety store offers a good example of the transfer of know-how across international borders. Many of the world's important contemporary retailers have borrowed innovative concepts and established these concepts in their home market. The variety store concept is a particularly interesting example because it allows evaluation over an extended period of time. Marks & Spencer today is in many respects a very different operation than it was when it epitomized the variety store concept in the 1920s and 1930s, although, it still retains important characteristics of the innovative variety store approach, which has in turn influenced the development of retailers who use very different formats. The term variety store is associated with the retailer F. W. Woolworth, whose pioneering operation was developed in the North East of the US in the 1880s and 1890s. The F. W. Woolworth Corporation was also responsible for internationalizing this concept. The company entered the Canadian Market in 1897, the UK in 1909 and Germany in 1926 (Woolworth, 1954). The variety store concept was been adopted within, and adapted to, the retail structures in a number of markets around the world.

Australia

Coles Myer was instrumental in developing the variety store concept in Australia. In the first store, Coles operated a three price point policy (Roberts, 1992). Goods were available for 3 pennies, 6 pennies, and 1 shilling. George James Cole, who founded the store, had observed developments in US and UK retailing. The first store was opened in 1914 in Victoria in the suburban area of Collingwood. Collingwood was populated by the same social groups that F. W. Woolworth addressed in the US: the urban labouring section of society. Five years later, Coles opened a larger store in the same area and set 2 shillings and six-pence – a half-crown – as the highest priced item in the store.

In 1927, having built a chain of eight stores in Victoria, Coles crossed the state line into New South Wales and opened a store in Sydney. By 1933, the company's chain of variety stores were in every Australian state. However, in 1938, in the face of inflationary pressure, the company was forced to abandon the 2/6d maximum price and instead adopt a refund policy if customers were not entirely satisfied with their purchase.

France

In France, Printemps became involved in operating limited price variety stores in 1931 (Jefferys, 1992a). A central buying group was established as SAPAC-Prisunic in 1932. Within three years, there were four Prisunic stores, operated by Printemps in Paris, and four in the regions, along with a further thirty stores operated by affiliated retailers. These affiliated stores enabled the central buying organization to negotiate favourable terms, thereby following Woolworth's established principles. The early Woolworth operation had been essentially a federation of store chains under the control of key personalities (Woolworth, 1954).

Galeries Lafayette also began developing a variety store operation in 1931 (Jefferys, 1992b). In that year, La Nouvelle Maison was established as a subsidiary company. Two stores, operating under the name of Lanoma, were opened in Paris, and by the end of 1932, a further two stores using the name Monoprix were operational outside Paris. The name Monoprix was adopted by all stores in 1932 and the structure of the company developed. La Nouvelle Maison was renamed Société Anonyme des Monoprix and Société Centrale d'Achats was formed as a buying organization.

Monoprix grew rapidly in the 1930s, but its early expansion was fraught with problems. The importance of the transfer of know-how between markets is exemplified by Max Heilbronn's visits to the UK to observe the operations of Woolworth and Marks & Spencer. Heilbronn even made direct contact with Simon Marks in order to gain advice (Jefferys, 1992b). Monoprix, like Prisunic sought development through both wholly owned operations and affiliated retailers.

Germany

In 1926, Karstadt AG, which had recently been formed to facilitate the merger of the Karstadt KG and Theodor Althoff KG operations, established a subsidiary operation EPA Einheitspreis AG (Mackervoy, 1992). The purpose of the company, under the direction of Heinrich Althoff, was the exploitation of the variety store concept. In the new stores, merchandise was offered at four price points. These were 10, 25, 50 and 100 Pfennigs. Growth was considerable, with 52 stores operational by 1932.

Kaufhof also recognized the importance of the variety store concept and established what was later to become Kaufhalle AG in the mid 1920s as EHAPE Einheitspreis Handels Gesellschaft mbh (Bauert-Keetman, 1992). This initiative, was taken by the founder's son Alfred Tietz, who had worked in American department stores. In 1925, he had visited the US with a team of Kaufhof employees to learn from American retail methods.

Japan

As was the case in France, in Japan, a department store operator Takashimaya began developing stores along the line of the variety store concept. Indeed, the growth of the low price operation must be understood in terms of the significance of department stores within Japanese retailing at that time and the intensely competitive environment. Ten Sen Kinitsu markets began operation in 1926 (Larke and Nagashima, 1992). These markets were originally sited in existing Takashimaya stores, but in 1931 the company established a separate chain of low price operations which grew to fifty-one stores within a year. The Kinitsu chain numbered 106 units by 1941.

United Kingdom

At the same time that variety store operations were being developed in Australia, but at a slightly earlier date than developments on mainland Europe, the variety store format was making an impact in the British Isles.

Woolworths opened a store in Liverpool in 1909 (Woolworth, 1954). However, under the direction of Michael Marks, Thomas Spencer, and William Chapman, an indigenous brand of the variety store approach had already begun to take root. The Marks & Spencer operation drew on the American model with the adoption a single price approach to merchandising. Indeed, Marks had adopted the 'Don't ask the price, it's a penny' before the turn of the century. By the time Woolworth entered the UK market, Marks & Spencer under the management of William Chapman, was already established as a variety chain operation. The most successful store in the group, the Liverpool store, for example had reached a turnover of £9,857 by 1906 (Briggs, 1992). It is hardly surprising, therefore, that it was the economically important port and prosperous city of Liverpool that F. W. Woolworth targeted for their first operation outside North America.

Using the pricing points of a penny, threepence and sixpence, the Woolworth operation, in Liverpool, attracted 60,000 people in the first two days of trading (Briggs, 1992). Within a year, the company was operating ten stores in the North of England, and by 1939 operated 759 British outlets. Simon Marks was to become concerned at the rapid development of the Woolworth operation and sought to revitalize his stores through the study of US retail operating practices. Tse (1985, p. 20) quotes Simon Marks' recollections of his visit to the US in 1924:

> It was there that I learned many new things. It was about my first serious lesson in the chain store art.

In the UK, other operators, such as Littlewoods, followed the example of Woolworths and Marks & Spencer. However, by the time stores such as Littlewoods began operating fixed outlets in the mid-1930s, the concept had moved on, as may be seen from the experience of operators noted above.

Concept as catalyst

The variety store concept was the vehicle for both the development of an international operation – F. W. Woolworth – but also the development in world markets of local versions of the concept. What these markets had in common was the social and economic structure to support the development of chain organizations selling the limited price merchandise offered by these establishments. The subsequent decline, or major remodelling of the chains noted above, illustrates the appropriateness of such retail forms to specific periods of economic and social development. As Kaynak and Cavusgil (1982, p. 250) have observed:

> The retailing systems that have evolved in the developed and developing economies of the world clearly share certain common characteristics, but they also differ

from each other in many important ways. What differentiates the more advanced economic systems from the less developed ones is the difference in the nature of their basic retailing institutions.

This flow of know-how, whether diffused or transferred, continues in the contemporary retail environment, although, it is often difficult to discern which new formats or systems will have a substantial impact. The warehouse clubs and discount store operations have proven to be dynamic in different market contexts and a threat to indigenous older retail forms. The flow will occur from markets with relatively developed economies and high levels of GDP per capita to markets with less developed economies and lower levels of GDP per capita. French retailers have successfully exported the hypermarket into Spain and into Latin America, but have been less successful in the US. The flow of know-how occurs from a higher to a lower level of economic development.

CONCLUSION

The national retail environment is crucial to the development of international retail enterprises. The distribution channels within the national context will help to support but also constrain international development. The two markets illustrated in figures 4.1 to 4.6 above, developed at a similar pace, independently of each other. Thus, the development of a common retail structure was made easier. If a simple structure, or even a radically different structure had existed in market B to that in market A, the process of internationalization would have been different. Thus, in the contemporary environment, while the markets of Eastern Europe offer West European retailers market opportunities, the structure, or lack of distribution structure, makes expansion problematic. The international retailer has to start building basic channel relationships or establishing channel structures, which could be taken for granted in other markets. Thus the market may not be ready for certain retail formats.

When internationalizing, retailers must be aware of the market conditions which have supported the development of their domestic operation and the difference in the structure of retailing in markets around the world. Thus, retailers have tended to expand into markets which reflect their domestic markets, unless other influential factors are present in the new market.

QUESTIONS – DISCUSSION POINTS

1   Has international retailing occurred as a natural response to the development of international manufacturing operations?

2   What is the retailer's new role in the distribution channel?

3   In what way does the variety store concept illustrate the importance of the international flow of retail skills and the international development of retail operations?

REFERENCES

Alderson, W., (1954) Factors Governing the Development of Marketing Channels, *Marketing Channels for Manufactured Products*, R. Clewett (ed.), Irwin, Homewood, Illinois.

Bauert-Keetman, I., (1992) Kaufhof Holding AG, A. Hast, D. Pascal, P. Barbour, J. Griffin (eds) *International Directory of Company Histories*, Vol. V, St James Press, Detroit, pp. 103–5.

Briggs, A., (1992) Marks and Spencer P.L.C., A. Hast, D. Pascal, P. Barbour, J. Griffin (eds) *International Directory of Company Histories*, Vol. V, St James Press, Detroit, pp. 124–6.

Gist, R., (1968) *Retailing: Concepts and Decisions*, John Wiley, New York.

Jefferys, J., (1992a) Au Printemps SA, A. Hast, D. Pascal, P. Barbour, J. Griffin (eds) *International Directory of Company Histories*, Vol. V, St James Press, Detroit, pp. 9–11

Jefferys, J., (1992b) Galeries Lafayette S.A., A. Hast, D. Pascal, P. Barbour, J. Griffin (eds) *International Directory of Company Histories*, Vol. V, St James Press, Detroit, pp. 58–9.

Kacker, M., (1988) International Flow of Retailing Know-How: Bridging the Technology Gap in Distribution, *Journal of Retailing*, Vol. 64, No. 1, pp. 41–67.

Kaynak, E., and Cavusgil, S., (1982) The Evolution of Food Retailing Systems: Contrasting the Experience of Developed and Developing Countries, *Journal of the Academy of Marketing Science*, Vol. 10, No. 3, pp. 249–69.

Larke, R. and Nagashima, K., (1992) Takashimaya Co., Limited, A. Hast, D. Pascal, P. Barbour, J. Griffin (eds) *International Directory of Company*, Vol. V, St James Press, Detroit, pp. 193–6.

Mackervoy, S., (1992) Karstadt Aktiengesellschaft, A. Hast, D. Pascal, P. Barbour, J. Griffin (eds) *International Directory of Company Histories*, Vol. V, St James Press, Detroit, pp. 100–2.

Piercy N, and Alexander N, (1988) The Status Quo of Marketing Organisation in UK Retailers: A Neglected Phenomenon of the 1980s, *Service Industries Journal*, Vol. 8, No. 2, April, pp. 155–75.

Pommering, D., (1979) Brand Marketing: fresh thinking needed, *Marketing Trends*, Vol. 1, pp. 7–9.

Roberts, J., (1992) Coles Myer Ltd., A. Hast, D. Pascal, P. Barbour, J. Griffin (eds) *International Directory of Company Histories*, Vol. V, St James Press, Detroit, pp. 33–5.

Tse, K., (1985) *Marks & Spencer, Anatomy of Britain's Most Efficiently Managed Company*, Pergamon, Oxford.

Walters, D., (1979) Manufacturer/Retailer Relationships, *European Journal of Marketing*, Vol. 13, No. 7, pp. 179–222.

Woolworth, (1954) *Woolworth's First 75 Years: The Story of Everybody's Store*, New York, Woolworth.

Multinationalization to Globalization

▌ OBJECTIVES ▌

This chapter chronologically considers the development of modern international retail activity and places institutional and corporate development within that context.

INTRODUCTION

A brief consideration of the literature on international retailing may leave the reader with the impression that international retailing is essentially a product of the last ten, twenty or thirty years. The more commercially oriented publications will frequently emphasize the contemporary nature of this activity.

> It is clear . . . that cross-border retailing in Europe is overwhelmingly a phenomenon of the 1980s and of the late-1980s in particular. (CIG, 1991, p. 3)

Academic articles will tend to place international retailing within a longer time frame.

> during the past three decades, retailers have increasingly concerned themselves with the international market (Salmon and Tordjman, 1989, p. 3)

> ... over the last 20 or so years an increasing number of retailers have been active in developing an international presence. (Treadgold, 1988, p. 8)

There has been a dramatic increase in international retail activity in recent years, but international retailing is not a product of recent decades, although, it may be said to be a distinguishing characteristic of retailing in the 1980s and the early 1990s. There is not a distinct dividing line between a period of nationally based activity and a period of international activity. To suggest this would not only be incorrect but would imply a uniqueness about the more recent phase of international development which would lead to misleading conclusions about international activity.

International retailing is not a new phenomenon:

> For many years there have been retail firms in Europe that operated in a number of different countries. (Jefferys and Knee, 1962, p. 70)

Earlier periods have also seen international activity. It is the environment of these periods and the development of retail operations within those environments, which provides an opportunity to consider international retailing in greater depth. To consider the recent period of activity as unique is to infer common causes of recent international activity and thereby invest the process with a unity which it does not have. If international retailing is seen essentially as a recent development then, in consequence, insufficient consideration will be given to the particular conditions which have brought about the latest stage in the development of international activity.

Care must be taken both to avoid the assumption that international activity is a phenomenon of the last twenty to thirty years and to avoid adopting a contemporary perspective, that is, based on the cognitive framework suggested by the events of the last ten years. To do so would be to make assumptions which would inhibit an understanding of the nature of international retailing and retailers' changing attitude to international activity. Unless this contemporary, and essentially myopic perspective is avoided, the activity will be continually replaced in the minds of observers with contemporary developments. Thus, internationalization will be interpreted for some time to come as a product of recent years. In consequence, idiosyncrasies of recent activity will be given excessive weight and come to define and explain the activity. Contemporary international expansion may not be representative of the development of sustained and sustainable international operations, particularly in a context where a considerable number of retailers are developing international interests, and there may be something of a 'me-too' effect in the nature of such expansion.

Retailers are attracted by different markets over time. They withdraw from foreign markets. A study of European retailing at the end of the 1980s would reveal a surprisingly limited number of US operations. The US impact on European retailing, however, has been considerable and of fundamental importance to the growth of international retail activity. However, it was the product of particular conditions. There is a danger in taking a snap-shot in time.

The events of the more recent past should not be perceived as fundamentally unique, nor a single development. By investing such events with a unique quality, they take on a significance and their causes are interpreted, without the appreciation of other contexts and other phases of development, which in themselves shed light on the direction, nature and motives of internationalization, and the changing context within which managers must operate in the international environment.

The most recent wave of international activity occurred as a response to new, as well as old, stimuli within national and international environments. It was also a product of familiar and less familiar influences from within retail operations. Thus, it may be more appropriate to view the international activity of the 1980s and 1990s either as a renaissance of international retailing, or the emergence of new retailers from markets which had previously not played an important role in the internationalization of retailing rather than *the* period of international activity.

CHRONOLOGY

Genesis, (1880–1945)

This period of international retail expansion coincided with the early development of retailing within industrialized and urbanized societies in North America and Western Europe. It was a period in which modern retailing has its roots. It was characterized by the growth of large retail organizations in the context of urbanization, improved educational facilities and communication systems, and a rising demand for consumer goods.

During this period, a number of key retailers developed from local, to regional and consequently national operations. However, development was uneven, so that some retailers achieved national operations at a very early date. The Liptons organization grew rapidly in the UK at the end of the nineteenth century and at the beginning of the twentieth century. While most of the company's overseas interests were non-retail, the Liptons organization did establish some international retail operations. The earliest development was in the US, where Thomas Lipton had worked in the retail trade in his youth. Impressed by retail practices in the US, he had vowed to himself that he would one day return and trade in the US. This he did in the early 1890s (Mathias, 1967).

The development of large retail operations, while uneven within markets, was also uneven between markets. The UK saw an early development of large retail operations, while other markets, such as Italy, retained a large number of small independent traders. However, even in markets where large retail organizations came to control large market shares, the success of different formats, or organizational types, varied considerably. In Scandinavia, consumer cooperatives gained considerable market share, while in Belgium and Germany, the department store format attained greater relative significance (Jefferys and Knee, 1962). In the UK, while the consumer cooperative, the department store and the variety store all gained market share at the expense of the independent trader, it was the multiple organizations that achieved the greatest share of the market by the middle years of the twentieth century.

Within this period, retailers began to develop international operations and thereby play a part – arguably a particularly important part – in the development of retail structures within industrialized markets around the world. The international development of stores as dissimilar in their target market as Harrods and Woolworths contributed to the development of retail structures internationally. The contribution of Woolworths to international retailing was discussed in chapter 4, but the department store has also contributed to the internationalization of retail know-how. In the early part of the twentieth century, the contribution of department stores was particularly significant.

European and US retailers were instrumental in developing the department store sector in Central and South America (Hollander, 1970), an area which has not been an important target of internationalizing operations in recent years – although the example of the hypermarket is an interesting exception – but which attracted considerable interest in the early years of the twentieth century. French retailers contributed to the development of Mexico's department store sector. Casa Tow, which developed into a chain of stores in Argentina, was established by a citizen of the US, Martin Tow, in 1912. This chain came into British hands in 1930, and remained so for thirty years. A branch of Harrods was established in Buenos Aires, and the company's Argentinean subsidiary Gath & Chaves had outlets in Chile. Similarly, Anglo-Brazilian Mappin Stores contributed to the development of retailing in the Brazilian market (Hollander, 1970).

The development of large-scale operations on the national level was an important prerequisite of international expansion in many cases, but it was by no means essential. Many of the early international operations did not have extensive chains of stores in the domestic market.

At the luxury end of the market, and in the form of such specialist operations as Van Cleef & Arpels (jewellers) and Christies (art dealers), retailers have long recognized cosmopolitan consumers as a group that they should seek to serve in key centres around the world.

> the dealer in expensive merchandise is one who may expect to meet his customers in the principal tourist capitals of the world. (Hollander, 1970, p. 16).

Foreign travel has been an important influence on the expansion of such retail outlets. Berlin, Geneva, London, Milan, New York, Paris and Rome are major cities which are associated with the growth in such luxury retail operations. The list itself is indicative of the cosmopolitan nature of this theme within international retailing.

Retailers who open a store in Milan or Rome are not necessarily targeting the average Italian consumer. Such cities support retail structures that are a product of high income levels and international tastes.

Foreign travel is important in the internationalization of retailing in two ways.

- First, nationals of one country making purchases in another may encourage the retailer from whom they make purchases to locate in major centres in the tourist's home market.

- Second, while travelling consumers will wish to make purchases from familiar retail outlets.

Burberry and Liberty are early examples of stores which have been prompted by foreign visitors to domestic stores to expand internationally. Characteristically British retailers, they established international outlets for customers familiar with their UK operations and merchandise. Burberry's first opened an outlet in Paris in 1909, while Liberty's first store in Paris was opened in 1890.

Organizations such as W. H. Smith, the UK stationer, newsagent and bookseller, when embarking on international expansion chose 'to provide for its customers the same distributary service it produced at home' (Wilson, 1985, p. 429). Smith's first shop outside the UK was in Paris on the Rue de Rivoli. Acquired in 1903, the store had previously had an English customer base. As part of the sale arrangement the previous owners were required not to establish a similar business in Paris, or other towns in France such as Cannes, that is, towns which were the vacation destination of English tourists. The fascia of the store and lettering in the tearoom were designed and painted by Eric Gill, thereby providing a distinctly English Arts and Crafts quality to the store and contributing a typographical style that W. H. Smith used and retained throughout the organization for a number of years (MacCarthy, 1989). The need to provide familiar products and surroundings was understood by W. H. Smith, an early pioneer of international retailing:

> Their [customers'] homesickness was abated by prompt and regular supplies of *The Times* or the *Morning Post*, plenty of books to buy or borrow at the well-stocked library, familiar stationery on which to write home and, perhaps above all, a tearoom where real English tea and buns could be drunk and eaten. (Wilson, 1985, p. 429)

This type of international expansion was evident before the more recent phases of international expansion; in many senses it was more typical of international retail activity before the 1950s. It is important to emphasize this fact, as it helps to explain the fundamental motivations which lie behind internationalization and emphasizes that this type of activity must be considered in tandem with that represented by the 'national' chain organizations which are a familiar contemporary feature of the retail landscape.

While mass merchandise retailers with innovative formats did establish international operations with the intention of securing national coverage in non-domestic markets, such operations were limited in number. Essentially, this period was characterized by a restricted group of retailers, usually operating a small number of outlets, utilizing traditional store formats, and selling merchandise in specialized ranges and often up-market products.

Emergence, (1945–74)

This period saw major changes in the global political-economy which had a fundamental effect on the development of retailing on an international level. Conditions were laid down in this period which would help to define international retailing until the end of the 1980s. These factors were:

- economic and political restructuring in Europe

- international economic and political role of the US

- Japan's emerging place in the global economy

- the growth of international trade

- the emergence of the consumer society

This period may, however, be further divided into two phases of internationalization. The first of these was strongly influenced by the innovative qualities of US retailing and the international activity of US retailers. The second phase saw the emergence of European retailers in greater numbers on the international stage.

1 'Packs' Americana, (1945–60)

The role of US companies in this period was crucial to the development of international retailing. While US retailers, concepts and innovations had been important in the earlier period of development, this period saw an enhancement of the US's role on the international stage.

The importance of US retailing was partly due to the comparative weakness of other markets. In Europe, the dislocation of economic activity, social disruption and the physical devastation experienced in the period 1914–45, precluded a general challenge being offered to US companies in the international market-place. In Japan, economic rebuilding and social reorientation provided a context in which the US, and its various agencies, were to have a considerable impact on post-war development.

The GNP of the US far outstripped the GNP of European countries and Japan, and the large 'single market' of the US was a major advantage in the development of aggressive and internationally relevant international operations (see table 5.1).

Both European and Japanese retailers experienced a disruption in the development of retail operations in the middle years of the twentieth century. Between 1945 and 1960, retailing in these markets experienced a major restructuring and reorientation. This occurred on a national level but the international agenda was also changing.

Table 5.1 Comparison of gross national product: 1960

	$m (000)
Germany	72.0
France	61.1
Italy	34.9
Netherlands	11.2
Belgium and Luxembourg	11.9
United Kingdom	72.2
United States	511.4
Canada	38.7
Japan	43.1

Source: Eurostat, 1971.

Europe   These were years of restructuring in Europe. The US, through the Marshall Plan, was instrumental in the resuscitation of European economies. The US's influence in Western Europe in the immediate post-war period was not merely economic; it had a considerable political and cultural influence. Within this wider context, European retailers looked to the US for inspiration and examples of successful retail operations. The US's influence on the spread of innovative formats has already been noted, and predates the period 1945 to 1960, but in this period the pre-eminence of US retailing was particularly striking. Although retailers experienced difficulties in introducing the supermarket format into some European markets, because of the restrictions on building due to post-war shortages of materials and the generally limited post-war supply of goods, conditions did not create the pressures which would later force retailers to rethink spatial issues within store. It was the late 1940s and early 1950s that saw retailers bringing back to Europe the concept of the supermarket. For example, Sainsbury's was instrumental in introducing the supermarket to post-war Britain. In 1949, Alan Sainsbury was joint-general manager of J. Sainsbury, the UK grocery retailer. He visited the US in that year and was impressed by the alternative approach to grocery retailing that the self-service system represented (Boswell, 1969). The first self-service Sainsbury store was opened in the UK in the following year.

The mainland of Europe, however, faced one problem that the UK had not faced. Occupation both of France and Germany contributed to the need for new initiatives and new beginnings. In France the Galeries Lafayette S.A. had suffered considerable disruption during the occupation period of the war, including confiscation of the company from its owners (Jefferys, 1992). Hertie, the German retailer found itself at the end of 1945 in possession of only 20 per cent of its store properties (Barbour and Fuchs, 1992). The rest had either been destroyed or were in the Soviet sector. Other retailers, such as C&A, found their international retail empire disrupted by occupation, with stores located in Britain, Germany and occupied territories. After the occupation of the Netherlands in 1940, the company was unable to retain contact with the stores in the UK. At the end of the war, their German operation literally lay in ruins with only two sites undamaged (Siewart, 1992).

By the end of this period, some European markets were developing concentrated retail structures that would establish the conditions that would see an increase in international actions in the 1960s. While in Western Europe as a whole, the cooperatives, multiples, variety and department stores controlled only 20 per cent of the market, in the UK over 40 per cent of market share was in the hands of such organizations, with multiple retailers alone controlling over 20 per cent by 1960 (Jefferys and Knee, 1962). The only other markets which saw a substantial share of the market in the hands of operations other than the independent trader were Finland and Iceland, where the cooperatives controlled over a third of the market. Only in Switzerland, where the multiples held 11 per cent market share and the department store sector 5 per cent, did concentration levels come anywhere near those in the UK. In other major European markets, such as France and Germany, the independent retailers still controlled a considerable market share. However, in those markets which were to see the emergence of a number of international retailers in the ensuing decades, an increasingly large market share was beginning to be achieved by the multiple store sector. In France and Germany, 6 per cent of the market was held by multiple organizations and in the Netherlands the figure was moving up toward 9 per cent by 1960 (Jefferys and Knee, 1962).

Japan   In Japan, the US was to have a fundamental impact on the development of retailing. US troops occupied Japan from 1945 until 1952. In this period, Japanese retailing was to be strongly influenced by US tastes and retail operating techniques. Some of this influence was strikingly direct. In the late 1940s, as more products returned or came into stores for the first time, Japanese women could respond to changing fashions. In this context of a greater availability of goods, a military look became popular amongst Japanese women, a style inspired by the women in the occupation forces (Lloyd-Owen, 1992). A similarly direct influence, although, in this case in terms of the organization of Japanese business, was to be achieved as the occupying forces were eager to dismantle the large organizations that had contributed to the entry of Japan into the war (Roberts, 1973). Large organizations, or zaibatsu, were reconstructed as partially independent companies (Classe, 1992). This control extended to the retail sector and included the Tokyo Department Store Company Limited, which like many department stores in Japan, such as Mitsukoshi (Moore, 1992), adopted Western merchandise ranges, and in this way gained an advantage over smaller operations which could not source such fashionable items. Sueko Suzaki, the founder of the retail operation Kotobukiya, recognized the dominance of US tastes during the 1940s and 1950s and began importing goods from the US and developed an American ambience in her store (Tanner, 1992a).

It was not only Western styles that were adopted. The early development of the Ito-Yokado retail operation in Japan owes much to Masatoshi Ito's recognition of the importance of US operating techniques. His observation of US retail chains convinced him that Japanese retailers, if they were to succeed in future years, must do so through the adoption of chain store operating techniques. Retail operations based on US chains selling food, clothes and household items were developed by Ito in the early 1960s on the basis of his observation of US retailing (Tanner, 1992b). Tadao Aoi visited the US to find out more about the use of credit in US retailing. The son of the founder of the Japanese retailer Marui, he established on his return Marui Advertising, later to become the AIM Create Company Limited for promotional purposes and Maruishinpan to provide customers with credit facilities and in due course an in-house credit card (Tanner, 1992c). Kohachi Iwata, the founder of Nagaskiya Company Limited also travelled to the US in a party of innovative retailers to observe operations in America (Tanner, 1992d). He was particularly impressed by the use of a single brand name in retail stores and the use of vending machines, then comparatively unknown in Japan, but destined to become an important aspect of Japanese distribution.

European expansion   In this immediate post-war period, European retailers sought international expansion, but their target markets were often those which were becoming increasingly unimportant as trading partners. This is particularly noticeable in the British context, where retailers continued to invest in the Commonwealth at a time when the European markets were becoming increasingly important. This was a continuation of the trade that Hollander (1970) recognized as an important aspect in the development of international retailing; that is, trade with politically and economically linked, but geographically dispersed, regions of the world.

In 1945, Great Universal Stores, the largest British owned UK retailer by the end of this period (Jefferys and Knee, 1962), acquired a controlling interest in a larger number of Cavendish and Woodhouse stores in Canada (Crompton, 1992).[1] Earnings from the company's international operations in Canada and South Africa in this period were profitable but not spectacular. By contrast, other European retailers who concentrated on building up a European operation laid important foundations. C&A saw rapid growth in the 1950s, and this growth continued on into the next decade, so that between 1952 through 1971, C&A saw an increase in clothing and textile stores from seventeen to seventy-two in Germany alone (Siewert, 1992). C&A built up strong relationships with small suppliers, which allowed the company to centralize buying, develop specialized buying teams and thereby provide the increasingly prosperous market it served with the low-cost fashion option with which the company became synonymous.

By the end of the 1950s, the markets of Western Europe were developing to a level which would prompt intra-European cross-border expansion. European retailers would consequently emerge as major international retailers. From 1960, Europe emerged as a market which could not only attract outside investment, but as a market that was increasingly capable of supporting retail operations which would seek expansion both in Europe and elsewhere. In part, this may be ascribed to the political and economic integration within Europe, which helped to create the conditions which allowed cross-border activity, a market which was both prosperous and one relatively free of restrictions. The internationalization of retailing between 1960 and 1990 is, to a considerable extent, the internationalization of European retailing and European retailers.

2 Mature markets (1960–74)

In this period, an increasing number of retail operations outside the US began to feel the constraints of their national markets. This was particularly evident in Europe. Increasingly, it was the mass merchandisers who sought new markets. For such retailers, internationalization would be very different from those European retailers of previous years who had operated at the luxury end of the market. These retailers were not following expatriates or the cosmopolitan consumers around the world.

European retailers began to play a greater role in international activity. French, German and UK grocery retailers began to make a number of international moves in the late 1960s, and continued to increase their activity into the early 1970s (Burt, 1991). In the UK, retailers such as the Burton Group, Electronic Rentals, EMI, Granada, Great Universal Stores, Marks & Spencer, Mothercare, and Thorn Electrical Industries began to develop international operations. This was a period of rapid, and often large-scale, expansion. In the 1960s, Great Universal Stores' entry into the United States market and mainland Europe helped to increase the non-domestic market contribution to profits to around 10 per cent by the end of the decade (Crompton, 1992).

Three factors lay behind the increase in international activity.

- A large number of retail operations had reached a stage in their development which allowed for international activity.

- Prosperity in the home market and non-domestic markets had created conditions which encouraged expansion and provided cash-rich companies capable of funding it.

- Barriers to international activity were being lowered or removed.

These three fundamental factors must, however, be considered carefully and fully understood. It is possible to misinterpret the connotations and significance of these factors.

The size of the retail operation must be considered on two levels. One is the company's internal resources; the other is the position of the company in the domestic market. While, as has been noted, relatively small operations, if they recognize the international relevance of their product may seek and successfully achieve an international presence, for most retailers, increased size has allowed for the development of specialized management functions which has allowed for the planning and implementation of international business activity.

The size of the retail operation also draws attention to the issue of growth opportunities within the domestic market. This has led to the conclusion that international retailers are motivated by saturation in the domestic market. Saturation is usually interpreted as an absence of growth opportunity (Treadgold, 1988),

Table 5.2 Acquisitions and mergers of retail companies in the UK: 1969–75

Year	Number of companies acquired	Expenditure £m[a]
1969	40	24
1970	33	26
1971	44	53
1972	66	196
1973	84	148
1974	16	5
1975	16	18

[a] Current prices: where a merger, rather than an acquisition occurred, the value of the smaller company within the new company structure constitutes the takeover value.

Source: CSO, 1976.

Table 5.3 Retail sales by volume, UK: 1967–75

	1971 = 100				
Sector	1967	1969	1971	1973	1975
All	95	97	100	111	108
Food	100	102	100	101	99
Non-food	91	94	100	118	114
Clothing	93	96	100	109	108
Durables	87	89	100	127	121
Other non-food	92	96	100	118	115

Source: CSO, 1976.

although, this in itself is open to interpretation. It may, however, be more appropriate to think in terms of the level of concentration which exists within the market. Certainly, it is easier to measure than the less precise term saturation.

Retailers internationalize during periods of prosperity at home. This statement is partly contradicted by interpretations of internationalization which put undue emphasis on push and pull factors. However, observation and financial realities suggest that this is not the case. The growth of international activity in Europe during the 1970s, followed a period of considerable economic development and prosperity. Economic prosperity at home allowed retailers to develop the kind of organisation that was capable of international activity and generated the funds needed to support such development. During poor economic conditions, retailers will not be as active in acquisition activity at home, so they will be less inclined to acquire operations outside the market (see table 5.2 and table 5.3).

The reduction in international barriers to trade may be considered in a number of contexts, but some of the most evident are examples such as the GATT agreements and the establishment and extension of Free Trade Areas. GATT has had a major impact on world trade. In Europe, the development of the European Economic Community and European Free Trade Area at this time contributed to a lowering of barriers to international trade.

It is, however, not simply on the level of inter-governmental agreements that trade barriers are lowered. With an increase in travel and the growth of the propensity of individuals to move for work-related purposes, the cultural barriers to internationalization have been partly eroded. This had begun to appear as a factor behind internationalization at an earlier period, as has been noted, but this tendency has increased. Between 1950 and 1980, tourists arrivals world wide grew by a factor of ten, from little more than 25 million arrivals in 1950 to 278 million in 1980 (Latham, 1994). In 1992, it has been estimated, arrivals reached 476 million. Tourism has depended upon the increasing level of affluence within Western markets. Thus, in Europe, residents of countries such as Belgium, Germany, the Netherlands and Sweden will be particularly inclined to spend their holidays abroad (Burton, 1994). Likewise, some markets such as France – 51.4 million arrivals in 1990 (Burton, 1994) – will attract a particularly high number of tourists. Indeed, on a global basis, Europe and the Americas have attracted the overwhelming majority of tourist arrivals in the post war period. In 1950, 30 per cent of arrivals were in the Americas and 67 per cent in Europe (Latham, 1990). In 1990, the Americas saw 21 per cent of arrivals and Europe 62 per cent (Latham, 1994). East Asia and the Pacific saw the greatest growth in the period, from around 1 per cent to nearly 12 per cent.

The effect of tourism on the internationalization of retailing has not been fully examined, but clearly remains a factor which has encouraged the flow of ideas across national boundaries. The figures noted above underline the importance in this transfer of ideas of North America, Europe and, increasingly, East Asia. The growth of tourism in the 1950s and 1960s was particularly marked, indicating fundamental developments in the changing psychological horizons of many people.

It was in the 1960s and early 1970s that European retailing began to emerge as a force in the international market place. Key Western European countries' GDP rose dramatically in this period. Between 1952 and 1964, Germany's GDP per capita doubled from DM 4,335 to DM 8,918, when calculated at 1970 prices (Flora et al., 1987). On the same basis, the figure had risen to DM 12,343 by 1974. This economic development was not limited to Germany. Italy's GDP per capita rose from L 455 in 1952 to L 1,212 in 1974. Not all growth was quite so dramatic, but nevertheless, other European countries saw substantial improvements in economic development, France's GDP per capita rose from Ff 7,569 in 1952 to Ff 18,103 in 1974.

The increase in international activity in Europe at the end of the 1960s and during the early 1970s was, however, to be short lived. The 'Oil Crises' of the mid 1970s and the second oil price increase at the end of the decade, would change the character of European expansion for a decade, before it resumed its growth in the mid 1980s.

Crises, (1974–83)

The previous period of international activity was truncated by the economic shocks of the mid to late 1970s. For example, UK international retail activity peaked in the early 1970s. In 1973, there were over sixty separate international actions by UK retailers, while between 1976–9 there were comparatively few actions, less than

Table 5.4 European investment in US retailing: 1972–80

Year of investment	US retailer	European acquirer
1972	Kohl	BAT (UK)
1973	Gimbel Brothers	BAT (UK)
	Grand Union	Cavenham (UK)
1974	Food Town Stores	Delhaize 'Le Lion' (Bel)
	Schwartz	Franz Carl Weber (CH)
1975	Fedmart	Mann (Ger)
1976	Dekon	Mothercare (UK)
	Pacific Gamble	Franz Haniel (Ger)
1977	Bi-Lo	Ahold (NL)
	Lil' Champs	Docks de France (F)
	Scrivner	Franz Haniel (Ger)
1978	Colonial Stores	Cavenham (UK)
	Dillard Stores	Vroom & Dreesmann (NL)
	Maurices	Brenninkmeyer (NL)
1979	Albertson's	Albrecht Group (Ger)
	Applebaum's	Lobaw (Can)
	Atlantic & Pacific	Tengelmann Group (Ger)
	Benner Tea Co.	Aldi (Ger)
	Furr's	Rewe (Ger)
	Korvettes	Agache-Willot (F)
	Pronto Markets	Albrecht Group (Ger)
	Ups 'n Downs	Tootal (UK)
	Winn's Stores	Heinrich Bauer Verlag (Ger)
1980	Alterman Foods	Delhaize 'Le Lion' (Bel)
	Hop-In Food Stores	Silverwood Inds. (Can)
	Hub Distributing	Brenninkmeyer (NL)
	3 Guys	Albert Gubay (UK)
	Macks Stores	KBB (NL)
	Red Food Stores	Promodes (F)
	Weingarten	Cavenham (UK)

Source: Ball, 1980; Seigle and Handy, 1981.

10 per cent of the peak figure annually (Burt, 1993). The economic crises of the 1970s disrupted the internationalization of retail operations. These years did not see a halt to the process, but a fundamental reorientation of motives and, to some extent, the direction of expansion.

Given the influence of US retailing and the attractions of the US market, retailers from outside the US had long been attracted to the opportunities afforded by this market. The UK company Liptons had a small retail operation in the US in the fourth quarter of the nineteenth century as has been noted (Mathias, 1967), while the Canadian Company Lobaw acquired the National Tea operation in the US in 1956, thereby becoming a substantial investor in the US food retail sector (Seigle and Handy, 1981). European retailers in the 1970s were particularly attracted to this market (Ball, 1980) because of the unattractive conditions which existed at that time in the European market in general (Kacker, 1985). Table 5.4 illustrates the considerable interest shown in US retailers by European operations.

Analysis of European retail activity in the US (Ball, 1980; Kacker, 1985), has suggested that European retailers have often succeeded in the US market through the recognition, and subsequent exploitation of, indigenous company strengths, and have often failed where radical change has been attempted or where the acquired company was simply a poor acquisition target. For European retailers attempting expansion in the US the market has often proved problematic and by no means an easy route to internationalization. Mothercare and the Early Learning Centre are examples of UK retailers' failure to understand the US market. This has even been the experience of Canadian companies, who it may be argued have had the advantage of both greater cultural and geographic proximity.

Nevertheless, the US market remains an important factor in the internationalization of retailing, both as a source of internationalizing operations and as an attractive market in which non-US retailers seek expansion.

Renaissance, (1983–9)

It was in this comparatively brief period that retailing saw a dramatic increase in the number and variety of retailers seeking expansion outside domestic markets. This period is characterized by economic growth which enabled retailers who were trading successfully at home to consider expansion in new markets. This was particularly marked in the UK, where economic recovery and even boom in the mid to late 1980s fuelled a rapid development in retailing and encouraged expansionist traits in UK retailers. The boom and bust nature of UK economic life since the 1940s has been, to some extent, replicated in the history of international retail development. Emerging from a period of economic recession, the UK economy's rapid expansion saw retailers eager for growth both at home and abroad. The late 1980s saw a curtailment of such activity.

Table 5.5 shows the rise and decline of UK international takeover activity in the 1980s. The importance of the US is illustrated. UK retailers continued to invest heavily in the US market. Other European retailers also saw the North American Market as attractive, but UK investments outstripped those of other nations. Of

Table 5.5 Major international acquisitions and mergers by UK retailers: 1986–91[a]

Year	Target company	Acquiring company	Price £m
1986	Hermans Sporting Goods (USA)	Dee Corp.	278
	LCP Holdings (USA)	Ward White	175
	M & H Sporting Goods (USA)	Dee Corp.	45
	H. Williams & Co. (Ireland)	Tesco	15
	Hot Sam (USA)	Rowntree	14
	Apparel Affiliates (USA)	Mackays Stores	13
	NASA (France)	Granada Group	11
	La Vie Claire/Herbier de Provence (France)	Booker	10
1987	Rent A Center (USA)	Thorn EMI	371
	Cyclops Corp (USA)	Dixons Group	240
	Shaws Supermarkets (USA)	Sainsbury	132
	Galerias Preciados (Spain)	Mountleigh Group	127
	Sterling (USA)	Ratners Group	126
	Liquor Barn (USA)	Majectic Wine	63
	Granada Grp European Stores	Thorn EMI	53
	Westhall (USA)	Ratners Group	29
	Tipton Centers (USA)	Dixons Group	19
	National Video Corp. (USA)	Granada Group	17
	Horst A. Werner (Ger)	European Home	11
1988	Brooks Brother (USA)	Marks & Spencer	440
	Kings Supermarkets (USA)	Marks & Spencer	64
	Ostermans (USA)	Ratners Group	32
	Digsa (Spain)	Ashley Trust	30
	TV & Telephone (USA)	Granada Group	22
	R & S Strauss (USA)	Ward White	20
	Jacadi (France)	Storehouse	16
	Granada HK & Australia Ops.	Thorn EMI	13
1989	Weisfields (USA)	Ratners Group	39
	Wee Three (USA)	W. H. Smith Group	10
1990	Kays Jewellers (USA)	Ratners Group	234
	Wall to Wall (USA)	W. H. Smith	12

[a] Acquisitions and mergers of £10m or more

Source: CIG, 1993.

foreign direct investment in retailing US in 1988, 58 per cent was accounted for by UK retailers, 13 per cent by Dutch and 8 per cent by German retailers (Treadgold, 1991). Japanese retailers accounted for 2 per cent of investment.

In Europe, considerable cross-border activity occurred. The large, developed retail markets of France, Germany and the UK were attractive targets but so were smaller markets such as Belgium, the Netherlands and Switzerland, as well as the relatively undeveloped market of Spain (CIG, 1991). Much of this activity was movement into contiguous national markets with, for example, German retailers continuing to build up a presence in Austria, Belgium, Denmark, the Netherlands and Switzerland. This geographical proximity was compounded by cultural proximity. German retailers continued to develop a major interest in the Austrian market. By far the largest international retail investors in the Austrian market have been German retailers. Food store fascias such as Aldi, Lowa and Zielpunkt, operated by Albrecht-Aldi, and Tengelmann were familiar to the Austrian consumer before the 1980s, when Huma and Supermagazin, operated by Metro Kaufhoff, were introduced to the market. For example, during this period, in other retail sectors, German retailers opened Parfumerie Douglas (1986) and Sankt Paul (1988) outlets in the beauty and health sector, Bauhaus (1985) in the DIY sector, Toy and Joy (1989) in the 'other non-food' sector and Modern Muller (1989) in the mail order sector (CIG, 1991).

However, geographical and cultural proximity were not the only distinguishing marks of European international development. Japanese retailers were showing an interest in European retailing, particularly in UK retailing. This interest included the opening of Japanese operations such as mixed good retailer Mitsukoshi or the fashion retailers Ichi Ni San and Yuzo, but also the acquisition of Acquascutum and an interest in Laura Ashley. Japanese retailer Ito-Yokado acquired an interest in UK retailing through the acquisition of the US 7-Eleven convenience store franchise operation.

Japanese retailers have shown an interest in US and European retailing not least because of the limited opportunities available to Japanese retailers in East Asia. Countries in East Asia have raised various barriers to exclude international investment and control of local facilities. This has not been restricted to retailing but has affected retail investment. Restrictions have effectively taken three forms and have, of course, affected not only Japanese retailers (Davies, 1993a):

- Communism in the People's Republic of China, North Korea and Vietnam.

- Ethnic tension which restricted ownership of enterprises to particular groups in Malaysia and Indonesia.

- Protection of local and small, if growing, enterprises in Japan, South Korea and Taiwan.

Some markets have remained relatively open such as those of Hong Kong, Singapore and Thailand. Therefore, activity has tended to focus on such markets.

The development of Japanese international retailing has to some extent mirrored the actions of European retailers in the 1980s. Japanese retailers made seventy-three international actions in the period 1980–9, compared with twenty-nine actions in the previous ten years (1970–9) (Davies, 1993b). Reflecting global trends, Japanese international actions between 1975 and 1978 were comparatively few in number. However, Japanese internationalization has been characterized by the high number of department store groups active in the international market-place. In the 1980s, 53 per cent of Japanese international retail actions were made by department store groups. Between 1950 and 1980, however, an even higher proportion (89 per cent) of actions were made by such retailers.

Regionalization, (1989–2000)

There are three main reasons for seeing international retailing before 1989 as fundamentally different to international retailing after 1989.

- Economic recession.

- Opening up of new markets in Eastern Europe.

- Single European Market and the North American Free Trade Area.

The economic recession of the late 1980s did not see the collapse of international activity, although, as noted above, a slowing did occur. This in itself suggests that retailing had passed through an essentially vulnerable stage in its development and that sustained growth could be expected. The 'fall of Communism' in Eastern Europe, while not the herald of rapid international retail expansion, opened up those markets in Europe which might, in due course, be expected to provide attractive markets for large retail enterprises. The opportunities were not to be realized as soon as some may have thought and decades rather than years will see the development of these markets. By the end of the 1980s, the advent of the Single European Market was already prompting retailers to expand across national boundaries. Retailers have shown themselves to be reluctant to admit the importance of the European Communities as a significant factor in their international planning, but observation would suggest that retailers have recognized the opportunities of planning on a wider European basis. One fundamental reason for this has been the restructuring of manufacturing companies on a multinational basis and the subsequent need for retailers to think on the same geographical basis. In Europe, the growth of strategic or buying alliances is indicative of the European agenda which retailers have adopted. In North America, the Free Trade Agreements between the US, Canada and Mexico have given further emphasis to the regional nature of the global economy.

Retailing is not global, but is increasingly macro-regional in nature and structure. Ironically, it is the increase in international activity which has contributed to this. As more and more retailers seek international expansion, a regional structure is developing, not least in the context of Free Trade Areas. In Europe, the EU, one of the world's most integrated global-regional free trade areas, regional development has been particularly pronounced. Between 1991 and 1994, the number of European retailers moving into other EU markets has continued to rise (see table 5.6). As more and more retailers cross the internal boundaries of the EU, a common European distribution system has begun to evolve. Its evolution is, however, still in its infancy.

If global-regional retail structures are still in their infancy, then global structures are still very much a theme of the future rather than the contemporary environment. That is not to say that inter-regional internationalization has not taken place,

Table 5.6 EU retail operations in European host countries

| Host country | *Number of international retail operations* | | | |
	Germany 1991–4	*France 1991–4*	*Netherlands 1991–4*	*UK 1991–4*
Belgium	15–22	47–64	20–41	20–25
Denmark	9–7	2–2	0–1	12–12
France	25–28	*	6–8	27–38
Germany	*	30–35	10–11	21–27
Greece	4–5	11–14	0–1	8–7
Ireland	0–1	6–4	0–0	37–34
Italy	8–18	26–35	1–1	10–9
Netherlands	28–30	28–20	*	22–26
Portugal	3–5	16–20	2–7	5–8
Spain	10–15	47–57	5–6	20–24
UK	10–14	40–32	3–3	*

Source: CIG, 1991; CIG, 1994.

but that such developments should be seen for what they are rather than over emphasized. The number of US retailers operating in Germany rose from nine in 1991 to twenty-two in 1994, and from twenty-four to forty in the UK, but the number of Japanese retailers rose from one to two in the same period in Germany and fell from thirteen to eleven in the UK (CIG, 1991, 1994). US retailers are making something of a comeback in Europe while Japanese retailers are still very much focused on markets closer to home around the Pacific Rim.

The greatest degree of globalization may be observed with respect to the market coverage of a limited number of retailers. These are the omnipresent retailers such as the Body Shop and Benetton, whose franchise operations have taken them to a wide variety of markets around the world. There are increasingly aggressive inter-national retailers who are building impressive lists of markets in which they oper-ate, but they have still a considerable task ahead of them before they could be said to have reached anything like a truly global geographical coverage. The logic expressed in Treadgold's (1988) description of international activity in the mid-1980s has only been modified not superseded. There are companies who may rightly claim to be global in orientation and thinking but, for the moment, global retailing in the structural sense has not truly arrived.

CONCLUSION

Of the four types of fixed retail operation which developed either before or during the first phase of international development discussed above, some have played a greater role than others in different periods of international retail activity, which, in itself, reflects the changing environment in which they operated, the limitations of the retail forms themselves and their role in the international environment. The cooperatives, since the middle years of the twentieth century, have not only conspicuously failed to retain a sufficient level of competitiveness on the national scale but have also singularly failed to address the international agenda. In some respects, this may be considered to be a product of their origins, but, arguably, these could have given them a head start in developing international operations. The department store has had a major impact on the retail structures of developed markets but characterizes earlier rather than later periods of internationalization. The variety store, likewise, had an important role in the early development of international activity, but what may be described as the heirs to the variety store style of retailing, the superstore, hypermarket and discount operation, continue to play an important role in the process. More recent international activity is characterized by the multiple organization as represented by the high street and shopping centre specialist store. The importance of different formats and retail types in different stages of the internationalization process is evidence of the changing nature of international retail activity.

The stages in the development of international retailing outlined above indicate a changing geographical focus of international activity. The role of the US retailers, important contributors to international activity until the early 1970s, has somewhat diminished. Europe, from being the focus of much US retailer activity in the middle years of the twentieth century, became the 'exporter' of retail operations, not least to the US itself. Asia grew in importance as a potential market during the 1980s and early 1990s. Likewise, Asian markets are increasingly the home of international operators.

Therefore, it is arguable that the dominant role of the US has been diluted, and will continue to be diluted in the future, by the international development of European and Asian operations and the development of retail structures within European and Asian markets.

NOTE

1 The other large UK based retailer at this time was F. W. Woolworth of the UK, in which the American parent company owned 52.7 per cent of the shares at the end of 1959 (Kirkwood, 1960; Jefferys and Knee, 1962).

QUESTIONS – DISCUSSION POINTS

1 The role of American retailing in the development of European retailing was fundamentally different in the period 1945–60 compared with the period 1974–83. How did these two periods differ, and what does this tell us about the internationalization of retail operations?

2 What factors led to the renaissance in international retail activity in the mid-1980s?

3 Are Japanese retailers the new force in international retailing?

4 Has retailing reached a stage whereby it may be considered to be essentially global in nature?

REFERENCES

Ball, R., (1980) Europe's US Shopping Spree, *Fortune*, 1 December, pp. 82–8.

Barbour, P., and Fuchs, K., (1992) Hertie Waren- und Kaufhaus Gmbh, A. Hast, D. Pascal, P. Barbour, J. Griffin (eds) *International Directory of Company Histories*, Vol. V, St James Press, Detroit, pp. 72–4.

Boswell, J., (1969) *JS 100, The Story of Sainsbury*, J. Sainsbury Ltd.

Burt, S., (1991) Trends in the Internationalisation of Grocery Retailing: The European Experience, *International Review of Retail, Distribution and Consumer Research*, Vol. 1, No. 4, pp. 487–515.

Burt, S., (1993) Temporal Trends in the Internationalisation of British Retailing, *International Review of Retail, Distribution and Consumer Research*, Vol. 3, No. 4, pp. 391–410.

Burton, R., (1994) Geographical Patterns of Tourism in Europe, *Progress in Tourism, Recreation and Hospitality Management*, C. Cooper, A. Lockwood (eds), Vol. 5, pp. 3–25.

CIG, (1991) *Cross-Border Retailing in Europe*, The Corporate Intelligence Group, London.

CIG, (1993) *Retail Rankings*, The Corporate Intelligence Group, London.

CIG, (1994) *Cross-Border Retailing in Europe*, The Corporate Intelligence Group, London.

Classe, A., (1992) Tokyo Department Store Co., Ltd., A. Hast, D. Pascal, P. Barbour, J. Griffin (eds) *International Directory of Company Histories*, Vol. V, St James Press, Detroit, pp. 199–202.

CSO, (1976) *Annual Abstract of Statistics*, Central Statistical Office, HMSO.

Crompton, G., (1992) The Great Universal Stores P.L.C., A. Hast, D. Pascal, P. Barbour, J. Griffin (eds) *International Directory of Company Histories*, Vol. V, St James Press, Detroit, pp. 67–9.

Davies, K., (1993a) The International Activities of Japanese Retailers, *7th International Conference on Research in the Distributive Trades*, Institute for Retail Studies, University of Stirling, 6–8 September, pp. 574–83.

Davies, K., (1993b) Trade Barriers in East and South East Asia: The Implications for Retailers, *The International Review of Retail, Distribution and Consumer Research*, Vol. 3, No. 4, pp. 345–66.

Eurostat, (1971), *Basic Statistics of the Community*, Statistical Office of the European Community.

Flora, P., Kraus, F., and Pfenning, W., (1987) *State, Economy, and Society in Western Europe 1815–1975*, Vol. II, Macmillan Press, London.

Hollander, S., (1970) *Multinational Retailing*, Michigan State University, East Lancing, MI.

Jefferys, J., (1992) Galeries Lafayette S.A., A. Hast, D. Pascal, P. Barbour, J. Griffin (eds) *International Directory of Company Histories*, Vol. V, St James Press, Detroit, pp. 58–9.

Jefferys, J., and Knee, D., (1962) *Retailing in Europe: Present Structure and Future Trends*, Macmillan, London.

Kacker, M., (1985) *Transatlantic Trends in Retailing*, Quorum, Connecticut.

Kirkwood, R., (1960) *The Woolworth Story at Home and Abroad*, The Newcomen Society in North America, New York.

Latham, J., (1990) Statistical Trends in Tourism and Hotel Accommodation, up to 1988, *Progress in Tourism, Recreation and Hospitality Management*, C. Cooper (ed.), Vol. 2, pp. 117–28.

Latham, J., (1994) International Tourism Statistics, 1991, *Progress in Tourism, Recreation and Hospitality Management*, C. Cooper, A. Lockwood (eds), Vol. 5, pp. 327–33.

Lloyd-Owen, J., (1992) Isetan Company Limited, A. Hast, D. Pascal, P. Barbour, J. Griffin (eds) *International Directory of Company*, Vol. V, St James Press, Detroit, pp. 85–7.

MacCarthy, F., (1989) *Eric Gill*, Faber & Faber, London.

Mathias, P., (1967) *Retailing Revolution*, Longmans, London.

Moore, B., (1992) Mitsukoshi Ltd., A. Hast, D. Pascal, P. Barbour, J. Griffin (eds) *International Directory of Company Histories*, Vol. V, St James Press, Detroit, pp. 142–4.

Roberts, J., (1973) *Mitsui: Three Centuries of Japanese Business*, Weatherhill, New York.

Salmon, W., and Tordjman, A., (1989) The Internationalisation of Retailing, *International Journal of Retailing*, Vol. 4, No. 2, pp. 3–16.

Seigle, N., and Handy, C., (1981) Foreign Ownership in Food Retailing, *National Food Review*, Winter, pp. 14–16.

Siewert, C., (1992) C&A Brenninkmeyer KG, A. Hast, D. Pascal, P. Barbour, J. Griffin (eds) *International Directory of Company Histories*, Vol. V, St James Press, Detroit, pp. 23–4.

Tanner, D., (1992a) Kotobukiya Co., Ltd., A. Hast, D. Pascal, P. Barbour, J. Griffin (eds) *International Directory of Company Histories*, Vol. V, St James Press, Detroit, pp. 113–14.

Tanner, D., (1992b) Ito-Yokado Co., Ltd., A. Hast, D. Pascal, P. Barbour, J. Griffin (eds) *International Directory of Company Histories*, Vol. V, St James Press, Detroit, pp. 88–9.

Tanner, D., (1992c) Marui Co., Ltd., A. Hast, D. Pascal, P. Barbour, J. Griffin (eds) *International Directory of Company Histories*, Vol. V, St James Press, Detroit, pp. 127–8.

Tanner, D., (1992d) Nagasakiya Co., Ltd., A. Hast, D. Pascal, P. Barbour, J. Griffin (eds) *International Directory of Company Histories*, Vol. V, St James Press, Detroit, pp. 149–51.

Treadgold, A., (1988) Retailing Without Frontiers, *Retail and Distribution Management*, Vol. 16, No. 6, pp. 8–12.

Treadgold, A., (1991) The Emerging Internationalisation of Retailing: Present Status and Future Challenges *Irish Marketing Review*, Vol. 5, No. 2, pp. 11–27.

Wilson, C., (1985) *First with the News: The History of W. H. Smith 1792–1972*, Cape, London.

PART

III

Theoretical
Parameters

Retail Internationalization in its Theoretical Context

▌ OBJECTIVES ▌

This chapter considers the foundations of international trade and retail development theory. It covers a wide academic area and must therefore be considered an introduction to the concepts considered rather than a full presentation of them. An appreciation of the wider theoretical material is important to an understanding of international retail development.

INTRODUCTION

The internationalization of retailing must be considered in the context of theories of international trade and generic theories of retail development. International retailing does not exist in an academic vacuum: therefore, it is essential that those theoretical developments which already exist within the literature should contribute to the development of a framework within which international retailing may be analysed.

It is also essential to understand the basis on which international trade exists because international retailing depends on the international trade in goods. As trade in manufactured products has grown, so international retailing has developed. Some international retailers depend on the international recognition their goods have achieved. Retailers who possess strong brands are often pulled into markets through customer demand for their goods. Such recognition has stimulated the growth of international retailing. It has drawn them into markets and, to a considerable degree, determined their success in those markets. Many clothing retailers when they move into new markets do so on the basis of their distinguishable and clearly positioned products, not on the basis of an innovative format. Retailers' outlets provide a packaging but it is often the products not the service that customers essentially seek.

This chapter is initially concerned with theories of trade. Without an appreciation of the development of trade theory, it is difficult to understand some of the assumptions that economists and managers make when analysing world trade. From a retailer's perspective, unless there is an understanding of the foundations of economic thought, there is a danger that false assumptions will be made.

This chapter also considers generic theories of retail development and institutional change. These theories of retail development have been primarily concerned with examples of retail change within the nationally defined context. They are, nevertheless, helpful in explaining the changes which are observable on an international level. Similarly, changes in the international environment are useful in refining the theoretical constructs which are available to the student of retailing.

FREE TRADE

From the perspective of the late twentieth century and from 'Western' markets, free trade may appear to be the norm. For many consumers around the world, imported products are a feature of their everyday lives. Australians buy German cars, Japanese eat New Zealand lamb, Canadians listen on Japanese compact disc players to Italian opera recorded in the US, while French men and women buy English country style clothing. Such apparent indications of an international market which acts freely and sees the ready flow of goods around the world is, in many cases, an illusion rather than a reality. Freedom of trade is neither universally established, nor is free trade commonly understood and valued in all circumstances. Governments around the world employ instruments which will allow them to control imports to protect industries at home. They may be considered appropriate in certain circumstances but the effects of such control should be understood. The restriction of trade leads to inefficiencies. It may be attractive for governments to protect operations in their own country, political expediency may demand it, but the end result may be a less efficient industry which does not provide society with the growth rates it could achieve.

In figure 6.1, the production of beer in Germany is considered. The demand curve D indicates the price that the consumers in the market are willing to pay for the product and hence, at different prices, the quantity they will buy. The supply curve S1 indicates the indigenous German producers' willingness to sell, and hence the quantity they will produce at a given price. In this example, if Germany does not permit imports, then the brewers will produce at P1 and Q1 and the consumers will buy beer at this price level and in this total quantity. On this basis, it is possible to calculate the surplus that the consumer and the producer derives from this situation. These surpluses are the difference that the consumer pays and the price the consumer is willing to pay and the difference the producer is willing to accept and the price the producer receives. Therefore, the consumer surplus in figure 6.1 at price P1 is described by the area beneath the demand curve and above the price ABP1. The producer surplus in figure 6.1 at price P1 is described by the area above the supply curve and below the price EBP1.

If Germany decides to open its markets to international producers and the world price is P2, then the quantity of the goods bought will rise to Q2 and there is a new supply curve at S2. The price in this example will fall and German consumers will buy beer in greater quantities but German producers will not be willing to produce as much beer as they had previously produced. The consumer surplus in figure 6.1 at price P2 is described by the area beneath the demand curve and above the price

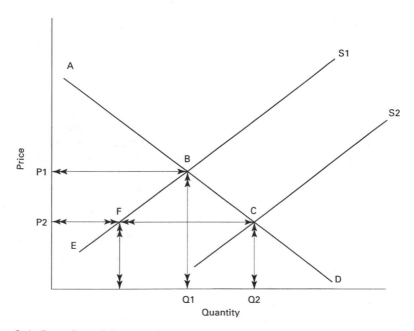

Figure 6.1 Benefits of free trade

ACP2. The domestic producer surplus in figure 6.1 at price P2 is described by the area above the demand curve and below the price EFP2.

In this example, Germany's decision to allow imports may be considered to constitute a local economic disaster. While the consumer has benefited from lower prices, the brewers have had their production cut dramatically because they cannot compete with 'cheap foreign imports', a refrain that is not uncommon in markets around the world. However, the opposite might be true. German brewers may be able to produce beer at lower costs than brewers in other countries. The removal of restrictions may have no effect on domestic sales as German brewers are cheaper. Foreign competitors may sell at a price above that established by demand and supply curves in Germany. If this were the case then German brewers would be losing out in a situation where free trade does not exist.

Free trade is established when it is in the country's interest to trade freely in products and possible for the country to gain benefits from that trade. This in itself begs the question; when do such conditions occur? The theories discussed below help to explain when those conditions occur, and why commercial operations engage in international business activity. These theories are well established in texts which address general international management issues (for example, Toyne and Walters, 1993) and are given due and able consideration, but they are less well established within the retail literature. These theories need to be considered with reference to the particular experience of international retailers.

CLASSICAL THEORY

The classical theories of international trade provide an understanding of the merits of the international exchange of goods and how such exchange creates greater wealth.

Absolute advantage

In the absence of previous theoretical material, or at least where such material was relatively limited, the theory of absolute advantage was a clear and logical statement of the reason why international trade should occur. In his book *The Wealth of Nations* published in 1776, Adam Smith (1723–90) described the conditions necessary for free trade and the reason why countries should specialize in the production of certain products for export.[1] Smith suggested that specialization should occur where a country enjoyed absolute advantage in the production of a particular product. There is a basic and sound logic in this. This is effectively what individuals do in their every day lives. They specialize in those activities in which they do well, while others carry out those tasks for them for which they are not well suited, or it is not cost effective for them to perform. Medical doctors treat patients, in turn they do not build the cars in which they travel to attend patients. Such specialized activity depends, however, on a context where exchange is possible. Thus, individuals within a society will only be able to specialize where other individuals are prepared to specialize in different areas. In international trade relations, specialization is possible only where other countries are willing to engage in free trade. Without free trade, societies will operate in a context of self sufficiency or autarky.

Comparative advantage

David Ricardo (1772–1823) recognized that while absolute advantage provided a useful underpinning to an understanding of international trade, there existed conditions where absolute advantage was not necessary to create conditions conducive to trade. Ricardo's *The Principles of Political Economy and Taxation* published in 1817, was to make an important contribution to the development of economic thought and provided, through its consideration of comparative costs, an important contribution to the understanding of international trade.[2] He recognized that there were advantages in specialization even when absolute advantage did not exist, that there were opportunity costs associated with production which enabled production to occur on the basis of relative advantage.

IMPLICATIONS FOR TRADE

A country's comparative advantage will alter according to changes in the national and global economic situation. The productivity achieved in the employment of land, labour and capital, the input factors, will affect a country's comparative advantage. If a country produces less for the same inputs, then its comparative advantage will be affected, as indeed it will be if productivity increases at a slower rate than that of other countries. If the cost of input factors rise, then the comparative advantage achieved by a country will be eroded. It will cost more to produce the product in the local currency and this will in turn have implications for the rate of exchange. Comparative advantage is also affected by external developments and the changes in other countries. Changes in the foreign exchange rate will affect a country's comparative advantage.

The theory of comparative advantage, therefore, shows how a country which does not have an absolute advantage in the production of products may benefit from free trade. While these classical theories provide a useful basis for the consideration of international trade, they must be qualified in the light of other theoretical material.

NEOCLASSICAL THEORY

It is unlikely that a country will achieve complete specialization in those products in which it has comparative advantage and will stop production of those in which it does not have such an advantage. The economic theory in its simplest form suggests that opportunity costs are constant: however, in reality it is recognized that opportunity costs will increase as production of a product falls. In reality, to stop producing beer in one market and produce wine instead will see a much higher opportunity cost as the last litre of beer is produced. This effect is described by the law of diminishing returns. This law considers the short-run and shows that, where one factor, such as technology remains fixed but other input factors are variable, a point will be reached where adding other input factors does not produce a benefit and indeed may produce a fall in the level of production.

Consideration of Ricardo's theory of comparative advantage has highlighted the problem of labour productivity, on which Ricardo places considerable emphasis, but which he failed to explain in terms of the reasons for the difference in labour productivity. Ricardo asserted that the quantity of labour used in production, and hence its cost, was the principal determinant of price. Dissatisfaction with Ricardo's lack of explanation for the reasons how comparative advantage occurs led Bertil Ohlin to develop an explanation of market difference. Ohlin (1933) attempted to integrate theories of international and domestic trade on the basis of spatial location theory, which concluded that trade was a consequence of unequal endowment of resources. Ohlin, in contrast to Smith and Ricardo, sought to explain why trade occurred and not to identify its benefits. Ohlin's work suggests that different relative factor endowments give rise to observable and measurable advantages. Therefore, where a country has an abundance of one factor, it would be reasonable to expect that the country in question would produce goods which intensively utilize that factor. Therefore, in terms of international trade, a country will export those products which demand the intensive use of those factors in which the country has an abundance. This has become known as the Hecksher-Ohlin principle, and the 'factor equalization problem evolves the views of Hecksher and Ohlin' (Wan, 1982, p. 147). The relationship between factor prices and factor endowments was an issue that had been raised by a number of economists in the first half of the twentieth century (Chipman, 1966); however, it was Samuelson who, in a series of articles, developed the factor price equalization theorem and who in his '1953 article essentially completed the Hecksher-Ohlin-Samuelson paradigm' (Wan, 1982, p. 149).[3] His theorem considers the proposition that free trade substitutes for the free mobility of factors of production. Here, free trade reduces the differences in commodity prices and thus equalizes the prices of factors of production.

The Hecksher-Ohlin principle, while further developing an understanding of the issues which underlie international trade, failed to fully account for the fact that technology is not the same in all countries and that non-price competition plays an important part. The principle has also been seriously undermined by Leontief's (1953) analysis of international trade patterns, which showed that countries do not necessarily export products which demand intensive inputs of the factors in which they are well endowed and import products which demand the intensive use of factors of which they do not have an abundance. In his work, Leontief recognized that a market did not necessarily conform to the laws established by previous trade theories. For example, the US imported capital intensive products and exported labour intensive products. The US was, and is, a capital intensive country and therefore should not have acted in this way, according to previous trade theory.

CLASSICAL AND NEOCLASSICAL INHERITANCE

Neoclassical theory, while qualifying and refining the basic theories of international trade, does not provide retailers with an immediately accessible body of knowledge through which to explain the events in the international trading environment. Rather, it provides an appreciation of the basic assumptions which explain the reasons for the international trade on which retailing relies and a framework within which other interpretive developments may be placed. However, these other approaches will always suffer from the lack of universal application which the classical and neoclassical theories attempted to provide. The following theories must therefore be considered in that light.

The classical and neoclassical theories attempted to describe economic conditions that were very different from those pertaining today. David Ricardo was not attempting to explain an industrial or service economy but an agriculturally based economy. The work of Hecksher, Ohlin, Samuelson and Leontief, while carried out in the context of industrialized society, were dealing with a body of theory which was rooted in the production of primary products; such as those produced by the extractive industries and agriculture. For a fuller explanation of the environment in which international retail companies operate, it is necessary to turn to other theories of international trade.

FACTOR ENDOWMENTS

Linder (1961) identified a fundamental difference in the trade of primary and manufactured products. In the context of primary products, he recognized the importance of factor endowments, while in the context of manufactured products, he suggested, that it was not factor intensities but demand factors which lay behind patterns of international trade. Linder suggested that international trade was effectively an extension of domestic trade, not only in that products are initially launched in the domestic environment, but that domestic production subsequently limits international production. Here Linder recognized the importance of international markets which have reached similar levels of GDP per capita and other factors which facilitate the ready adoption of the exported product.

Linder has provided a useful framework for the interpretation of international retail activity. In retailing, international activity is commonly an extension of domestic activity. The options available to retailers internationalizing their format and merchandise are often limited to markets which exhibit similar levels of economic development to the market in which the product originates; that is, where consumer tastes are similar and the retail operation is subsequently more readily accepted. In many instances, international retailers have expanded their domestic operation only to find that the market into which they have moved is not entirely suited to the domestically defined operation. Indeed, all retailers who have attempted to export an established format, rather than acquire or develop a new format in the host market, will to some extent have had to come to terms with the limitations and preconceptions which their domestic experience has placed upon their operation and their managerial attitude to store development. This will be especially true of retailers who have taken some time to develop their operations in the domestic market.

INTERNATIONAL PRODUCT LIFE CYCLE

The relationship between the market of origin and the market of destination is further explored in the International Product Life Cycle (IPLC), which addresses the issues of Foreign Direct Investment (FDI) and international trade (Vernon, 1966). This theory of international trade and FDI utilizes the now familiar life cycle approach to interpreting the development of products. The Product Life Cycle (PLC) has much to recommend it. Products, newly introduced onto the market, are seen to follow an S-shaped curve, which passes through an initial phase of adaptation and hence through other stages of maturity and decline. That is, as the product becomes accepted in the market, a period of rapid growth is followed by a period in which growth slows and eventually declines, unless environmental conditions change or action is taken to rejuvenate the product. Vernon used this fundamental schema to interpret the development of products in the international environment through the identification of three phases of development. They are, a phase of new product development, a phase of product maturity, and a phase of product standardization.

As Linder's (1961) interpretation began by looking at the development of a product in the market of origin, so Vernon (1966) identifies the importance of the market of origin in determining the characteristics of the product. Research and development occurs in more sophisticated markets and the product is, in time, transferred to markets which are also economically advanced. Initially, local demand, that is, demand in the market of origin, is small, but grows in due course, as the product is developed to meet the needs of the home market and the very limited export market which develops in the product development stage.

In the product's mature stage, the product's uniformity and standardization facilitates the manufacture of the product in markets which do not have the same research and development conditions, such as a skilled workforce. Under such conditions, the product in its developed form may be produced. In such markets, where costs are lower than they are in the home market, and barriers to imports exist then the establishment of production units in non-domestic markets is encouraged.

Overseas production will increasingly be the preserve of other companies that have begun production of the product, as well as the overseas units of the company which developed the product in the market of origin. This will lead, not only to the importation into the country of origin of the product from units owned by the original exporter located in other markets, but also to the importation of products produced by other companies based in other markets.

As the product enters a phase of standardization, then the product will demand less research and development and will spread further into markets around the world which do not show the same level of development as the market of origin or those markets into which the product was first exported and in which it was subsequently manufactured. Production costs will determine the location of production units and these will increasingly be newly industrializing countries. Exhibit 6.1 describes what occurs in the IPLC in the different markets.

This model is useful in explaining the development of particular products but is not universal in its application. Accepting this qualification in respect of manufactured products and transferring some of the key components of the model to the retail context, it will again be seen that it does not offer a universal explanation of international activity, but it does offer an insight into the international development of retail activity. As in the manufacturing context, it is possible to see the US market as a source of innovation and US firms as the exporter of innovative products, so it is possible to see the US market and US firms in the same light as far as retail innovation is concerned.

US companies, such as Woolworths, have exported innovative concepts into markets which exhibit similar levels of economic development and have consumers with similar tastes. In the case of the British operation of this company, it is possible

Exhibit 6.1 The international product life cycle

New product stage

Primary market: Product development. Small market in country of origin. Exports begin to develop to other economically developed and similar markets.

Secondary market: Imports from innovating market begin.

Tertiary market: Limited imports from innovating market begin.

Mature product stage

Primary market: Growth in home market. Exports reach maximum levels.

Secondary market: Imports from innovating market reach maximum and begin to decline as home production grows rapidly and exports are made.

Tertiary market: Imports increase.

Standardized product stage

Primary market: Production in the home market declines as imports rise and exports decline.

Secondary market: Imports from tertiary markets rise rapidly as home production declines and exports fall.

Tertiary market: Imports decline, production and exports rise rapidly.

Source: Vernon, 1966.

to observe the concept then being subsequently transferred to other markets such as South Africa. The expansion of French hypermarket operations into less developed European and in turn developing markets such as Taiwan and Malaysia also shows the diffusion of retail formats to secondary and tertiary markets.

It is also possible to consider the expansion of European retailers in the 1970s and 1980s in the US and draw parallels with Vernon's theory of the IPLC. US retailers exported their retail formats and operations to Europe in the 1950s and 1960s. In the 1970s, European retailers began acquiring operations and exporting their operations to the US. Thus, the market which saw initial innovations became, in turn, the recipient of non-domestic operations.

FOREIGN DIRECT INVESTMENT

The IPLC is a theory of Foreign Direct Investment (FDI): however, it does not fully explain the reasons for FDI. It is a theory which involves FDI, rather than a universal explanation of the circumstances in which FDI will occur. FDI describes many different types of international investment. It may concern the ownership of sources of raw materials, that is primary industries: extractive industries or agriculture. FDI may also involve the ownership of service based operations and may take the form of marketing subsidiaries. Therefore, the reasons for FDI will vary as to the resource or subsidiary that has been acquired. In some instances, as is implied in the IPLC, FDI may occur as the result of a management's desire to protect market share by investing in production in a particular non-domestic market. It may be initiated as a result of a need to acquire sources of scarce inputs, which if left in independent hands, may lead to difficulties of input sourcing for that particular producer. Conversely, FDI may be prompted by a desire to learn from innovative markets.

Investment by European retailers in North America may be seen as an example of the last of these motives. First-hand experience of operating in the market, or at least having a subsidiary which operates in the market, may be beneficial to a company in its home market and other non-domestic markets. Similarly, FDI may derive from a desire to acquire intangible assets, such as trademarks or in retailing fascias which would otherwise not be available to the company. The Japanese retailer Aeon's acquisition of the British company Acquascutum is an example of the purchase of a valuable trade name and fascia.

As Knickerbocker (1973) has recognized, FDI may occur in response to FDI carried out by rivals in the same home market. Knickerbocker's (1973) research was based on US multinational enterprises, covered the period 1948–67 and concerned 'data on 23 countries within which approximately 83 per cent of all foreign manufacturing subsidiaries of U.S. firms (excluding those in Canada)' (Knickerbocker, 1973, p. 33). Canada was excluded because of the high level of integration of the Canadian operations of US firms. His research shows that there was in this period a temporal bunching of international actions by companies within industry classifications and in respect of specific countries under consideration. Half the international actions so constrained were carried out in a three year period, three-quarters in a seven year period (Knickerbocker, 1973). He noted that evidence suggests:

> that neither random events nor the overall trend of U.S. investment abroad accounts for the bunching of foreign direct investment. (Knickerbocker, 1973, p. 193)

Such oligopolistic rivalry may be identified in retailing, where, in the UK grocery sector, both Sainsbury and Tesco have acquired international operations in a manner which suggests that this type of rivalry may not be far beneath the surface and may form a strong basic motivation behind expansion. Similarly, the bursts of international retail activity which have been characteristic of the internationalization process suggests the Knickerbocker's thesis may have some validity in the retail context. However, in retailing such a study remains to be carried out in the same depth as Knickerbocker's original study.

FDI may also be stimulated by a desire to spread risk. Certainly, there are examples of this in the retail environment and Kacker's (1985) work on the motives behind international investment in the US in the 1980s shows that retailers have expanded into other markets in order to avoid the problems, both economic and regulatory, that they had experienced or were concerned might occur in their domestic markets. It is also important to recognize that, over time, a company will develop within the international context of its operation. Therefore, over time, the nature of the benefits and the direction in the flow of benefits will change as the company's international relations evolve.

CONTRIBUTION OF TRADE THEORIES

The fundamental theoretical parameters of international economic business theory are important in the understanding of the actions of international retail operations. There is a danger in focusing exclusively on international retail activity to the exclusion of a wider understanding of trade theory and multinational business activity.

The internationalization of service industries offers a challenge to existing theories of internationalization. For example, Dawson (1994) has considered general interpretations of international activity with respect to the internationalization of retailing. In particular, he noted the work of Dunning (1981, 1988) and the eclectic paradigm. Dunning's individual and collaborative work (Dunning, 1981, 1988; Dunning and Norman, 1985) has identified three important factors behind direct investment in the international market place. These advantages are: (1) ownership specific, where a company has competitive advantage through such aspects of its business as its product; (2) location specific, where the host market has particular advantages; (3) and internalization, where the company or the environment sets conditions in which the other two factors may be fully realized. Dawson recognizes the advantages of Dunning's approach and the insights it provides, but notes that it also highlights the differences between manufacturing and retailing. Dunning (1988) has also recognized this limitation of the eclectic paradigm when referring to the specific but maintains that it has a general relevance. These issues may be further explored by attempting to reconcile theories of retail development with general theories which have been constructed with particular reference to the manufacturing sector or to construct frameworks for considering the broader service environment. This may be achieved either through considering the service sector as a whole (Edvardsson et al., 1993) or through considering two areas, such as retailing and the hotel sector, in conjunction (Alexander and Lockwood, 1995).

Adam Smith and David Ricardo's theories of international trade provide a basis of understanding within the context of which work by neoclassical economists and business theorists may be placed and used to understand the activities of retail operations in the global economy. However, much of this work has yet to be integrated into the retail literature.

RETAIL DEVELOPMENT THEORIES

There are many theories of retail development. No single theory of retail development is either universally applicable or universally acceptable. From the considerable body of literature which now exists in this area, it is only possible to extract those theories which have had a major impact on retail thought and those which appear to be useful in the interpretation on specific trends relevant to an understanding of international retailing.

While much of the available theory is relevant to the international environment, it has not had the objective of explaining and interpreting the internationalization of retailing operations. Where it has explicitly addressed trans-national issues, it has tended to address the diffusion of concepts and technical skills. It is, therefore, essential that in the consideration of international retailing, an appreciation is achieved of those forces which are considered to have had a fundamental impact on retail structures in the national context and should, therefore, be considered from an international perspective.

Brown (1987) has suggested that theories of retail development may be placed in three broad categories:

- cyclical, where change occurs in a rhythmic pattern, where phases that have definable and identifiable associated characteristics are repeated;

- conflictual, where the issue of institutional conflict and the responses to innovation by existing organizations within the retail structure is seen as a fundamental determinant of change;

- environmental, where emphasis is placed on the environment in which retailers operate and change is explained as a response to developments in the environment.

Retail theories do not always fall neatly into these categories, and some contain a mixture of elements which could place them in more than one category, however, this three part categorization system is a useful method of interpreting the dynamic forces within retailing.

Cyclical theories

The most well known, and often misused, theory of retail change must be the Wheel of Retailing theory. The Wheel of Retailing, as described by McNair (1958) is a useful framework in which retail change may be described and understood. The Wheel of Retailing, illustrated in figure 6.2 describes the movement of retailers through three stages of development. In the initial entry stage, the retailer operates from a low status position, moves through an intermediary stage where the retailer occupies a traditional, or standard, position in the market, to a mature, high status, vulnerable stage.

The most important problem associated with the Wheel theory is that it is often expected to offer a universal explanation of retail change. This it does not do and should not be expected to do. There are retail forms, such as the department store and the supermarket, which may be seen to follow the logic of the Wheel of Retailing, while there are other forms which do not, such as shopping centres and those specialist retailers who by their very nature and market stance operate permanently at what is described in the Wheel theory at the mature end of the spectrum.

Another major problem associated with this theory is that the changes, even where they are observable, may be the result of numerous and very different causes. Explanations for the observable phenomenon of trading up may range from a deterioration in the quality of management to an interpretation which suggests the action of a law of nature. However, as Brown notes: 'the two most widely embraced explanations of trading up have their roots in the environmental and conflict-based traditions of institutional thought' (Brown, 1987, p. 11). That is:

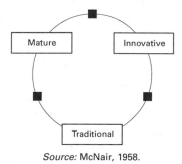

Source: McNair, 1958.

Figure 6.2 Wheel of Retailing

- environmental – increasing affluence and subsequent desire for increased service levels amongst consumers encourages retailers to develop their operations through the addition of services which in turn increase operational costs and force prices upward. This interpretation may be associated with Bucklin (1972), Hollander (1960) and Lewis (1945);

- conflictual – through the need to differentiate their operation, retailers may be obliged to compete on non-price terms, improving services adding merchandise ranges and hence seeking advantage in an operational response to competition which while improving services increases costs and in turn prices. This interpretation may be associated with Bartels (1981), and Dreesman (1968).

It has been recognized that the Wheel theory does not explain developments in all markets. While some markets may conform to the pattern of an institutional form, other markets do not. In less developed markets, introduction does not necessarily occur at the low price, low status end of the market but may occur at the higher end of the market (Cundiff, 1965; Goldman, 1982; Hollander, 1960). However, in economically and socially more developed markets, the introduction of an institutional form may conform to the basic principles of the Wheel.

From an international perspective, the Wheel of Retailing theory offers a means by which to understand the development of an institutional format in a particular market, and may, in part, be employed to explain certain features of the international context in which retailing develops and internationalization occurs. In developed markets, such as the UK or Germany, when an institutional format is introduced from the US, while adaption will occur and the introduction will not necessarily follow the same form as it has in the US, it will be introduced in a recognizable form and aimed at a similar customer group or retail need. In less developed markets, with different social and economic conditions such similarity of entry mode can not be expected. Indeed, the retail format may be introduced for very different reasons and appeal to very different customer groups. As a representation of a more developed market, the image associated with the form will recommend it to a more cosmopolitan group and the format may with perhaps the non-domestic merchandise that it would thereby sell occupy the position of a luxury retail operation rather than a mass merchandiser. This has certainly been the case with the introduction of supermarkets into less developed markets such as Chile and Saudi Arabia (Bennett, 1966; Alawi, 1986).

The Wheel of Retailing is a useful interpretive framework in certain circumstances. In markets with similar economic and social profiles, and thus where retailing has developed in a particular form, it is possible to use the Wheel of Retailing as an indicator of change that is or will occur in a market as a result of the introduction of a new format, or indeed identify the need for such an introduction. Thus, in the context of 1950s Britain, the supermarket was a logical development, given the environmental changes that were occurring in the market at that time. The response of specialist retailers within the market was to focus on the service they gave and by which they might differentiate themselves conforms to the

6.1 Message in a Bottle

French wines represent 60 per cent of Japanese wine imports but elsewhere in the world, other producer countries are eroding the market share of traditional producers. In the US, Australian and Chilean wines achieved an 8 per cent market share in 1993 and in the UK they reached a combined 14 per cent of market volume.

Australian wine exports have increased dramatically in recent years. In 1986, the country exported US$20m worth of wine, in 1993 the figure reached US$200m, and it is estimated the figure could be US$700m by 2000.

This remarkable success may not be matched by other exporting countries, but both the US and Chile have also seen exports rise considerably. Between 1986 and 1993 US exports rose by 500 per cent to US$182m and Chilean exports by 600 per cent to US$135m.

Respectively, Australia, the US and Chile achieved 2.6 per cent, 2.2 per cent and 1.6 per cent of global market share by 1993.

One of the reasons why Australian wines are relevant in the international market is the concentrated nature of the wine industry in Australia. Of Australian wine exports, 75 per cent is in the hands of four companies. This contrasts with the fragmented nature of the wine industry in markets such as France. The larger operations are therefore better placed to serve the needs of large retail chains who demand consistent quality and high volumes.

Modern technology is also an important aspect of the new wine producing countries' ability to compete in the global arena. Thus they are able to provide higher quality at more competitive prices.

The new exporters are also benefiting from the reduction of tariffs and export subsidies accepted by the EU and the US in the Uruguay Round of the GATT talks. Likewise, Asian countries offer attractive export opportunities but high import taxes and excise duty still stand in the way of their full exploitation.

With increased wine quality in the new wines from new markets, the traditional exporters no longer have a clear advantage.

Source: Maitland, 1996.

pattern of trading in the food trade in the UK in the 1960s through to the 1980s. While other specialist food retailers saw dramatic declines in earlier years, some retailers, such as those in the butchery trade, managed to resist the challenge of the supermarket and superstore for some time. It was not until the recession of the late 1980s and 1990s that the butchery trade finally succumbed to the full impact of the large superstore operations by which time the superstore where providing a high service butchery counter options to the customer.

In the UK, the superstore operators themselves became vulnerable to threats from innovative low price low status operations in the late 1980s as their margins rose, their product ranges expanded and developed and their services were enhanced. The discount stores and the warehouse club concept was perceived to represent a considerable threat to those retailers which had achieved dominance within the grocery sector. Increasing affluence in the UK market in the 1980s had encouraged the superstore operators to move away from a low status position. This is particularly well illustrated by the Tesco operation which sought from the late 1970s to shed its low status format and develop a chain of stores out of town which competed with its rivals which already possessed a more high status position. By the late 1980s, of the 'big five' grocery operators in the UK, three – Sainsbury, Tesco and Safeway – had achieved relatively high status positions within the market while the remaining two – ASDA and Gateway – were becoming marginalized, in part as a result of their failure to establish themselves in the segment of the market occupied by the other three retailers. There was a considerable gap toward the low price end of the market which the discount stores appeared so well placed to fill.

The experience of the UK grocery sector in the early 1990s illustrates the usefulness and relevance of the Wheel of Retailing. It illustrates the importance of environmental change and the role of management's strategic vision in creating the conditions which lead to low status innovative introductions but it also illustrates the international dimension of the Wheel theory. The UK market could not be taken in isolation and the importance of economically developed markets such as the US and Germany which had seen the development of warehouse operations and discount formats relevant to economic conditions in similar markets shows the international level on which the Wheel of Retailing must be understood.

Conflict theories

Change is a constant feature of retailing (Markin and Duncan, 1981). This change is a product of conflict which is always present within retailing but which is emphasized more at certain times than other. Conflict always exists between the operators of similar formats and within broad retail categories. At times, however, this conflict becomes inter-institutional and the intra-institutional conflict which is accepted as given recedes into the background.

Retailing is prone to periods of challenge as new formats appear to threaten old formats with extinction. Such cataclysms are however modified by the response of the individual retail organizations as they adapt to the challenge of the new. Organizational responses to challenges mirror the response of individuals. Fink, Beak and Taddeo's (1971) work which extended Fink's (1967) earlier model concerning individual experience to the organizational context, provides a structure in which to consider the reaction of retail organizations to the international innovator.

The organizational response to innovation will be shock, in that the organization does not have a set of responses with which to combat the threat posed (Fink et al., 1971). In the commercial environment, the more innovative the retailer is, the less the existing retailers will be able to cope with the challenge (Stern and El-Ansary, 1977; Martenson, 1981). There are four phases in the crisis change model.

1   Shock: in this phase the organization's response is characterized by panic, random action and paralysis. The threat of the innovative form is seen as overwhelming and there is a strong sense of helplessness and an inability to cope with the innovator. Consequently, any response is ill-conceived and as Stern and El-Ansary (1977) suggest in the retail context, a response is likely to be non-competitive and the formulation of a strategy to address the real threat of the new operation is not established.

2   Defensive retreat: in this phase, those organizations who perceive themselves to be under threat will seek to maintain the familiar structure of the industry. In this phase the organization may choose not to recognize the real implications of the threat and, through mechanistic resistance to change, avoid taking the planning decisions which would in the long term provide a coherent coping strategy.

3   Acknowledgement: in this phase, the organization is forced to face up to the reality of the threat and relinquish hopes of reestablishing the familiar structure and to begin to rationalize the new conditions which the organization faces.

6.2 Promises

On 1 February 1996, a trade agreement between the EU and Russia came into force. Just six weeks later, Russia ignored the agreement by raising minimum import prices for Vodka.

The agreement had sought to increase trading links between the EU and Russia by increasing access to the Russian market for car producers and alcoholic drink companies. In return, Russia gained access to EU markets through the removal of key restrictions on trade.

Russia set a minimum price of US$8.20 per litre for EU products compared with a price of US$3.80 for vodka from former Soviet Republics.

The consequences could be considerable for Russia. The move will not improve the EU's inclination to support Russia's application to join the World Trade Organisation. It will also help to undermine confidence in Russia's general attitude on trade and the countries desire to join the OECD.

Source: Tucker, 1996.

Planning and leadership qualities within the organization will reassert themselves as the organization begins to explore the available options.

4   Change: in this phase, having survived the threat of the innovator, the organization will, through a greater understanding of the new environment, reorganize in the new and increasingly familiar context. The organization will begin to achieve a new place in the changed order. Planning processes will be more integrated and consequently more comprehensive in contrast to the earlier phases when planning was dormant.

Some firms will be able to respond better in the change phase than others. The organization must be flexible enough to be able to accept the new realities and learn from the new experiences and to identify its own advantages in responding to the changing conditions in which it finds itself.

Stern and El-Ansary (1977) have suggested that there is another phase which follows the change phase described above. They suggest that, following the change phase, a shock phase occurs which is felt by the innovator. However, there is a danger that to accept this new shock phase in this light is to lose some of the validity of the earlier model; and if a further shock wave is identifiable, it is experienced by those firms unable to cope with the decline of the old structure and the new structure which replaces it (Martenson, 1981).

Responses to external threats range from imitation to differentiation. Thus, the challenged format will develop distinctiveness as a result of the challenge and the imitators will adopt the innovation. In the international environment, the imitator will be a local retailer adopting an innovation developed in a different market which will lead the retailer within the market into which the format has been introduced to bring a local management and understanding which will be distinctive and will frequently lead to the development of a more relevant concept in due course. It is observable that retail innovation, far from reducing the number of formats available to the consumer will lead to the development of more formats.

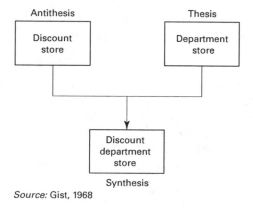

Source: Gist, 1968

Figure 6.3 Gist's dialectic model

Gist's (1968) employment of the dialectic in understanding conflict and the structural resolution of conflict illustrates the diversity that institutional conflict produces. Figure 6.3 depicts the thesis of the department store and the antithesis of the discount store and the synthesis of these two concepts in the discount department store. The transfer of a retail format from one market to another may, therefore, be expected not only to result in the establishment of that new format in the new market but the synthesis of old and new, in addition to the development of a format differentiated in the light of the new introduction. In the UK, following the introduction of the discount operations in the early 1990s, the indigenous retailers responded by establishing other formats which they may not have been expected to establish at that time. ASDA, for example, established the Dales operation.

Environmental theories

Retailing does not occur in a vacuum. In consequence, changes in the retail environment stimulate change. Poor economic trading conditions will force retailers to respond, as will increasing affluence, as noted above in respect of the Wheel theory, which will lead retailers to add services to their operations. If an environmental approach to retail change is adopted, however, there is the danger that the environment itself will appear to be the determining factor behind innovation. From a marketing perspective retailing is very much a product of its environment. There is, however, a danger that the adoption of an environmental perspective at the effective expense of other interpretive approaches will lead to a level of determinism that may be both intellectually unsatisfactory as well as being commercially inappropriate.

There have been successful attempts to measure the environment and predict change. Arndt's (1972) study of conditions in Sweden and his predictions

6.3 Papa Don't Preach

My father's background as a grocer is sometimes cited as the basis for my economic philosophy. . . . My father was both a practical man and a man of theory. He liked to connect the progress of our corner shop with the great complex romance of international trade which recruited people all over the world to ensure that a family in Grantham could have on its table rice from India, coffee from Kenya, sugar from the West Indies and spices from five continents. Before I read a line from the great liberal economists, I knew from my father's accounts that the free market was like a vast sensitive nervous system, responding to events and signals all over the world to meet the ever-changing needs of peoples in different countries, from different classes, of different religions, with a kind of benign indifference to their status.

Source: Thatcher, 1993.

concerning the development of self-service in Norway lend credibility to an approach, however, if taken to its logical conclusion such an approach treats the development of retail markets mechanistically. That is, Arndt (1972) following in the footsteps of Cundiff (1965) asserted that retail development will follow in the wake of economic development. Arndt sought, through the measurement of environmental determinants of retail structure, to predict developments in the retail structure. In this, personal consumption expenditures per capita, passenger car ownership and the geographical concentration of population determined the number of inhabitants per retail outlet and retail sales per outlet. While, Arndt's predictions for the Norwegian market on the bases of existing structures in the Swedish market may be said to show the process which does occur in different markets, and points toward the main determinants of change, it is nonetheless true to say that such predictive approaches neither account for fundamental breaks in development, which occur from time to time, nor the qualitative factors which may not be fitted into equations.

Emphasis on the retail environment has led to ecological (Markin and Duncan, 1981) and more specifically, Darwinian (Dreesman, 1968) interpretations of retail development. There is much to recommend these approaches, reflecting as they do both the competitive and cooperative and mutually beneficial context in which retailing occurs. The C-store (Convenience store), as it developed in response to the superstore is threatening on one level to the superstore, but in practice has cohabited with the superstore and provided the customer with a different time and place utility the superstore did not seek to provide. This cohabitation, however, is breaking down as superstores extend opening hours and develop smaller formats and wider distribution.

The Darwinian approach to retail development, while firmly rooted in the environmental context also embraces the conflict which is inherent within retail structures. Dreesman (1968) has recognized the periods of sudden change which characterize the retail environment and the development of phenotypes around the genotype in those periods which follow rapid development.

The environmental approach to interpreting retail change has its attractions, and even validity, if treated with care and if the problems of retail introductions into different cultures are recognized and economic and social factors are not treated in isolation. International retailing is essentially the product of markets that have reached critical levels of economic and social development. Therefore, international activity indicates that transfers of formats will occur where key conditions exist, where a suitable habitat exists. However, to this must be added the retail structure, the regulatory environment and the cultural context before decisions may be taken as to the suitability of one market over another for international operations.

CONTRIBUTION OF RETAIL THEORIES

The classic retail theories which have emerged in the last forty years, often from American academic institutions, and often based on the US experience, have not explicitly dealt with issues of internationalization. Rather, international themes have emerge through comparative studies. Arndt's (1972) consideration of temporal lags is an example of this. However, it could also be argued that Arndt (1972) represents a strand of European retail thought which because of the size of European markets has been forced to embrace the comparative retailing agenda. However, it has not been only geography, but also time, which has and will determine the internationalization of theory development. As retail structures integrate across national boundaries, particularly within Free Trade Areas, the international dimension will become a prerequisite of study in a way it was not when the early progenitors of retail thought began to develop theories of retail change.

CONCLUSION

Recent work by Dawson (1994) and Whitehead (1992) shows that the growth of international retail operations and an increasing academic interest in this area will lead to an accommodation of retail experience within general theories of international business. In this, retailing is part of international trends towards internationalization in the service sector (Alexander and Lockwood, 1995). It may, however, prove difficult to accommodate retailing within broad theories of service sector internationalization as it is to accommodate retailing within general theories of internationalization based on research into the experience of manufacturing industry. Nevertheless, efforts to provide a general interpretation of service sector development such as those by Edvardsson, Edvinsson and Nystrom (1993) are helpful contributions to an overall understanding of those factors which are important in the development of international operations and implementation of international development programmes. Theories of retail development in the international environment will also have to accommodate theories of structural development.

NOTES

1   For an edited and easily accessible edition of Smith's book see: Smith, A., (1776) *An Inquiry into the Nature and Causes of the Wealth of Nations*, R. Campbell and A. Skinner (eds), Clarendon, Oxford, 1976.
2   For an edited and easily accessible edition of Ricardo's book see: Ricardo, D., (1817) *The Principles of Political Economy*, P. Sraffa (ed.), University Press, Cambridge, 1962.
3   For edited and easily accessible editions of Samuelson's work see: Samuelson, P., (1966) *The Collected Scientific Papers of Paul A. Samuelson*, Vol. 1, J. Stiglitz (ed.), MIT Press, Cambridge Mass. Samuelson, P., (1966) *The Collected Scientific Papers of Paul A. Samuelson*, Vol. 2, J. Stiglitz (ed.), MIT Press, Cambridge Mass. Samuelson, P., (1972) *The Collected Scientific Papers of Paul A. Samuelson*, Vol. 3, R. Merton (ed.), MIT Press, Cambridge Massachusetts. Samuelson, P., (1972) *The Collected Scientific Papers of Paul A. Samuelson*, Vol. 4, H. Nagatani and K. Crowley (ed.), MIT Press, Cambridge Massachusetts.

QUESTIONS – DISCUSSION POINTS

1 What are the underlying principles of free trade?

2 How does the international product life cycle help to explain the transfer of retail skills and operations across national boundaries?

3 Is there evidence of oligopolistic rivalry in international retailing?

4 Does the 'Wheel of Retailing' help to explain the means by which international retailers enter a market?

5 How does Fink, Beak and Taddeo's (1971) crisis change model provide a basis on which the reaction of retailers in a host market may be explained and understood when internationalization occurs?

REFERENCES

Alawi, H., (1986) Saudi-Arabia: Making Sense of Self Service, *International Marketing Review*, Vol. 3, No. 1, pp. 21–38.

Alexander, N., and Lockwood, A., (1995) Internationalisation: A Comparison of the Hotel and Retail Sectors, *Marketing Education Group Conference*, Ulster, 4–6 July.

Arndt, J., (1972) Temporal Lags in Comparative Retailing, *Journal of Marketing*, Vol. 36, October, pp. 40–5.

Bartels, R., (1981) Criteria for Theory in Retailing, in R. Stampfl, E. Hirschman (eds) *Theory in Retailing: Traditional and Non-traditional Sources*, Chicago, American Marketing Association, pp. 1–8.

Bennett, P., (1966) Retailing Evolution or Revolution in Chile, *Journal of Marketing*, Vol. 30, July, pp. 38–41.

Brown, S., (1987) Institutional Change in Retailing: A Review and Synthesis, *European Journal of Marketing*, Vol. 21, No. 6, pp. 5–36.

Bucklin, L., (1972) *Competition and Evolution in the Distributive Trades*, Prentice Hall, Englewood Cliffs.

Chipman, J., (1966) A Survey of the Theory of International Trade, Part 3, *Econometrica*, Vol. 34, No. 1, pp. 18–76.

Cundiff, E., (1965) Concepts in Comparative Retailing, *Journal of Marketing*, Vol. 29, pp. 143–62.

Dawson, J., (1994) The Internationalization of Retailing Operations, *Journal of Marketing Management*, Vol. 10, pp. 267–82.

Dreesman, A., (1968) Patterns of Evolution in Retailing, *Journal of Retailing*, Vol. 44, Spring, pp. 64–81.

Dunning, J., (1981) *International Production and the Multinational Enterprise*, Allen and Unwin, London.

Dunning, J., (1988) The Eclectic Paradigm of International Production: A Restatement and Some Possible Extensions, *Journal of International Business Studies*, Vol. 19, No. 1, pp. 1–31.

Dunning, J., and Norman, G., (1985) Intra-Industry Production as a form of International Economic Involvement: An Exploratory Analysis, in A. Erdilek (ed.) *Multinationals as Mutual Invaders: Intra-industry Direct Foreign Investment*, Croom Helm, London.

Edvardsson, B., Edvinsson, L. and Nystrom, H., (1993) Internationalisation in Service Companies, *The Service Industries Journal*, Vol. 13, No. 1, pp. 80–97.

Fink, S., (1967) Crises and Motivation: A Theoretical Model, *Archives of Physical Medicine & Rehabilitation*, Vol. 48, November, pp. 592–7.

Fink, S., Beak J. and Taddeo, K., (1971) Organisational Crises and Change, *Applied Behavioural Science*, Vol. 7, No. 1, pp. 15–37.

Gist, R., (1968) *Retailing: Concepts and Decisions*, Wiley and Sons, New York.

Goldman, A., (1982) Adoption of Supermarket Shopping in a Developing Country: The Selective Adoption Phenomenon, *European Journal of Marketing*, Vol. 16, No. 1, pp. 17–26.

Hollander, S., (1960) The Wheel of Retailing, *Journal of Marketing*, Vol. 24, July, 1960, pp. 37–42.

Kacker, M., (1985) *Transatlantic Trends in Retailing*, Quorum, Connecticut.

Knickerbocker, F., (1973) *Oligopolistic Reaction and the Multinational Enterprise*, Division of Research Harvard Business School, Boston.

Leontief, W., (1953) *Studies in the Structure of the American Economy*, Boston.

Lewis, W., (1945) Competition in Retail Trade, *Economica*, Vol. 12, November, pp. 202–34.

Linder, S., (1961) *An Essay on Trade and Transformation*, Wiley, New York.

Maitland, A., (1996) New wine exporters threaten to bottle up old producers, *Financial Times*, 14 March, p. 3.

Markin, R., and Duncan, C., (1981) The Transformation of Retail Institutions: Beyond the Wheel of Retailing and Life Cycle Theories, *Journal of Macromarketing*, Vol. 1, No. 1, 1981, pp. 58–66.

Martenson, R., (1981) *Innovations in Multinational Retailing: IKEA on the Swedish, Swiss, German and Austrian Furniture Markets*, Gothenburg, University of Gothenburg.

McNair, M., (1958) Significant Trends and Developments in the Post War Period, in A. Smith (ed.), *Competitive Distribution in a Free High Level Economy and its Implications for the University*, University of Pittsburg Press, Pittsburg, pp. 1–25.

Ohlin, B., (1933) *Interregional and International Trade*, Harvard University Press, Cambridge Massachusetts.

Ricardo, D., (1817) *The Principles of Political Economy and Taxation*, P. Sraffa (ed.), University Press, Cambridge, 1962.

Samuelson, P., (1966) *The Collected Scientific Papers of Paul A. Samuelson*, Vol. 1, J. Stiglitz (ed.), MIT Press, Cambridge Massachusetts.

Samuelson, P., (1966) *The Collected Scientific Papers of Paul A. Samuelson*, Vol. 2, J. Stiglitz (ed.), MIT Press, Cambridge Massachusetts.

Samuelson, P., (1972a) *The Collected Scientific Papers of Paul A. Samuelson*, Vol. 3, R. Merton (ed.), MIT Press, Cambridge Massachusetts.

Samuelson, P., (1972b) *The Collected Scientific Papers of Paul A. Samuelson*, Vol. 4, H. Nagatani and K. Crowley (ed.), MIT Press, Cambridge Massachusetts.

Smith, A., (1776) *An Inquiry into the Nature and Causes of the Wealth of Nations*, R. Campbell and A. Skinner (eds), Clarendon, Oxford, 1976.

Stern, L., and El-Ansary, A., (1977) *Marketing Channels*, Prentice Hall, New Jersey.

Thatcher, M., (1993) *The Downing Street Years*, Harper Collins, London, p. 11.

Toyne, B., and Walters, G., (1993) *Global Marketing Management: A Strategic Perspective*, second edition, Allyn and Bacon, Needham Heights, Massachusetts.

Tucker, E., (1996) Vodka move 'breaks spirit of trade deal', *Financial Times*, 14 March, p. 3.

Vernon, R., (1966) International Investment and International Trade in the Product Cycle, *Quarterly Journal of Economics*, May.

Wan, H., (1982) Samuelson and Trade Theory: From the Methodological Perspective, *Samuelson and Noeclassical Economics*, G. Feiwel (ed.), Kluwer Nijhoff, Boston.

Whitehead, M., (1992) Internationalisation of Retailing: Developing New Perspectives, *European Journal of Marketing*, Vol. 26, No. 8/9, pp. 74–9.

Motives for Internationalization

▌ OBJECTIVES ▌

This chapter considers the reasons behind the development of international retail operations and the motivations which stimulate the process of internationalization. Frameworks into which different retailer responses to the internationalization process may be placed are described and discussed. A theoretical approach is taken to the development of retail operations.

INTRODUCTION

Although, for the sake of confidentiality, he shall remain anonymous, a senior retail analyst based in the City of London, once confided, with at least a hint of seriousness, when in conversation with the author of this book, that the reason why retailers move abroad is to make money. This is undoubtedly true. Retailers are in business to be profitable; without profit they will not survive, therefore, markets in which they believe they will make a profit will be attractive to them and markets in which they will not make a profit will not be attractive to them. However, while profit is the ultimate objective, the motivations or reasons which lie behind internationalization are varied and will affect the success of international actions, and are important in understanding the stage the retailer has reached in the internationalization process and the general conditions within the retail sector.

The motives which lie behind an international move reveal much about the retailer undertaking international development, as well as helping to shed light on general developments in the international market and conditions within the retailer's market of origin. Frequently, retailers' initial moves in the international environment are poorly thought out and often reflect conditions at home more than they reflect opportunities in the new market. Retailers, once they have achieved a given level of market coverage or market share in their domestic market, will often start to consider international operations. Their thinking will be dominated more by limited or diminishing opportunities at home rather than profitable opportunities elsewhere. International activity may also mask a retailer's failure to address important problems in the domestic market. The retail environment is a dynamic environment. Retailers must therefore be aware of changing customer needs and the new requirements customers seek from retail outlets. While international expansion may provide an opportunity for format replication or a transfer of skills across national boundaries, it should not be allowed to distract management from the task of up-dating domestic operations. Thus, the motivations which lie behind internationalization must not be viewed in isolation from the issues of domestic development and expansion.

This chapter considers the theoretical material that has emerged on the development of international retail operations and the motivations which lie behind the process.

WHY INTERNATIONALIZE?

Why should the company internationalize? Which market should the company consider? Are there core market opportunities to exploit at home? Are there diversification opportunities in the domestic market? Does the European market offer the company longer term growth opportunities than the US market? Should sourcing opportunities in South East Asia encourage the company to expand retail operations in the region? The way in which the question of international expansion is addressed will indicate not only the stage in the development of the retail operation but the fundamental perspective adopted by senior management toward the global market-place.

A retail operation considering international activity for the first time may well adopt an ethnocentric approach to the issue. The issue will be addressed from the perspective of the retailer's market of origin and the development of the retailer's operation in that market. A retail operation which has already accrued considerable international experience may be capable of a geocentric approach toward the issue. The issue will be addressed with reference to the development of retail operations in a number of markets and with reference to an international perspective.

For the retailer considering international activity for the first time, international activity may be perceived as nothing more than one of the options available. It is enshrined within strategic management thought that businesses may pursue four fundamental objectives (Ansoff, 1957, 1988):

1   the business may seek to further penetrate the market in which it already operates;

2   the business may expand into new product areas in the same market in which it already operates;

3   the business may maintain its present product lines and expand into new markets in which it is not currently operating;

4   the business may expand into new product areas and expand into new markets in which it is not currently operating.

These fundamental positions may be further elaborated. Omura (1986), has suggested, on the basis of this fundamental schema, twenty fundamental product and market strategic alternatives may be identified. These positions will be determined by market and market needs against merchandise and service provision. In respect of markets and needs, businesses may seek to:

• continue to serve the present market with present needs;

• or seek to serve different needs within the present market.

Also, the business may seek to:

• serve different markets where customers' needs are served in the same way as they are served in the core market;

• serve different needs in different markets.

These four basic market orientations may then be qualified by product and service alignment. Thus:

• a merchandise mix which is marketed in the core market may be altered;

• delivery systems may be altered;

• new merchandise may be introduced with similar service support, either through the manipulation of assortment or the extension of merchandise lines;

• new merchandise with new service support requirements may be adopted.

Retailers remain within a series of borders or boundaries, of which only one is political or regulatory. Therefore, retailers do not internationalize because they do not wish to cross these boundaries. However, where a retailer does not have to cross boundaries of considerable dimensions or, indeed, greater boundaries exist within the confines of the national market, then the question logically becomes, why not internationalize? There is a logic inherent within this argument which dictates, if it is risk avoidance with which the retailer is primarily concerned, then as a consequence, is internationalization a risk avoidance strategy in itself: is the risk greater where internal expansion is considered or where external expansion is proposed? Essentially, if the retail planner's mental map is constrained within the geographical context of the state, the question is, why internationalize? However, if the retail planner seeks to access markets which will be served by and will support a retail operation of given characteristics, the question is, why not internationalize? That is, if the growth or the survival of the company is better served by an international, rather than a purely domestic, operation, then international growth not only becomes attractive but imperative.

The development of retailer thought in this area has been determined by the first rather than the second perspective. This has been the result of intellectual and historical factors. It is therefore instructive to follow the development of this debate before constructing a framework in which the reasons for internationalization and the process of internationalization may be understood.

TRANSITION

Figure 7.1 describes the national development of a retail operation. The operation is based on a concept which is either borrowed or an innovation that is the product of the company. The concept, if an adaptation, will either be a concept that is borrowed from another market or from another operator's use of a concept in the domestic market. Three phases of the operation may be observed.

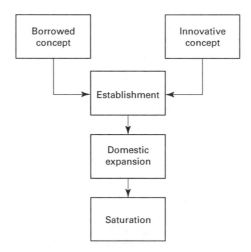

Figure 7.1 Retail operational development: in the domestic market

1 Establishment: in this phase, the company experiments with the concept and eventually develops a format which meets immediate market needs.

2 Domestic expansion: in this phase, the retailer will expand the operation geographically within the domestic market. The retail format will come into conflict with other retailers operating in the market and operators who exploit the same format.

3 Saturation: in this phase, the retailer reaches a point of national development where further growth will provide only limited benefits. At this stage, the geographical market will be covered and market share will be relatively high compared with other operators.

These three phases describe the fundamental process of national development. However, it should also be recognized that national development is not a linear process and retail operators are continually re-evaluating their operation. Small changes occur regularly so there is, at the very least, incremental change. There will also be periods when rapid change occurs, or fundamental changes in operating procedure, merchandise ranges and format occur. The introduction of the supermarket meant that many large grocery operators in markets around the world had to transform their operations, replacing the old, out-moded formats with the supermarket format. In the grocery sector, a second fundamental change occurred with the move to out of town sites and the superstore or hypermarket format. Figure 7.2

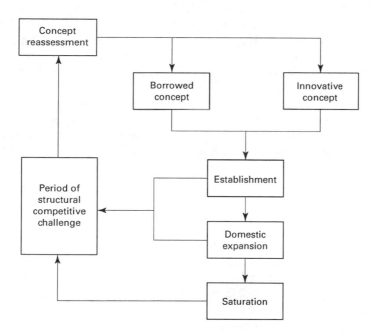

Figure 7.2 Retail operational development: conceptual reassessment in the domestic market

describes these fundamental shifts diagrammatically. Having reached a level of domestic expansion, a retailer may be faced with the type of challenge discussed above in chapter 4. This will call for reassessment of the concept within the domestic context. This may lead, as discussed, to the adoption of features associated with the new competitors, or wholesale adoption of the new concept. It may lead to innovative responses which create an inherently new format to withstand the new competition. A challenge or need for reassessment may occur as the retailer reaches a point of saturation. Thus, the need for the reassessment of domestic operations may also preclude internationalization or other strategic options. Failure to recognize this need may lead to decline within the national context and a need for domestic reassessment in less than positive circumstances.

A retailer, having reached saturation will then face, it is assumed, two options.

- Diversification into new product areas: Retailers will often choose this route, preferring to remain within the wider retail structure with which they are familiar. This may, however, only gain the company time before it has to take a decision to expand internationally. It may also lead the company into commercial contexts which are not fully understood and weaken the company through the draining of financial resources and diverting strategic vision.

- Internationalization: Having reached a point of saturation, the company may look for international opportunities. Certainly, there are examples of retailers who have only internationalized once they have exploited national markets, but just because such retailers exist does not mean that retailers will only internationalize after they have reached this point. Indeed, retailers who wait until opportunities have become limited in the domestic market may internationalize too quickly and make an initial error which may lead to withdrawal and the loss of confidence in the international market-place and long term damage to the company.

Internationalization is neither a direct corollary of saturation nor the only or direct consequence of it. Internationalization, however, has often been seen as the product of saturation and this has lead to a particular school of thought on this matter.

REACTION

One school of thought suggests that internationalization is a reaction to limited opportunities in the domestic market. This interpretation of the internationalization process is based on negative factors in the domestic market. This approach recognizes the reasons why retailers are attracted to, or 'pulled' toward, international markets, but places primary importance on those factors which push a retailer out into the international environment.

Push and pull factors appear throughout the literature on international retailing. These factors indicate the reasons why retailers decide to move away from one market and to another. They may be categorized in terms of the five boundaries of international development described in chapter 2 (see table 7.1).

These push and pull factors are not absolute but are relative, and must therefore be considered in relation to each other. They describe the general political, economic, social and cultural environment, all of which have a direct influence on retail operations, as well as retail specific and retailer specific factors. Table 7.1 lists the most commonly cited examples of push or pull factors but this list could be extended to include factors which may have an important influence on retailers in specific situations. In particular, there will be retailer-specific issues which will encourage expansion in markets which on the basis of other factors might not appear attractive. A mass merchandise retailer will not be able to operate in markets which specialist retailers with smaller formats will be able to access. In a relatively small market, specialist retailers who expand through franchise operations may be

Table 7.1 Push and pull factors behind internationalization

Boundary	Push	Pull
Political	Unstable structure, restrictive regulatory environment, anti-business culture dominant, consumer credit restrictions	Stable structure, relaxed regulatory environment, pro-business culture dominant, relaxed consumer credit regulations
Economic	Poor economic conditions, low growth potential, high operating costs, mature markets, small domestic market	Good economic conditions, high growth potential, low operating costs, developing markets, property investment potential, large market, favourable exchange rates, depressed share prices
Social	Negative social environment, negative demographic trends, population stagnation or decline	Positive social environment, positive demographic trends, population growth
Cultural	Unfamiliar cultural climate, heterogeneous cultural environment	Familiar cultural reference points, attractive cultural fabric, innovative business/retail culture, company ethos, homogenous cultural environment
Retail structure	Hostile competitive environment, high concentration levels, format saturation, unfavourable operating environment	Niche opportunities, company owned facilities, 'me too' expansion, favourable operating environment

Source: Kacker, 1985; Treadgold, 1988, 1991; Alexander, 1990a,b; CIG, 1991; McGoldrick and Fryer, 1993.

7.1 What in the World's Come Over You?

In 1986, the Dee Corporation plc, a major UK grocery operation at that time, made a number of acquisitions. In June, the company purchased Fine Fare from associated British Foods for £686m, thereby gaining considerable market share in the UK grocery sector. In April of the same year, the company had acquired further trading space through the purchase of twelve Woolco superstores from Woolworth Holdings for £26m. These were domestic acquisitions. Through these purchases the company extended its market base in the UK and placed itself amongst a small group of grocery retailers who were increasingly coming to dominate the grocery sector. However, in March of the same year, the Dee Corporation also purchased Hermans Sporting Goods in the US for £278m. The acquisition, for £45m, of M & H Sporting Goods, the US retailer, followed in July. The company's move into the US leisure goods market may have appeared a reasonable move, given the buoyancy of the US economy and the growth in the sports good market within the lifestyle culture of the 1980s. However, irrespective of these apparent reasons for expansion, the company had made an international move into a sector in which the company did not operate domestically. The company may have employed the funds used in the funding of the US move to rationalize its store portfolio which, after domestic acquisitions, needed some attention.

An investment of more than £300m in US sports goods retailing by a UK based grocery retailer looked surprising at the time. Following the acquisition of the Gateway Corporation, the new name for the Dee Corporation, by Isosceles plc in July 1989 for £2,000m, the international operation was sold off. By the end of the 1980s, the rapid expansion of the company, both domestically and internationally, had come to a dramatic end, leaving the new owners to cope with a considerable debt problem and an increasing difficult trading environment in which the company's outlets were often less than able to compete with such rivals as Sainsbury and Tesco. To understand why the Dee Corporation would consider such an international move, it is necessary to understand the reasons why retailers internationalize, and the threats and opportunities which they perceive, or should perceive, at the time of international development.

Source: CIG, 1993.

able to reach a market segment that is inaccessible to the larger operator whose expansion occurs through acquisition of organic growth. Therefore, the importance of a large market may not be as great. The Body Shop will be able to operate in small markets around the world such as Bahrain, the Cayman Islands and Qatar, while retailers such as Tengelmann will prefer to expand in large markets such as the US and the EU.

The interpretation of internationalization as reactive assumes a fundamental retailer reluctance to leave the security of the national market and hence the interpretation places a primary emphasis on push factors. This interpretation was followed by Kacker (1985), who considered that an important stimulus behind the international activity of European retailers in the late 1970s and early 1980s were the push factors which existed within the European environment. To some extent, Kacker (1985) identified time-specific factors, but the logic of his analysis is that the push factors were creating an environment which forced retailers out. This sentiment was shared by Treadgold who has commented: 'For many . . . retailers . . . the principal motivation for expanding internationally has been the limited opportunities for sustained domestic growth' (Treadgold, 1988, p. 8). This view has been challenged by research which has emphasized the importance of pull factors.

PROACTION

The reactive interpretation of internationalization has been challenged by empirical research carried out in the late 1980s and early 1990s on both sides of the Atlantic (Alexander, 1990a, 1990b, 1994; Williams, 1992a, 1992b, 1994). Williams argued that those factors associated with the reactive response to internationalization were 'not the major reason behind the recent RI of UK retailers' (Williams, 1992a, p. 278). In this new research, retailers emphasized the importance of their own operations and the opportunities available to them in other markets to exploit those operations, rather than the negative factors which existed in their home markets. Therefore, Williams concluded:

> the major motives behind the RI of UK-based international retailers originate from a perceived internationally appealing and innovative offering and growth oriented and proactive motives. (Williams, 1992a, p. 279)

The results of the empirical research emphasized the importance of such factors as the retailer's format and the relative lack of importance attached to issues such as saturation, as tables 7.2 and 7.3 illustrate. The retailers surveyed were far more inclined to emphasize their proactive response to the international environment. The results show a high level of agreement.

SYNTHESIS

The reactive and proactive interpretations of internationalization are, in part, the result of the research methodology employed, the period of time under study and initial assumptions. The reactive school have tended to be observational, the proactive school empirical in their approach. Much of the work carried out by the

Table 7.2 Reasons for internationalization: Williams (1992)

Motive	Strong or very strong effect (%)
Retail formula has international appeal	75.6
Possessed unique competitive advantage	66.7
Knowledge of overseas market opportunities	61.9
Capitalize on innovative retail formula	59.5
Future growth prospects of overseas markets	47.7
Saturated UK retail sector	27.5
Dominant firm in UK retail sector	27.5
Increased competition in UK sector	12.5
Excessive restrictions in UK market	7.5

Source: Williams, 1992a.

Table 7.3 Reasons for internationalization: Alexander (1990)

Motives	Average significance score
Niche opportunities in new market	3.6
Size of new market	3.5
Economic prosperity in new market	3.4
Retailer's operating format	3.2
Retailer's product lines	3.2
Underdeveloped new market	3.1
Favourable exchange rates	2.9
Favourable operating environment	2.8
Saturation in home market	2.2
Real estate investment, new market	2.1
Favourable labour climate, new market	2.1
Share prices, new market	2.1

1 = unimportant; 2 = low importance; 3 = moderate importance; 4 = high importance; 5 = utmost importance.

Source: Alexander, 1990a.

reactive school concerned relatively negative economic conditions and specific historical conditions. The reactive school made assumptions based on the size of retailers entering the international arena, while the proactive school's empirical research reflected the assumptions of practitioners.

However, even the methodologies applied by the proactive school indicate that retailers do react to limited opportunities in the domestic market while observation of retail activity also shows that proactive internationalization occurs at a surprisingly early stage in some retailer's development. Benetton's second retail outlet was not in its domestic market of Italy but in Paris. Both approaches recognize the importance of saturation in the domestic market and the importance of a retailer's operation to its ability to expand internationally. Therefore, taking these as fundamental to an understanding of the motives behind internationalization, it is possible to construct the matrix illustrated in figure 7.3 (Alexander, 1995).

In figure 7.3 four positions are given, they are defined thus:

Autochthonic: the retailer has reached a point in the development of the domestic operation where saturation in the market of origin is unimportant, and the retailer's operation has limited potential within the global environment.

Reactive: the retailer has reached a point in the development of the domestic operation where saturation in the market of origin is important, and the retailer's operation has limited potential within the global environment.

Expansive: the retailer has reached a point in the development of the domestic operation where saturation in the market of origin is important, and the retailer's operation has considerable potential within the global environment.

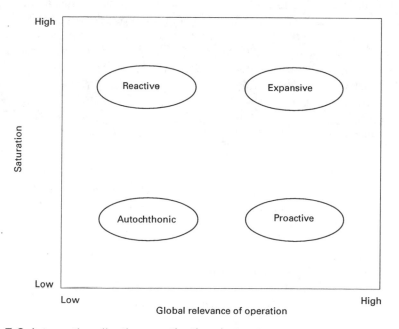

Figure 7.3 Internationalization: motivational structure

7.2 Norwegian Wood

Ikea is a globally recognized retail brand name, and its founder, Ingvar Kamprad, is respected as an innovative retailer entrepreneur. In the 1950s, however, it was a relatively small retail operation based exclusively in the Swedish market.

Ikea is known for its furniture warehouse showroom concept and its attractive product range, but in the early years of the company, the mail order side of the business was an important element in its approach to its market.

The first showroom was opened in 1953 in Sweden, and radically expanded in 1958. The second store opened by the company was in Oslo, Norway, in 1963. At that time, the company had a healthy but relatively small share of the Swedish market (6 per cent). It was not until 1965 that Ikea opened a store readily accessible to the Stockholm market at Kungens Kurva. A store was opened in the Danish market in 1969, so that when Ikea moved into the Swiss market in 1973, it had seven stores in Scandinavia and a market share in Sweden of 18 per cent.

In 1973, Kamprad moved to Copenhagen in Denmark, in order to be closer to the large European markets which the company had set its sights.

The development of Ikea shows a proactive approach to international development. While it must be said that there are considerable similarities in the Scandinavian markets, the company's willingness to think on an international basis early in its retail store development is indicative of an attitude of many that has the potential to build truly international operations.

By 1994, the company was operating in Austria, Belgium, the Czech Republic, Denmark, France, Germany, Hungary, Iceland, Italy, the Netherlands, Norway, Poland, Slovakia, Spain, Switzerland and the UK in Europe. Further, afield Ikea was operating in Australia, Canada, Hong Kong, Kuwait, Saudi Arabia, Singapore, UAE and the US.

Source: Jefferys, 1992; Martenson, 1981; CIG, 1994.

Proactive: the retailer has reached a point in the development of the domestic operation where saturation in the market of origin is unimportant, and the retailer's operation has considerable potential within the global environment.

Internationalization may occur when a retailer finds itself in any one of these positions, although the stage in the retailer's development and the subsequent nature of the retailer's international development will be affected by the position which it occupies at the time of internationalization.

It is, therefore, possible for retailers to internationalize at different stages in their domestic growth: it is not just large retailers who move into non-domestic markets

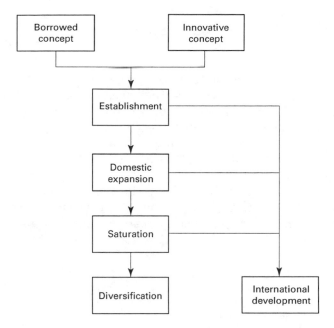

Figure 7.4 Retail operational development: internationalization

and neither is it only negative factors which motivate retailers. Therefore, as figure 7.4 indicates, recognition of international opportunities may occur at any stage in a retailer's domestic development. Indeed, some of the most internationally relevant retail formats have emerged at a relatively early stage.

POST-INTERNATIONALIZATION

The theoretical material discussed above has grown out of a debate which assumed that the individual retailer, and hence the motivations of the individual retailer, were determined and developed by an essentially ethnocentric state of collective management thinking. This was based on an implicit, yet essentially unrecognized, but understandable assumption, that a retailer's first international move was an important determinant in the construction of a theoretical framework which attempted to provide an explanation of the internationalization process. In an increasingly international retail environment, this is no longer a satisfactory assumption. Although, it may be unwise to ignore the importance of market of origin based thinking, as a retailer develops in the international environment, it is inevitable that the international environment will increasingly determine management thinking. Therefore, it may be necessary to conceptualize retailers' motivational thinking within a time frame and hence stages of internationalization.

7.3 Young Americans

The first Woolworth Store was opened in Utica, New York, 1879. In 1897, the first store of what was to become, in 1912, the F. W. Woolworth Co. opened in Canada, in Toronto. Another store was opened shortly, afterwards, in Montreal. Within fifteen years, the company had thirty-one stores in Canada.

The first store in the British Isles opened in Liverpool, England, in 1909. Within five years, the success of the operation had led to the opening of forty-four stores in England, Scotland, Wales and what are now Northern Ireland and the Republic of Ireland.

Whether in Canada or in the British Isles, the Woolworth concept was readily accepted by customers at the turn of the twentieth century. Frank Woolworth was proved correct when he said in 1890, on a buying trip to Britain:

> I think a good penny and six pence store run by a live Yankee would create a sensation here

Source: Woolworth, 1954.

Treadgold (1990) has suggested that a retailer's international development has three stages.

Stage 1:   Reluctance: In this stage, retailers are essentially domestic operations who are reluctant to develop internationally, and will only do so where there exists in their home market an 'absence of long term growth opportunities' (Treadgold, 1990. p. 21).

Stage 2:   Caution: In this stage, retailers have increased their international exposure and are cautious in their approach to foreign markets. Consequently, retailers look for expansion opportunities in geographically close markets which have operating environments similar to those found in the domestic market.

Stage 3:   Ambition: In this stage, retailers are more ambitious and aggressive in the identification of attractive international markets. The emphasis moves away from the need to locate in close geographical or culturally proximate markets and to the need to identify attractive markets.

These three stages suggest that, over time, retailers become more inclined to seek out opportunities in distant markets as they gain confidence in the international arena. There are two principle determinants, those of 'time' and 'geographical presence' within this perceptual framework. Over time, retailers move from reluctance through cautious to ambitious positions, and in so doing attain a greater willingness to access geographically distant markets. There is a prima facie logic to these stages, but this interpretive framework begs further questions:

- is it correct to assume that retailers are forced out of their markets by limited opportunities at home?
- how should geographical presence be measured?
- is time or some other factor, such as experience, being measured?

The answers to these questions must then be considered in the light of answers to the others.

This first question has already been addressed in the discussion above. While some retailers may internationalize because they no longer have opportunities for expansion in their domestic market, other retailers internationalize at a relatively early stage in their domestic development. Nevertheless, without accepting that retailers are reactive or reluctant to internationalize, it is possible to assume that they may be hyper-cautious in their approach to the international environment and this may lead them to consider geographically or psychologically proximate markets within which to expand. This does not indicate, by inference, that the retailer is placing greater emphasis on push rather than pull factors, rather that the choice of international market may be circumscribed by a lack of international experience. It is, therefore, reasonable to assume that as retail managers gain experience in the international environment they are willing to consider markets at a greater geographical distance.

The second question relating to the measurement of geographical presence may be better expressed with respect to psychological distance but is more easily measured with reference to geography. Essentially, what is being measured is psychological distance but geography is a useful proxy. Internationalization is therefore measured in terms of the distance of markets and the number of such markets from the domestic market.

The third question relates to time, yet it is experience that is essentially being measured. Here again a measurable entity stands proxy for a less definable concept. Nevertheless, as with the issue of geography, the length of time an organization operates within the international environment will affect corporate thinking and hence attitudes toward different market opportunities. This factor will also be affected by the internationalization of the sector in which the individual retail firm operates as this will in itself affect the attitude of individual managers.

Research carried out among European food retailers has shown that Treadgold's suggestion of stages of internationalization has some validity (Myers and Alexander, 1995). This research has shown that the attitudes of directors of European food retailers toward international expansion does vary according to the levels of internationalization achieved within their domestic market and the length of individual activity. Thus, French food retailers exhibited an essentially ambitious approach to internationalization, while UK food retailers were more cautious.

7.4 Handyman

To describe the GIB operation as a Belgian operation would be inaccurate but, although the company has a collection of international interests, it remains constrained by its national market.

Internationally, the company has interests in food retailing, Do-It-Yourself retailing, restaurants and speciality retailing. Its DIY interests are particularly widely spread, with a 100 per cent interest in Obi in France and Scotty's in the US, a 65 per cent interest in A-OK of Delaware in the US, a 55 per cent interest in Aki Bricolage in Spain and Portugal, and a 25 per cent interest in Homebase in the UK. However, in international food retailing, it has only a small interest, in the Polish market, through Precowa, which runs Globi stores. Likewise, its restaurant business is focused strongly on Belgium with only Quick outlets in France and its speciality retail operations, apart from its Disport stores in France, are all in Belgium. Three-quarters of its turnover still comes from the relatively small Belgian market.

GIB is the product of two mergers. The first occurred between the department store and variety chains, Innovation and Bon Marche, in 1969. The second occurred in 1974, between the group established in 1969 and the department store, supermarket, hypermarket retailer GB Enterprises. The resulting company was to become the leading retail enterprise in Belgium and was to achieve diversification into a number of attractively expanding retail subsectors.

However, like a number of large retail operations with long histories and considerable operational baggage, the company has had to undergo a process of major restructuring in recent years.

Retailers such as GIB face a major challenge in the international retail environment of the 1990s. While they have considerable management skills to draw on, they are operations with numerous interests, many of which have been the result of diversification at home rather than internationalization abroad.

Source: Euromonitor, 1996.

This reflects the international experience of food retailers in the UK compared with their counterparts in France and hence the international geographic spread of French and UK operations.

This empirical research was carried out amongst food retailers and this in itself may affect the results. Food retailers face problems which non-food retailers do not face, therefore, this may make them more cautious when it comes to geographical development, nevertheless the empirical research in this context supports the observational material.

CONCLUSION

The motivations which lie behind individual retailer internationalization are complex. The schools of thought discussed above and the framework of motivations described are simplifications of internal and external influences which affect decisions to operate in the international environment. Nevertheless, the reactive-proactive debate and the 'push and pull' factors, while simplifications, identify important fundamental issues associated with the internationalization process and the motivational factors which lie behind it.

Motivations change over time, both in the context of the macro-economic environment but also in terms of individual retailer experience. The motivations behind international retail developments are a complex mixture of commercial, sectoral, economic and psychological influences.

QUESTIONS – DISCUSSION POINTS

1 What are the fundamental alternatives available to a retailer seeking operational development?

2 What are push and pull factors?

3 What is the fundamental difference between a 'reactive' and 'proactive' response to internationalization?

4 Treadgold (1990) has suggested three stages of international development. Do these stages presume a 'reactive' or 'proactive' interpretation of internationalization?

REFERENCES

Alexander, N., (1990a) Retailers and International Markets: Motives for Expansion, *International Marketing Review*, Vol. 7, No. 4, pp. 75–85.

Alexander N., (1990b) Retailing Post-1992, *Service Industries Journal*, Vol. 10, No. 2, pp. 172–87.

Alexander, N., (1994) NAFTA and the EU: UK Retailers' Strategic Response, *Recent Advances in Retailing and Services Science Conference*, Banff, Alberta, Canada, 7–10 May.

Alexander, N., (1995) Expansion within the Single European Market: a motivational structure, *The International Review of Retail, Distribution and Consumer Research*, Vol. 5, No. 4, pp. 472–87.

Ansoff, H., (1957) Strategies for Diversification, *Harvard Business Review*, September–October, pp. 113–24.

Ansoff, H., (1988) *New Corporate Strategy: An Analytical Approach to Business Policy for Growth and Expansion*, John Wiley, New York.

CIG, (1991) *Cross-Border Retailing in Europe*, The Corporate Intelligence Group, London.

CIG, (1993) *Retail Rankings*, The Corporate Intelligence Group, London.

CIG, (1994), *Cross-Border Retailing in Europe*, London: The Corporate Intelligence Group.

Euromonitor, (1996) GIB Group, *Retail Monitor International*, February 1996.

Jefferys, J., (1992) The Ikea Group, A. Hast, D. Pascal, P. Barbour, J. Griffin (eds) *International Directory of Company Histories*, Vol. V, St James Press, Detroit, pp. 82–4.

Kacker, M., (1985) *Transatlantic Trends in Retailing*, Quorum, Connecticut.

McGoldrick, P., and Fryer, E., (1993) Organisational Culture and the Internationalisation of Retailers, *7th International Conference on Research in the Distributive Trades*, Institute for Retail Studies, University of Stirling, 6–8 September.

Martenson, R., (1981) *Innovations in Multinational Retailing: IKEA on the Swedish, Swiss, German and Austrian Furniture Markets*, Gotenburg, University of Gotenburg.

Myers, H., and Alexander, N., (1995) Direction of International Food Retail Expansion: An Empirical Study of European Retailers, *8th International Conference on Research in the Distributive Trades*, Milan, 1–2 September, pp. A7.1–10.

Omura, G., (1986) Developing Retail Strategy, *International Journal of Retailing*, Vol. 1, No. 3, pp. 17–32.

Treadgold, A., (1990) The Emerging Internationalisation of Retailing: Present Status and Future Challenges *Irish Marketing Review*, Vol. 5, No. 2, pp. 11–27.

Treadgold, A., (1988) Retailing Without Frontiers, *Retail and Distribution Management*, Vol. 16, No. 6, pp. 8–12.

Williams, D., (1992a) Motives for Retailer Internationalization: Their Impact, Structure, and Implications', *Journal of Marketing Management*, Vol. 8, pp. 269–85.

Williams, D., (1992b) Retailer Internationalization: An Empirical Inquiry, *European Journal of Marketing*, Vol. 26, No. 8/9, pp. 8–24.

Williams, D., (1994) *Recent Advances in Retailing and Services Science Conference*, Banff, Alberta, Canada, 7–10 May.

Woolworth, (1954) *Woolworth's First 75 Years: The Story of Everybody's Store*, New York, Woolworth.

Determinants of International Expansion

Expansion Patterns

OUTLINE

▌ OBJECTIVES ▌

This chapter places the other chapters in part IV in context. Patterns of international expansion are described and discussed. Determining factors behind patterns of international retail development are identified.

INTRODUCTION

This part is concerned with patterns of international expansion and those factors which determine market choice. Retailers, when faced with the prospect of internationalization, are constrained by a complex interplay of market and organizational factors. When considering international market alternatives, retailers must consider the suitability of their operations to new markets. In many markets around the world, opportunities either do not exist, or would create problems which retailers are not willing to address. International expansion is, therefore, concentrated on a relatively limited number of international markets. Key characteristics of internationalization are therefore identifiable.

MARKET GEOGRAPHICAL PROXIMITY

It has become generally accepted that international retailers will look to geographically proximate markets before they start to expand into more distant and distinct markets (Burt, 1993; Treadgold, 1988, 1991). This means that retailers will engage in 'border hopping' activity, particularly during the early stages of their development. Thus, a large retail operation which has begun to look at the strategic option of non-domestic operations, will commonly look to neighbouring markets as a first step toward international expansion.

Some markets have seen the development of large numbers of international retail operations; France, Germany, Japan, the Netherlands, the US and the UK are all markets which have supported the growth of international retail operations. In turn, other markets which border these markets have become important markets of destination for retailers based in those markets which have nurtured the development of international retail operations. In this way, French retailers have focused much activity on the Spanish market, German retailers have developed operations in Austria, Dutch retailers have looked to expansion in Belgium, and UK retailers have viewed Ireland as an initial target.

European retailer expansion in Europe

Table 8.1 illustrates the geographical expansion of mainland European retailers by the beginning of the 1990s. The markets in table 8.1 are categorized on the basis of geographical proximity. Zone A refers to markets which have a land border with the country of origin. Therefore, with respect to French companies, Spain, Belgium, Germany, Switzerland, Italy are in zone A. Zone B refers to markets which have a land border with countries in zone A but not with the country of origin. For example, Austria which borders Germany, does not border France and so is categorized as a zone B market as far as French retailers are concerned. The table clearly illustrates that European retailers have favoured expanded their market of origin into markets which are adjacent to their domestic markets in preference to those further away.

French retailers have shown themselves to be particularly inclined toward international expansion. While their domestic market is well placed to allow French retailers to expand into both the less developed retail markets of southern Europe

Table 8.1 Geographical preference of mainland European retailers

Country of origin	Zone A: number of active retailers		Zone B: number of active retailers	
France	Spain	47	Portugal	16
	Belgium	47	Netherlands	28
	Germany	30	Denmark	2
	Switzerland	27	Austria	10
	Italy	26		
	Average =	35	Average =	14
Germany	Austria	33	Spain	10
	Netherlands	28	Italy	8
	France	25		
	Switzerland	23		
	Belgium	15		
	Denmark	9		
	Average =	22	Average =	9
Netherlands	Belgium	20	France	6
	Germany	10	Switzerland	3
			Austria	2
			Denmark	0
	Average =	15	Average =	3
Switzerland	Austria	8	Belgium	3
	France	8	Netherlands	2
	Germany	5	Denmark	1
	Italy	0	Spain	0
	Average =	5	Average =	2

Zone A: national markets which have a land border with the country of origin and are within the European Economic Area.
Zone B: national markets which have a land border with countries in zone A but not with the country of origin that are within the European Economic Area.

Source: CIG, 1991.

and the more developed retail markets of northern Europe, French retailers have also displayed a willingness to expand into distant markets.

The Groupe André based in Paris, is Europe's largest footwear retailer, with 2,589 outlets in total and 740 international outlets (CIG, 1994). In 1991, the group entered into a commercial arrangement with the Sears operation based in the UK which combined the two companies' footwear retail operations in the Benelux and German markets, thereby creating an operation of over 450 outlets. André also owns operations in Canada and the US along with operations in Hungary.

French retailers are also an important element within the retail buying groups which have developed in Europe during the 1980s and 1990s. These buying groups have emerged in the food sector to improve buying information and power but they have also provided members within opportunity to share information and marketing skills on a far wider basis. These alliances are often called buying groups but it is generally accepted that their objectives are not limited to sourcing issues. These alliances include the European Retail Alliance, established in 1989 by Ahold of the Netherlands, Argyll in the UK and Casino in France; Duero/MIAG which brings together Metro the Swiss-German operation and the French retailer Carrefour and associates; SEDD which involves Sainsbury in the UK, Delhaize Le Lion in Belgium, Docks de France in France and Esselunga in Italy.

Through such alliances, European food retailers have recognized that adopting a pan-European outlook and sharing information with operations with which they are not in direct market competition provides them with the opportunity to better understand the important changes which are tasking place across the European market. This is indicative of the changing attitude of European retailers to the opportunities which exist throughout the EU and in East Europe.

Japanese retailer expansion in Asia

Retailers' interest in geographically proximate markets is evident elsewhere around the globe. Japanese retailers have moved into Pacific Rim markets such as Hong Kong and Taiwan.

Japanese retailers are geographically isolated from many of the markets around the world which are host to international retail operations. Japanese retailers have, therefore, expanded into the markets of the Asian seaboard. Of 271 international retail actions by Japanese retailers, from the 1950s through to the 1990s, 59 per cent of those actions were represented by moves into East or South East Asia (Davies and Fergusson, 1995). Japanese department stores have played an important role in the internationalization of Japanese retail practice. The most popular cities in Asia for expansion have been Hong Kong, Singapore, Bangkok and Kuala Lumpur (Davies and Jones, 1993).

Japanese department store operations have exploited the opportunities of rapidly developing major urban centres such as Hong Kong and Singapore, markets into which Daimaru (Hong Kong, 1960) and Yaohan (Singapore, 1974) (Goldstein, 1988) both moved at a relatively early stage in the development of recent international activity. In the Hong Kong market, Japanese retailers have successfully positioned themselves to appeal to the younger market through the development of a fashion conscious image and aided by the associations which Japan has with 'high technology, affluence, modernity and efficiency' (McGoldrick and Ho, 1992, p. 72).

The Asian market has also involved Japanese retailers in the development of underdeveloped retail structures. In Taiwan for example, through management contracts, department store retailers such as Matsukoshi, Matsuya, Seibu, and Tokyu have facilitated the transfer of retail technology and skills to local stores such as Today, Evergreen, Hsin-Hsin and Hsin-Kuang (Chang and Sternquist, 1993; Chen and Sternquist, 1995).

US and Canadian retailer expansion in North America

It is not surprising that US retailers have sought expansion in the Canadian market. While it would be inaccurate to describe the markets as essentially the same in terms of social and economic characteristics, the considerable similarities have proved an advantage for US retailers seeking an initial international move.

In recent years, the signing of the NAFTA has further encouraged US retailers to consider expansion in Canada. This agreement 'led to a greater awareness of neighbouring markets by both Canadian consumers and US retailers. The number of American retailers entering Canada, many with new formats, increased dramatically as did the flow of Canadian cross-border shoppers' (Jones, et al., 1994, p. 2). New retail format operations have followed other US retailers into this geographically proximate and accessible market. Category killers, such as Toys RUs, Winners (owned by T. J. Maxx), Lenscrafters (owned by the US Shoe Corp.), The Office Place (owned by Office Depot), Michaels, and Value Village have a considerable stake in Canadian retailing as do Membership Club retailers, such as Price Club and Costco (Jones et al., 1994). These new format retail operations from the US are seen as dynamic market leaders (Hallsworth et al., 1995).

While US retailers have been successful in exporting their retail operations to Canada, Canadian retailers have been less successful in their moves south of the 49th parallel. As Hirst (1991, p. 77) has noted:

> Time after time, Canadians who succeed splendidly in their own country stumble badly when they succumb to the allure of the US market place.

Canadian retailers have seen considerable success in their domestic market turned into failure in the US. Mark's Work Wearhouse was a successful retailer of clothing for blue-collar workers in Canada; however, in 1987, after six years trading in the US, it filed for bankruptcy (Lane and Hildebrand, 1990). Like the Canadian Tire Corporation, which also entered the US market in the early 1980s, Mark's Work Wearhouse found that US operating conditions were not hospitable to their style of operation. This may, in part, be the product of long term structural differences. As Burns and Rayman (1995) have noted, both in terms of department store and chain store development, Canadian retailing has historically lagged behind the US. Such examples of failure may also be the product of different conditions such as a greater degree of price sensitivity in the US, demand for higher service and quality levels, different purchasing patterns, sophisticated comparative shoppers, and distinct tastes which undergo rapid change (Lane and Hildebrand, 1990).

These problems are characteristic of a market which neighbours a market where there is a more dynamic retail structure. Canada, while a wealthy market in many respects, will be vulnerable to the dynamic commercial sector of its larger and wealthier neighbour. Likewise, its domestic retailers will have difficulty trading up to the demands of the more developed market. This issue of core and peripheral market interaction is based on relative levels of socio-economic development.

West European retailer expansion in East Europe

Since the process of market liberalization began in East Europe in the late 1980s, West European businesses have looked to the markets of East Europe with some interest. While many of the hopes of the first years after the collapse of centrally planned economies in East Europe have not been realized, there have been major initiatives in some of these markets by West European retailers who see considerable opportunities in this geographically close market.

In East Europe, potential West European retail investors were initially discouraged by complex regulatory systems, intolerable levels of bureaucracy and limited consumer purchasing power (Drtina, 1995). However, as the 1990s progressed, retail operators began to make sizeable investments in the markets of East Europe. In the Czech Republic, the development of the Spar operation is a good example of the importance of geographical proximity for non-domestic market development where the new market lacks an advanced distributive infrastructure. Spar has developed in the Czech Republic from two centres on the border in Linz in Austria and Passau in Germany. Three local wholesale bases were established in Susce, Ceske Budejovice and Brno to serve the 100 Spar shops which were established by the beginning of 1995 (Drtina, 1995).

GEOGRAPHICALLY PROXIMATE OPPORTUNITIES

In some markets, the impact of a neighbouring market has been limited by the strength of indigenous retail operations and the proximity of other advanced retail structures. For example, although a large number of Dutch retailers have moved into the Belgian market, the market is also home to large retail companies, such as GIB and Delhaize Le Lion. The Belgian market has also attracted French and German retailers seeking expansion opportunities in geographically proximate markets. In other markets, such as Spain, retailers from a core market have been particularly influential in one retail sector. French retailers, through their development of Spanish food outlets in the 1970s and 1980s, had a major impact on the development of food retailing in Spain. In other markets, such as Ireland, a neighbouring market, such as the UK, with a highly developed retail structure has dominated international investment.

Sectoral impact: the example of French food retailers in Spain

When Promodès and Carrefour began developing hypermarkets in the Spanish market in the 1970s, the retail structure was underdeveloped and offered considerable opportunities to non-domestic advanced retail operations. Following the imposition of regulations concerning the development of large retail operations in

France, French Hypermarket retailers turned to the geographically and culturally proximate market of Spain.

For Carrefour, however, Spain was not the first option for international expansion. Early international growth had focused on more developed markets (Burt, 1986). Carrefour had looked initially to the Austrian, Belgian, German, Swiss and UK markets. Joint operations were established with Kastner and Öhler in Austria, Delhaize in Belgium, Mercure in Switzerland, and with Wheatsheaf distribution in the UK. Penetration of the German market involved the extension of the existing relationship with Delhaize, established for Belgium, to include the German companies Kaufpark and Stüssgen. These markets offered considerable market opportunities within Europe. However, it was not only European markets which attracted the company. At the same time as the company was developing its interests in Europe, some consideration was given to establishing an operation in the US. However, the expected arrangement with a US retailer did not develop (Burt, 1986). Likewise, as the company's relationship with retailers in the more developed retail markets of northern Europe were established between 1969 and 1977, the company turned to the opportunities offered by the less developed markets in Europe of Italy and Spain, as well as Latin American opportunities in the Brazilian market.

Carrefour's management soon began to realize that there were considerable opportunities to be exploited in the less developed markets and considerable problems to be faced when operating in more developed, and essentially more competitive, retail structures. The problems of expansion in markets where planning restrictions were becoming increasingly restrictive and competition from indigenous retailers was becoming acute, encouraged the company to turn its attention to less developed markets. Thus, the company began a period of sustained divestment, as financial resources were channelled away from the more developed markets and the proceeds from the sell off of operations provided funds for growth elsewhere (Burt, 1986). Between 1978 and 1983, Carrefour sold interests in its Austrian, Belgian, German and UK operations. The company, after a period of intense and even frenetic activity, began to focus on the development of stores in which it held at least a 50 per cent share and in the markets of Spain and Latin America. As Burt (1986) has noted, in 1975, the company only controlled 50 per cent of four of the twelve stores with which it was involved outside France: in 1985, of thirty-four stores, the company had a majority holding in thirty-two. By 1985, Carrefour had twenty stores throughout Spain held through various subsidiaries.

For Carrefour, the Spanish operation became an important aspect of its international activities. The company had found a market in which it could develop a Spanish version (Pryca) of the retail form that had proved so popular in the French market when it was introduced twenty years previously. The geographical proximity of Spain helped facilitate the company's international growth as it facilitated the international growth of other French hypermarket operators.

In the mid 1990s, French retailers predominate in the food and particularly the large store sector of the Spanish food market. Retailers from other European markets have, nevertheless, established operations. The Dutch, through the Karry and Super operations, have a role in the cash and carry sector, and in supermarket retailing through El Abol and Spar food stores. Likewise, in the mid-1990s, the German retailers Tengelmann, with the Plus fascia, and Lidl and Schwarz, with the Lidl fascia, entered the market. However, French retailers such as Promodès, with around 1,500 Dia supermarkets, and Carrefour, with forty-three Pryca Hypermarkets, remain important players in this market (CIG, 1994). Through the Alcampo (Auchan), Continente (Promodès), Hyper L (Leclerc), Intermerca (Docks de France), Mamut (Docks de France) and Pryca (Carrefour) fascias, French retailers operate over 100 hypermarkets in the market. The only other non-indigenous hypermarket operator in the market is Jumbo, owned by the Portuguese retail organization Pao de Açúcar.

While some fascias, such as Mamut, which trades in San Sebastien through 7,345 sq m, are only represented by one outlet in Spain, the Alcampo, Continente and Pryca fascias are well represented (LSA, 1992). There are three Alcampo stores in and around Madrid alone, operating a combined selling space of 26,229 sq m and with parking provision for 7,500 cars. Two Continente stores serve Seville with 20,748 sq m of selling space. In the Barcelona catchment area, Pryca operates five stores at Prat del Llobregat, Tarras, Cabrera del Mar, San Adrian del Besos and Manresa with a combined selling space of 49,078 sq m and provision for 9,388 cars. For French hypermarket retailers, Spain has become an extension of the core market. The core market has expanded into the less developed and, hence over time, peripheral market.

General impact: the example of British retailers in Ireland

The influence of British retailers on Irish retailing has been general. To some extent this influence must be interpreted in the context of political changes that occurred during the twentieth century: for some retailers, expansion into Ireland was domestic expansion because it took place before Irish independence. The Irish Free State was established in 1922. However, these political changes occurred during the early phase of national retail chain developments.

British (England, Scotland and Wales) based retailers had long been part of the Irish retail environment. Liptons were operating in Ireland in the late nineteenth century (Mathias, 1967), as were W. H. Smith (Wilson, 1985). Smith withdrew its operations at an early date as a result of trading tensions; but also because of political factors. The W. H. Smith retail operation in Ireland had not been as successful as had been hoped. Despite the capable management of Charles Eason from the mid-1860s, the business had not been allowed to develop. Eason's enthusiasm for growth was not shared by William Henry Smith the second. Support for expansion was not forthcoming from London. Finally, in 1886, on William Henry Smith becoming Chief Secretary to Ireland, the Irish outlets were sold to Charles Eason. It was considered a possibility that the business might suffer as a result of William Henry Smith's conflicting political and commercial interests.

8.1 All Around the World

By 1993, the Body Shop had been in the international market-place for only a decade and a half, yet it had achieved an international operation of 667 stores, which stood alongside its UK operations of 233 stores. In total, the company had reached the 900 store level in a surprisingly short period of time.

The first international outlet was in Belgium in 1978. This was followed a year later by operations in Austria, Greece and Sweden. Throughout the 1980s and early 1990s, the company entered a number of new markets:

1980 – Canada, Iceland
1981 – Denmark, Finland, Republic of Ireland
1982 – France, Netherlands
1983 – Australia, Cyprus, Germany, Singapore, Switzerland, UAE
1984 – Hong Kong, Italy, Malaysia
1985 – Bahamas, Bahrain, Norway
1986 – Kuwait, Oman, Portugal, Spain
1987 – Antigua, Bermuda, Malta, Qatar, Saudi Arabia
1988 – Gibraltar, Taiwan, US
1989 – Cayman Islands, New Zealand
1990 – Indonesia, Japan
1991 – Luxembourg

By 1993, the company had an extensive geographical spread of operations, and in some markets a considerable number of stores. The number of stores in different markets varied considerably:

More than 100 outlets: UK (233), US (120), Canada (104)

25–100 outlets: Australia (43), Netherlands (40), Germany (37), Italy (37), Spain (33), Sweden (34)

10–24 outlets: Greece (23), Switzerland (19), France (16), Finland (15), Norway (15), Denmark (11), Japan (11), Singapore (11), Republic of Ireland (10), Malaysia (10), Saudi Arabia (10)

1–9 outlets: Austria (8), Belgium (8), Hong Kong (8), Portugal (8), New Zealand (7), Taiwan (5), Bahamas (4), Luxembourg (2), Iceland (2), Indonesia (2), Kuwait (2), Oman (2), UAE (2), Antigua (1), Bahrain (1), Bermuda (1), Cayman Islands (1), Cyprus (1), Gibraltar (1), Malta (1), Qatar (1)

Between 1992 and 1993, the company's international outlets increased from 517 to 667. This, coupled to the rate of growth in the previous fourteen years, was impressive. By the mid 1990s, the company was entering a new stage in its international development. It is a stage where consolidation is an important aspect of international development.

Source: The Body Shop, 1993.

Some British retailers found themselves inadvertently becoming an international operation as a result of the establishment of a Free State in the south of the island in 1922. This included the British subsidiary of Woolworths, the recently arrived US owned retail operation which had established outlets on the island of Ireland, north and south, by the outbreak of the First World War in 1914 (Woolworth, 1954). Marks and Spencer were also operating in Ireland at this time (Tse, 1985), as were Burtons, the men's clothing operation (Sigsworth, 1992). However, the political changes of the 1920s preceded much of the multiple store development in British retailing, as Jefferys (1954) researches show, and therefore UK retailer development in the south of Ireland is, in great part, a product of the years after independence.

To some extent, William Henry Smith's caution in Ireland has been mirrored in subsequent periods of retail expansion in Ireland. While the market has appeared one into which British retailers might relatively easily – even absent-mindedly – expand, the size of the market is limiting. Also, retailers have not always found Ireland a soft option. Tesco acquired 51 per cent of the 3 Guys operation in Ireland in 1978 for £4.2m and the remaining share of the company for £5.5m in 1979 (Lord et al., 1988). The operation that Tesco bought included eight operational sites, five under construction and other sites on which there were planning applications. Tesco proposed an operation of 25 outlets, where both food and non-food items would be sold. The company, however, immediately encountered problems. It has been calculated that, in 1979, the company lost £0.5m on a trading base of £10m (Lord et al., 1988). This was, in part, the result of interest charges and currency fluctuations as a result of the Irish punt and Sterling parting company after a period of forty years during which time the two currencies had been linked on the international exchange markets. Tesco, in consequence, was obliged to import UK-produced merchandise in order to maintain a price advantage at the point of sale. This tactic, however, only succeeded in uniting local commercial interests. Wholesaler and retailer trade associations became united in opposition to the company and, in particular, to its store development plans and applications. Despite Tesco's attempts to move toward UK type operations, the company remained an unsuccessful outsider in the Irish retail game; even the new superstore built at Dundalk covering 7,000 sq m failed to meet the company's expectations. Eventually, part of the selling area at the Dundalk store was closed off as the non-food lines were dropped (Lord et al., 1988). Having operated a dispersed chain of stores from Sligo in the north west to Tralee in the south west, Cork in the far south and Dundalk in the North east, the company sold the operation in 1986 to the H. Williams organization for IR£17m, and at a loss somewhere in the range of IR£6m to IR£20m (Parker, 1986; Lord et al., 1988). The company was happy to forget the Irish expedition, certainly there is no mention of the operation in the recently published company history (Powell, 1991).

UK retailers' experiences in Ireland have not always been as costly as Tesco's. UK retailers continue to dominate the international contingent of retailers operating in Ireland. That is not to say non-UK international retailers are not present; Yves Rocher, the French beauty retailer operates a store in Ireland as do Cenoura

8.2 Waking Up the Neighbours

Aldi are one of Germany's largest and most well known food retailers. Founded in 1948 by two brothers, Karl and Theodore Albrecht, the company has developed a considerable presence in the European market-place.

The Aldi operation is shrouded in secrecy, so reliable figures on the trading operation are difficult to obtain. However, it has been estimated that, in 1992, the company had a global turnover of DM35bn of which DM9.5bn was the result of operations outside its domestic market.

The company serves all its international operations from its own retail distribution centres. This may, in part, explain the pattern of the company's retail development.

Operation	Market	Outlets in 1994	Year of entry
Hofer	Austria	180	1967
Aldi-Combi	Netherlands	270	1972
Aldi	Belgium	260	1976
Aldi	US	340	1976
Trader Joe's	US	27	1976
Aldi-Marked	Denmark	115	1977
Albertson's	US	600	1980s
Aldi	France	100	1988
Aldi	UK	100	1989
Aldi	Poland	1	1991

Source: CIG, 1994.

Lojas (Portugal) and Jacardi (France) the maternity and childrens' wear retailers, Escada (German), Liz Claiborne (US), Oilily (Netherlands) and Rodier (France), all fashion retailers, Brioche Dorèe (France) the food specialist retailer, and Ciro (US) the jewellers (CIG, 1994). Likewise, others chains, such as the Minit Corporation, based in Belgium (20 outlets), and Benetton (15 outlets), based in Italy, operate in the Irish market. Other retailers have, or have had some UK connection. Associated British Foods is UK and Canadian owned, while Virgin Megastore has US and UK associations. Acquascutum with its archetypical British merchandise is now owned by Renown the Japanese retailer. Otherwise, familiar British retail names such as Marks and Spencer, HMV, Texas Homecare, Laura Ashley, Falmers, Tie Rack, Wallis, Saxone and Thorntons typify the international retail presence.

The movement of retailers across the UK-Irish border is not merely one way. Dunnes Stores have expanded in to the Northern Ireland market and the British mainland. Likewise, Waterford glass, which does not operate a chain of Waterford retail outlets in Ireland, has acquired, through the purchase of Wedgewood, which is based in the UK, over 170 shops in the UK and around thirty stores – selling china and glass – outside the UK, including the Republic of Ireland (CIG, 1994). While these developments indicate that the flow in international retail traffic is not all in one direction and, as the examples given above show, UK retail expansion into Ireland has not always brought the rewards that had been anticipated, the two retail markets remain closely connected by cross-border retail developments which are dominated by British based enterprises. To describe the Irish retail structure as dependent on that of the UK would be both provocative and inaccurate; nevertheless, it is undoubtedly true to say that UK companies have seen and, in many cases, continue to see their operations in the Republic of Ireland as essentially an extension of their UK operations.

ATTITUDES TO INTERNATIONAL DEVELOPMENT

Survey work has also shown that retailers' attitudes to international expansion differ according to the environmental pressures to which retailers are subject, both

Table 8.2 European market evaluation ranking

| All | Market of Origin | | | |
	France	Germany	Netherlands	UK
Spain	2	=11	=1	=1
Italy	1	=13	4	3
Portugal	3	=11	=1	=4
Czech Republic	=5	=7	3	=8
Hungary	=5	=5	=5	=4
France	*	=5	11	=1
Poland	7	10	9	=8
Germany	8	*	=7	7
Belg/Lux	9	1	=5	10
Netherlands	=11	2	*	=4
Austria	10	=7	=7	=11
Greece	4	=18	19	19
UK	=11	=3	=12	*
Denmark	=11	=3	10	=13
Switzerland	=16	9	=12	=16
Norway	=11	=15	=12	=13
Russia	19	17	17	=13
Sweden	=11	=15	=15	=16
Finland	=16	=13	=15	=16
Ireland	=16	=18	18	=11

Source: Myers and Alexander, 1995b.

in the domestic and international environment. Myers and Alexander (1995a, 1995b) have shown that European food retailers' attitude to international expansion will be influenced by the retailer's market of origin. Within Europe, retailers were inclined toward border hopping activity. Table 8.2 shows the relative attraction of different markets within Europe according to food retailers' market of origin. While different influences will have exerted different pressures, it is possible to identify patterns and to show that the observable trends are supported by retailers' assessment of markets.

French retailers placed an emphasis on those markets with developing or under-developed retail markets such as Italy, Spain, Portugal, the Czech Republic and Hungary, and a particular emphasis on those markets which also possessed geographical and cultural proximity such as Italy, Spain and Portugal. German retailers ranked contiguous markets higher than geographically distant markets, hence the Benelux countries were considered favourably. The German retailers surveyed were particularly strongly inclined toward expansion within a ring of markets which surrounds their domestic market. Dutch retailers showed an orientation toward the less developed markets within the EU and emerging markets such as the Czech Republic and Hungary outside the EU. British retailers were attracted to

Table 8.3 Expansion opportunities by global region and country of origin

Europe		*North America*	
Germany	4.4	Netherlands	3.4
France	3.8	UK	3.4
Netherlands	3.6	Germany	3.2
UK	3.4	France	2.1
Italy	3.0	Italy	1.1
Far East		Latin America	
France	3.8	France	3.5
Netherlands	2.5	Germany	1.7
Germany	2.3	UK	1.6
UK	1.9	Netherlands	1.5
Italy	1.1	Italy	1.1
Australasia			
France	1.9		
Netherlands	1.8		
Germany	1.7		
UK	1.6		
Italy	1.0		

1 = no real opportunity, 2 = little opportunity, 3 = possible opportunity, 4 = good opportunity, 5 = extremely good opportunity.

Source: Myers and Alexander, 1995b.

opportunities in less developed markets but were also drawn to markets with geographical proximity. For British retailers, France was considered one of the most attractive options, while Ireland, although it was not rated high on the UK list, ranked far higher on the UK list than on the Dutch, French and German lists.

These results reflected observable sectoral trends of international retailers based in these four countries of origin, and also the general observable trends of international activity within the European global region. Similar responses were seen on a global basis, when European food retailers evaluated the opportunities in global regional markets. Overall, Europe was seen as the market which provided the greatest opportunity. However, for some retailers other regions were also perceived to be attractive. As table 8.3 illustrates, German food retailers were far more inclined toward European expansion than Dutch or UK food retailers. Outside Europe, French retailers were more ambitious with regard to the Far East Market. UK retailers, who might have been expected to evaluate the Australasian market highly for reasons of cultural associations, did not do so. Thus, while these results confirm that geographical proximity does influence retailers' perceptions of international opportunities, there are other factors such as cultural proximity and economic development which influence strategic decisions.

GEOGRAPHY, CULTURE OR ECONOMICS?

The pattern of expansion described above, where retailers expand into geographically proximate markets, is partly explained by the realities of distribution and the relative ease with which expansion across land boundaries may be expedited when compared to expansion to geographically distant markets. The same logic applies to international expansion into geographically proximate markets as pertains to expansion within a state into geographically proximate regions. It is, however, also a product of the fact that geographically contingent markets are also more likely to be culturally similar. In table 8.4, markets are divided according to the their cultural affinity with the market of origin. This is represented in the table by language. Thus French, as part of the Western Romance group gives France a cultural affinity with Italy, Portugal and Spain and with significant parts of Belgium and Switzerland (Crystal, 1987). Dutch and German, as part of the West Germanic group, gives The Netherlands and Germany an affinity with each other, and with Austria. Again, observable development supports the contention (Burt, 1993) that cultural proximity encourages expansion from one market into another.

Markets will also be attractive to retailers in respect of the economic development attained within a market. However, while in many respects economic development is easier to measure than cultural proximity, market attraction on the basis of economic development may be encouraged both by a relatively high level of development or a relatively low level of growth when measured against the domestic market. As Hollander (1970) noted with reference to international development earlier this century, international operations may develop where markets have reached a stage where high spending consumers will encourage expansion between

Table 8.4 Cultural preference of mainland European retailers

Country of orign	Zone A: number of active retailers		Zone B: number of active retailers	
France	Spain	47	Germany	30
	Belgium	47	Netherlands	28
	Switzerland	27	Denmark	2
	Italy	26	Austria	10
	Portugal	16		
	Average =	33	Average =	18
Germany	Austria	33	France	25
	Netherlands	28	Spain	10
	Switzerland	23	Denmark	9
	Belgium	15	Italy	8
	Average =	25	Average =	13
Netherlands	Belgium	20	France	6
	Germany	10	Spain	5
	Switzerland	3	Portugal	2
	Austria	2	Italy	1
			Denmark	0
	Average =	9	Average =	3

Zone A: national markets which have a linguistic association with the country of origin, are within the European Economic Area and are connected by land with the country of origin.
Zone B: national markets which do not have a linguistic association with the country of origin, are within the European Economic Area and are connected by land with the country of origin.
Source: CIG, 1991.

markets such as New York, London and Paris. Conversely, the underdeveloped nature of retailing may attract trading companies to develop retail operations in the third world markets because of the very lack of developed retail operations where there existed some form of demand for them.

As has been noted above, the development of the Spanish food retail structure has been strongly influenced by French hypermarket operators. Spain was geographically close, it was relatively culturally proximate and it also had an underdeveloped retail structure, which was in part the result of an economy which lagged behind that of the domestic market of the French retailers. Conversely, the North American market has been attractive to European retailers because of its high levels of economic development. It has been particularly attractive to UK retailers, who have been, and continue to be, attracted by the cultural proximity which they perceive to exist between their home market and the US. Nevertheless, and as a fundamental prerequisite, while retailers will be attracted by markets which demand retail structural development, markets into which retailers expand will usually have reached critical levels of economic development or contain pockets of consumer demand which will support sophisticated retail operations before expansion occurs. Markets outside the EU, NAFTA and Japan will only appeal to retailers where market development is occurring. Thus the developing markets of Asia may be attractive but markets in Africa will not be so attractive.

Markets are attractive to retailers for three fundamental reasons.

- They are attractive where they are geographically proximate.

- They are attractive where they are culturally proximate.

- They are attractive where they have reached an appropriate level of economic development.

The ideal market for an internationalizing retailer would be one where geographical proximity is combined with close cultural associations and an economy which is similar to the economy in the domestic market but where the retail structure has yet to undergo a modernization process. In this, some retailers are more fortunate than others.

A German retailer contemplating international activities for the first time may consider operating in the Austrian market. This market is geographically proximate, and culturally close to the market of origin, it is also economically developed to a level comparable with the market of origin. The German retailer may even perceive a gap in the retail competitive structure which the retailer's format will fill. Few retailers will, however, be faced with markets which fulfil these key criteria to such a degree. Markets will often meet one requirement but not another. Australia was an attractive market to some UK retailers in the 1960s (Burt, 1993). However, as retailers came to discover, while cultural and economic proximity encouraged expansion, geographical distance was a considerable drawback. Management control was simply weakened. Thus, as noted above, it is not surprising to see survey work in the 1990s reflecting an unenthusiastic attitude amongst UK food retailers toward the Australasian market (Myers and Alexander, 1995a, 1995b).

These three factors of geographical, cultural and economic proximity may be represented as three points of a triangle. Retailers will usually find that one point or corner of the triangle is further than the others. In figure 8.1, the points of the triangle labelled C1, E1 and G1 represent the Austrian market from the perspective of a German retailer. In this example, the Austrian market is described by a compact equilateral triangle. The Australian market from the perspective of a UK retailer will be differently described. While the points on the triangle represented by culture and economics may stand in a similar relationship to the retailer at position X, the point representing geography, G2, will be further away. Hence an isosceles triangle is described.

Markets of retailer origin may, therefore, be seen to stand in relative relationship to the market of destination. Geography may be measured by contiguity, absolute

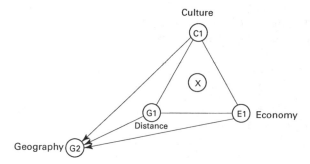

Figure 8.1 Market proximity triangle

distance or travel time from core economic regions within the market of origin to core economic regions in the market of destination. Economic proximity may be measured by such factors as levels of differences in levels of gdp. Cultural differences, while not easily quantified, may be indicated by such factors as interlingual distance.

DETERMINING FACTORS

The three factors of geography, culture and economic development provide a basis on which to consider the direction of international expansion. However, these three factors do not sufficiently encapsulate fundamental issues which determine international expansion. In chapter 2, five boundaries were considered to be important when defining international activity: regulatory boundaries, economic boundaries, social boundaries, cultural boundaries and retail structural boundaries. By considering social conditions and regulatory conditions or public policy independently, it is easier to separate fundamental determining issues and consider determinants of internationalization in a more meaningful way.

It was noted above, that economic measures will not always explain patterns of development. This problem is somewhat overcome if consideration is given separately to regulatory conditions, cultural conditions and retail structural development.

Public policy: regulatory conditions are determined by public policy. They are influenced by cultural assumptions, economic development and social conditions. Public policy toward economic and social development will indirectly affect retail development. Regulatory constraints will effect both incoming and indigenous retailers but it will not necessarily do so in the same manner.

Social conditions: cultural differences will often manifest themselves through social change and the conditions of life in a community and, therefore, separate consideration may be given to social factors. Similar levels of economic development may have been reached in two markets but cultural value systems may alter the social response in one market compared with another. Thereby, such differences will affect patterns of development of retail structures. Likewise, social conditions which do not conform to conditions in a retailer's market of origin may well be indicative of underlying market factors which would cause considerable problems for the organic development of a retail operation.

Retail structure: retail structural development may be considered separately, for although it is a product of public policy, economic development, social conditions and cultural values, it is also a product of managerial initiative and intra-industrial competitive conditions which will in turn impact on public policy as well as the other key determinants of international expansion.

These other factors of public policy, social conditions and retail structure will shape retail expansion patterns, and they may, therefore, be used to analyse market attractiveness. They may be added to the list of key factors which retailers must consider when moving into new international markets. They may also be seen as indicators and interpreters of existing expansion patterns. They replace the geographical factor but stand, with the remaining factors, as proxy for psychological proximity which is, in itself, a product of market contiguity.

In an extension of the market proximity triangle described earlier, it is possible to think in terms of a pentagonal market proximity framework. Figure 8.2 provides a diagrammatic representation of this conceptualization. Thus rather than taking culture and economic factors to be representative of public policy regulation, social conditions and retail structure a further refinement may be achieved.

In figure 8.2, two markets are represented. Points P1, E1, S1, C1 and R1 represent a market of greater attraction than points P2, E2, S2, C2 and R2 which represent a less attractive market. The second, less attractive, market will be

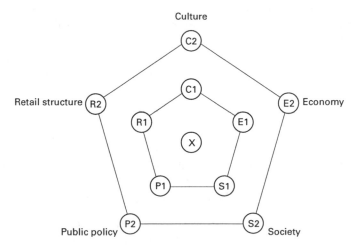

Figure 8.2 Market proximity pentagon: spatial difference

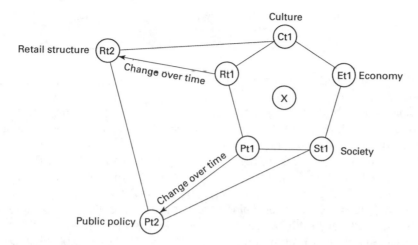

Figure 8.3 Market proximity pentagon: temporal difference

perceived by retailers in the market of origin, represented diagrammatically at position X, to be less psychologically close. The market will often be less geographically close, although this will not always be the case, although there will be a tendency toward such patterns because of the permeable nature of state boundaries within the historical continuum.

Different markets may also be described over time. In figure 8.3, change has occurred where changes have brought about a less attractive public policy and retail structural environment and has led to a situation in which market entry is a more formidable exercise. Thus Pt1 moves to Pt2 and Rt1 to Rt2. This change has occurred in the UK large store food retail sector, where increased levels of market coverage has led to public policy change, of planning laws, and which has curtailed entry opportunities for out-of-town formats.

CONCLUSION

An important theme of the internationalization process is the inherently cautious nature of the process. Retailers will tend, at least in the early stages of their international development, to seek expansion in familiar markets. This search for familiarity may often mean that retailers seek expansion in geographically contiguous markets. Such markets are psychologically proximity. However, this geographical proximity, and consequent psychological proximity, is itself a product of similarities in approaches to public policy, shared cultural norms, comparable levels of economic development, social values and relative levels of retail structural development. Conducive markets are therefore often found immediately across national boundaries, where political barriers may artificially separate markets.

8.3 American Pie

European retailer interest in North American retailing is not just a feature of the 1970s and 1980s. European retailers continue to take an interest in US retailing.

Ahold, the Dutch retailer announced the acquisition of the biggest supermarket in New England in the spring of 1996. Stop & Shop is an innovative chain which is known for its sound management.

The acquisition for $2.9 bn, the largest single acquisition in Ahold's development, will make the retailer the fifth largest supermarket operator in the US. The Stop & Shop operation, which includes 159 supermarkets operating under the Stop & Shop fascia, along with seventeen Mel's Foodtown supermarkets, twenty-eight Purity Supreme supermarkets, and sixty-four Li'l Peach convenience stores, had a turnover of $4.1bn in 1995. This will boost the company's US turnover which was $8.3bn in 1995, on the basis of 650 stores.

Since 1977, the year in which Ahold acquired Bi-Lo supermarkets, the company has pursued an acquisition policy in the US. Giant supermarkets attracted its interest in 1981, Edwards supermarkets in 1983, Finast Ohio supermarkets in 1988, Tops supermarkets in 1991 and Red Food Stores supermarkets in 1994.

Ahold is not content to look only at the US market. The company has operations in the Czech Republic, Poland and Portugal. The Asean market is also seen as an attractive international opportunity.

The company's president Cees van der Hoeven recently remarked:

We will continue to actively pursue growth opportunities both in central and southern European markets, Asia and the United States.

Source: van der Krol and Urry, 1996; Lex, 1996; CIG, 1994.

QUESTIONS – DISCUSSION POINTS

1   What is 'border hopping' in the international retail context?

2   Why, as Hirst (1991) suggests, do Canadian retailers 'stumble badly when they succumb to the allure of the US market place'?

3   French food retailers have played an important role in the development of Spanish retailing. Why was this possible?

4   Are British, Dutch, French and German food retailers likely to find European and global markets attractive to the same degree?

5   Is geography, culture or economic development more important in determining the direction of international expansion?

REFERENCES

Body Shop, The, (1993) *Annual Report and Accounts*, The Body Shop, London.

Burns, D., and Rayman, D., (1995) Retailing in Canada and the United States: Historical Comparisons, *The Service Industries Journal*, Vol. 15, No. 4, pp. 164–76.

Burt, S., (1986) The Carrefour Group – the first 25 years, *International Journal of Retailing*, Vol. 1, No. 3, pp. 54–78.

Burt, S., (1993) Temporal Trends in the Internationalization of British Retailing, *International Review of Retail, Distribution and Consumer Research*, Vol. 3, No. 4, pp. 391–410.

Chang, L., and Sternquist, B., (1993) Product Procurement: A Comparison of Taiwanese and US Retail Companies, *International Review of Retail, Distribution and Consumer Research*, Vol. 4, No. 1, pp. 239–57.

Chen, Y., and Sternquist, B., (1995) Differences Between International and Domestic Japanese Retailers, *The Service Industries Journal*, Vol. 15, No. 4, pp. 118–33.

CIG, (1991) *Cross-Border Retailing in Europe*, The Corporate Intelligence Group, London.

CIG, (1994), *Cross-Border Retailing in Europe*, The Corporate Intelligence Group, London.

Crystal, D., (1987) *The Cambridge Encyclopedia of Language*, Guild, London.

Davies, B., and Jones, P., (1993) The International Activity of Japanese Department Stores, *The Service Industries Journal*, Vol. 13, No. 1, pp. 126–32.

Davies, K., and Fergusson, F., (1995) The International Activities of Japanese Retailers, *The Service Industries Journal*, Vol. 15, No. 4, pp. 97–117.

Drtina, T, (1995) The Internationalization of Retailing in the Czech and Slovak Republics, *The Service Industries Journal*, Vol. 15, No. 4, pp. 191–203.

Goldstein, C., (1988) The Bargain Hunters, *Far East Economic Review*, 26 May, pp. 82–5.

Hallsworth, A., Jones, K., and Muncaster, R., (1995) The Planning Implications of New Retail Format Introductions in Canada and Britain, *The Service Industries Journal*, Vol. 15, No. 4, pp. 148–63.

Hirst, N., (1991) How to Succeed in US Retailing, *Canadian Business*, Vol. 64, No. 10, pp. 77–84.

Hollander, S., (1970) *Multinational Retailing*, East Lansing, MI: Michigan State University.

Jefferys, J., (1954) *Retail Trading in Britain 1850–1950*, Cambridge University Press, Cambridge.

Jones, K., Evans, W., and Smith, C., (1994) *New Formats in the Canadian Retail Economy*, Centre for the Study of Commercial Activity, Ryerson Polytechnic University, Toronto, Ontario Canada.

LSA, (1992) Hypers Français a L'Etranger, *LSA*, No. 1331, 17 December.

Lane, H., and Hildebrand, D., (1990) How to Survive in US Retail Markets, *Business Quarterly*, Vol. 54, No. 3, pp. 62–6.

Lex, (1996) Royal Ahold, *Financial Times*, 29 March, p. 28.

Lord, D., Moran, W., Parker, T., and Sparks, L., (1988) Retailing on Three Continents: The Discount Food Store Operations of Albert Gubay, *International Journal of Retailing*, Vol. 3, No. 3.

McGoldrick, P., and Ho, S., (1992) International Positioning: Japanese Department Stores in Hong Kong, *European Journal of Marketing*, Vol. 26, No. 8/9, pp. 61–73.

Mathias, P., (1967) *Retailing Revolution*, Longmans, London.

Myers, H., and Alexander, N., (1995a) European Food Retailers' Global Expansion: An Empirical Consideration of the Direction of Growth, *2nd Recent Advances in Retailing & Services Science Conference*, Brisbane – Australia, 11–14 July.

Myers, H., and Alexander, N., (1995b) Direction of International Food Retail Expansion: An Empirical Study of European Retailers, *8th International Conference on the Distributive Trades*, Università Bocconi, Milan, 1–2 September.

Parker, A., (1986) Tesco Leaves Ireland, *Retail and Distribution Management*, Vol. 7, No., 6, pp. 36–9.

Powell, D., (1991) *Counter Revolution: the Tesco story*, Grafton, London.

Sigsworth, E., (1992) The Burton Group PLC, A. Hast, D. Pascal, P. Barbour, J. Griffin (eds) *International Directory of Company Histories*, Vol. V, St James Press, Detroit, pp. 20–2.

Treadgold, A., (1988) Retailing Without Frontiers, *Retail and Distribution Management*, Vol. 16, No. 6, pp. 8–12.

Treadgold, A., (1991) The Emerging Internationalisation of Retailing: Present Status and Future Challenges *Irish Marketing Review*, Vol. 5, No. 2, pp. 11–27.

Tse, K., (1985) *Marks & Spencer: Anatomy of Britain's Most Efficiently Managed Company*, Pergammon Press, Oxford.

van der Krol, R., and Urry, M., (1996) Ahold to pay $2.9bn for Stop & Shop, *Financial Times*, 29 March, p. 28.

Wilson, C., (1985) *First with the News: The History of W. H. Smith 1792–1972*, Cape, London.

Woolworth, (1954) *Woolworth's First 75 Years: The Story of Everybody's Store*, New York, Woolworth.

Public Policy

▍ OBJECTIVES ▍

This chapter considers political environments and the means by which they may be assessed as a market opportunity. Consideration is given to the regulatory issues which retailers face in different markets around the world.

INTRODUCTION

The student of international business has to consider the global operational environment from a number of perspectives. One perspective is that of the observer of domestic and international politics. Political issues are important in the domestic business environment but, in the international environment, the problems are multiplied by the number, nature and type of markets in which the retailer operates.

As the political environment is a product of the economic, social, cultural and commercial environment, so are the economic, social, cultural and commercial environments affected by the political environment. The political environment is both a reflection, and the determinant, of other important factors that must be assessed in non-domestic markets. Whether the political environment is the most important factor is open to debate and will depend on different philosophical assumptions, but it should certainly be considered a crucial factor when considering different markets.

This chapter considers political environments and their assessment as well as the regulatory issues which retailers face in different markets around the world.

THE POLITICAL STRUCTURE

An individual's perception of political structures within the global trading environment will be greatly influenced by that individual's country of origin and the perceptual framework which has been established in their own minds on a formal and informal basis during their lives. The rapidly changing nature of the international environment in the 1990s emphasizes the difference, not only of national perceptions, but also the perceptions of individuals within different age groups, from different social backgrounds and of different educational attainment levels within the same country.

At different times during the twentieth century, the markets of the world have been variously defined within imperial trading blocs, nation-states and global-regional free trade areas. The pattern of international relationships, and hence the interplay of international political entities, is constantly evolving. Thus, the perception that the global international political environment may be simply, and only, considered in terms of the nation-state is flawed. The nation-state is only one of many bases on which the international environment may be assessed.

The global political structure may be considered on three levels:

- inter-state, where states combine to regulate trade and may have agreed to some form of economic and/or political union;

- state, where a unitary or federal state regulates trade within set, internationally recognized, boundaries;

- local, where local government regulates trade within boundaries accepted or set by the state of which the locality is a constituent part.

INTER-STATE

In the global environment of the 1990s, there are a number of international state associations which help to regulate the trading environment of markets. The aims and objectives of these associations of states will vary enormously. Likewise, at any one time, some associations will be witnessing a strengthening of bonds, while others will see the weakening of bonds. Some of these associations will be the product of historical power political circumstances, while others will be the product of current trends and influences and entered into voluntarily.

In recent decades, the UK has been associated with two formal associations of states where the establishment of a free trade area has been a primary concern. The UK has been a member of EFTA (European Free Trade Area). EFTA was always geographically marginalized within Europe, and over the years, was increasingly economically marginalized by the EC. Consequently, from the 1970s through to the 1990s, its members have left the organization in order to become party to, and benefit from, the EC or EU. The UK followed that path. These were voluntary associations which the UK joined in order to facilitate trade in Europe. Also, the UK remains a member of the Commonwealth, the product of the UK's imperial past. While the Commonwealth continues to exist, its economic influence has diminished considerably since the 1960s, as the regional trading blocs of the world, or other individual non-Commonwealth markets, have attracted the constituent members of its association.

International associations

There are a number of international associations around the world which are geographically defined within global-regions. In Africa, there are the Organization for African Unity, the Franc Zone, the Southern Africa Development Committee, the Preferential Trade Area for Eastern and Southern Africa and the West African Economic and Monetary Union. In the Arab world, there are the Arab League, and the Organization of Arab Petroleum Exporting Countries. In the Middle East, there is the Gulf Cooperative Council. In Asia, there are the Association of South East Asian Nations and the South Asian Association for Regional Cooperation. In the Caribbean, there is the Caribbean Community and Common Market. In

Europe, there are the European Union and the European Free Trade Area. In Latin America, there are the Andean Pact and Mercosur. In North America, there is the North American Free Trade Area and across the Pacific there is the Asia-Pacific Economic Cooperation organization.

Also, there are a number of organizations which may be described as world groupings. The Commonwealth, the Organization for Economic Cooperation and Development, the Organization of Petroleum Exporting Countries and the United Nations may be so described. Their origins, and membership requirements may be very different but one factor they have in common is that they bring together a geographically disparate group of states.

These organizations, whether of a global-regional or global-interest nature have varying ambitions and impacts on trade. Some, like the EU, have ambitious plans for political and social integration as well as economic cooperation and convergence. The regional nature of many of these organizations is an important aspect of their role in the modern trading environment and what may be considered to be the regionalization of world trade. From the perspective of retailers entering the international environment, two associations are particularly important. Those are, the EU and NAFTA. This is because a tremendous exchange of retail activity occurs between, and within, these markets.

European Union

The EU, or the European Economic Community, as it was previously described, was to a considerable extent the product of European conflicts in the first half of the twentieth century. While the EEC was based on federalist objectives, or at least, many of the founders of the community shared a federalist vision, the EU has grown incrementally. The Union has its formal roots in the European Coal and Steel Community which was established in 1951. It was cooperation in the area of fundamental products required to rebuild war-torn Europe which led the six founding members – Belgium, France, Germany (West), Italy, Luxembourg and the Netherlands – to establish the EEC in 1957, following discussions in Messina in June 1955 and the publication of the Spaak Report in 1956 (Litner and Mazey, 1991).

The ECC, was formally established in 1957 with the aim of reducing internal quotas and duties on trade, and the establishment of common external tariffs: however, such changes could not be achieved immediately and a period of adjustment was set. Therefore, the history of the EU has been a gradual process of harmonization and integration with the express purpose of establishing cohesion through the convergence of economic development and the eradication of discrepancies in living standards in regions of the community. The '1992' legislation associated with the establishment of the Single European Market is a recent example of this process.

As the Community has gradually increased its role in the economic and social development of Europeans, so the number of European nations encompassed by the community of states has grown. The original six increased in 1973 to nine, with the accession of Denmark, Ireland and the UK. Greece joined the community in 1981 and Spain and Portugal in 1983. The community was enlarged in 1990 with the union of the two Germanies and the inclusion of the eastern Länder. The community continues to grow. The one-time EFTA countries of Austria, Finland and Sweden have also now joined the Union.

Many of the powers associated with the regulation of trade at state level are now coming under the auspices of the EU, as exhibit 9.1 illustrates. Merger regulations came into force on 21 September 1990. By the end of June 1993, the Commission

---

Exhibit 9.1 EU mergers regulations from 21 September 1990

Notification
If a merger is of sufficient magnitude the Commission of the European Communities must be notified.

Conditions
Where any of the following apply:

General threshold: aggregate global turnover of new operation is more than ECU million 5,000.

De minimus threshold: turnover in the EU of at least two of the businesses concerned with the merger is more than ECU million 250.

Two-thirds rule: the businesses concerned achieve more than two-thirds of their community wide turnover within the same member state.

Procedure

1 Notification of merger.

2 Three weeks must elapse before merger, Commission may impose a suspension of merger while merger is considered.

3 Within one month after notification Commission must make first decision:
    (a) no serious doubts;
    (b) serious doubts, Commission must launch investigation.

4 Commission must report within four months.

Decision
The Commission may prohibit a merger or require the companies concerned to adjust their portfolio in order to avoid unacceptable market presence.

Source: European Economy, 1994a.

had been notified of 164 mergers, of which seventeen were considered not to fall within its scope, 129 were not considered to be a serious impairment of competition and a further eleven were examined in detail because the mergers were considered after initial consideration to pose a prima facie danger to freedom of trade (European Economy, 1994a). One case, involving Aérospatiale and Alania and the take-over of de Havilland was prohibited. In the main, merger regulations at the EU level are not currently of great concern to the retail operations, because of the scale of retail cross border activity in Europe. Compared with the industrial sector, the size of retail acquisitions, and their impact on the freedom of trade, are relatively small. However, retail organizations have been considered by the Commission. Decisions have been taken on a number of service operations including retailers. As yet retailers have raised no serious doubts at the Commission: Promodès and Dirsa, supermarkets (decision, 17 December 1990); Otto and Grattan, mail order (21 March 1991); Redoute and Empire Stores, mail order (25 April 1991); Spar and Dansk Supermarked, discount stores (3 February 1992); Promodès and BRMC, wholesale and supermarkets (13 July 1992) (Morgan, 1994).

The EU has created an environment in which retailers may more easily extend their geographical coverage. It would be inappropriate to suggest that the EU has removed all barriers to trade. Some barriers, such as cultural barriers are not so easily removed. Nevertheless, it is the case that political integration has facilitated international retail expansion by providing a common regulatory environment at an international level and convergent economic development. As economic integration and regulation has facilitated expansion within the EU, so it will facilitate expansion into the EU by retailers based outside the EU, who will be able to operate on a European rather than a national basis.

North American Free Trade Area

The NAFTA does not have the same federalist agenda as the EU. The association is based on recognition of the advantages to be gained from a free trade area in North America. To some extent, the NAFTA will bring the same benefits to the economies of Canada, Mexico and the US as the large internal market has brought to the US. The large US market has facilitated the development of corporations with a large domestic market capable of competing in the global environment.

The free trade area encompasses considerable economic and social differences. While there are many prosperous consumers within Mexico, the country contains considerable variations in living standards. Therefore, the poorer sections of the Mexican population living in the south of the country have a very different social experience from Canadian citizens who pride themselves as being a competitive but caring society.

Many Canadians expressed considerable concern over the Canada-US free trade area when it has established as a precursor to the NAFTA. They have been concerned that their larger neighbour would be able to exercise greater influence in a country which was to a great extent already dependent on trade with, and hence the economy of, the US. In 1993, 67 per cent of Canadian imports came from the US; 81 per cent of exports were sent to the US.

The NAFTA has not created a single market, and retailers expanding into North America should be aware that the arrangements have perhaps only further served to emphasize that, in North America, apparent similarities may mask fundamental differences. The US alone contains vast economic, social and cultural differences.

STATE

The state, or more colloquially in this context, the 'nation', is usually taken to be the fundamental unit for consideration when international business is discussed. However, as has been noted above, the state is increasingly subject to regional trading and political arrangements. The sovereign nation state, while not a redundant entity, is increasingly hedged around with international agreements and constraints if it wishes to participate in global economic development.

The nature of states varies considerably. Germany and the UK are both states. Germany is a federal state; the UK is a unitary state. Both possess the essential qualities of statehood. Both are members of the European Union. Both Germany and the UK therefore possess sufficient political cohesion to be judged to be sovereign states. Therefore, questions may be asked regarding the political conditions within the state, and hence the influence of such conditions on public policy and the regulatory environment.

- Are these states politically stable?

- What are the current or likely, politically disruptive issues within the political environment?

- Are these democracies?

- Does the party of government have general support for its economic policies within the state legislature.

- Is the party of opposition opposed to fundamental economic principles of the government?

Retailers may be particularly exposed to the political environment in which they operate. Retailers who use their own fascias and own their outlets will be particularly vulnerable to political changes which threaten property rights or where animosity toward the company is present in the non-domestic market, because of the contemporary actions or past actions of the company. Shell's experience of negative public reaction over its plans for the North Sea oil platform Brent Spar is an example of such exposure. Likewise, a retailer's association with its home market, and hence the politics within the home country, may attract negative attitudes within the market of destination. French nuclear testing in the Pacific is an example of the type of international events which may cause considerable negative reaction, and indeed campaigns, among consumers, directed not only toward the national government in question, but also the products and enterprise of the society which the national government represents. Aggression toward the government of the domestic market of a retail company may lead to the seizure of property or the boycotting of the operation.

It has tended to be manufacturing or extractive industries which have experienced this type of negative international experience. The 1995 controversy over the disposal of the North Sea oil platform, the Brent Spar, by Shell led to a firebomb attack on one of the company's retail facilities in Hamburg, Germany (Gedye, 1995). Demonstrators also spray-painted slogans on the walls of filling stations, and in Frankfurt gun shots were fired at a filling station. By the middle of June 1995, Shell filling stations experienced a fall in fuel sales of 20 per cent. In other markets, such as the UK, protestors distributed leaflets at petrol stations in an attempt to dissuade customers from purchasing fuel and other goods at those retail outlets. Retail companies have not tended to be so high profile and hence they have not attracted the same level of publicity and negative action as manufacturing or extractive industries. However, retailers have seen the seizure of assets by regimes antipathetic to them. C&A lost property in the communist takeover in East Germany. Not only did this affect the company in the 1940s, but also in the 1990s. The company showed a reluctance to move back into that market until property rights issues had been clarified (Siewart, 1992). Harrods had a very successful operation in Buenos Aires before the Peronist period of government in Argentina (Hollander, 1970). US retailers have found themselves caught in the political machinations of governments and the chaos of political movements in markets close to home. Sears Roebuck's 'short-lived attempt to sell sewing machines in Mexico in the early 1900s foundered on fears of political instability' (Hollander, 1970, p. 22). Likewise, the same company's 'profitable Cuban branch, opened in 1942, was eventually closed by the Castro government' (Hollander, 1970, p. 22).

Public policy

The public policy issues affecting retailing have received limited attention in the literature. Kirby (1992a) has suggested this is because marketing academics are not used to dealing with the specific complexities of political issues and that marketing academics prefer more definable subject areas which are more easily quantified, rather than the intractable problems of politics. Nevertheless, public policy has a profound effect on retail development. Public policy may affect retailers directly through those regulations which government may impose from time to time on planning bodies or impose through legislation or directives on retail prices and merger and acquisition activity. Public policy may also have an indirect effect:

> Postwar American policies that have encouraged highway construction and the development of suburban one-family housing have probably done as much as any other phase of action in shaping contemporary retailing. (Hollander, 1972)

Therefore, in one sense, all government policy will have an effect on retailing as it supports or promotes developments which build the economic and social fabric in which retailers operate, and in the international contexts in which they choose to operate. However, as far as retailing itself is concerned, governments will have two specific roles. Governments will endeavour to control competition as well as encouraging fair competition. How they achieve this will depend on the political outlook of the government and the political issues of the day. Therefore, in the international environment, retailers will, or will not, have the opportunity to operate in markets where there is limited regulation and where regulation is extensive. Some markets will be controlled to such a degree that retailers will simply be unable to operate within them. The command economies of Eastern Europe and China were, until relatively recently, inaccessible to 'Western' retailers. Other markets, while ostensively open to retailers, may be unacceptably economically and commercially regulated.

Political interference

The UK Industrial Development Committee (IDC) of the mid-1970s was based on a manifesto commitment of the Labour government of the day to bring companies into public ownership 'where they had failed their workers' (Benn, 1989, p. 350). On the 20 March 1975, the IDC discussed two retail companies, Mothercare and Boots. Although, neither company was considered for public ownership, the tenor of the reported debate displays the context in which business may be discussed and even affected by politicians.

In 1975, a large number of jobs were threatened at the Triang Toys factory in Merthyr in the UK. It was debated whether government money should be used to save the firm:

> Harold Lever said the plan was outrageous. 'What we want is another firm to buy it, Mothercare would be perfect, they produce baby products. As a matter of fact, [he said] my wife Diane has a cousin who owns Mothercare – I'll ask her to do it.' Everybody laughed. (Benn, 1989, p. 350)

The discussion turned, in due course, to Bearbrand, a manufacturer of hosiery tights. The Cabinet Minister, Tony Benn, was asked if Boots had been approached as a potential buyer:

> 'As a matter of fact', I answered, 'Boots were approached, and when they were told Bearbrand were in trouble, they exploited their knowledge of Bearbrand's weakness to force them to make a price cut, which is why the firm has gone bankrupt. That is capitalism. Everybody is out for themselves and nobody gives a damn about people who lose their jobs'. (Benn, 1989, p. 350)

While rhetoric clearly had not only crept into these discussions, but had strode confidently into them, rhetoric will often create an environment in which fundamental decisions are made in government and hence affect the direction of future policy. Likewise, it will affect decisions made in the board-room and influence major investment decisions. As Kacker (1985) has noted, European retailers were anxious to move investments into North American retailing in the 1970s as the political climate across Europe gave them cause for concern with respect to future public policy and regulatory decisions.

Regulatory control

The political position adopted by government and opposition parties may, in time, lead to the establishment of legislative programmes and the establishment of regulatory frameworks which will directly and indirectly affect the retailer. Retailers must be conscious of regulations concerning the products they sell as well as the context in which the products are sold. Retailers may be directly affected by a wide variety of laws. In the retail literature, the Robinson-Patman Act in the United States, the Loi Royer in France, the Loi de cadenas in Belgium and Resale Price Maintenance in the UK, are often referred to as examples of regulation which have had a major impact on the course of retail structural and competitive development. In the sections below, some of the important areas of retail business in which the state has become involved are discussed.

Vertical relationships

The negotiating power of large retail operations is synonymous with growth of large retail organizations. The development of large retail chains has been a feature of retailing since the late nineteenth century. Such organizations as Liptons in the UK, Woolworth and A&P in the US developed their operations on the basis of innovative and cost reducing sourcing policies. In retail distribution channels, the ability of the retail buyer to reduce the length of that channel, to source directly from the manufacturer and to buy in bulk sufficient quantities to allow substantial discounts has facilitated the development of retail structures. However, not all participants in the distribution channel view such developments as desirable.

Keiretsu are a feature of the Japanese distribution system (Marvel, 1993). Manufacturing companies exercise considerable control in Japan and through a network of contractual arrangements (keiretsu) have come to exercise control over distribution channel members. This is one of the products of the Large Stores Law discussed below. The retail sector has not been free to develop large retail operations in the last fifty years as retailers in Europe and North America. Indeed, to some extent, given the influence of department store retailers in Japan, which has only begun to be seriously challenged in recent years, retailers from outside Japan face a retail sector which has something in common with retail structures which were observable elsewhere in the 1930s.

Even in the US market, considerable restrictions have been imposed on retailers and manufacturers in the negotiation of trade discounts. The Robinson-Patman Act of 1936 is one of the best known examples of retail regulation. The

Robinson-Patman Act was an attempt to protect the small retailer against the large chain store organization through the control of the advantages large organizations had when negotiating with suppliers. However, as Wrigley (1992) notes, it was only part of a sequence of legislation which sought to regulate the competitive environment. Both the Sherman Act of 1890, and the Clayton Act of 1914, were designed to control economic power and form the legislative background to the Robinson-Patman legislation. Such legislation was to create a regulatory environment in which A&P, the large food chain operation, was fined $1,750,000 in 1949 for achieving anticompetitive discounts and selling to its customers goods at prices which were not prevalent in the market-place.

This wish to control the development of large retail operations in the US was not limited to issues of trade discounts. Later legislation, the Celler-Kefauver Act of 1950, also contributed to the form which retail structural change would take in the US through the regulation of merger activity.

Regulations which were not introduced are sometimes more indicative of the level of control some parties would wish to introduce to control the growth of large retail operations. Patman proposed a bill which would have taxed retail chain operations on the basis of the number of branches operated, with the tax rising progressively, and would have inflicted crushing taxes on a chain which operated in more than one state of the US (Wrigley, 1992). For an operation such as A&P, it has been calculated that, this would have led to taxes of $523m (Adelman, 1959); this figure would have been twenty-six times greater than the company's annual profits.

Planning regulations

The Loi Royer and the Loi Cadenas were both directed at the large supermarket or hypermarket operations. In the years preceding this legislation, the supermarket and hypermarket were challenging the market position of the small trader in Belgium and France. In Japan, the Large Stores Law has restricted the development of new stores (Larke, 1992).

Belgium
The Loi Cadenas or Padlock Law, as it is often called, had a long history and reflects the historical context in which decisions concerning retail development are taken. Boddewyn's (1971) classic work in this area provides an insight into the historical development of public policy toward retailing from the late eighteenth century. While within the nineteenth and twentieth century period of industrialization in Belgium there were a number of short lived factors which influenced public policy toward retailing, two connected factors dominated policy formulation in this period:

> The first was the intermittent development of new, aggressive retailing firms that generated intertype competition, and the second was the coming of age of the middle classes. (Boddewyn, 1971, p. 216)

The economic conditions of the mid 1930s and the ensuing pressures on the community brought these two factors together to prompt the passing of the Padlock law of 1937. The law forbade the development of large department stores. Initially seen as a short term measure, the policy was maintained until 1961. The Belgian retail sector, as a result of this curtailment of growth, failed to develop in the new markets of the immediate post war world. With the repeal of the Padlock law, pressures were unleashed within the distribution channel. There was a subsequent growth in supermarkets and shopping centres. This occurred despite the 1962 law which controlled land use and could be used to restrict retail development.

This reaction to deregulation in turn led to demands, support for which built up built up during the 1960s, to regulate late closing which the large retailers in urban centres used to increase their profitability and against which the small shopkeepers felt unable to compete. In consequence, late night shopping was restricted in 1973. Shops had to close at 8 p.m. and could not open before 5 a.m. (Francois, and Leunis, 1991). This was a clear attempt, no matter how liberal the restrictions might appear, as far as labour force rights were concerned, to control the competitive advantages of large operations (Hollander and Boddewyn, 1974).

The restrictions on opening hours were only the first attempt to respond to the concerns of the 'small shopkeepers' lobby. The restrictions on opening hours were followed in 1975, by the Business Premises Act, which sought to restrict store development (see exhibit 9.2). Applications were subsequently considered on the basis of four criteria:

1   the proposed store's relative position to other retail facilities and contribution to the local retail structure

2   the needs of the local consumers

3   employment levels within the community

4   impact on existing retail operations

Leunis and Francois (1988) have suggested the fourth criteria has the most impact on the final decision.

The law has had an effect on the development of supermarkets and hypermarkets. How great an effect, however, is open to interpretation. On the basis of their research, Francois and Leunis (1991, p. 482) suggest that the law 'has had a major impact upon the evolution of the number of supermarkets and the number of hypermarkets'. Between 1969 and 1975, the number of supermarkets increased by 350 to 709 outlets, while the number of hypermarkets rose by fifty-seven to seventy outlets. Between 1975 and 1980, the number of supermarkets rose by 147 and the number of hypermarkets by seven. Nevertheless, it is possible to suggest that the surge of development activity in the late 1960s and early 1970s was a response to the fear that public policy would become more restrictive and that development should occur sooner rather than later and that the limited growth in hypermarkets after 1975 may reflect the fact that a level of saturation had been reached by this date (Dawson, 1982).

Exhibit 9.2 Business Premises Act, 1975: Belgium

Application
Zone 1 (high density of population): where planned stores exceed 3,000 sq m or selling space exceeds 1,500 sq m.
Zone 2 (high density of population): where planned stores exceed 1,000 sq m or selling space exceeds 750 sq m.

Procedure
Where planned store exceeds the size appropriate to the zone in question

1   application presented to the relevant local Council of the municipality;

2   application sent to the Social Economic Committee for Distribution (SEC) within 5 days;

3   SEC advises on suitability within 90 days.

4(a)   where SEC supports proposal advise must pass to Provincial Committee for Distribution (PCD) within 7 days

4(b)   where SEC does not support proposal advise must pass to the municipal Council within 7 days

5(a i)   PCD advises within 30 days and advice passed to municipal Council within 5 days

5(b)   where no support forthcoming from the SEC municipal Council must reject the proposal

5(a ii) municipal Council decides within 30 days informing applicant thereafter within 5 days

6   appeals to Interministry Committee by applicant where proposal rejected or National Commission for Distribution (NCD) where accepted

Source: Francois and Leunis, 1991.

France
At the same time that the small shopkeepers of Belgium were concerned about the developments of large operations under the fascia of multiple store organizations and Belgian policy makers were wrestling with the problems of planning control, French policy makers were facing the same problem. Indeed, in France, a law was introduced earlier than in Belgium, in 1973, to cope with the tensions which had been aroused in local communities and amongst local traders against the larger retailers. The Belgian legislation has strong echoes of the legislation passed in France. In France, the Commissions Departmentale d'Urbanisme Commercial

(CDUC) dealt with applications of 1,500 sq m or 1,000 sq m in communes with a population of less than 40,000 (Dawson, 1976). The evidence from France, however, according to Burt (1984), was that the Loi Royer did not have as great an impact as had been anticipated, and therefore as great an impact as the Loi Cadenas had in Belgium. As Burt (1984) notes, while the annual growth in hypermarket openings fell from sixty-two outlets in 1972 to a figure of around thirty for the rest of the 1970s and the early years of the 1980s, the overall growth in hypermarket numbers increased at a healthy rate in the same period, to the extent that such stores doubled their market share of retail sales to 12 per cent between 1972 and 1982.

When such laws do have an effect on the number of planning applications which are given permission to progress, there will be a knock-on effect. It will lead to an increase in horizontal acquisition activity, as businesses seek new outlets for their goods through what may be he only available option for them. This has been one of the factors behind acquisition activity in France in the food sector in the early 1990s (Schwarz, 1993).

Japan

In Japan, the Large Stores Law (LSL) has been a determining factor in the development of retailing (Larke, 1994). The law was introduced in 1937 in its original form. Apart from a period when it was not effective, during the US occupation of Japan (1945–52) after the Second World War, the law has been in place, albeit in modified forms, since that time. In recent years, 1992 and 1994, the law has under gone major revision as a result of the SII (Selective Impediments Initiative) talks with the US (Rodger, 1990). The law made it very difficult to introduce new retail operations into Japan. The large US retailer, Toys R Us were particularly anxious that they should be given access to the Japanese market and have since developed their operations in the market.

As in Belgium, the small shopkeepers in Japan have been an important political lobby group and have been effective in persuading governments to support their position. While the law has imposed various stages on planning proposals 'it was the operation of the law which attracted the most criticism' (Larke, 1994, p. 105). It was possible for delays to kill the proposal. It was also possible for the new mass merchandisers of the 1960s to circumvent the 1956 law by the useful fiction that in buildings over the 1,500 sq m mark contained a number of 'businesses' within them and not just one retail business. In 1974, the law was tightened up and the retail premises not the retail business became the controlled entity.

As in Belgium and France, store size thresholds were imposed in Japanese cities of different sizes. The 1974, law required permission for premises of 3,000 sq m or more in the eleven largest cities in Japan, and a threshold of 1,500 sq m elsewhere. This threshold was lowered to 500 sq m in 1979 but these applications below the previous threshold were dealt with at the prefectorial or local level rather than by MITI, and created a Type 2 store application procedure. However, critics of new store openings were not satisfied, so that by the end of the 1980s, the guidelines imposed had increased the complexity of the law to such an extent that it was a considerable problem for Japanese stores but an effectively unfathomable issue for foreign retailers with limited knowledge of, and influence in, Japan.

It might be considered somewhat politically insensitive that the US should have championed the relaxation of restrictions on new store developments, given the fact that the only time in the last half a century Japan had been released from such restrictions was during the US occupation of Japan. Yet, the US government has been influential in the relaxation of these laws. The Japanese government, while remaining implacable in its opposition to the law's abolition, was prepared to see MITI implement changes in the law which, to some extent, satisfied US requests.

The new regulations, which came into effect in 1992, have been further relaxed since. From the end of 1994, new stores could increase their operating area by up to 10 per cent or 50 sq m without implementation of the law. A time limit was also placed on the application process (see exhibit 9.3). Depending on the type of store, type 1 or 2, the threshold rose to 6,000 in the larger cities and 3,000 in other areas for the type 1 store and 1,000 for type 2 stores (Larke, 1994).

While the law facilitated new store development, it was perhaps not as thorough as the US negotiators would have liked, but nevertheless, the relatively stream-lined procedures and control of local delays was an important relaxation of the law. For the foreign retailer, an interesting aspect of the law, is that retailers may

Exhibit 9.3 Large Stores Law 1992: Japan

Process

1   Submission of proposal by the developer.

2   (a)   Presentation and preliminary explanation of proposal;
     (b)   the public announcement of the proposal.

3   Submission of proposal by the retailer.

4   Large Retail Store Deliberation Council (LRSDC) receives the views of:
     (a)   consumer groups;
     (b)   retailers;
     (c)   experts;
     (d)   other interested groups such as local; chambers of commerce.

5   LRSDC considers proposal and submitted opinions.

6   Recommendations sent to the Ministry for Trade and Industry (MITI).

7   Decision by MITI which must be made within a year of the developer's original submission and eight months from the time of the retailer's submission.

Source: Larke, 1994.

develop up to 1,000 sq m of sales space devoted to imported goods. This may prove an interesting opportunity for non-domestic retailers seeking space in existing Japanese stores.

Summary

Planning regulations are, at times, as overtly stated as these examples of retailing in Belgium, France and Japan illustrate. However, retailers may also, through the use of innovative formats place themselves in anomalous positions in respect of the law which might act to their advantage and this may cause them considerable problems when establishing operations in a new market. Costco's legal problems in the UK are an example of a business challenging the accepted practices in one country. The legal issue was one of definition; that is, was Costco a retail organization or a wholesaler? While the courts were to support Costco's claim to be a wholesaler and thereby able to operate from sites which retailers would not be able to operate from, the Department of the Environment in the UK was soon to indicate that warehouse membership clubs should be considered to be retail operations (Hallsworth et al., 1994).

Opening hours

Some of the most notorious retail opening hours in Europe are those in Germany. The Ladenschlussgesetz (Shop Opening Hours Act) restricts shops to opening between 7 a.m. and 6.30 p.m. on weekdays and requires them to remain closed on Sundays. Usual shopping hours on Saturdays are 7 a.m. until 2 p.m., although shops may stay open longer one Saturday in the month. An extension was given in 1989, which allowed late openings on Thursdays until 9 p.m. This, however, was not entirely well-received by unions, politicians and retail executives, who argued that this was an unnecessary relaxation of the regulations governing opening hours. Wulf Ridder, speaking for the large retailer Kaufhof, noted that, outside the main shopping areas, retailers did not even take advantage of the extended hours on Saturdays (Randlesome, 1993). In the west of Germany, pressure for change has not been as strong as might be expected given these restricted hours. Ironically, support for longer trading hours has emerged from the Eastern Lander, where customers, under the communist regime, were used to shops opening until 10 p.m. (GB, 1993). The West German law was passed in 1956 and has become well established, reflecting the strength of the unions, but also the social environment and cultural expectations of West Germans. The demands for legislation from the East serve only to show how, once established, such laws may have a profound effect on consumer expectations as much as retailer operating practices.

In France, the UK based Virgin Megastores came into conflict with French opening hours regulations. The store on the Champs Elysees had permission to open on a Sunday; however, its permit to open on Sundays expired in the summer of 1993. Nevertheless, the store continued to open, to the dismay of small shopkeepers and trade union officials, although customers continued to use the store and the workforce, perhaps not a little inspired by double pay, were prepared to turnout (Laushway, 1993).

Opening hours will vary considerably within different markets. However, some indication is given of opening hours in most of the markets of the EU in table 9.1. The table suggests that the weighted average of store opening hours in Spain is the shortest at forty-six and the longest in Greece with fifty-nine. The hours retail outlets open will be affected by local custom in more traditional markets, as well as legal requirements which may have more effect amongst the larger retailers in more developed retail structures.

Employment law

Another issue with which state governments are closely involved is the regulation of the relationship of employer and employee. This may involve government in the formulation of regulations which directly relate to retailing, as in the UK in respect of Sunday trading, or indirectly, as in the US with President Clinton's health care reform proposals.

One of the major concerns of lobbyists in the debate over Sunday Opening in the UK was the protection of employee rights. The Sunday Trading Act of 1994, apart from regulating opening hours of large shops, also sought to provide rights to those employees who did not wish to work on a Sunday (IRRR, 1994). However, as the union USDAW have noted, pressure may effectively be placed on part-time workers who will be unable to pursue dismissal claims if they refuse Sunday working hours (Keen, 1994).

In the US, health care is an important labour issue. President Clinton's 1993 health care programme proposals, while not directed at retailers, would indirectly raise the cost of employing part-time workers, since the proposals recommend that employers should pay 80 per cent of employees basic health insurance programmes

Table 9.1 Retail opening hours in Europe: 1994

	Hours stores open			*Not known*	*Weighted average*
	<50	*56–65*	*>66 (%)*		
Spain	84	8	6	2	46
Italy	69	28	1	2	47
France	76	13	11	0	49
Germany	81	12	2	5	50
Netherlands	85	10	5	0	51
Portugal	76	3	21	0	51
Denmark	66	17	17	1	53
UK	64	14	21	0	54
Belgium	51	18	30	1	56
Greece	50	22	28	0	59
EU 12	74	15	9	2	59

Source: European Economy, 1994b.

(Stores, 1994). Such recommendations are important to an industry such as retailing, which employs relatively large numbers of staff, due in part to staff turnover, during an accounting period.

Working conditions will be influenced by the activities of shopworker unions where they are influential. In Germany, as the issue of opening hours shows, unionized labour has been able to contribute to a campaign of retaining a system which might be considered restrictive and out of date in other parts of Europe. In the UK, as Kirby's (1992b) research on this issues indicates, there was considerable concern amongst shop staff as far as Sunday Trading was concerned. In the UK, the union USDAW represents only 250,000 shop workers (Keen, 1994). Thus retailers like Allied Maples, the carpet and furniture retailer, has been able to introduce 'key-time' employees who are called in when necessary, such as busy periods, but who are provided with zero-hour basic contracts. This has caused concern amongst full-time employees who have expressed concern over the affect of such workers on their commissions (IRRR, 1993).

LOCAL

Local or regional government may exert independent policies, especially where federal structures exist. This may include the right to levy local taxes on incomes and purchases. It may also include the ability to affect decisions taken at the federal level, which the regional government may delay or influence. Even within a unitary state such as the UK, where regional governments are not present, local authorities, through measures such as planning policy, may exert considerable influence over the development of retail operations.

Governmental influence at the local or regional level may prove an important factor in the development of Europe in the next decade and beyond. As power moves to the centre of the EU, so there is pressure to ensure that, where possible, decisions are taken at the lowest level possible. That is, the Community is developing on the basis of the principle of subsidiarity. This suggests that, not only will powers move away from the national government to the supra-national organization in Brussels, but that power will also devolve to the regions. While local or regional aspirations have long been a feature of European politics, the European environment, as it emerged in the 1980s, has helped to fundamentally alter the nature of regional aspirations. Regions aspiring to local autonomy are not simply characterized, as they once were, as putative or ancient nations in their own right.

> Far from being the geographical anthologies of cultural particularism and social obsolescence, certain regions (largely but not exclusively drawn from the 'core', London-Frankfurt-Milan-Paris quadrilateral, and including all three EC 'capitals': Strasbourg, Luxembourg and Brussels) now seemed the 'sharp end' of European consciousness: areas of sophisticated technology, environmental awareness, local democracy, and a culture and society which integrated the intimate and the cosmopolitan. (Harvie, 1994, p. 2)

Therefore, while retailers may, on one level, wish to think increasingly of Europe on a supra-national level, they may also wish to think of Europe on a regional basis as well. Indeed there is evidence to suggest that they are already recognizing the declining importance of national government and national boundaries within the EU. Directors of leading European food retail operations have indicated in a survey carried out in 1994, that they would still consider that national boundaries are influential in determining expansion programmes but such boundaries are becoming less important (Myers, 1995). In contrast, they suggest that regional boundaries are retaining their influence.

Bavaria is a Free State and constituent part of the Federal German State. The Free State is a champion of the rights of the Länder in Germany and prides itself on this fact. Information published by the Bavarian State Chancellery while acknowledging that 'Bavaria emphatically supports the unification of Europe' emphasizes the importance of local involvement in European decision making:

> under pressure from Bavaria, the Bundesrat [Federal Council] has won an important say for the states in European policy matters. The Federal Government has to hear the states and consider their comments, when it negotiates in Brussels on matters which affect the competence of the states. (Bavarian State Chancellery, 1988)

To this end, Bavaria has established its own offices in Brussels in order to ensure that it is able to communicate with decision makers at the heart of the EU. In this way, the Free State of Bavaria is recognizing the importance of European integration and helping to build an enhanced role for the regions in Europe. However, this is not the only way that Bavaria has contributed to the development of transnational associations of regional-states. The Community of Alpine States was founded in 1972 and the Community of the Eastern Alps in 1978, with the aim of establishing cooperation on ecological, economic, social and cultural issues. The Community of the Eastern Alps involves cooperation between Austrians, Croatians, Germans, Italians, Slovenes, and Swiss. It is an association at the regional-state and not national-state level, although political changes in the former Yugoslavia have altered the original balance in this respect.

The power of the individual state has long been recognized within the US context. State governments have played an important role in the development of legislation affecting the development of retailing. The history of Resale Price Maintenance (RPM) in the US is inextricably linked to state rights and statutes. The importance of the states in this matter was, in part, due to the 1890 Sherman Anti-trust Act, which prohibited restraints on commerce between the states of the Union and the US Supreme Courts judgement that the 1890 Act and the common law forbade 'agency contracts' or RPM (Hollander, 1966). In consequence of this, and of pressure from the manufacturer, retail, and consumer groups, state legislation was passed in order to facilitate RPM where the product remained in one state from production to retail sale. This was extended after the Miller-Tydings Enabling Amendment in 1937 to allow RPM if the state from which the product was supplied and the state in which the product was sold both had RPM legislation, then RPM was permissible. Many states then introduced legislation, often based on the Californian Statute. However, not all states allowed such control, so that consumers are able to travel to retail outlets with lower prices by crossing state boundaries, most notoriously, perhaps, into the District of Columbia to buy alcohol, and thereby increase the average purchase per local head of population, to the delight of newspaper journalists writing about their sober federal legislators.

ASSESSMENT

As the preceding discussion shows, retailers operating in the international arena will need to be aware of the regulatory context in which they operate. The retail company will need to be aware of the differences in regulation which it faces in the new environment. It will need to appreciate the regulatory distance which exists between past and anticipated experience. When assessing the political environment, the retailer must consider new markets on the basis of the market of destination, the country in which it considers operation, in the light of the market of origin, the country in which it is based and with which it is associated, and its company history, associations and ethical stance. All considerations of the market of destination must be understood in this context, otherwise assumptions will be made about the environment in which operations are planned which may lead to limited success or outright failure. Where retailers perceive discontinuity, they should consider whether they wish to continue with the development of an operation in the market concerned or if they wish to radically alter the means by which they intend to address that market.

Some retail products will be closely associated with their market of origin. Hence, retailers may benefit or be hindered by the general reputation of their market of origin. British retailers such as Aquascutum, Austin Reed, Burberrys and Laura Ashley may benefit from their association with an English style. Conversely, retailers may not wish to emphasize their country of origin, in case there is a detrimental rather than a positive effect.

The market of destination may be considered on the basis of key questions about the political and legal environment.

What type of government does the country have?

Retailers will be familiar with the political system in which their organization has initially developed. Therefore, they will often seek to expand into contexts with which they are familiar. Retailers operating in liberal democracies will face new challenges by moving into markets where other systems operate.

Recent developments in Eastern Europe have given retailers the opportunity to access new markets which may in time prove very lucrative, especially to those retailers who have built up an operating structure in the early days of

9.1 I'm a Tiger

The enthusiasm for investment on the Pacific Rim is considerable among retailers. The Tiger economies, with their rapid economic growth, are attractive to retailers based in markets with much lower growth rates. The new consumers of South East Asia are, therefore, an attractive target for American, European and Japanese retailers alike. However, such attractive growth rates must be set against other uncertainties, some of which are political.

It may not be of particular interest to retail executives that General Chiang Kai-shek abandoned the Chinese mainland in 1949 and set up a Nationalist government in Taiwan, but in 1996 with the first totally free and direct Presidential elections in Taiwan, Chinese history came back to haunt the election campaign and undermine investors' confidence in Taiwan.

The rising tensions with China led to considerable net capital flows out of Taiwan in 1995 ($6.77bn), and in turn, led to a record balance of payments deficit of $3.93bn compared to a surplus of $4.62bn the previous year.

While an outflow of capital is one indicator of rising tension in the area, arms sales are another. This has not just affected Taiwan but the Asean area. Asean defense expenditure is expected to rise by 2 per cent a year in real terms of the next ten years. This in itself will have an effect on economic development.

With Chinese warships posturing in the waters close to Taiwan, the damaging consequences of international conflict and political uncertainty brought home the wider political issues which all international businesses face.

Source: *Financial Times*, 1996; Luce and Bardacke, 1996.

'liberalization'. However, in the meantime those retailers are faced with considerable problems as those countries develop a political system to meet their needs.

China is a large market, but Western commentators were shocked when student demonstrators were forcibly removed from Tianmen Square in Peking following demonstrations which the Chinese government clearly believed threatened their position as similar demonstrations had threatened the old regimes in Eastern Europe. Different systems of government will respond in different ways to both political developments and economic change. International businesses should be fully aware of this.

How strong are the centrifugal and centripetal forces within the body politic?

Retailers may at times find themselves operating in more than one market simply because secessionist pressures have led to the establishment of a new state.

9.2 High Hopes

It may look a long way off, but a Free Trade Agreement for the Americas is gaining support. One strong element of that support is the private sector which is increasingly putting pressure on governments to make concrete advances in the direction of a hemisphere-wide agreement.

Cartagena, was the venue for a meeting of 34 trade ministers from the Americas in March 1996. High on the agenda was a set of recommendations from business representatives also meeting in Cartagena.

As Mr Renato Martins of the Brazilian based Magnesita company put it, the region is made up of a wide variety of economies: 'a mixture of elephants, dinosaurs, snakes and rabbits'. This provides planners with considerable problems, but the success of existing agreements is fuelling plans for a bigger FTA. Mercosur with a population of 204m people spread through Argentina, Brazil, Paraguay and Uruguay was not initially given much hope. However, as Renato Martins acknowledges, once it came into being: 'there were 600 Brazilian companies in Buenos Aires with their phones ringing' (Kendall and Dunne, 1996).

Negotiations will build on the Denver talks of 1995, and will focus on such issues as market access, customs regulations, investment, technical barriers to trade, sanitary concerns, subsidies to smaller economies, anti-dumping measures and countervailing duties. To this list the Cartagena talks added government procurement, intellectual property rights, services and competition policy.

While there is much enthusiasm in many quarters, the scale of the task before negotiators should not be underestimated. Along with Mercosur, with a total GDP of $1,014bn, and the Andean Pact countries of Bolivia, Colombia, Ecuador, Peru and Venezuela, with a combined GDP of $240bn, there is the NAFTA with Canada, Mexico and the US with a combined GDP of $8,059bn. Whatever they are called, there are some very different economies in the Americas.

Source: Kendall and Dunne, 1996.

Hollander (1970) has described this as inadvertent internationalization. K-mart had this experience when Slovakia and the Czech Republic separated. However, even where major constitutional developments such as those in the state of Czechoslovakia have not occurred or are unlikely to occur, localist tensions within states must be considered in all parts of the world. Even within long-established political communities, this issue may have important implications for retailers, which, in the context of civil unrest and violence, may not only make trading difficult but also very costly. Centrifugal political forces are felt within stable democracies, as well as third world dictatorships, indeed both within the trading areas of the EU and NAFTA, local political movements are challenging the established political structure. In Canada, Quebec separatism remains a live, and potentially very significant, factor in the development of Canada. In the EU, divisions exist within Spain, tensions between interests in Madrid and Cataluña, Madrid and the Basque country, within Belgium, between Wallonia and Flanders, within France between Paris and Bretagne, Paris and Corse, and, within the UK, between London and Wales, London and Scotland. While not all the examples cited here are of the same magnitude of importance in terms of their threat to existing political institutions, they all represent a political agenda of which retailers should be aware. Such agendas may in turn lead to changes in the commercial operating environment, as is evident in Northern Ireland where political conflict has had an impact on the retail structure and competition (Alexander and McFetridge, 1995).

How many parties are found in the legislature and the government?

Where there are two or more parties in a legislature, government action will be open to stronger criticism. One party states may offer stability, in that changes of policy may be less likely in the short term, and the threat of turbulent political periods is also a possibility. Single party government may also provide clear policy objectives but lead to radical shifts in policies after elections. Multi-party or coalition government may reduce the likelihood of radical policy shifts but it may also lead to comfortable 'arrangements' which do not encourage open government. At the beginning of 1995, with the establishment of Lomberto Dini as Prime Minister of Italy, the country saw its 54th government since the Second World War: however, in that time, the personnel to be found in government posts did not always change radically from one government to another and surprising continuity was maintained.

How long has the political system been in place?

Longevity is no guarantee of stability, but the fact that the US constitution has been in place for more than 200 years during a time of rapid geographical, economic and demographic expansion would lead most commentators to presume that the US is sufficiently politically stable to support international operations. Other markets, those, for example, in the so called Third World, may be treated cautiously, simply because they have only recently emerged as states in their own right. This is a fraught area for judgements, as some markets' political institutions and traditions have not been sufficiently tested over time. Spain has attracted retailers in considerable numbers from the US and other European countries, yet its present democratic political system is relatively young. Spain has, however, been part of the European political system for centuries, and for much of its history, a particularly important part of that system. Spain is also part of the EU and thus very much part of the new integrated Europe.

What are the country's relations with the international community of states?

In the late twentieth century, this question may imply what associations is the country involved with and therefore who are the guarantors of stability? That Mexico is part of the NAFTA agreement can not fail to go some way toward reassuring prospective investors that, by inference, without any substantial changes in Mexican politics, the country is a sounder option than if it was not part of that agreement.

This may lead investors to be wary of countries that show signs of leaving international associations. The rather confused rhetoric which UK governments and opposition parties alike have voiced in respect of the EU, while clearly not stemming the investments of non-UK retailers, represents the kind of uncertainty which in other circumstances, or where statements were taken more seriously, will lead companies to investing elsewhere, if the association and not the secessionist country is seen to be implementing those policies which will support buoyant markets.

Countries must also be considered on the basis of their international relationships with other states which are often their neighbours with whom there may be disputes. Kuwait and the state of Yugoslavia are cases in point. This aspect of international trade can not be ignored, although it may seem far from the considerations of day to day business activity.

How does the government approach fundamental economic issues and hence regulate commercial and financial activity?

While commentators have for much of the twentieth century been content to use language such as 'left wing' and 'right wing' economic policies, in reality a far more complex picture exists, and left wing governments may find themselves initiating policies that would have been considered right wing a few years before. The reverse is also true. In the UK, Heath's Conservative government's (1970–4) prices and incomes policies were not only unacceptable a few years earlier to key cabinet members in the government itself but were certainly anathema to the Conservative government of the 1980s. However, governments may be categorized, in general terms, as interventionist or non-interventionist, and while circumstances may force short term policy reversals, fundamental positions will often reassert themselves.

In many markets around the globe, simplistic notions of interventionist and non-interventionist policy divisions are eclipsed by local divisions which fundamentally align the political life of the country. In African states, such as Nigeria and Zimbabwe, ethnic allegiances are important political factors. In South Africa, while the electoral franchise has become one of universal suffrage, major divisions remain within the community. While these are extreme and thus clear examples, sectional interest and hence the largesse which sectional interest distributes is a feature of all communities. Governments look after their own. Incoming businesses may not be their 'own'; however, they may in some way serve the interests of their in-group.

What legal requirements are there as far as property rights, including patents and copyrights?

Retailers who have a distinct merchandise brand may find their products replicated in markets where copyrights and patents are not respected. Retailers must be conscious of the level of exposure they have to risk as far as heir property portfolio is concerned. Problems over ownership of property in Eastern Europe in recent years has made companies cautious of the potential problems of identifying the real owners of, or those that may have a prior claim on, property.

The US is a large market with an attractively affluent customer base. However, retailers operating in the market need to be aware of the legal regulations which control trade in that most litigious of societies. The Body Shop was wary of entering the market for legal reasons. As Anita Roddick (1991, p. 134) notes, there are 'an amazing mass of rules and regulations that circumscribe the activities of every company hoping to trade in the Land of the Free'. The company was very anxious to conform to the regulations monitored by the Food and Drugs Administration, a Federal body, based in Washington DC. The Body Shop's refill system was nearly dropped because advisors warned there could be insurance problems. Likewise, the company was advised against stating that products were not tested on animals, as reprisals might be taken by cosmetics companies in the form of legal action. Lawyers in their various guises throughout the world are capable of costing legitimate enterprises a considerable amount of money.

Are there restrictions on the repatriation of profits?

In some markets, the repatriation of profits will be restricted. While the movement of funds is acceptable in many markets around the world, even in those markets such as the UK, restriction on the movement of funds has been restricted historically, and this issue is one that retailers may have to face during their operations in a market. Where repatriation of profits is restricted, retailers may have to source locally or engage in complicated export deals from the market of destination, if they are in some way to see benefits on the balance sheet at home. Retailers operating in East Europe have had to use such means to repatriate profits. The Littlewoods operation in Russia has had to resort to such means.

What commercial codes are there?

Entry into some markets may be restricted by the regulations on takeover activity. It may be difficult for aggressive takeovers to occur. Likewise, retailers may find that the amount of information that a retailer must divulge in some markets is relatively limited compared to its own. Thus, a retailer seeking expansion may find that these is relatively limited information available on the performance of some companies. In Germany, retailers are not required by law to consult independent advisers when making an acquisition. The German banks play an important part in dealing with and funding such activity (Shearlock, 1994). In the UK, conversely, retailers may be able to establish a presence through acquisition with relative ease. Indeed, as concentration increases in retailing in the UK, it is possible that a non-UK acquisition in some sectors would be more acceptable than a bid by a competing company in the UK market which already has a substantial market share and would find itself in a politically unacceptable monopolistic position were merger to occur.

Retailers must also be aware of general operating codes to which companies must adhere. Germany has strict regulations concerning waste packaging. As a result, retailers and manufacturers have organized a system whereby packaging is collected and recycled. The system is known as the Duales System Deutschland. The system was initially a disaster, as companies which had not paid to join the scheme use the Green dot system which is placed on packages to indicate that they were part of the system (Kennett, 1993). This overburdened the system to breaking point.

What planning, operating employment restrictions are there?

Such problems have been discussed in some detail above and relate directly to the service provision offered by retailers. Planning restrictions will vary within markets but overall assessments may be made. For some retailers, planning issues may not be a problem, particularly where their operation may be fitted into stock units within shopping Malls or other developments. Conversely, retailers may choose to purchase companies already operating in a market, as a means of acquiring a stock of properties which may then be used as units for the retailers' operations. Retailers who depend on long opening hours will find that there will be some markets in which they will experience particular problems.

Because labour costs are such a large proportion of a retailer's costs this issue will be of particular concern. Retailers may find that there are hidden costs such as those of training or redundancy payments which may amount to considerable expenditure. UK retailers moving to the rest of the EU will find that the contribution they are expected to make to staff welfare and training programmes will be greater than in the UK.

CONCLUSION

The political environment is an important aspect of global market assessment and has had an important role in determining the direction of international retail development. Indeed, it would not be an exaggeration to suggest that retail organizations as they are perceived in the contemporary environment and those enterprises such as trading companies who were an important part of early international retail activity, have sought to operate, where possible, under the umbrella of international political associations. This has not always been possible, but the direction of international retail development within Commonwealth countries was an important aspect of the internationalization of UK retail enterprises at one time. Today, the EU attracts a considerable number of internationalizing UK operations.

Where political umbrellas do not exist, retailers will often seek out, and, in certain circumstances, should be advised to seek out, markets where government structures and systems are similar to those in the domestic market. Retailers' initial familiarity with such systems will enable retailers to overcome some of the cultural problems which different political environments will present. Business practice in one political culture will be different from business practice in another, and commercial enterprises may find themselves asked, or forced, to make what they would consider to be ethical compromises, which, even if the individual executive is prepared to make, may not be considered acceptable to shareholders at home.

As far as the regulation of retail activity is concerned, governments have often regulated issues important to the development of retail structures and operations but as Hollander and Boddewyn (1974, p. 55) have recognized, 'government policies toward retailing are usually fragmentary, unconnected and even inconsistent'. Specific examples of regulations designed to control or inhibit the development of new retail operations or large organizations are a common feature of retailing across the world. Sometimes, such restrictions are found in markets such as Japan, which have become, rightly or wrongly, associated with distribution controls, but they have also been a feature of other markets such as the US which have become, rightly or wrongly, associated with freedom to trade without undue interference. When entering new markets, retailers will need to consider not only the regulatory framework which is in place but also the history of regulation within the market. They should also be aware of the influential lobby groups within the political structure. In some markets, the complexity of interest group influence, may lead retailers to consider joint-ventures in order to make contact with local networks.

QUESTIONS – DISCUSSION POINTS

1 On what levels should the global political environment be considered?

2 Is the European Union typical of international regional associations?

3 How may retailers be affected by changes in public policy?

4 Are strict planning regulations the last refuge of uncompetitive retailers?

5 How may retailers evaluate the political environment?

REFERENCES

Adelman, M., (1959) *A&P: A Study in Price-Cost Behaviour and Public Policy*, Harvard University Press, Cambridge MA.

Alexander, N., and McFetridge, D., (1995) Viewpoint: The Northern Ireland grocery sector – retrospect and prospect, *International Journal of Retail Distribution Management*, Vol. 23, No. 9, 4–7.

Bavarian State Chancellery, (1988) *Information about Bavaria*, Bayerische Staatskanzlei, Munich.

Benn, T., (1989) *Against the Tide, Diaries 1973–76*, Hutchinson, London.

Boddewyn, J., (1971) *Belgian Public Policy Toward Retailing Since 1789*, Michigan State University, East Lansing.

Burt, S., (1984) Hypermarkets in France: Has The Loi Royer had any Effect?, *Retail and Distribution Management*, January/February, Vol. 12, No. 1, pp. 16–19.

Dawson, J., (1976) Control Over Larger Units in France The Loi Royer and its Effects, *Retail and Distribution Management*, July/August, Vol. 4, No. 4, pp. 14–18.

Dawson, J., (1982) A Note on the Law of 29 June 1975 to Control Large Scale Retail Development in Belgium, *Environment & Planning*, A 14, pp. 291–6

European Economy, (1994a) *Competition and Integration: Community Merger Control Policy*, Commission of the European Communities, Brussels.

European Economy, (1994b) *Business and Consumer Survey Results*, No. 12, December, Supplement B, Commission of the European Communities.

Financial Times, (1996) Capital flow hits Taiwan payments balance, *Financial Times*, 28 February, p. 6.

Francois, P., and Leunis, J., (1991) Public Policy and the Establishment of Large Stores in Belgium, *The International Review of Retail, Distribution and Consumer Research*, Vol. 1, No. 4, pp. 469–86.

GB, (1993) Shopping in Germany: A Consumers Nightmare, *German Brief*, Vol. 5, No. 44, 5 November, pp. 6–7.

Gedye, R., (1995) Firebomb attack on Shell station, *Daily Telegraph*, Saturday 17 June, p. 7g.

Hallsworth, A., Jones, K., and Muncaster, R., (1994) New Retail Formats in Canada and Britain – The Planning Implications, *The Service Industries Journal*, Vol. 15, No. 4, pp. 148–63.

Harvie, C., (1994) *The Rise of Regional Europe*, Routledge, London.

Hollander, S., (1966) United States of America, in B. Yamey (ed.), *Resale Price Maintenance*, Weidenfeld and Nicholson, London, pp. 65–100.

Hollander, S., (1970) *Multinational Retailing*, Michigan State University, East Lancing, MI.

Hollander, S., (1972) Retailing and Public Policy: Retrospect and Prospect, in D. Allvine (ed.) *Public Policy and Marketing Practices*, p. 342.

Hollander, S., and Boddewyn, J. (1974) Retailing and Public Policy: An International Overview, *Journal of Retailing*, Vol. 50, No. 1, pp. 55–66, 91.

IRRR, (1993) 'Key-time' working at Allied Maples Group, *Industrial Relations Review & Report*, No. 546, October, pp. 12–16.

IRRR, (1994) Sunday Trading Act 1994: Employment Protection Rights, *Industrial Relations Review & Report*, No. 566, August, pp. 2–6.

Kacker, M., (1985) *Transatlantic Trends in Retailing*, Quorum, Connecticut.

Keen, S., (1994) Big Stores Set Standards for Wider Sunday Trading, *Personnel Management*, Vol. 26, No. 1, January, p. 19.

Kendall, S., and Dunne, N., (1996) Business spurs all-America free trade accord, *Financial Times*, 22 March, p. 3.

Kennett, J., (1993) Manufacturers should Heed German Lessons in Retail 'take-back' Programs, *Environment Today*, Vol. 4, No. 12, December, pp. 3, 19.

Kirby, D., (1992a) Government Control in Retailing, W. Howe, (ed.) *Retailing Management*, Macmillan, Basingstoke.

Kirby, D., (1992b) Employment in Retailing: Unsociable Hours and Sunday Trading, *International Journal of Retail & Distribution Management*, Vol. 20, No. 7, November/December, pp. 19–28.

Larke, R., (1992) Japanese Retailing: Fascinating, but Little Understood, *International Journal of Retail & Distribution Management*, Vol. 20, No. 1, pp. 3–15.

Larke, R., (1994) *Japanese Retailing*, Routledge, London.

Laushway, E., (1993) Paris – Row over Virgins Sunday sales, *Europe*, No. 330, October, pp. 40–2.

Leunis, J., and Francois, P., (1988) The Impact of Belgian Public Policy upon Retailing: The Case of the Second Padlock Law, E. Kaynak (ed.) *Transnational Retailing*, Walter de Gruyter, New York, pp. 135–53.

Litner, V., and Mazey, S., (1991) *The European Community: Economic and Political Aspects*, McGraw-Hill, Maidenhead.

Luce, E., and Bardacke, T., (1996) Fear of Beijing fuels Asean arms spending, *Financial Times*, 28 February, p. 6.

Marvel, H., (1993) Contracts and Control in Japanese Distribution, *Managerial & Decision Economics*, Vol. 14, No. 2, March/April, pp. 151–62.

Morgan, E., (1994) European Community Merger Control in the Service Industries, *The Service Industries Journal*, Vol. 14, No. 1, pp. 62–84.

Myers, H., (1995) The Changing Process of Internationalisation in the European Union, *The Service Industries Journal*, Vol. 15, No. 4, pp. 42–56.

Randelsome, C., (1993) *Business Cultures in Europe*, Butterworth-Heinemann, London.

Roddick, A., (1991) *Body & Soul*, Edbury Press, London.

Rodger, I., (1990) Stores Group Challenges Retail Law, *Financial Times*, 2 April, p. 2.

Schwarz, M., (1993) Land of the Giants, *Marketing Week*, Vol. 16, No. 29, 24 September, pp. 14–17

Shearlock, P., (1994) Not the Dream Ticket, *Banker*, Vol. 144, No. 818, April, pp. 47–8.

Siewart, C., (1992) C&A Brenninkmeyer, A. Hast, D. Pascal, P. Barbour, J. Griffin (eds) *International Directory of Company Histories*, Vol. V, St James Press, Detroit, pp. 23–4.

Stores, (1994) Health Care Reform – How Much Will It Cost You?, *Stores*, Vol. 75, No. 11, November, pp. 22–6.

Wrigley, N., (1992) Antitrust Regulation and the Restructuring of Grocery Retailing in Britain and the USA, *Environment and Planning*, A24, pp. 727–49.

Economy

OUTLINE

▌ OBJECTIVES ▌

The economic trading context in which retailers operate is examined in this chapter. It considers international retailers' place within that environment. The importance of the economic conditions within which retailers choose to operate is considered, together with those factors which create such environments.

INTRODUCTION

This chapter considers the economic environment in which retailers operate. Sophisticated retail formats require critical levels of economic development within markets to have been reached before operationalization is feasible. Although, retailers will be attracted to markets where retail structures have lagged behind developments in their market of origin, they will seek to expand in such markets only when those markets show indications of developing toward levels of economic development with which the company is familiar or where there are pockets of development which will support their operational requirements. Therefore, retailers have developed retail operations within a relatively limited set of economic circumstances in the recent phase of internationalization. Expansion has occurred in advanced economies or at specific locations in less advanced economies which have experienced urbanization and industrialization to an extent that more elaborate service facilities are viable.

This chapter also considers the economic trading environment of which international retailers are a part. The international trading environment which exists in the 1990s is supported by a number of regional institutions which were discussed in the previous chapter but also international institutions and agreements, such as the IMF and GATT, which are discussed in this chapter. Economic activity requires stability and this is particularly emphasized in the international trading environment in which concern over the financial insecurity of both countries and firms will be acute.

The economic conditions within countries are often taken to include a number of factors which are discussed in a separate and following chapter on social conditions. The economic issues discussed here are those factors which pertain to general market conditions. Specific issues of socio-economic development will be considered separately.

THE ECONOMIC TRADING ENVIRONMENT

International retail activity must be understood in the context of general patterns of international trade. There is a danger that by merely considering the direction of international retail activity too much emphasis is placed on the peculiarities of the retail trade and not enough emphasis is placed on the context in which retailers operate. Retailers within their national market are part of a wider commercial community. They are influenced by the same economic conditions as other sectors within their domestic economy. They are constrained by the same regulatory environment. They are influenced by the same cultural or sub-cultural environments which influences managers in other service businesses, manufacturing organizations, and primary industries.

Table 10.1 illustrates the changing trading relationships of France, Germany, the Netherlands and the UK. All three countries have seen their international trade become increasingly focused on their trading partners in the EU. At the same time, their trade with developing countries has declined as a percentage of their total trade. All four countries had strong trading links with distant parts of the world in the first half of the twentieth century. In the period 1958–91, the total international trade of these countries has grown considerably but there have been major shifts in trading partnerships, most notably toward other EU members.

Table 10.1 Structure of EU exports (selected countries): 1958 and 1991

	Fr	*Ger*	*Nl*	*UK*	*US/Can*	*Jap*	*Aust*	*Developing countries*
Percentage of total exports/imports								
France exports								
1958	–	10.4	2.0	4.9	6.7	0.3	0.5	46.7
1991	–	20.7	4.7	8.9	7.0	2.0	0.5	16.7
Imports								
1958	–	11.6	2.5	3.5	11.0	0.2	2.4	45.6
1991	–	20.7	6.6	7.6	9.1	2.9	0.3	12.8
Germany exports								
1958	7.6	–	8.1	3.9	8.5	0.9	1.0	20.9
1991	13.1	–	8.4	7.6	7.1	2.5	0.5	11.0
Imports								
1958	7.6	–	8.1	4.3	16.7	0.6	1.2	23.9
1991	12.2	–	11.8	6.4	6.8	5.3	0.3	10.8
Netherlands exports								
1958	4.9	19.0	–	11.9	6.4	0.4	0.7	17.6
1991	10.6	29.3	–	9.3	4.2	0.9	0.4	7.8
Imports								
1958	2.8	19.5	–	7.4	12.7	0.8	0.2	24.4
1991	7.0	23.5	–	8.0	9.0	5.4	0.4	15.6
United Kingdom exports								
1958	2.4	4.2	3.2	–	13.6	0.6	7.2	33.6
1991	11.0	13.7	7.9	–	12.6	2.2	1.3	15.8
Imports								
1958	2.7	3.6	4.2	–	17.6	0.9	5.4	34.7
1991	9.2	14.7	7.6	–	14.1	5.7	0.7	12.3
EU 12 exports								
1958	4.7	7.6	5.3	5.9	10.2	0.6	2.4	27.4
1991	11.2	14.5	6.3	7.4	7.2	2.0	0.6	12.8
Imports								
1958	4.4	8.7	5.2	5.4	15.0	0.7	2.6	29.5
1991	9.6	14.3	8.2	6.5	8.5	4.3	0.4	12.5

Source: European Economy, 1993b.

Outside the EU context, France, Germany, the Netherlands and the UK have witnessed a considerable increase in trade with Japan. German imports from Japan in 1991 represented nearly nine times the percentage of total German imports they did a third of a century earlier at the inception of the European Community in 1958. Conversely, UK exports to and imports from Australia have fallen dramatically. UK imports from Australia were nearly eight times higher as a percentage of total imports in 1958 compared with 1991.

The member countries of the EU send a high proportion of their traded goods to other member states. This may be interpreted as a strength of the Community which has facilitated concerted and closer development. It is also an important feature of trade within the developing global environment. However, not all regional associations have seen intra-regional trade attain as important a role in their trading practices. Table 10.2 shows how other trading bloc nations have failed to achieve high levels of intra-regional trade.

This failure to build intra-regional trade has often been the result of an unwillingness to open up markets and a lack of concerted effort on the behalf of the regional associations. While many in Europe may complain at the bureaucracy in Brussels, which is associated with the EU and its regulatory policies, lack of institutionalization in other regional associations has stifled attempts at integration and development. This has in itself led to a failure to establish ultimate objectives for the regional association. Governments come and go within regional associations but an established institutional framework has the ability to provide stability and consistency.

Among other regional associations, the Asean group has attained a relatively high level of intra-regional trade but this trade has not grown rapidly. The Asean group of Indonesia, Malaysia, Philippines, Singapore, Thailand and from 1984 Brunei, was established in August 1967 through the Bangkok Declaration, although, it was not until the Bali Concord of 1976 that a permanent Secretariat was established (European Economy, 1993a). There are a number of reasons why further intra-regional trade has not been achieved. While the organization has tried to establish a system of preferential trading arrangements, the commodities which were included in the agreements were of little importance to other members. The tariff reductions were also of limited magnitude, and non-tariff means of limiting trade were permitted to persist in a context where an institutional framework had not been established to ensure, or at least work toward, the success of these arrangements.

The Andean Pact, involving Bolivia, Colombia, Ecuador, Peru and, from 1973, Venezuela was established in October 1969 on the basis of the Acuerdo de

Table 10.2 Intra-regional trade of regional trading groups

	Percentage of total exports			
	1970	*1980*	*1990*	*% change 1970–90*
Andean pact	2.3	3.5	3.8	+65
CEAO	9.1	6.9	12.1	+33
Asean	14.7	17.8	18.5	+26

Source: European Economy, 1993a.

Cartagena of that year. However, political problems in the region and a reluctance of some countries to reduce barriers to trade have seen limited developments and intra-regional trade remains at a relatively low level. These problems, while by no means missing from the CEAO (Communauté économique de l'Afrique de l'Ouest), which was reconstituted in 1974 with Benin, Burkina Faso, Côte d'Ivoire, Mali, Mauritania, Niger and Senegal as members, have to some extent been overcome, at least in recent years. Despite considerable problems in the initial ten years of its existence, this regional association has made considerable headway toward integration. Apart from Mauritania, these states share a central bank and a common currency.

There are, therefore, a number of regional associations around the world that share in part, the integration envisaged by the EU. Nevertheless, despite some headway in the growth of intra-regional trade among some associations, the levels of intra-regional trade remains much lower than levels within the EU. When the figures in table 10.2 are compared with figures in table 10.1, it may be seen, for example, that 29.3 per cent of Dutch exports were sent to Germany alone by 1991, while 49.3 per cent of Dutch exports were sent to France, Germany and the UK. Other regional associations have a long way to go before they achieve the levels of integrated trade seen in the EU.

For international retailers, world trading blocs will offer an important opportunity for future expansion, as the cross-border activities of retailers within the EU illustrates. Retailers will follow general trading patterns as they exploit international opportunities. Thus, retailers will initially exploit opportunities within their own trading blocs unless there exist particular reasons for doing otherwise. Likewise, retailers will also be a part of general trends in Foreign Direct Investment (FDI). Table 10.3 shows the four most important sources of global FDI in the late 1980s. It illustrates the growth in importance of the economies of Germany and Japan, but it also illustrates the importance of the North American, European and Japanese markets as sources of investment within the context of world trade. Canada, France

Table 10.3 Global FDI

	Percentage				
	1960	*1980*	*1985*	*1988*	*% change 1960–88*
US	47.1	40.0	35.1	30.3	−35.6
Japan	0.7	7.0	11.7	16.9	+2,314.3
UK	18.3	14.8	14.7	16.3	−10.9
Germany	1.2	7.8	8.4	8.2	+583.3
Total (4)	76.4	69.6	69.9	71.7	
RoW	24.6	30.4	30.1	28.3	

Source: UNCTC, 1990.

Table 10.4 Fastest growing EU trading partnerships:
imports 1980–90

	1980–90 Cumulated growth (%)	*1990 Share (%)*	*1990 Value ECU m*
Turkey	464.4	1.3	5,943
China	437.1	2.3	10,603
Taiwan	308.7	2.0	9,159
Former Yugoslavia	251.8	1.7	7,684
Japan	230.9	10.0	46,224
Thailand	225.0	0.9	4,105
South Korea	215.4	1.4	6,557
Pakistan	212.8	0.3	1,461

Source: European Economy, 1993a.

and the Netherlands all had a share greater than 4 per cent of global FDI. These patterns are mirrored by international retail investment.

Trade between trading blocs is a significant proportion of world trade. The EU and the countries of the NAFTA illustrate this point. As important trading nations in their own right, the trade between these groups is doubly significant. In 1990, 21 per cent of EU imports came from the US, Canada and Mexico (European Economy, 1993a). If the trade between Japan and the EU is added to this calculation, a considerable proportion of imports is accounted for. In 1990, 10 per cent of EU imports came from Japan. The EU, NAFTA and Japan are major trading partners and also the major trading partners of other countries (see table 10.4). This makes these markets a focus of world trade.

Retailers operate within this context. Therefore, it is not surprising to find that retailers have expanded within this context into certain key markets. European retailers have invested considerable sums in North America and North American retailers have done likewise in Europe. Increasingly, North American and European retailers are taking an interest in the Japanese market. Therefore, while retailer activity mirrors these trends, it is also possible to say that international retail activity has tended to lag behind trends in trading patterns.

INTERNATIONAL AND NATIONAL DEVELOPMENTS

The reasons for the patterns of trade described above is the international trading structure which has been established during the second half of the twentieth century and the economic development of international markets. Consequently, the economic trading environment may be considered on two levels: those agreements and institutions which have been established at the international level to facilitate the movement of goods and those conditions which are imposed at the national level to restrict trade.

International financial and trade structures

There are three important institutions or agreements that facilitate world trade: GATT, the World Bank and the IMF. These entities are important in providing the stability that international businesses needed in the trading environment as it developed in the late twentieth century. Without these supports, trade would be short-termist in many cases and international retailers in particular would face considerable problems in developing international chains of stores.

GATT

The General Agreement on Tariffs and Trade is a recognition of the interrelationship of trading operations which exist within the global trading environment. As chapter 6 explained, free trade enables markets to specialize in the production of products to the benefit of the domestic and foreign market.

The GATT dates from 1947. The members of the GATT are responsible for more than 90 per cent of world trade. The objective of the agreement is the incremental reduction in tariffs. Thus, the GATT is periodically renegotiated and extended to other areas of international trade interest and a reduction in tariffs negotiated. Essentially, when tariffs are reduced in respect of imports from an individual country then, on the basis of the agreement, tariffs must be reduced for all signatories of the agreement. However, unequal agreements are permitted under GATT where countries are associated in a trading bloc. However, bilateral agreements such as the CUFTA, while they occur, may be considered to be essentially against the spirit of the agreement.

The World Bank

The World Bank, or to give its full title, the International Bank for Reconstruction and Development, grew out of the turmoil of the Second World War and, like the IMF, was conceived at the Bretton Woods negotiations in 1944. Its founding purpose was to provide long term capital investment to developing economies. Thus, in conjunction with the International Development Agency, which the World Bank established and which is particularly concerned with the development of the least advanced economies, the World Bank has funded projects in markets which would otherwise not attract investment, and in time, trade, which such markets need in order to stimulate development. Thus, international businesses are able to trade with markets which would otherwise not be of interest to them because of the higher risks involved.

IMF

The International Monetary Fund was a response to the problems of currency value fluctuations in the inter-war period as countries came off the gold standard. Like the World Bank it was established by the Bretton Woods agreement of 1944 and has contributed to the stability of the international trading system from that date, although the means by which it has achieved this has changed over the years. Until 1973, since when currencies have not been so rigorously pegged, the IMF member states were required to maintain the value of their currency within plus or minus 1 per cent of a par value that was pegged to the value of the dollar.

Within this early period, currencies such as Sterling (UK pound) were devalued, but this in itself was something of an economic and political event. In the 1960s and 1970s, apart from the structural changes in the world economy which required revaluation of currencies, the banking sector was increasing capable, through the increasingly large funds held, to move money from one currency to another and thereby put pressure on currency values which national banks were unable to support, because they were simply unable to match the funds that were determining new currency values.

As a consequence of this fundamental change in the banking world, currencies now float relative to each other. This raises problems for international businesses which were less significant in a period of pegged and stable currency values. Companies must now be aware of the currency changes which may have a significant effect on their profits when they are repatriated and on their operating costs when items such as merchandise is moved from one market to another.

The changes in the way currency rates are managed has had an effect on the IMF's role in the world. Nevertheless, it remains an important stabilizing factor in the global financial sector. The fund supports countries which have trade problems, although its support is linked to measures which the countries who benefit from its support must take in order to rectify their problems. The IMF, therefore, is an institution which has considerable financial influence and remains a focus of cooperative activity in financial markets.

Retailers and international trade structures

International trade agreements may seem remote from the everyday sales activity of retail operations but the influence of trading agreements on retailers may be immediate and dramatic. In the US, retailers will be directly affected by that countries series of trade agreements: NAFTA, GATT and the establishment of China's trading status as Most Favoured Nation (Liebeck, 1994). These agreements affect US retailers and in turn consumer prices which the retailers will pass on. The National Retail Federation, which has been campaigning for a greater say for retailers in the formulation of government policy, was very keen to see the federal administration sign the NAFTA and the GATT (Hartnett, 1993). They were also anxious that certain amendments should be voted down. US clothing retailers could have seen their costs rise if one amendment to the GATT legislation had been made: the so called 'Fruit of the Loom Amendment'. If the amendment had not been defeated, in the US Senate, imported supplies to US retailers would have been restricted and prices would have risen (Mundy, 1994). While, all of these agreements are important, Robin Lanier, who is vice president concerned with international trade issues for the International Mass Retail Association, has suggested that the GATT agreement will have a greater effect than NAFTA on the associations members, as it will lower prices in a problematic area of international tariffs and quotas. He has expressed particular concern that China should retain its Most Favoured Nation status, as this stops tariffs rising by 40 per cent (Roach, 1994).

Free trade agreements will benefit non-service sectors of the economy and hence have a beneficial effect on retail sales and the profitability of retail organizations. The bilateral trade agreements between Australia and New Zealand are particularly important to the New Zealand economy. Australia is New Zealand's main trading partner, and therefore, although, the latest GATT agreement, which was signed in April 1994, will bring benefits as far as its wider trading activities are concerned, many of the benefits of free trade are to be felt in respect of Australia. New Zealand has a number of manufacturing advantages that Australia does not possess. That is good for the New Zealand economy and that is consequently good for the New Zealand consumer. In such contexts, the retail sector has benefited. Thus, by the middle of 1994, New Zealand retailers were experiencing strong consumer demand and healthy low stock levels (Yarwood, 1994).

Likewise, free trade agreements will facilitate the development of infrastructure which in turn will allow retailers to operate on the basis of commercial assumptions with which they are familiar. Real Estate Investment Trusts in Canada, for example, will be able to access opportunities in Mexico under the NAFTA agreement which would not otherwise appear as attractive. A Canadian consortium are, for example, developing a large area in Mexico City which, while also having residential, office and hotel properties, will include retail units (Palm, 1994).

The GATT agreement, where it is geographically extended, may bring in large markets to the free trade arrangements. China is one such market. Manufacturing operations such as Singer Shanghai, part of International Semi-Tech Microelectronics Incorporated, are seeking new opportunities in this market at an early date in order to avoid the problems of market entry once the market has become more established as a target amongst international operations (Banks, 1994). The company includes the Singer operation which was an important early player in the internationalization of retailing in Europe.

The Far East promises to be an important market for international retailers in the future. The lifting of trade restrictions are an important element in the development of these markets by international retailers. At the GATT talks, in December 1993, South Korea announced that it intended to lift some of the country's restrictions on international trade. South Korea's representatives announced a plan to lift totally restrictions on the number of stores permitted to one retailer and maximum floor space restrictions (Business Korea, 1994).

While the GATT does bring benefits to world markets, it does not mean that retailers will not find the tariff and non-tariff restrictions noted above. Mexico is a member of GATT, but imports are subject to a number of formal and informal controls. Import taxes of around 20 per cent are not unusual, and may be higher, while customs duties will add 5 per cent to costs, before the imposition at the point of sale of a 10 per cent sales tax (Silverstein, 1993). The relatively undeveloped Mexican distribution system and retail structure will informally restrict retail distribution developments. While Mexican department stores have reached a certain level of development, they only account for 20 per cent of retail sales. Thus, distributors will find accessing the small local traders an expensive activity. At this level, it may be argued, especially with the signing of the NAFTA, that international retailers will have an important role to play in easing some of these problems.

Likewise, local regulations on copyright may frustrate trade in various ways. In Japan, a new copyright law came into force at the beginning of January 1992. The law allowed both Japanese and international companies operating in Japan the right to prohibit renting of compact discs for one year after their release onto the market and the legal right to claim royalties on rentals for fifty years after a compact disc's original release date (Tanaka, 1992). While this may be welcomed by Japanese shop owners, US compact disc producers believed it would lead to illegal copying and thus, far from supporting sales in the first twelve months of the compact disc's life, it would actually lead to a decrease in sales.

How important are free trade areas to retailers?

While the discussion above has emphasized the importance of free trade areas to retailers, there will always remain some doubt as to the their absolute importance. Schools of thought tend to vary between the belief that international expansion would have happened anyway, despite the establishment of free trade agreements, and, the alternative belief that, free trade agreements are fundamentally important and stimulate international activity. Press statements will tend to anticipate huge benefits, post hoc academic analysis will often attempt to repudiate their effect and retailers will claim that they would have done whatever they did anyway.

It has been suggested that the arrival of the NAFTA will have a major impact on retail operations in Mexico, with indigenous retailers being forced to take note of the technological advances of US retailing such as credit and debit card services, bar-coding, improved layouts and lighting systems and the operating systems expertise of the incoming US operations, who would surely see in the Mexican market an ideal opportunity for expansion (Malkin, 1994). Conversely, academics may suggest that retailers, when asked their opinion may be more sanguine about the advantages of the free trade area at the same time as they take advantage of it (Alexander and Morlock, 1994).

Mexico has been of long term interest to US retailers. Sears Roebuck first entered the market in 1947 (Hollander, 1970). Nevertheless, the recent interest shown in retail opportunities in Mexico will inevitably be assessed in the light of the NAFTA. The fact that recent international moves across the border into Mexico have been described as a flood, in contrast to the previous trickle, would suggest that such agreements have had a positive effect (Stores, 1994). Nevertheless, bilateral or trilateral agreements may not have as great an impact as multilateral agreements such as the GATT (Roach, 1994).

10.1 Identity

In many parts of Europe, regional democracy and locally inspired economic initiatives have increased the opportunity to attract industrial development and create wealth amongst consumers. There is, however, a negative side to such developments, where revenue needs encourage regional governments to take money out of the pockets of consumers.

The Institute of Fiscal Studies in the UK published a report in 1996, which looked at the revenue needs of regions of the UK, if funds had to be raised locally. In Scotland, the UK government spends 14 per cent per capita more than it does in the south east of England, and 4 per cent more in the north of England than the English regional average. If Scottish income tax payers were to directly fund government expenditure, in Scotland the basic rate of income tax would rise to 37 per cent. This would be an increase of 13 pence in every pound. A similar approach in the north-west of England would bring local income tax to 27.9 per cent. If VAT rather than income tax was raised in Scotland the new rate would be 27 per cent rather than 17.5 per cent.

Although, some political groups in Scotland would argue that Scotland did not see the benefits it should have done from North Sea oil exploitation, in the context of a political debate where increased devolution is on the agenda, such issues are relevant to international retail expansion in even the most apparently politically stable markets.

Soruce: Tett and Buxton, 1996.

What free trade agreements such as the SEM and NAFTA often achieve is a reorientation of economic geography. Retailers will play a primary role in this reorientation. In Europe certain 'border' areas, such as the German side of the Danish-German border have benefited from the movement of shoppers across the border to avoid higher levels of value added tax in Denmark. In Europe, the central belt of regions from the South East of England through Eastern France and through Western Germany to Northern Italy, the Dorsal, is evidence of economic integration and in turn cross-border trade and the development of a core area for future economic growth.

In North America, the same type of cross-border consumer traffic has also occurred, but with the NAFTA will continue on a more sure footing. Most of the Canadian population live within relatively easy driving distance (200 miles) of the US border. Thus, cross border traffic in consumer goods has become an important aspect of their retail trade for some border towns. Mexican consumers have sought consumer products in US towns such as El Paso and Brownsville in Texas. Likewise, as the NAFTA takes effect, the San Antonio to Austin corridor may see substantial development given is relationship to the Mexican-US border (Hazel, 1994).

10.2 Taxman

On 25 March 1996, many Italian shopkeepers closed their stores to protest against taxation levels in Italy. The shopkeepers, many of them supporters of Silvio Berlusconi's right-wing alliance, were protesting against the level of taxation in the Italian economy.

The shop closure occurred in the run up to the Italian general election of April 1996, where Berlusconi faced the centre-left alliance of Romano Prodi.

The issue, while important to small traders like shopkeepers, was not one that either of the political opponents would necessarily be able to address with any vigour. Italy's budget deficit has placed it in a difficult position with respect to the Maastrict criteria for European Union. If Italy is to meet the criteria, it must maintain a level of fiscal management which will not warm the hearts of Italian shopkeepers eager for lower taxation.

Source: Hill, 1996.

As Mexican retailers face the operational sophistication of US retailers (Malkin, 1994), Canadian retailers are also reacting to the threat of US intruders. Zellers the Canadian retailer is planning to use large formats and develop EDI systems as a part of an attempt to be more competitive in the context of increased activity in the Canadian market by US firms (Roach, 1993). For Zellers, though, the NAFTA is not merely a threat but also an opportunity in that it provides the company with new sourcing opportunities. Clearly, however, such a response by an established firm is possible, whereas in Mexican retailing, such a response, while desirable may not be possible given relative size of retail operations in Mexico.

Sourcing is an important issue in the context of free trade areas and the assessment of their value to cross-border retail activity. US retailers will benefit considerably from the sourcing opportunities in Mexico in the next few years as US retailers recognize the new trading relationships (Silva, 1993). This type of relationship between Mexican suppliers and US retailers will increase the likelihood of retailers moving operations into the market from which they source. The US Hagger Apparel Company clothing supplier was operating in the Mexican market for more than a decade before the NAFTA took effect and illustrates the advantages that the Mexican market has been seen to have, namely as a manufacturing opportunity. However, increasingly retail opportunities are being recognized (Cedrone, 1992).

One of the most important economic benefits of a free trade area, which is easily overlooked in the consideration of the more detailed advantages to be gained in specific sectors, is that it provides a large market in which to operate. The ASEAN free trade area, for example, provides Singapore and incoming investors with a large market which the city of Singapore does not provide. Singapore in this respect provides a good base for operations within the ASEAN area (Business Asia, 1993a). The ASEAN area offers opportunities to food retailers and suppliers alike as the market shows a growth potential not available in some regions of the world (Business Asia, 1993b).

National barriers to trade

Barriers to trade may take different forms. Some barriers, such as tariffs and quotas are overt, others which may be described as non-tariff barriers may not be immediately obvious to potential market entrants.

Tariffs are designed to protect local industry and also provide government revenue. They may take different forms. An 'ad valorem' tax will increase according to the value of the product. Therefore, a retailer bringing goods into a country to sell in its outlets will have to pay £100 on goods worth £1,000 where the tariff rate is 10 per cent . Rather than the 'ad valorem' rate, there may be a specific rate which applies. Therefore, a tax of £100 may be levied on a product irrespective of its cost. A retailer bringing in a product valued at £500 or £1,000 would therefore attract the same level of tax as long as it conformed to the same general specification. These two taxes may be combined as a compound tariff so that in the example above, a £100 charge as well as a 10 per cent charge would be levied.

Quotas may also be imposed. They will limit imports to a specific quantity or value. Retailers would in this instance have either to be aware that their supply might be erratic or restricted, in which case retailers may wish to consider sourcing locally.

Non-tariff barriers may cause international operations considerable problems. This may include subsidies to local organizations, inappropriate anti-dumping regulations, foreign exchange controls, product standard regulations, as well as customs and documentation requirements. They are the type of problems that retailers must be very conscious of when entering a new market as they may make it very difficult to use the retailer's operating techniques, especially where the retailer has a particular format or distinct, and brand specific, product line.

MARKET CLASSIFICATION

Government control

It is usual in descriptions of global trading conditions to discuss markets in terms of 'market economies' and 'command economies'. While events of recent years have undermined the statement that the world's economies may be divided amongst these two groups, it is still possible to observe that economies lie somewhere, as indeed they always have done, between those two extremes: that is, where market forces are dominant and where market forces have a limited role to play. The position which countries occupy across this spectrum is, however, an important factor in determining international trade. International retailers have clearly favoured those markets where controls are limited, although, as in the case of the Republic of China, retailers will be aware that even partial liberalization provides access to a potentially large market.

Demographics

Market size

The population of a market is also important in determining its attractiveness. Although a large market with limited economic activity will not be attractive for its own sake, markets with large populations will be attractive in their own right as they will avoid international business having to adapt to numerous regulatory conditions in a number of different markets. Thus, the US market is attractive because of its size and the high levels of disposable income within it, and why EU is more attractive than the individual markets of which it is constituted.

Table 10.5 provides demographic data for markets around the world. It is clear from the table why China is seen as a market with considerable potential. With a population of over 1 billion people, it is much larger than the combined population of the EU and NAFTA. Conversely, in Singapore, with a high population density of over 4,000 people per square kilometre and a buoyant economy, the market is small at only 2.8 million. The annual rate of population increase is indicative of one of the factors that encourages international retail expansion. The European markets included in table 10.5 have less than 1 per cent annual population growth, with some markets barely replacing (Belgian, Denmark Spain, UK) or failing to replace (the Eastern German Lander) their populations.

Market growth

Population projections provide important indicators for international businesses. If international retailers were to limit themselves to those markets which they have primarily targeted in the thirty years 1965–95, in the following thirty years 1995–2025, they would be serving a declining proportion of the world population. Table 10.6 shows the considerable differences in the future populations of world markets. The growth in the Chinese population between 1995 and 2025 is projected to be greater than the current EU population. In contrast, many of the countries of the EU are predicted declining populations. The Western Lander and Eastern Lander figures are given separately but the theme is the same: a declining German population throughout the next thirty years. If the EU is to see an increase in the number of consumers in its domestic market then it will have to look to expansion to the east; although, the markets of Eastern Europe are not themselves experience large population increases and the inclusion of such markets would not add considerable population numbers.

In Asia, there are contrasts as far as population growth is concerned. While Japan will experience Western European growth figures, other industrialized markets in the Far East, such as South Korea, will see a substantial increase in its population. The markets of Africa and Latin America will also see considerable growth. The Brazilian market alone will be a similar size to the current EU in the year 2025. In

Table 10.5 Population statistics: 1992

Country	Mid year estimates millions	Annual rate of increase (%)	Density per sq km
Nigeria	115.7	2.7	125
South Africa	39.8	2.4	33
Uganda	18.7	3.1	77
Zaire	39.9	3.6	17
Canada	27.4	1.2	3
Mexico	89.5	2.0	46
US	255.0	1.0	27
Argentina	33.1	1.2	7
Brazil	156.3	2.0	18
Chile	13.6	1.6	18
Venezuela	20.3	2.2	22
China	1,188.0	1.5	124
Hong Kong	5.8	0.9	5,406
India	870.0	2.1	265
Japan	124.3	0.4	329
Korea South	43.7	1.0	440
Saudi Arabia	15.9	3.6	7
Singapore	2.8	1.8	4,560
Hungary	10.3	−0.3	111
Poland	38.4	0.4	119
Ukraine	52.1	0.3	86
Belgium	10.0	0.2	328
Denmark	5.2	0.2	120
France	57.4	0.6	104
Germany (W)	64.8	0.9	261
Germany (E)	15.7	−0.8	145
Ireland	3.5	0.0	51
Netherlands	15.2	0.7	372
Spain	39.1	0.2	77
UK	57.9	0.3	237
Australia	17.5	1.5	2
New Zealand	3.4	0.8	13

Source: United Nations, 1994.

North America, the increase in the Mexican population will surpass the figure for the entire Canadian population.

In those countries with lower birth rates, formal female employment rates are much higher and contribute to the trend whereby mothers give birth later than

Table 10.6 Population growth projections (medium variant): 1995–2025

Country	1995 (millions)	2005 (millions)	2015 (millions)	2025 (millions)
Nigeria	127.7	174.3	228.8	280.9
South Africa	39.4	48.1	57.2	65.4
Uganda	22.7	31.7	42.6	53.1
Zaire	41.8	57.8	78.1	99.4
Canada	27.6	29.3	30.9	31.9
Mexico	98.0	116.3	133.8	150.1
US	258.2	273.5	288.3	299.9
Argentina	34.3	38.2	42.1	45.5
Brazil	165.1	193.6	221.0	245.9
Chile	14.2	16.3	18.1	19.8
Venezuela	22.2	27.3	32.7	38.0
China	1,222.6	1,354.2	1,435.7	1,512.6
Hong Kong	6.1	6.5	6.5	6.5
India	946.7	1,134.7	1,304.0	1,442.4
Japan	125.9	130.5	130.4	127.5
Korea South	68.6	76.0	81.1	84.7
Saudi Arabia	17.1	24.9	34.6	44.8
Singapore	2.9	3.1	3.2	3.3
Hungary	10.5	10.5	10.4	10.2
Poland	39.4	41.5	43.5	45.1
Belgium	9.9	9.8	9.6	9.4
Denmark	5.2	5.1	5.0	4.9
France	57.1	58.9	59.8	60.4
Germany (W)	61.1	60.0	57.8	55.1
Germany (E)	16.2	16.2	16.2	15.8
Ireland	3.9	4.3	4.6	5.0
Netherlands	15.4	16.2	16.6	16.9
Spain	40.0	41.3	41.9	42.3
UK	57.9	58.7	59.3	59.7
Australia	17.9	19.8	21.5	23.0
New Zealand	3.5	3.8	4.0	4.1

Source: United Nations, 1991.

mothers in those countries where early marriages are more usual. In Brazil, children are very likely (31 per cent) to be born when their mother is in the age group 20–4 (United Nations, 1994). In the Western Lander of Germany children are more likely (41 per cent) to be born to mothers in the 25–9 age bracket. In some countries, such as Germany, changes in fertility rates in different age groups has changed rapidly in only a short space of time. In 1983, 37,711 children were born to mothers in the age group 35–9, by 1990 that number had risen to 61,243. In comparison, the number of births to women in the 20–4 age group fell from 169,145 to 143,361.

Urbanization

The percentage of the population living in the urban environment is an indicator of economic development and is clearly the precursor of the type of retail structural development which has emerged in the twentieth century in the US and West European countries. Urbanization levels when set against life expectancy figures provide an indication of the economic well being of the population and the market environment.

Table 10.7 illustrates the considerable differences which exist in urbanization levels and life expectance figures. High urbanization figures combined with high

Table 10.7 Urbanization and life expectancy at birth

Country	Year	Urban Population (%)	Year	Life expectancy	
				Female	Male
Nigeria	1988	16.1	1985–90	52	49
South Africa	1991	56.6	1985–90	64	58
Uganda	1991	11.3	1985–90	46	43
Zaire	1985	39.3	1985–90	53	50
Canada	1991	76.6	1985–7	80	73
US	1990	75.2	1989	79	72
Argentina	1992	86.4	1980–1	73	66
Brazil	1992	76.1	1985–90	68	62
Chile	1992	85.1	1985–90	75	68
Venezuela	1990	84.0	1985	73	67
China	1990	25.2	1985–90	71	68
Hong Kong	1986	93.1	1990	80	75
India	1992	26.0	1981–5	56	55
Japan	1990	77.4	1991	82	76
Korea South	1990	74.4	1989	75	67
Hungary	1992	63.1	1991	74	65
Poland	1991	61.9	1991	75	66
France	1990	74.0	1990	81	73
Ireland	1986	56.4	1985–87	77	71
Netherlands	1990	88.7	1990–1	80	74
Australia	1986	85.4	1991	80	74
New Zealand	1991	84.9	1989–91	78	72

Source: United Nations, 1994.

life expectancy figures are associated with those markets that international retailers have already begun to exploit. The Netherlands, with 88.7 per cent of its population living in the urban environment with a female life expectancy of 80 years, is an example of such a market. In comparison, the low life expectancy levels and low urbanization levels of much of Africa are representative of environmental conditions unsuited to the type of operations which retailers have recently transferred from one market to another in Europe, North America and the Far East. The high urbanization levels and relatively high life expectancy levels of Latin America may be indicative of markets that may in the future once again attract international retailers in some numbers as Eastern Europe has attracted retailers in the 1990s.

While urbanization is certainly not a guarantee of a sophisticated retail structure, consideration of national markets will soon reveal opportunities for retail development. The US has the kind of urban environment that will support a sophisticated retail system. The US not only has a large number of cities with populations in excess of 100,000, but also has smaller city locations with extensive urban or suburban development to support the city retail facilities. A town like Fayettevill, North Carolina, may only have a population of 76,000 but it is part of an urban agglomeration of 275,000 people (United Nations, 1994). Boston has a population of 574,000 but the urban agglomeration of which it is a part is 5.5 million.

Economic output

Markets may also be classified in terms of economic development. Common measure of development are GNP or GDP per capita figures. In countries with a high GNP/GDP per capita figures there will be a different economic structure to those with a low GNP/GDP per capita figures. In the former markets, service industries make a far more significant contribution to GDP calculations than in the latter, where agriculture will contribute a higher share of economic activity.

Table 10.8 Unemployment rate in selected major world economies

| | *Percentage* | | | | |
	1960	*1970*	*1980*	*1990*	*1993*
France	0.7	2.4	6.2	9.0	10.8
Germany	1.0	0.5	2.7	4.8	6.0
Netherlands	0.7	1.0	6.4	7.5	7.6
EU 12	2.5[a]	2.4	6.0	8.3	10.6
US	5.4	4.9	7.1	5.5	7.2
Japan	1.7	1.2	2.0	2.1	2.2

[a] Europe of the 9.

Source: European Economy, 1993b.

Table 10.9 Economic indicators in selected markets: annual change to the end of 1995

	GDP growth (%)	Rate of inflation (%)	Retail sales volume (%)
Australia	+3.3	+5.1	+4.8
Canada	+1.9	+2.1	+1.2
France	+2.1	+1.9	+4.8
Germany	+1.5	+1.7	+5.0
Japan	−0.2	−0.7	+0.5
UK	+2.1	+3.1	+1.1
US	+3.3	+2.6	+4.0

Source: Economist, 1996.

International retailers, as part of the service sector, will tend to enter more developed markets. Specific local conditions or associations may encourage some international retail expansion but international activity is primarily focused on developed markets with relatively high levels of GDP per capita and a developed service sector and those markets where GDP growth and the associated need for service sector development encourages expansion. Other important economic measures such as productivity, inflation, balance of payments, reserves, savings, interest rates, money supply and the purchasing power parity (ppp) within a market must also be considered before international expansion is considered.

These different indicators will have important implications for retail operations. For example, inflation is an important factor for any international business but this will be particularly important for international retailers. Retailers operating in inflationary economies will not only face the operational problems such as constant price alterations but also the exchange rate implications which will face an inflationary economy. This will therefore be an important consideration for retailers in markets outside the core international trading regions. Table 10.8 and table 10.9 provide some comparative market indicators for a selection of markets from around the world.

CONCLUSION

The markets of Africa have not seen international developments in recent years not least because of the political uncertainty in these markets, yet they have attracted operations in the past. Likewise, South America has attracted international retail expansion. Carrefour's operations is evidence of some interest being shown in these markets. However, they remain outside the interest of many international operators.

International retail expansion is still essentially a feature of the more developed markets of the world. The indicators used above are extensively used by businesses considering operations in non-domestic markets. For the retailer, it is particularly important that these indicators should be considered over a relatively long time frame. This is because retailers will be more exposed than other businesses which simply export products to non-domestic markets. The retailer is often in the same position as the manufacturing business which owns production facilities in the non-domestic market. Therefore, retailers who are uncertain about the long term opportunities in a market, may seek market presence through such methods as franchised operations, which thereby limit their exposure within a market.

QUESTIONS – DISCUSSION POINTS

1   How is the GATT important to retailers?

2   By what measurements should retailers evaluate economic conditions?

3   Are regional associations making international trade less global in nature?

4   Which area has the most attractive long term investment potential for retailers, the Far East or Europe?

REFERENCES

Alexander, N., and Morlock, W., (1992) Saturation and Internationalization: The Future of Grocery Retailing in the UK, *International Journal of Retail & Distribution Management*, Vol. 20, No. 3, 1992, pp. 33–9.

Banks, B., (1994) One billion Buyers, Easy Credit Terms, *Canadian Business*, Vol. 67, No. 6, June, pp. 33–5.

Business Asia, (1993a) Singapore: Boring but Buoyant, *Business Asia*, Vol. 25, No. 3, 1 February, p. 9.

Business Asia, (1993b) Lining Up at the Banquet, *Business Asia*, Vol. 25, No. 23, 8 November, pp. 6–7.

Business Korea, (1994) Wholesale Changes, *Business Korea*, Vol. 11, No. 7, January, pp. 26–7.

Cedrone, L., (1992) Why Wait for NAFTA? *Bobbin*, Vol. 33, No. 10, June, pp. 14, 16.

Economist, (1996) *Economist*, London, 13 January.

European Economy, (1993a) *The European Community as a World Trade Partner*, No. 52, Commission of the European Communities, Brussels.

European Economy, (1993b) *Annual Economic Report*, No. 54, Commission of the European Communities, Brussels.

Hartnett, M., (1993) Call to Action, *Stores*, Vol. 75, No. 2, February, pp. 20–2.

Hazel, D., (1994) Stars Shine on the Lone Star State, *Chain Store Age Executive*, Vol. 70, No. 3, March, pp. 181–4.

Hill, A., (1996) Italy's irate shopkeepers offered new tax policies, *Financial Times*, 26 March, p. 2.

Hollander, S., (1970) *Multinational Retailing*, East Lansing MI: Michigan State University.

Liebeck, L., (1994) Legislation and Regulatory Burdens Place Potholes in Path of Mass Retailers, *Discount Store News*, Vol. 33, No. 10, 16 May, pp. 39–45.

Malkin, E., (1994) Mexico Retail Feels Nafta Pinch, *Advertising Age*, Vol. 65, No. 3, 17 January, pp. 1–4.

Mundy, A. (1994) Fruitless, *Brandweek*, Vol. 35, No. 32, 8 August, pp. 1, 6.

Palm, L., (1994) The Canadian Connection, *Commercial Investment Real Estate Journal*, Vol. 13, No. 1, pp. 20–1.

Roach, L., (1993) North of the Border, *Discount Merchandiser*, Vol. 33, No. 11, November, pp. 32–6.

Roach, L. (1994) The Trade Horizon: NAFTA, GATT, and China, *Discount Merchandiser*, Vol. 34, No. 5, May, pp. 92–4.

Silva, F., (1993) Mexico: The Making of a New Market, *Bobbin*, Vol. 34, No. 12, August, pp. 38–46.

Silverstein, J., (1993) What's the Price? The Arbitrary Science of Determining Markup, *Business Mexico*, Vol. 2, No. 10, 2 October, pp. 11–12.

Stores, (1994) Major Chains Look to Mexico for Growth Opportunities, *Stores*, Vol. 76, No. 8, August, pp. 33–4.

Tanaka, R., (1992) GATT Proposal May Satisfy Foreign Companies: Japan's CD Rental Shops Find Hope for Survival, *Japan Times Weekly International Edition*, Vol. 32, No. 6, p. 7.

Tett, G., and Buxton, J., (1996) Scots rule 'would push basic tax to 37p', *Financial Times*, 28 March, p. 8.

UNCTC, (1990) *Regional Economic Integration and the Transnational Corporations in the 1990s*, United Nations Centre on Transnational Corporations, United Nations, New York.

United Nations, (1991) *World Population Prospects 1990*, United Nations Publication, New York.

United Nations, (1994) *Demographic Yearbook 1992*, United Nations Publication, New York.

Yarwood, V. (1994) Manufacturing: Driving the Economy, *Management-Auckland*, Vol. 41, No. 7, August, pp. 62–5.

Society

▌ OBJECTIVES ▌

This chapter is concerned with the social environment in which retailers operate. It is concerned with those issues which are the context for shopper behaviour and purchasing patterns and those characteristics of the market which contribute to the social context in which retailers recruit their workforce.

INTRODUCTION

The social environment is a synthesis of the economic and cultural influences which act on society. The social characteristics which are a product of these influences demand separate attention from the influences themselves. Economics will play a profound role in determining the social characteristics of a market; however, it would be shallow to conclude that all markets with specific levels of economic development will see the same social developments. These differences will be created by cultural influences. Similar patterns of social development may emerge, on the basis of economic conditions, but throughout the world there is sufficient divergence in social conditions to conclude that social difference is not simply a product of economic development and thereby requires separate consideration.

The social environment is measured and characterized by the artefacts of everyday existence, the physical representation of economic wealth, and an individual's personal interaction with the social environment, which is the social manifestation of cultural values. That is, individuals will own certain items such as books, cars, televisions, telephones and washing machines, they will live in household units, work in particular settings, have educational and intellectual aspirations, engage in leisure pursuits and visit places of entertainment. These characteristics will influence consumption patterns and shopping habits. It is therefore essential that the international retailer appreciates the significance of the social environment.

RETAILERS AND SOCIETY

In chapter 9, the role of the political environment in determining the context in which retailing develops and structural problems are created and addressed, has been discussed. The legal system will in part determine the interaction of retailer and customer, retailer and employee. In turn, the legal system, will have been influenced by the prevailing views of society which, in part, will have been formed through day to day relationships with retailers. In this, retailing is a reflection of contemporary culture (du Gay, 1993). The importance of this interaction has not been sufficiently developed within retail studies. Further emphasis for example could be placed on the sociological aspects of retailing in retail management study programmes (Jones, 1993).

The importance of retailers' sustained interaction with the social environment is easily forgotten in a context where management issues are considered within a narrow time frame. However, with a longer viewpoint, such interaction becomes a significant part of the retail landscape. For example, in the UK, in the mid-nineteenth century, when small retail operations served the public and could not be easily controlled, adulteration of food items was a considerable problem, not least because of the length of the distribution channel. The result was a body of legislation designed to protect the customer against such practices as adding chalk to flour in order to make up weight and profit. Such practices of adulteration were important factors behind the establishment of the early cooperative stores, as customers sought cheaper, reliable goods. Consumer cooperatives offered the nineteenth century consumer the type of guarantee that retail brands offer the consumer in the late twentieth century.

Employment law has evolved as social problems emerge. In the nineteenth century, long hours for shop staff were gradually reduced, and conditions improved. Abuse by retailers has resulted in legislation which protects staff, and, as may be seen from the German example of the regulation of opening hours, employment conditions are jealously guarded.

Retailers influence social change and are a reflection of those changes. Retailers are increasingly seeking to meet the needs of those customers and balance those needs with the needs of the workforce. In developed retail systems which have seen the introduction of the superstore or hypermarket operations, retailers have extended opening hours where possible to cater for dual income households which require opening hours outside the '9 'till 5' day. In some markets, such as the UK and the US, retailers have been able to extend their opening hours as employees seek work in the evenings or at weekends. Superstore retailers have been able to establish more suitable work patterns as employees seek part-time hours.

Out of town retail sites are a response to the increasingly mobile consumer. Such consumers have greater purchasing power and a limited amount of time in which to shop. Retailers have responded to these changes, but in so doing, they have fundamentally changed other consumers' shopping patterns and many would suggest they have left less prosperous members of the community isolated from essential services and retail requirements.

Retail opportunities arise as customers acquire new possessions. Grocery outlets have rapidly increased their provision of frozen and chilled food as customers acquire better facilities for storing such products. Indeed, sectors within retailing have merged as the customer's living conditions change. DIY centres are a product of increased home ownership and changing social habits, whereby services are not necessarily bought in, but carried out, by members of the household unit.

Therefore, when assessing a market, retailers should look for certain indicators which will provide a social picture of the consumer environment into which the retailer considers moving. These may be broadly classified as material possessions, household conditions, work as a lifestyle delineator, and leisure activities as lifestyle delineator.

MATERIAL POSSESSIONS

The wealth of any one market may be measured in terms of the gross domestic product of that market. The economic wealth of a market may also be measured by the material possessions which are owned in that market. Possessions, while not a direct reflection of wealth, are an indicator of it. However, such possessions hold an important key to understanding the social environment of that market. Consumption patterns and ownership figures are indicative of social conditions and lifestyle. These conditions and lifestyles may vary considerably between and also within markets as table 11.1 shows with reference to regional markets in the EU.

Differences in GDP per capita figures vary enormously within the EU. They vary considerably even within the 'national' markets of the EU, as the regional figures in table 11.1 indicate. These differences are reflected in the material possessions that the populations of those regions possess. In Spain, in the Sur, and in Italy, in the Sud, the ownership of private cars, telephones and TVs is much lower than

Table 11.1 EU material possessions (selected markets): 1985

	GDP in Ecu per capita EU 12 = 100	Private cars per per 1,000 capita	Telephone subscriptions per 1,000 capita	TV per 1,000 capita
France	115	387	402	327
Ile-de-France	171	358	477	323
Centre-Est	109	407	399	323
Nord-Pas-de-Calais	94	324	332	319
Germany	128	424	424	346
Hessen	148	451	417	356
Baden-Wurtenberg	135	440	412	348
Niedersachsen	110	414	437	348
Spain	69	231	136	267
Madrid	87	272	213	282
Noreste	80	231	176	271
Sur	54	183	81	253
Italy	103	394	274	254
Lombardia	135	447	326	291
Nord-Ovest	120	455	352	306
Sud	69	276	173	221

Source: Eurostat, 1993.

in other regions of the EU such as Hessen or the Ile-de-France. The importance of these indicators varies over time and must be considered in their temporal context. Telephones and TVs have become almost *de rigueur* in some parts of the world, but the incidence of such items may still indicate important social differences. In Niedersachsen, while GDP per capita is below that of Hessen, subscriptions to telephones is higher than in Hessen. In such a context, telephone subscriptions do not delineate social difference but, in Spain, the difference in GDP figures, and the absolute levels of GDP per capita, are crucial enough to delineate difference. Thus, Sur with a low level of GDP per capita is distinct from Madrid on other measures as well.

Housing facilities are also indicative of social conditions. It is important to remember that certain characteristics will not reflect the same values in two societies. The number of households with WCs, will to some extent, reflect levels of wealth, other factors will not. In the UK, home ownership has become associated with social aspirations and rented dwellings with lack of social achievement. The 1980s, in particular, were a time when home ownership became entwined with the political philosophy of self-help and success. As table 11.2 shows, in Germany, a country with high levels of GDP per capita, home ownership is relatively low because of the large number of rented properties. The legal framework, which

Table 11.2 EU housing characteristics (selected markets): 1985

	GDP in Ecu per capita EU 12 = 100	Rented dwelling (%)	Single family buildings (%)	Households with WC
France	115	34	45	70
Ile-de-France	171	47	22	77
Centre-Est	109	33	37	69
Nord-Pas-de-Calais	94	35	70	63
Germany	128	59	28	98
Hessen	148	58	28	99
Baden-Wurtenberg	135	54	28	99
Niedersachsen	110	53	37	98
Spain	69	19	33	91
Madrid	87	20	11	97
Noreste	80	20	34	83
Sur	54	16	46	87
Italy	103	28	23	79
Lombardia	135	37	16	87
Nord-Ovest	120	33	14	76
Sud	69	21	35	72

Source: Eurostat, 1993.

controls rental agreements, is obviously an important factor in determining the number of dwellings available for rent, but social assumptions are also important. In Germany, renting properties is socially acceptable. In table 11.2, the figures given for France show that in the Ile-de-France, while the level of GDP per capita is high, the level of rented properties is also high. The Ile-de-France includes Paris where levels of wealth are high compared to other parts of the country and where, in the urban environment, rented properties are more numerous and appropriate to social conditions. In contrast, in Sur in Spain the GDP per capita is low but the number of rented properties is also low. In an agricultural environment this is socially appropriate.

In the UK, buildings containing single family dwellings are considered socially desirable, yet as table 11.2 indicates, in Europe, particularly in metropolitan environments, multi-family dwellings are a common feature of the social landscape. In the rural and poorer areas, however, the number of single family dwellings rises. Thus, assumptions about housing conditions should be treated with care.

Retailers should, therefore, be aware that in some national markets, regional differences may be considerable. This will have an impact on individual consumer's ability not only to afford purchases but access certain formats, and information, as well as utilize the merchandise purchased.

11.1 Deutscher Girls

Reading reports on German retailers' attitudes to longer opening hours would be enough evidence to suggest that the consumer in Germany is not entirely well served by its retailers. If changing lifestyles, such as increased female participation in the paid workforce, lead to changing opening hours and service provision, then German retailing should have restructured long ago. However, there may be hope for the German shopper.

Claire Kent, Morgan Stanley's European retail analyst, suggests:

> Restructuring is finally taking place in an industry which cared little in the past about the consumer. But there needs to be further development if [it] wants to compete.

Because customers have reduced their expenditure in recent years, as they fear unemployment and experience increased taxation, turnover among retailers fell by 2 per cent in 1995. This is forcing retailers to think again about the needs of their customers, who live in an advanced socio-economic environment, where a failure to recognize lifestyle needs is undermining retail competitiveness. The accusations which could be levelled at German retailing was that it was, until comparatively recently, an environment in which the customer and service provision mattered little, design and layout was not considered to play an important role, and there was little price competition.

However, retailers are reacting. Metro announced in the Spring of 1996 that it would be merging its previously independently run subsidiaries Asko, Deutsche SB-Kauf and Kaufhof Holding. The reorganization was considered to be a platform for more competitive operations in the German market and international developments. As Ken Costa of SBC Warburg, and an advisor to the large German operator Metro, has indicated:

> Metro is competitive, offers cheaper prices and provides a service to the customer. This compares sharply with the old-fashioned nature of other German retailers. We see a change in attitude, with interior design as well as competition and pressure on prices playing a greater role.

Source: Dempsey, 1996a, 1996b.

HOUSEHOLD AND WORK

While standing in apparent juxtaposition, the relationship between the words 'household' and 'work' may be used to discuss much of the social changes that have affected, and are affecting, the provision of retail services within developed economies. There are two fundamentally important trends which affect retailing in the contemporary consumer markets. They are, the increase in the number and proportion of working women within a society, and the changing ratio of working to retired consumers. In this, the US may seen as the model on which other societies may be understood and social changes which are still occurring explained and future changes projected.

New family

The image of the 1950s suburban American family enshrined in the celluloid images of film, and early mass audience television, could accommodate a retail structure that had come into being in the previous 100 years. The dual income household of the 1980s with its self-expressive values and materialist certainties demanded a new structure. The latter, of course, is a product of the former. In America, between 1946 and 1954, the 'Rock and Doris' world of early consumerism saw the birth of 76 million Americans, the 'baby boomers', who were to define the youth culture of the 1960s and the early 1970s and the upwardly mobile commercialism of the 1980s. It is this group, who have now, in a scaled-down and restructured form, sought to reproduce on a yet more affluent scale, the 1990s version of the family environment of their parents. For these consumers, the new wants are comfort, quality, entertainment in the domestic setting and nostalgia (Fisher, 1992). These consumers place particular emphasis on control and security, and, as a consequence of this, value companies that provide good reliable and overt customer service provision (Clark and Lempert, 1993). Home furnishing catalogues are experiencing an increase in sales as baby boomers have families and build comfort into their newly significant domestic environment (Fisher, 1994).

Such social change has an impact on retail provision. The logic is simple. If, in dual parent households, one parent is in the home, and traditionally in many societies, this is the mother of the family, shopping is carried out within working hours. Frequent trips may be made to retailers. Trips will be of short duration and often made on foot: a baby cart or pram pushed to geographically proximate retail outlets. With the parent at work who has traditionally been in the home, the logic changes. The family shopper has to combine not only job but also family. Irrespective of the unfilled cohorts of 'new men' or the wishful thinking of political correctness, the shopping role has to a great extent remained with the female in the household. In consequence, opening hours have had to change to accommodate the '9 'till 5' routine that rules out the day time frequent shop, to be replaced with the evening fortnightly shop in the dual income supported car or cars.

Table 11.3 provides female employment figures for selected regions of the EU. The figures show that higher employment rates among women occurs in regions with high GDP per capita. This statement should be qualified, because in rural areas, female employment is often subsumed in family enterprises but not officially recorded: nevertheless, the broad statistics have implications for retailers. In social contexts where female employment is the norm, retailers may adopt employment policies which they will not be able to adopt in regions where there different social conditions and attitudes exist. Attitudes to female employment will affect the pool of part-time labour available to retailers. Part-time employment has been an

Table 11.3 GDP and EU female formal activity rates (selected markets): 1990

	GDP in Ecu per capita EU 12 = 100	Total	Age groups 25–34	35–44	45–54
France	115	45.4	74.8	73.3	63.6
Ile-de-France	171	53.5	80.6	79.6	75.4
Centre-Est	109	46.7	77.1	74.5	68.0
Nord-Pas-de-Calais	94	38.3	68.1	62.5	46.2
Germany	128	44.9	67.8	67.7	61.4
Hessen	148	45.8	68.5	69.1	62.7
Baden-Wurtenberg	135	48.6	69.2	71.7	67.7
Niedersachsen	110	42.1	65.0	65.9	59.4
Spain	69	31.9	60.6	44.6	31.7
Madrid	87	32.0	63.5	44.4	32.6
Noreste	80	31.0	68.1	44.2	26.6
Sur	54	28.6	50.2	36.9	26.8
Italy	103	34.5	62.4	54.3	38.2
Lombardia	135	36.9	73.6	59.2	36.7
Nord-Ovest	120	35.6	73.2	62.5	41.6
Sud	69	31.1	49.8	45.8	36.0

Source: Eurostat, 1993.

important part of the development of retailing in some parts of Europe, such as the UK, in recent decades.

Female activity rates are an important indicator of social attitudes as they affect and are closely related to family issues such as child birth and child-rearing. In Hessen Germany, 68.5 per cent of women, in 1990, in the age group 25–34 years, were recorded as economically active. Hessen had a GDP per capita above the EU average (see table 11.3). In Noreste Spain, 68.1 per cent of women, in 1990, in the age group 25–34 years, were recorded as economically active. Noreste Spain had a GDP per capita below the EU average. These two regions, with very different levels of recorded wealth, nevertheless display very similar female activity rates. In the age group 35–44 years, however, the figures were very different. In Hessen, female activity was similar at 69.1 per cent, but in Noreste Spain, the figure was appreciably lower at 44.2 per cent. In the older age group of 45–54 years, the Hessen figures remained high at 62.7 per cent while the Noreste Spain figure was much lower at 26.6 per cent. High activity rates have affected the time at which women have children and the size of families. This in turn has an important influence on consumer needs, both in terms of the products they buy and the time in their lives when they buy products but also the way in which they shop and use retail facilities. It also has an important implication for the age profile of the population.

Aging society

Likewise, the aging of consumers a little older or a generation older than the baby boomers is affecting the social environment and altering the conditions which retailers must address. The retail industry, however, remains focused on the youth or youth oriented market, whereas the 35–54 age group will represent 50 per cent of consumer spending by the year 2000 (Clark and Lempert, 1993).

Table 11.4 gives the demographic profile of the US in the early 1990s. A distinct bulge in the profile may be observed in the age groups between 20 and 44, with the peak in the 30–4 age group. These individuals were born in the consumer boom years from the late 1940s to the early 1970s. The higher birth rate of the post-war period and the years of economic growth was followed by relatively lower birth rates in the economically less buoyant years of the 1970s and early 1980s. If there is evidence that retailers are not reacting to demographic changes, then there are opportunities for innovative retailers.

The profile in table 11.4 also shows the way the gender balance changes in the different age groups. More males than females are born, but with improved health

Table 11.4 US demographic profile 1991

Age group	Male		Female		Total % of total
	% of male total	% of age group	% of female total	% of age group	
0–4	8.0	51.2	7.3	48.8	7.6
5–9	7.6	51.2	6.9	48.8	7.2
10–14	7.4	51.2	6.7	48.8	7.0
15–19	7.2	51.4	6.5	48.6	6.8
20–24	7.9	50.9	7.3	49.1	7.6
25–29	8.5	50.2	8.0	49.8	8.2
30–34	9.0	49.8	8.6	50.2	8.8
35–39	8.3	49.6	8.0	50.4	8.1
40–44	7.5	49.4	7.4	50.6	7.4
45–49	5.6	49.0	5.6	51.0	5.6
50–54	4.6	48.6	4.6	51.4	4.6
55–59	4.1	47.9	4.2	52.1	4.1
60–64	4.0	46.7	4.4	53.3	4.2
65–69	3.7	44.7	4.3	55.3	3.9
70–74	2.9	42.8	3.7	57.2	3.3
75–79	2.0	39.5	2.9	60.5	2.5
80–84	1.1	34.9	2.0	65.1	1.6
85+	0.7	27.9	1.8	72.1	1.3

Source: United Nations, 1994.

11.2 Champagne Supernova

What do Bouef du Maine, Mozarella di Bufala Compana, Noord-Hollandse Gouda, Rhenser Mineralbrunnen, feta cheese, Orkney Beef, Gloucester cider, Jersey royal potatoes, Newcastle Brown Ale and West Country Farmhouse Cheddar Cheese have in common?

They are a selection from 318 geographical trademarks which are protected by the EU. The list given above is a relatively short one. There are many other examples of geographically protected products, including 104 cheeses, sixty-four meats and thirty olive oil and fats.

Regulations mean that only producers from designated areas who reach certain production regulations will be allowed to use the type of designations indicated above.

While to some, such as Danish producers of feta cheese, this may be the type of EU regulation that is unnecessary and economically disruptive, it is an example of the social context in which products develop and the geographical branding on which customers are prepared to spend money.

Source: Southey, 1996.

care the male child is more likely to survive in developed economies. Where health care is less advanced male children die in greater numbers. Thus, in the US demographic profile, it is not until the twenties and thirties that an equilibrium in gender balance is observed. By the late forties, however, the proportion of females in the age group begins to rise steadily. In consequence of male mortality rates in certain age groups, over two-thirds of US citizens above the age of eighty are female. From the age of fifty, retail costumers are even more likely than usual to be female.

In 1994, the International Mass Retail Association's Annual Convention research project was 'Your Aging Consumer: Reality vs. Perception' (Rouland, 1994). The report suggested that retailers were not prepared for consumers over 50 years, although there was an awareness of this group. The group likes to engage in shopping activity but it is not being catered for. Aging baby boomers and those in the 50 years plus age group often shop three times a week (Discount Merchandiser, 1993), thereby reflecting the time older customers have available to them but also traditional shopping patterns. Older US customers are attracted to discount operations and are oriented toward familiar products and brands. They place an emphasis on price and quality. The older customer is not essentially a credit customer. For example, even the older baby boomers are aware of the increasing costs, such as education, which they face and are oriented toward credit accumulation. As far as the older customer is concerned, their purchases are often oriented toward grandchildren and they are therefore important customers in the children's wear and toys product categories.

These trends in the US market are also being felt elsewhere. European markets, as was noted in the previous chapter are experiencing, and will continue to experience, population decline or even stagnation. This means that the average age of these markets is rising rapidly. However, there are considerable differences in market profiles and rule of thumb assumptions should not be relied on when considering which markets will be most affected by these changes. Italy for example, which commentators often include in vague generalizations about Mediterranean markets, displays certain social trends that are more comparable with North European markets. In table 11.5 projected age group figures are presented for the year 2000 and 2025. African countries such as Uganda will see between a half and a third of their population under the age of fifteen in the first quarter of the twenty-first century, while West European markets such as Italy will see less than a sixth of their population in this age group. Conversely, many African countries, even in 2025, are projected to have only one in twenty of their populations over the age of sixty. In contrast, some European countries will see their citizens of 60 years or more representing nearly a third of their population.

National market figures should not be considered alone without reference to regional differences. Wide differences in population structures exist within markets. Indeed, increased mobility may increase demographic imbalances on a local level as individuals live out stages in their lives in different locations. In Australia there has been the wholesale development of retirement villages for Japanese nationals, while in Europe, Spain has become a popular destination for retired people from North European countries.

Differences in local population figures may be the product of different cultural values, different historical experiences and current economic conditions. Table 11.5 provides West and East German projections separately. Although the two Germanies are today part of one federal political structure, these two 'parts' of Germany will continue to exhibit differences, only some of which will be eroded by unification. As noted above, Italian population figures are not typical of many countries of Mediterranean Europe. However, when the figures are considered in further detail this may be seen to owe much to the considerable differences within Italy itself: while the south or the Mezzogiorno does resemble the figures for Spain the North does not.

Lifestyle

In some societies, the family meal occurs in the domestic environment, in others it is increasingly an event which occurs in the public setting. The US family will eat out in restaurants more often than their EU equivalents. Thus, in the US, retailers are looking increasingly to the selling opportunities afforded by the casual diner. Eating and shopping may develop as part of a bundle of services (Benezra, 1995).

With an increase in disposable income and leisure time, retailing and leisure pursuits have increasingly been combined in the same location. Shopping centres have an important social and recreational role to play in contemporary society (Brown, 1992). The West Edmonton Shopping Mall is one of the best known

Table 11.5 Population age projections (medium variant): 2000, 2025

	Year 2000		Year 2025	
Country	% population under 15	% population over 60	% population under 15	% population over 60
Nigeria	46.7	4.3	35.2	5.6
South Africa	35.6	6.9	27.2	10.8
Uganda	49.4	3.7	36.6	4.9
Zaire	46.0	4.3	38.3	5.5
Canada	18.7	17.0	16.4	28.4
Mexico	32.8	6.8	26.9	12.5
US	20.2	16.8	17.9	26.5
Argentina	27.3	13.6	23.6	15.8
Brazil	31.7	8.0	24.6	13.8
Chile	29.4	9.6	23.9	16.0
Venezuela	24.5	6.5	28.8	11.5
China	26.6	10.2	18.5	19.1
Hong Kong	17.6	15.1	13.0	31.9
India	34.5	7.8	23.3	12.3
Japan	16.9	21.8	14.9	29.9
Korea South	21.3	10.3	16.7	21.6
Saudi Arabia	45.7	4.2	38.0	6.1
Singapore	22.2	11.0	16.9	26.9
Hungary	17.9	19.9	16.4	25.2
Poland	21.4	16.0	19.6	22.2
Belgium	17.3	21.8	15.6	30.3
Denmark	16.3	20.6	15.3	30.9
France	19.4	20.0	17.0	27.2
Germany (W)	15.8	24.1	15.1	33.0
Germany (E)	17.4	21.1	15.8	28.1
Ireland	24.5	13.1	20.3	18.4
Italy	15.5	22.7	13.2	30.7
Netherlands	18.4	18.2	15.4	28.6
Spain	18.3	19.7	16.5	26.3
UK	19.6	20.0	17.3	26.8
Australia	20.6	15.8	18.0	23.7
New Zealand	22.0	15.3	18.0	23.7

Source: United Nations, 1991.

examples. The West Edmonton Mall encompasses retail outlets, hotels and leisure attractions. However, the relationship between the different facilities implies greater advantage to retailers in unplanned usage. Shoppers intent on making purchases at the beginning of their visit are less likely to make unplanned visits to the leisure facilities, although, visitors who come to use the leisure and social facilities are more likely to engage in shopping activities (Finn, 1994).

Changing leisure patterns or new tourist destinations will create changes in retail provision. In locations where the tourist industry has boomed, jobs have been created in retailing and new retail outlets have developed (Driggers, 1992). Shopping as a leisure activity is very much a subject of retailer concern. Past developments have suggested that the two combine symbiotically: however, predictions suggest that in the US, shopping will become a less important aspect of social life during the 1990s (Howard, 1994).

SOCIAL PROBLEMS

Retailers have to contend with social problems in the market in which they operate. The Sock Shop's problems operating in the subways in New York have taken on a somewhat legendary status of a retail experience which was so insensitive to the social context of its international market, the company was unable to replicate the success it had in the UK and ultimately foundered. Levels of crime in a New York subway station do not allow retailers to take advantage of passing trade in the same way as they might elsewhere.

Urban environment

The same urban problems of decay, however, may lead planners and developers to seek new solutions to social problems and hence create new opportunities for retailers. Cleveland, Ohio, was renowned for the social problems as it decayed in the 1960s and 1970s to the 'doughnut' logic of American urban decay. The town develops outward around a decaying centre. However, in recent years with the development of the Terminal Tower in the centre of Cleveland, a retail hotel and leisure complex has been created which offers opportunities for retailers to locate in a central but safe environment (Greengard and Solomon, 1994). Thus, as the mall has been a response to social changes in household shopping habits, it has also been a response to the inadequacy and unattractiveness of central urban shopping locations, and the development of a relatively safe but certainly controlled shopping environment. In some markets, the level of urban decay and negative social aspects of that decay will be less evident. In some markets however it may have a redefining effect on retailers' location strategies and format presentation.

Shrinkage

Retail shrinkage, or theft problems, are universal but each market will have its specific problems. In Canada, $20 billion is lost through employee theft each year. Research shows that only 20 per cent of employees will never steal, while 20 per cent are chronic thieves and 60 per cent will steal given motive and opportunity (Holt, 1993). Theft by shoppers is strongly influenced by peer groups, relations with parents and the moral setting in which they have grown up (Cox et al., 1993).

In the UK, within a price sensitive market, cost control is recognized as crucial, and theft is hence an important variable that needs to be controlled (Leaver, 1993). However, the social factors responsible are beyond retailers' control.

Unemployment

Equally beyond retailers' control are the social and economic effects of unemployment. High unemployment rates will depress retail sales. Retailers, particularly on a store by store basis are particularly vulnerable to high unemployment rates. Within local communities, factory closures will soon affect retail sales. In Elkhart, Indiana, Whitehall Laboratories Incorporated closed a pharmaceutical factory in 1991 making 800 employees redundant (Kelly, 1992). The effect on the local social fabric has had an immediate effect on the retailers as sales have decreased. Such changes are well beyond the control of retailers: all that retailers are able to do is understand the macro-economic and micro-economic changes which may affect the environment. In the case of the factory in Indiana, the former employees argued that the plant had been moved to Puerto Rico in order to avoid the $14 an hour wage rate negotiated in the Indiana plant and benefit from Federal tax breaks. Locating in developed markets may not always be the safe option.

Ethics

While macro-economic changes and macro-social trends may be beyond retailers control, ethical questions have certainly brought retailers to the fore in recent years as the consumer has shown interest, although the consumer has not always followed that interest up by purchases, in Green issues and other ethical concerns. Retailers are increasingly being challenged with the need to be socially and ethically responsible. This challenge comes from other retailers such as the Body Shop, which markets itself on its ethical stance, but also by observers (Glen, 1994) who predict the increasing importance of this aspect of retail business. In 1993, Kmart was the winner of the SAMMI Good Citizenship Award for Community Service for involving its employees and associates in local voluntary activities (Dealerscope Merchandising, 1993).

The emphasis on returning benefits to the community is one that is epitomized by the Body Shop. It is one way that retailers are able to respond to social problems. The response may often appear as little more than drops in oceans, despite large sums of money being involved, but it represents a commercial responsibility which, where suitably directed, may have some impact. While the Body Shop has built its reputation on its ethical image, it has also proved to be a profitable organization. The Cooperative Societies in the UK, however, have not shown the same capacity to make profits and thereby serve the community they were established to benefit. In the CWS (Cooperative Wholesale Society), this fact has been recognized and a new emphasis having been placed on profit so that fundamental social objectives able to be met (Bose, 1992). The Cooperatives, which were founded on the realization that money talks and that united consumers are able to force suppliers to provide good products at reasonable prices, failed to make sufficient profits. The Body Shop's soap factory in Glasgow is an example of the organization's willingness to identify social problems such as high unemployment, and continue to contribute by returning 25 per cent of the factories profits back into the local community through support for such projects as care for the elderly (Franssen, 1993).

Safety

Responsibility toward the community also means responsibility toward customers and the safety of customers. In litigious societies, retailers must be particularly aware not only of the costs of customers who consider store facilities unsafe, and shop somewhere else, but the high costs involved in meeting claims by customers who have been injured in stores. Retailers have long been familiar with the problems associated with customers falling in stores, but with increased service provision, problems may result which retailers had not anticipated. In a 12 month period of 1992–3, 22,975 children under 5 years were treated in US hospitals for falls from shopping trolleys (Rouland, 1993). Consequently, retailers have been forced, through the fear of expensive out of court settlements that they are having to meet, to improve safety in stores.

SOCIAL CONTINUITY AND HOMOGENEITY

International businesses will spend decades learning about a market, only to find that it is a dynamic environment that changes often imperceptively operating day by operating day. Some markets will retain a continuity for considerable periods of time while others will provide an uncertain and constantly changing social environment. The former market may prove the most problematic, for in it the retailer may be less prepared for the essential task of monitoring the social environment.

Some societies will exhibit a high degree of homogeneity. This may in part be the product of a single ethnic culture and identity but it may also be a product of a society where different social groups which share similar aspirations are the norm. Japanese society and the Japanese consumer have traditionally been perceived in this way. Japanese consumers desire for risk-free acceptable consumer decisions gave them a homogeneity that was unusual in the contemporary consumer environment. However, increasingly, the Japanese market is exhibiting signs of divergence, and in consequence marketers are having to pursue segmentation strategies (Raudabaugh, 1994). This has advantages for niche retailers in this market. Niche retailers are among the most successful international operations. The leisure market has increased in Japan in the early 1990s, particularly among men in their thirties (Focus Japan, 1993). Retailers such as department stores have developed their retail facilities for this market in a way they have not previously, although the opportunities for non-indigenous and indigenous retailers alike remains strong in such lifestyle markets. The relaxation in shopping development regulations and the rise of new indigenous large retail mass merchandisers as well as the influx of

11.3 Telling Tales

Some societies expected a high level of administrative openness and when societies come together to work cooperatively that may cause differences.

Ms Liala Freivalds, the minister for justice in Sweden's Social Democratic government has spearheaded a campaign to achieve more open access to documentation produced by the European Union. She noted, before the intergovernmental conference in Italy in the Spring of 1996:

> Openness and transparency are central to winning public confidence in the EU.

Ms Freivalds anticipated support from other EU member countries, but in particular she anticipated it would be ministers from Denmark, Finland and the Netherlands who would support the Swedish case.

Source: Carnegy, 1996.

international operations in feeding a desire by some segments of the Japanese consumer market to shop in stores that are different to those traditionally used. The new discounters, for example, are confronting the manufacturers and challenging the hold they have on distribution systems on the basis of price (Smith, 1994).

The growing diversity in Japanese society may be the product of similar tensions which developed in the consumer environment of Western Europe and North America in the 1960s and 1970; that is, a breaking down of set social patterns and cross generational responses to consumer opportunities.

Such changes in consumer behaviour are not limited to Japan. Also on the Pacific Rim, customers in Australia are changing their buying habits. The household has evolved considerably in recent decades and retailers and manufacturers have had to constantly respond to the changing social requirements. Household surveys of white-collar workers in Australia mirror the social changes that have occurred in both North America and Western Europe. The Australian based Keig & Co. agency consider three social trends have characterized the fundamental shifts in consumer profiles and hence their buying behaviour (Narayanan, 1994):

- an increase in educational levels;

- an increase in women in the workforce;

- increasing diversity in family composition.

Thus, David Keig, who is based in Sydney, considers these factors have led to the increasing value placed on service an inclination to buy from a group of acceptable brand names, rather than rely on one and hence to treat the staple product as little more than a commodity. This, he maintains, has increased the use of private brands.

Keig's views on the changing consumer are mirrored by the consumer research carried out by the Australian market research company AMR Quantum, which believes that the consumerism of the 1980s has been replaced by a new set of characteristics or the seven 'Cs' as the company describes them: confidence, choosiness, control, cynicism, caution, convenience, concern (Retail World, 1994). The first five 'Cs', the company believes, reflect a new maturity among consumers the last two changes in demographics, a changing social value system, and changing lifestyles. The consequence of these changes in consumer attitudes is placing new emphasis on time, price and quality.

Consumer buying behaviour is influenced by changing social conditions which may lead to sudden growth in product areas which would otherwise be unexpected and retailers must be prepared to react to that. The bicycle market in the UK went through a period of decline as lifestyle changes rendered it inappropriate or unattractive. However, with the mountain bike product innovation and the spin-off benefits for retailers as far as clothing and accessories are concerned, this has become a growth market (Wall, 1993). Four key social trends have been recognized which explain this reversal of market fortunes: green awareness, health consciousness, product development, urban traffic problems. Likewise, changing social relationships and work patterns have contributed to the development of other products such as the pager. In the US, for example, pagers are used by working mothers to keep in touch with their children and by 'singles' reluctant to give personal telephone numbers (Glasse, 1993).

Retailers must also be aware of the different markets which exist in any one community. In Saudi Arabia, the car market may be described as being made up of Saudi drivers and expatriates working in Saudi Arabia. The expatriates propensity for smaller cars is not shared by the Saudi market, which prefers larger cars, although increasingly the young are favouring Japanese products (Tuncalp, 1993).

Consumers will also become increasingly distinct as social change occurs within specific geographical regions. Increasingly, retailers are becoming aware of the need to recognize and cater for regional tastes:

> Be advised: fascination with local heritage, preservation efforts, rediscovery of regional culture, and concerns for the environment are not passing fancies. (Green, 1993, p. 30)

In the UK, the establishment of a Welsh language television channel, S4C, provided advertisers with the opportunity to communicate with their Welsh language customers through television advertising for the first time. The Midland Bank made a very positive impression as an early advertiser and hence financial supporter of the station. This was reflected in new business.

Social fragmentation is an aspect of global retailing that will help to characterize the social environment in which retailers operate in the 1990s. This may in part be a product of the mass media world of the twentieth century which is breaking down (Narayanan, 1994). However, more extremely, some commentators consider that consumers in some markets are experiencing consumer schizophrenia, where consumers exhibit mutually inconsistent even antagonistic motives which are created by economic, social, demographic and psychological influences (Kardon, 1992).

This leaves retailers with considerable problems. To simply identify socio-economic groups is no longer sufficient. Income levels and material possessions will take the retailer so far and may form the basis for much market evaluation but increasingly retailers have to be aware of the psychographic differences which exist in a market and between markets. For example, Mitchell's (1983, 1984) American lifestyle groupings will not directly translate to the European environment even though they may identify some key similarities and characteristics. For Mitchell, consumers could be described as a survivor, sustainer, belonger, emulator, achiever, I-am-me, experiential, societally conscious and integrated. In the French context the first three groups appear to merge, while in Germany the experiential and societally conscious consumer was seen as limited in number.

In the store environment, customers look for cues through which they will develop a perception of a store and the service quality they may expect (Baker et al., 1994). The social cues with which retailers provide customers should be sensitized to the local environment if the correct message is to be conveyed. In this retailers must learn to appreciate the idiosyncrasies of the local social language. This will be particularly important where the retailer is charging relatively high prices and needs the store environment to provide the correct ambience through socially acceptable design features as Grewal and Baker's (1994) research has shown.

CONCLUSION

Social conditions are the product of a mixture of economic and cultural factors. They are important to retailers when operating in a market. International retailers will be strongly influenced by the social conditions in their domestic market when they initially consider internationalization. This may lead them to assume that other markets in which they establish operations will also exhibit certain characteristics. These assumptions may be based on crude, assumed correlations between economic development and retail requirements.

International retailers should separate economic and social issues in their international planning activities. Retailers should also consider regional differences in social conditions carefully. These may be the product of cultural differences which are reflected in socially related data and other indicators.

QUESTIONS – DISCUSSION POINTS

1   When considering social development in Europe, is the region or the state the most appropriate basis on which to consider conditions?

2 What role has female employment played in the development of retail provision?

3 The ageing of society in developed markets is seen as an important issue. Is it important, and if so, in what ways will it affect retail operations?

4 How may retailers act 'ethically' and how profitable is social responsibility?

REFERENCES

Baker, J., Grewal, D., and Parasuraman, A., (1994) The Influence of Store Environment on Quality Inferences and Store Image, *Journal of the Academy of Marketing Science*, Vol. 22, No. 4, pp. 328–39.

Benezra, K., (1995) What's for dinner . . . tomorrow? *Adweek*, (Eastern Edition, pp. 48–52).

Bose, M., (1992) The Survival of a Social Institution, *Director*, Vol. 45, No. 7, February, pp. 50–4.

Brown, S., (1992) Tenant Mix, Tenant Placement and Shopper Behaviour in a Planned Shopping Centre, *Service Industries Journal*, Vol. 12, No. 3, July, pp. 384–403.

Carnegy, H., (1996) Stockholm to press openness on the Eu, *Financial Times*, 26 March, p. 2.

Clark, B., and Lempert, P., (1993) Riding the Age Wave, *Retail Business Review*, Vol. 61, No. 5, June, pp. 18–20.

Cox, A., Cox, D., Anderson, R., and Moschis, G., (1993) Research note: Social influences on adolescent shoplifting – Theory, evidence, and implications for the retail industry, *Journal of Retailing*, Vol. 69, No. 2, Summer, pp. 234–46.

Dealerscope Merchandising, (1993) When Money is not Enough, *Dealerscope Merchandising*, Vol. 35, No. 12, December, p. 34.

Dempsey, J., (1996a) Metro sees sharp rise after merger, *Financial Times*, 15 March, p. 27.

Dempsey, J., (1996b) German shops warm to the idea of customer as king, *Financial Times*, 29 March, p. 27.

Discount Merchandiser, (1993) America's Aging Consumers, *Discount Merchandiser*, Vol. 33, No. 9, September, pp. 16–18.

Driggers, K., (1992) Managing the Tide of Tourism, *Business & Economic Review*, Vol. 39, No. 1, October–December, pp. 7–11.

du Gay, P., (1993) 'Numbers and Souls': Retailing and the de-differentiation of Economy and Culture, *British Journal of Sociology*, Vol. 44, No. 4, December, pp. 563–87.

Eurostat, (1993) *Regions Statistical Yearbook 1993*, Eurostat, Brussels.

Finn, A., (1994) Residents' Acceptance and Use of a Mega-multi-mall: West Edmonton Mall Evidence, *International Journal of Research in Marketing*, Vol. 11, No. 2, March, pp. 127–44.

Fisher, H., (1992) Psychology of the Home: An Anthropological Perspective, *Retail Control*, Vol. 60, No. 2, February, pp. 3–7.

Fisher, C., (1994) Late Rush to Fuel Double-Digit Catalog Jump, *Advertising Age*, Vol. 65, No. 43, 10 October, pp. S2, S12

Focus Japan, (1993) Outdoor Recreation on the Upswing, *Focus Japan*, Vol. 20, No. 11, November, p. 4.

Franssen, M., (1993) Beyond Profits, *Business Quarterly*, Vol. 58, No. 1, Autumn, pp. 14–20.

Glasse, J., (1993) The Beep Goes On, *Dealerscope Merchandising*, Vol. 35, No. 3, March, pp. 59–63.

Glen, P., (1994) Ten Predictions for the New Year, *Chain Store Age Executive*, Vol. 70, No. 1, *January*, p. 182.

Green, J., (1993) Retail for the Year 2000, *Discount Merchandiser*, Vol. 33, No. 8, August, pp. 28–30.

Greengard, S., and Solomon, C., (1994) A City Rebuilds its Symbol – And Rejuvenates Itself, *Personnel Journal*, Vol. 73, No. 2, February, pp. 64–5.

Grewal, D., and Baker, J., (1994) Do Retail Store Environmental Factors Affect Consumers Price Acceptability? An Empirical Examination, *International Journal of Research in Marketing*, Vol. 11, No. 2, March, pp. 107–15.

Holt, A., (1993) Controlling Employee Theft, *CMA Magazine*, Vol. 67, No. 7, September, pp. 16–19.

Howard, K., (1994) Global Retailing 2000, *Business Credit*, Vol. 96, No. 2, February, pp. 22–4.

Jones, P., (1993) Some Thoughts on the Sociology of Retailing, *International Journal of Retail & Distribution Management*, Vol. 21, No. 4, pp. 29–32.

Kardon, B., (1992) Consumer Schizophrenia: Extremism in the Marketplace, *Planning Review*, Vol. 20, No. 4, July/August, pp. 18–22.

Kelly, K., (1992) A 'Living Hell' in Indiana, *Business Week*, No. 3255, 9 March, p. 33.

Leaver, D., (1993) Legal and Social Changes Affecting UK Retailers' Response to Consumer Theft, *International Journal of Retail & Distribution Management*, Vol. 21, No. 8, pp. 29–33.

Mitchell, A., (1983) *Nine American Life Styles: Who We are and Where We are Going*, Macmillan, New York.

Mitchell, A., (1984) Nine American Life Styles: Values and Societal Change, The Futurist, Vol. 18, August, pp. 4–13.

Narayanan, S., (1994) Working Women Losing Brand Loyalty, *Retail World*, Vol. 47, No. 7, 11 April, p. 5.

Raudabaugh, J., (1994) Opportunities for Customer Segmentation Strategies, *Planning Review*, Vol. 22, No. 6, November/December, pp. 36–8.

Retail World, (1994) Consumers have Rejected Consumerism, *Retail World*, Vol. 47, No. 7, 11 April, p. 5.

Rouland, R., (1993) There is Safety in Partnerships, *Discount Merchandiser*, Vol. 33, No. 9, September, pp. 14–15.

Rouland, R., (1994) Partners and Perceptions: The 50-plus Consumer, *Discount Merchandiser*, Vol. 34, No. 7, July, pp. 12–13.

Smith, C., (1994) Opening Time, *Far Eastern Economic Review*, Vol. 157, No. 18, 5 May, pp. 62–6.

Southey, C., (1996) Brussels cooks up plan to protect European recipes, *Financial Times*, 7 March, p. 1.

Tuncalp, S., (1993) The Automobile Market in Saudi Arabia: Implications for Export Marketing Planning, *Marketing Intelligence & Planning*, Vol. 11, No. 1, pp. 28–36.

United Nations, (1991) *World Population Prospects 1990*, United Nations Publication, New York.

United Nations, (1994) *Demographic Yearbook 1992*, United Nations Publication, New York.

Wall, N., (1993) Bicycles, *Retail Business Market Reports*, No. 425, July, pp. 40–55.

Culture

▌ OBJECTIVES ▌

This chapter considers the issue of culture. It does not attempt to didactically characterize or define elements of culture, but rather to raise questions. The most important attribute that any international marketer should be equipped with is the ability to keep asking questions and learning.

INTRODUCTION

> 'culture' ... is *collective mental programming*: it is that part of our conditioning that we share with other members of our nation, region, or group but not with members of other nations, regions, or groups. (Hofstede, 1983a)

Textbooks on international marketing frequently follow a set pattern when culture is considered. They attempt to identify those factors which characterize culture and discuss the differences which make business difficult in specific environments, while pointing out the amusing problems which have occurred as marketers fail to identify cultural nuances before they press on with advertising campaigns, packaging designs, the names of the products and the products themselves. Unfortunately, what this often achieves, apart from stereotypical reinforcement, are indications of cultural superiority or a form of intellectual imperialistic thinking which is misleading at best and distasteful at worst. However, to deny cultural difference is also flawed. Culture provides the individual with the opportunity for self expression.

While it is important to appreciate important influences on culture and how it may be defined, it is very difficult to use these factors as if they are part of a scientific equation. Even if it were possible to do that for one culture, different weighting would have to be used in others. Culture, to a great extent, is the imponderable in the international market-place, and defies simplistic characterization. Yet it is simplistic interpretations which influence decision makers. It is similarities of culture which encourage retailers to expand in some markets through organic growth; it is dissimilarities which encourage retailers to seek partners for joint-ventures in others. An appreciation of the market culture in which retailers operate will not be gained during a short operational period in the market. A culture may only be appreciated after considerable study of the nuances of that culture.

This chapter does not attempt to didactically characterize or define elements of culture, but rather to raise questions. The most important attribute that any international marketer should be equipped with is the ability to keep asking questions and learning, to take nothing for granted and not to assume some form of cultural superiority; to remember that in another market that she or he is the foreigner.

There is the well-known story, which bears repeating, of the English girl who wished to marry a Hungarian but was told by the young man that he could not marry her because she was a foreigner and his mother would not approve of him marrying a foreigner. Her reply to the young man:

> I, a foreigner? What a silly thing to say. I am English. You are the foreigner. And your mother, too . . . Truth does not depend on geography. What is true in England is also true in Hungary and in North Borneo and Venezuela and everywhere. (Mikes, 1962, p. 12)

WHAT IS CULTURE?

Culture, like a first language, is learnt through everyday interaction. Our own language and culture, therefore, become, through their unconscious assimilation, an index against which we measure other cultures and language. The more we are cut off from other cultures the more absolute, the more 'correct' our own culture becomes.

Culture and language define our picture of the world. One of the most frustrating or intriguing remarks that a translator of a language can say, is that this word or that phrase of a foreign language does not translate directly but is an attempt to convey this or that meaning. We are left floundering and challenged by the different allusions of the phrase outside the mind of the speaker, but the alternative is a translation which does not convey the value of the phrase. Such words have entered English because they convey a meaning which is not resonant in the vernacular but powerful in the original: *esprit de corps, jeu d'esprit, jeunesse dorée, Übermensch, Zeitgeist*. While some Frenchmen may cavil against the use of English or American-English words and phrases in their language, English has made a contribution to French everyday speech and, likewise, French has made a considerable contribution to English vocabulary. It has done this through the contact that as occurred between the two cultures and the propensity of English to absorb other languages (see exhibit 12.1). A language such as English is continually evolving and thereby provides an insight into the dynamic nature of culture and culture itself.

Culture is often associated with the national group but within such a group are many conflicting social groups and influences. The culture will at times take on a considerable amount of material from other cultures into which at least one group within the wider culture comes in contact. By looking at one culture over time, it is possible to appreciate the idiosyncrasies of that culture in our own time and hence the transitory cultural values that we may hold to be immutable. Political correctness is an exemplary case of language use and its evolution, as old meanings are found wanting and new usages attempted. James Garner's humorous and

Exhibit 12.1 English language borrowings

Languages	Words
Arabic:	alcohol, jar, sofa
Breton:	penguin
Chinese:	ketchup, tea
Dutch:	yacht, slim
Irish Gaelic:	brogue, galore, tory
North Indian:	bungalow, cot, shampoo, verandah
Hungarian:	goulash, hussar
Japanese:	tycoon
Malaya-Polynesian:	bantam, gong, launch
Persian:	caravan, shawl, bazaar
Scots Gaelic:	banshee, slogan
Spanish:	junta, tornado, cigar
South American:	chocolate, cocoa, hammock, potato
Turkish:	coffee, kiosk, tulip, vampire
Welsh:	coracle, crag, cwm

somewhat affectionate attempt to translate Bedtime Stories into the language of the politically correct, although as he puts it the 'original title, "Fairy Stories For a Modern World", was abandoned for obvious reasons' (Garner, 1994).

> Through the thicket, across the river, and deep, deep in the woods, lived a family of bears – a Papa Bear, A Mama Bear, and a Baby Bear – and they all lived together anthropomorphically in a little cottage as a nuclear family. They were very sorry about this, of course, since the nuclear family has traditionally served to enslave womyn, instill a self-righteous moralism in its members, and imprint rigid notions of heterosexualist roles onto the next generation. Nevertheless, they tried to be happy and took steps to avoid these pitfalls, such as naming their offspring the non-gender-specific 'Baby'. (Garner, 1994, p. 39)

Such stories, by their very nature, are not simply childish but for children to whom cultural messages must be conveyed and warnings given. The reinterpretation or setting of such stories in the contemporary cultural milieu serves only to emphasize the power of accepted cultural messages and the unconscious way in which cultural values are conveyed in both the informal and formal educational context, a context which a 'foreigner' does not have.

When looking at other cultures, before hands are held up in horror or fingers pointed in wagging condemnation, the value of the tradition should be placed in context and perhaps considered in alternative lights to that which the first instinctive, culturally specific, interpretation suggests. It is not an international marketer's place to judge but interpret the unfamiliar environment. It is very easy to look at facets of other cultures in the contemporary environment and judge them on the basis of contemporary cultural norms. However, the society from which the international observer comes may also have within it, or have had within it the capacity for similar nuances (see exhibit 12.2).

Our own cultural past may be as alien as someone else's cultural present. Our own culture is alien to others. Culture defines an individual's experiences and the manner in which they express themselves in the social environment. Culture is the product of shared values which lead to a form of behaviour that is recognized as acceptable to a group. The group does not have to be geographically defined, although they may often be associated with a particular location. The group may be a social group within a wider society but part of that society, influencing and being influenced by that wider group.

> La plus ancienne de toutes les sociétés, et la seule naturelle, est celle de la famille. (Rousseau, 1772, p. 240)

Man lives in groups. These groups give man the opportunity to form relationships which will allow the maintenance of life both on an individual but also group level. In such groups norms are established which regulate activity. Culture establishes boundaries over which members of the group are expected not to trespass. Culture liberates the individual from the need to continually learn and establish relationships from a basic level but it also restricts individual behaviour in that it requires conformity.

Exhibit 12.2 Household finance

In Britain

As soon as the whistle went they put chairs outside their front doors and sat there waiting till the men came up the Hill and home. Then as the men came up to their front doors they threw their wages, sovereign by sovereign, into the shining laps, fathers first and sons or lodgers in a line behind. (Llewellyn, 1939, p. 9)

In Japan

Before the age of electronic banking, husbands would bring home their pay packets every month, and, as their children looked on, solemnly present it to their wives over the dinner table. (Larke, 1994, p. 28)

In time

The past is a foreign country: they do things differently there. (Hartley, 1953, p. 9)

International marketers must, therefore, be very conscious of their own interpretation of cultural phenomenon but also their reaction to it, for they must also live within the confines of their own culture and the values imposed on them by that culture. Bribery may be acceptable in non-domestic markets, indeed a prerequisite of business and good intent, but it may not be acceptable to superiors and public attitudes in the domestic market.

Culture is shared. Individuals, when they come into contact with others from their own culture, in the midst of an alien culture, are often thrown together in a way which they would not achieve in the context of their own culture. Particularly where in the culture from which the individuals are drawn they may be from different sub-groups with subtly different cultural norms. Foreign outposts of domestic retailing are comforting. Japanese retailers have expanded abroad in recent years to serve not only new customers but expatriate communities of Japanese. This is part of a long tradition in retailing.

Expatriate groups and tourism has been an important influence on the expansion of retail outlets. W. H. Smith, the UK stationer, newsagent and bookseller, when embarking on international expansion chose 'to provide for its customers the same distributary service it produced at home' (Wilson 1985, p. 429). The first W. H. Smith shop outside the British Isles was in Paris on the Rue de Rivoli, and was acquired in 1903. The fascia of the store and lettering in the tearoom, designed and painted by Eric Gill, thereby provided a distinctly English Arts and Crafts quality to the store (MacCarthy 1989). The need to provide familiar products and surroundings to the expatriate community was understood by W. H. Smith.

To the outsider cultures may appear homogenous and differences will not be apparent. Thus retailers should be very careful that they are aware that cultures are more heterogeneous than they may at first appear. British retailers have been enthusiastic in their efforts to access the North American market only to find that the US is a *melange* of different cultures and different assumptions. In the retail context, it is the small differences which make the differences and offer prompts or do not offer prompts to customers. In US stores, customers are approached in fundamentally different ways than they are in the UK. This is not necessarily a product of training but ingrained attitudes toward the fundamental determinants of social relationships and interaction. It is ways of thinking, not broader similarities, which prove problematic. In a US store, there is an assertiveness which is less evident in the UK. There is a willingness to emphasize price. In the UK, there is a reluctance to make contact, there is a relative unwillingness to discuss prices. In the US, stores may look surprisingly basic or unfinished in appearance, in contrast to UK retailers' emphasis on appearance. The emphasis in US stores is on the practicalities. Arguably, this permeates the whole of US society.

> here (US) everything looked well-used. The verges were dusty and ragged; where road ended and verge began was a matter of real ambiguity. In England edges were distinct. . . . Here energies were directed to making the important things work – like telephones, food production, heating and cooling – not dissipated in buffing up road signs or polishing cat's eyes. By their verges and street furniture shall ye know them. (Boyd, 1984, p. 90)

Culture is comforting, it provides a stock of set responses to familiar situations. It is reinforced through various means, as it is a product of those means. Culture provides identity both to the individual with whom it is associated but also those who look on seeking to define characteristics of the group or groups with whom they will have to deal. International marketers are one set of individuals who have to define for their own purposes the groups to whom they wish to market.

IDENTITY

When retailers assess the global environment national culture will play an important role in their calculations.

Smith (1993) has defined a nation as:

> a named human population sharing an historic territory, common myths and historical memories, a mass, public culture, a common economy and common legal rights and duties for all members.

However, in the global political environment, as noted in chapter 7, it is relatively easy to visualize the world in terms of nation-states; the world may be divided into states but there are also supra-national institutions and associations as well as local institutions which redefine the role of the state. Thus the nation, which is in itself often misinterpreted as sharing boundaries with the state, is not sufficiently well defined to allow it crude use in identifying cultural identity.

Exhibit 12.3 Thomas Jefferson's view of his countrymen

I will give you my idea of the characters of the several states.

In the North they are	In the South they are
cool	fiery
sober	voluptuary
laborious	indolent
persevering	unsteady
independent	independent
jealous of their own liberties, and just of those of others	zealous for their own liberties, but trampling on those of others
interested	generous
chicaning	candid
superstitious and hypocritical in their religion	without attachment or pretension to any religion but that of the heart

These characteristics grow weaker and weaker by gradation from North to South and South to North, insomuch that an observing traveller, without the aid of the quadrant, may always know his latitude by the character of the people among whom he finds himself.

In correspondence with the Marquis of Chastellux, 2 September 1785.

Source: Ricks and Vance, 1994.

In assessing culture, international retailers will need to be aware of the same cross-border influences which affect political structures. Europe is not merely a geographical expression. While Europe is divided into what often purports to be a collection of nation-states, it shares a cultural identity and history which transcends the nation. The US has been brought into being in little under 400 years. It is often referred to in terms which would suggest a homogenous culture and identity yet it is a collection of hyphenates (Afro-American, German-American, Irish-American, Italian-American etc.), and regional identities. Indeed, if Thomas Jefferson is to be believed the US has always had its cultural differences (see exhibit 12.3)

LANGUAGE

Verbal

The linguistic map of Europe has something of the Jason Pollock about it, where splashes of linguistic expression clash. However, the distinct languages of Europe are often far from the separate entities they appear and purport to be. Language is partly political, developing as it does with reference to the political boundaries in which it is used as well as the cultural influences of a wider community (Chambers and Trudgill, 1980). While Norway and Sweden are two independent states and their languages are commonly perceived as different they share many similarities and owe much of their distinction to political boundaries than to linguistic ones. Languages are related. Most languages in Europe are part of an indo-European group which may be further subdivided into such categories as West Germanic, Scandinavian Celtic, South Slavic, West Romance before they are divided into German, Dutch, Swedish, Danish, Welsh, Irish, Bulgarian, Serbian, French and Spanish. The Altaic languages are spread across the Eurasian land mass from the Balkans to the Chukchi Peninsula. They are subcategories as Turkic, Mongolian and Manchu-Tungus and may be further subdivided into forty languages (Crystal, 1987).

Language is a means by which human beings communicate, some schools of thought would even suggest we require language to think. Language is a fundamental technology, without which further more elaborate human interaction and endeavour is more prohibited. It is not surprising therefore that retailers, when asked about the problems of international expansion, place language high on their list (Alexander, 1990a, 1990b). Or at least UK retailers do. An individual's awareness of language will depend on the culture they come from. In the Netherlands, 32 per cent of people claim that they are able to follow a conversation in two or more languages, 12 per cent say that they are able to do so in three languages (Eurobarometer, 1988). The comparable figures for the UK are 5 per cent and 1 per cent. These are figures which bring into question UK managers' ability to think globally, if they come from such a linguistically introverted culture, compared with their Dutch counterparts.

> (*He [Basil Fawlty] looks up to see a couple approaching the [Hotel] desk.*
> *He beams at them.*)

Elderly German:	Sprechen Sie Deutsch
Basil:	. . . Beg your pardon
Elderly German:	Entschuldigen Sie, bitte, können Sie Deutsch sprechen?
Basil:	. . . I'm sorry, could you say that again?
German lady:	You speak German?
Basil:	Oh, German! I'm sorry. I thought there was something wrong with you. Of course, the Germans!
German lady:	You speak German?
Basil:	Well . . . er . . . a little . . . I get by.
German lady:	Ein bisschen.
Elderly German:	Ah – wir wollen ein Auto mieten.
Basil:	(nodding helpfully) Well why not?
Elderly German:	Bitte.
Basil:	Yes, a little bit tricky . . . Would you mind saying it again?
German lady:	Please?

Basil:	Could you repeat . . . amplify . . . you know, reiterate? Yes? Yes?
Elderly German:	Wir . . .
Basil:	Wir? . . . Yes, well we'll come back to that.
Elderly German:	. . . Wollen . . .
Basil:	(to himself) Vollen . . . Voluntary?
Elderly German:	Ein Auto mieten.
Basil:	Owtoe . . . out to . . . Oh, I see! You're volunteering to go out to get some meat. Not necessary! We have meat here! (pause: the couple are puzzled) We haf meat hier . . . in ze buildink!! (he mimes a cow's horns) Moo! (Polly comes in) Ah, Polly, just explaining about the meat.

(Cleese and Booth, 1977, pp. 152–3)

Language, however, is varied within nations, both in terms of different languages being spoken within a state and differences in speech associated with geography and social groups. Such differences may contribute strongly to personal identity. Each individual is in possession of an idiolect, which distinguishes their speech patterns, together these form dialects and hence languages which are part of broader family groups. Language provides identity. Although, most people would be unable to emulate Shaw's Professor Higgins:

Simply phonetics. The science of speech. That's my profession: also my hobby. Happy is the man who can make a living by his hobby! You can spot an Irishman or a Yorkshireman by his brogue. I can place any man within six miles. I can place him within two miles in London. Sometimes within two streets. (Shaw, 1914, p. 26)

Such identification will help to establish an agenda as groups attempt to communicate. International marketers who have made the effort to master the language of the country in which they are operating have to be aware of their potential ignorance of the nuances of the local culture.

Non-verbal

Language may also be non-verbal. Individuals may convey much through the use of gestures and the way they stand or sit when talking. An Indian or Latin business partner may convey all the wrong messages to an English executive as he stands unexpectedly close. In the business environment, ownership of cars and office space may convey much in some cultures and leave those ill-attuned to such communication oblivious and ignorant of important factors. The English value the space they leave around them. A French manager who is used to using space efficiently so as to encourage a good working environment may be surprised by the power political importance of space in the English environment. German and Scandinavian regard for punctuality may be far from acceptable in a Latin environment and vice versa. Likewise, the contemporary belief amongst English managers that lateness is excusable if it has something to do with congestion on the M25 may not be fully appreciated by either group.

RELIGION AND EDUCATION

Religious observance reinforces values. Religion perpetuates ethical values which will inform social, economic and political conditions. It will not, however, be interpreted by the insider in the same way as it is interpreted by the outsider. A recently published book on business in Europe makes the following comments on religions' attitudes to gender roles and relationships:

> Muslim men may have more than one wife although the women are expected to remain monogamous;

> Jewish people have a strong sense of family loyalty and decision making tends to be more democratic than is the case in various other groups. (Welford and Prescott, 1994, p. 206)

Consider the statements from three perspectives: the Muslim, the Jew and the politically correct. First, it is impossible to do so adequately, it is only possible to assume various interpretations. The statements may, in any case, be disputed by those to whom the statements refer. They may be oversimplifications. Is it possible to encapsulate the role of different genders and their social and economic ramifications in short statements? The problem, of course, is that individuals choose to adopt reference points for religious groups which may not only be deeply offensive to those groups but may say far more about the holder of the views.

Religiously based values and attitudes have a profound impact on the society in which they are accepted and very soon are interpreted as 'good' or 'bad'. Consider the statements above again from your own perspective. Is one more acceptable than the other? If so, why is one more acceptable or partly unacceptable, or why are both acceptable or unacceptable? Do you know if the statements are accurate? What does that say about your own education and those subject areas with which your education was not concerned? Cultural differences neither emphasize what we know nor what we know we don't know; rather, cultural difference tells us more about what we didn't even know we didn't know.

It is difficult to separate religion and education. The development of education and religion in society has been linked throughout history. Attempts to claim that 'modern' education is secular, and, therefore, in some way unconnected with religion is to ignore the religiosity of rationalism and secularism. One of the first acts of political movements when they seize power through revolution is to wrest control of education from the religious groups which control it. Education may be considered to be a political act and statement. Education inculcates values; religions provide a value structure; revolutions seek to supplant value systems.

Religious values do not die easily, as indeed religions show an ability to gain strength from persecution. Such values are challenged by marketers at their peril. But marketers themselves may also find they are influenced by long-established value systems. Religion and education are strongly associated and are closely associated with the family both in the way the family nurtures religious observance and also in the way religion supports the family and concepts of the family. Individuals must therefore be aware of their own preconceptions.

KINSHIP AND HISTORY

> The falseness of an opinion is not for us any objection to it. . . . The question is, how far an opinion is life furthering, life preserving, species-preserving, perhaps species-rearing; and we are fundamentally inclined to maintain that the falsest opinions (to which the synthetic judgements *a priori* belong), are the most indispensable to us; that without the recognition of logical fictions, without a comparison of reality with the purely *imagined* world of the absolute and immutable, without a constant counterfeiting of the world by means of numbers, man could not live – that the renunciation of false opinions would be a renunciation of life, a negation of life. (Neitzsche, 1923, pp. 8–9)

Ask an Englishman the last time his country was invaded and the answer will probably be 1066. The Dutch Stadtholder William of Orange, who was to become William III of England, made a military landing in the west of England in 1688, and, with the help of what in the twentieth century would be called fifth columnists, seized the throne. In the late 1370s and early 1380s, in the south of England French and Castilian troops were 'harrying the coast with impunity' (Saul, 1995). The towns of Rye and Folkestone were burned in June 1377, and in July a major body of foreign troops landed on the Isle of Wight. In 1380, Winchelsea an important coastal town of the period was sacked. The examples do not end there, to suggest that they do would be to ignore the civil strife of the twelfth and the fifteenth centuries when bodies of foreign troops successfully marched into England, but that is not the material of popular myth.

While academic history as it developed in the nineteenth century might have attempted to enshrine, if not always succeeded in following, von Ranke's formula that history should be written as it was – 'wie es eigentlich gewesen' – such arid adherence to the facts of history is not the stuff of popular belief, of kinship myths and cultural identity. To quote one contemporary and eminent Oxford historian:

> Social memory and written history represent two very different, though sometimes not unrelated, ways of engaging with the past. They operate on different assumptions and through very different agencies; their views of the past often bear little relation to each other. (Davies, 1995, p. 338)

Groups need their myths and they need their heroes enshrined in those myths. The question 'what were you doing when Kennedy was assassinated?' did not merely make reference to an event but invited the individual, to whom the question was addressed, to express the shared values of a subset of a generation. The Kennedy memorial at Arlington cemetery is not merely a grave, it is a shrine, replete with improving texts. National identity may be seen as the logical progression from tribal or ethnic identity but it also requires self-conscious recognition and may even as some would suggest be little more than an artificial product so that 'Nationalism is not the awakening of nations to self consciousness; it invents nations where they do not exist' (Gellner, 1964, p. 168).

From the family to the nation, useful, indeed life-furthering, historical perceptions bind members of the group together. This will create barriers to relationships with other groups as it will help to build inter-group associations. The historical associations of the UK and the US, or perhaps more accurately the political aristocracy of the UK and the US, was a factor which helped to frustrate the initially unsuccessful attempts by the UK to gain membership of the European Community. Historical associations and popular historical belief structures and myths are not abstract issues that are of no concern to the international marketer. National identity is important not only in terms of the propensity of members of that nation to trade internationally but also in terms of other national groups and hence consumer groups to recognize qualities in the nation from which products come which will affect those consumers' willingness to buy products. Thus when marketers look at international markets, it is important that they appreciate not only the formalized and structured understanding of a market development and the formalized historical narrative but the informal traditions, the social memory, upon which perceptions amongst consumers are based.

> Social memory – in the sense of the common collective memory of human groupings from the neighbourhood to the nation – operates on very different principles. It is, in the admirable Welsh phrase for it, *cof gwlad*, the memory of the community or pays. It is not structured or generalized; rather it is selective and episodic. (Davies, 1995, p. 338)

When Sainsbury, the UK superstore operator, announced it was moving into the Northern Ireland market in June 1995, the company may have had many perceptions about the historical context into which it was moving. A ceasefire had been announced in the previous year after 25 years of conflict. The company is based in Great Britain (England, Scotland and Wales) and could be expected, if anything, to be associated in the minds of Northern Ireland consumers with historical links within the UK, rather than between the two Irelands, North and South. This is a market where shopping patronage will divide along political lines. However, following Sainsbury's announcement of its intention to open seven stores, a political issue arose which was ostensibly around the issue of planning permission and town development. Accusations were made concerning Sainsbury and special privileges provided by the UK government to encourage inward investment in Northern Ireland. Both 'Loyalist' (pro-UK political connections) and 'Nationalists' (pro-Irish Republic political connections) politicians made statements that were negative toward the Sainsbury development. While planning issues were of some concern, Northern Ireland had not seen the same level out of town developments which had occurred in the rest of the UK, and Sainsbury appeared to be confident in its aspirations to develop out of town sites, there were other issues associated with social memory which coloured views on the matter. During the 25 years of 'the troubles', Northern Ireland retailers had suffered considerable damage to their retail properties and had maintained town centre operations in accordance with planning policy. Sainsbury were therefore seen by many as coming into the market after the cessation of conflict and pushing aside those retailers who had maintained their presence in troubled times. Sainsbury therefore encountered a situation which was far more complex than structured observation would suggest.

ATTITUDES AND VALUES

Attitudes and values are a product of a number of factors: language, religion, education, aesthetics, kinship and history. To distil the variations of such factors in a few paragraphs is a futile effort which unfortunately texts often attempt to achieve and instead provide a crass commentary of popularly held misconceptions. What may be attempted, however, is a recognition of those contexts in which the international retailer must appreciate the problems of culture.

Part-time work in Northern Europe is well established but in Italy it has only recently been formally recognized in law (1984, law number 863) and is therefore a far from generally accepted part of the working culture. The phrase used to describe this phenomenon is 'part-time' not something like 'il lavoro a tempo parziale' (Brierly, 1993) thereby indicating the associations that such developments have. Part-time work in the UK in the retail sector is strongly associated with female employment. In Italy women have not been inclined to take up part-time work, rather they prefer to take up full-time employment.

The Code Napoleon in France is synonymous with the Anglo-Saxon derivative 'if it isn't allowed its forbidden'. French wages are embedded in a corporatist mind set which evaluates jobs on the basis of coefficients and rewards workers accordingly. This has led to a rigid remuneration structure which has controlled rewards for effort and innovation. However, an Act of 1986 now permits generalized bonuses to be paid on the basis of productivity and cost reductions. These bonuses may be paid immediately and are referred to as intéressement and are to be distinguished from participation payments which are held for five years before they are paid (Gordon, 1993).

Figures for Dutch international trade were used earlier in this book for sound reasons. The Netherlands, while only a relatively small country in terms of both population and land surface has been historically an important world trading nation. Its international retail activities continue that long tradition. Vendex and C&A continue its international tradition. C&A is so international, its Dutch roots have been subsumed in other identities. It is, therefore, perhaps not surprising that Dutch business culture lies somewhere between the American, the British and the

German. The business culture is reflected in the saying 'hij is handig, he makes good manoeuvres', that is judgement rather than dogmaticism is the more important quality (King, 1993).

Employees

Retailers when directly operating in another market will have to employ a local workforce. If the cultural barriers are too great for the company then the retailer should employ one method or another to access the market which does not involve recruitment of a workforce. Thus retailers should consider, joint-ventures and franchising, especially where there is a local main franchiser.

Employees will bring cultural attitudes and values to their place of work which will not necessarily be compatible with the operating systems and management style that a retailer has forged in another cultural context. As social groups whether economically culturally or geographically defined will vary within a national market, company culture will also vary. Thus a company that has recruited in its home market may find that some of its company culture as well as its national culture will profoundly influence its operational procedures. In a new market, it may not be able to rely on the same source of labour with the same values and will be unable to inculcate fundamental values in the way it may have anticipated.

Particularly where the retailer wishes to maintain a definitive image it will have to reinterpret that image through its local employees. Even where franchising is adopted as a growth strategy, the company will need to be conscious of the image that the employees in non-domestic stores are conveying to customers. Retailers such as the Body Shop will be able to appeal to the global values which are associated with its products and modes of operations. How though does a store with a general market coverage seek to achieve the same effect? What are the store's fundamental values?

In markets in West Europe and North America, while differences in employee attitudes are perceptible they are often graduated rather than absolute differences. This is not the case in East Europe, where attitudes to service are diametrically opposed to perceptions of service to be found in commercial operations in markets where their is a tradition of serving market needs. The experience of using a store in East Europe, even after the opening up of those markets, is to experience the mentality of rationing. It is not the customer who is the focus of attention, rather it is the product and its availability. In part this is the product of inefficiencies and shortages in the distribution system but it also an attitude of mind among shop staff. In 'free' markets, bulk purchasing may be used as a pretext for reduced prices. By buying more, the customer expects the value of the transaction to the supplier to be recognized and given some acknowledgement. In markets which have been command economies, the attitude of shop staff is not based on this assumption. To them larger orders represent more work per customer and may result in a higher unit price being charged because of the extra work involved. In such circumstances, international retailers have to address fundamental and in-grained ways of thinking.

Suppliers

Unless the international retailer intends to source all its merchandise from outside its new market, the company will have to deal with local suppliers. This may lead the retailer into a situation which it had not anticipated, particularly in markets which are fundamentally different not only in terms of everyday culture but in terms of business culture as well.

Spanish business culture, which to many, is characterized by an aura of mañana – although, as many Irishmen will be proud to tell you, in Ireland there is no word which conveys the same degree of urgency – has been subject to considerable changes in recent years, but it still poses fundamental challenges to retailers seeking to develop in the market. There are a large number of conservatively inclined small companies, a low level of management and shop floor training, a weak technological and service infrastructure and conflict between government and unions (Bruton, 1993).

Retailers may, therefore, find themselves unable to follow procedures which they would take for granted in their domestic market. Consequently, the retailer may need to become more involved with suppliers or find suppliers reluctant to accept the same level of cooperation and advice from retailers as the retailer has come to expect in the home market. Technological systems may be incompatible or simply not exist. Thus, the retailer may be faced not only with the physical reality of limited technology but a failure on behalf of the local suppliers to recognize the need for the technology. This should not imply that the retailer is the bearer of superior operating systems and comes from a market which is more advanced, merely that systems have developed differently. Sainsbury has found in New England that the development of supplier-retailer technologies and ware-housing systems has not matched the development in the UK. If the retailer believes that the systems used in the domestic market are essential to foreign operations then the retailer will have to educate the suppliers and change the business culture.

This alteration of business culture may not, however, prove particularly easy to bring about. Ahold, the Dutch food retailer with substantial operations in the US, has introduced a system of centralized distribution called 'cross-docking' in the US. The system involves vehicles being unloaded at one side of a warehouse and almost immediately another vehicle being loaded at the other side of the ware-house. The system is common in the European environment and saves warehouse costs. The system has fallen foul of the Teamsters trucking union in the US. On 10 January 1996, they placed advertisements in Dutch newspapers accusing Ahold of introducing a system which hurt the 'poor and elderly' (van de Krol, 1996, p. 2). As far as the Teamsters were concerned, the system did not permit them to make deliveries to small stores along their route and this damaged small operations and the shopping facilities of small communities. The Dutch company did not feel they had a case to answer and believed the union was focusing on their distribution changes rather than indigenous US retailers' introduction of the system because as a non-US company they were an easier and more attractive target.

In conducting business with suppliers, retailers may find they make certain assumptions which are not made in their new market. This may be as simple as the way business negotiations are conducted. Experienced negotiators may find themselves confused in a new cultural environment. Negotiations with Japanese businesses has long been a source of concern for negotiators more familiar with the 'American way' of business negotiation. Negotiations involve various types of social procedures which draw on cultural perceptions of politeness. Negotiating skills do not necessarily travel well. Indeed, the whole process of negotiation may be more acceptable in some cultures than in other cultures. Cultural assumptions may lead some individuals to think of negotiation in very different ways. As Wood and Colosi (1996, p. 6) have observed, many Westerners, 'notably those with an English-speaking background . . . consider negotiation as an adversarial process'. The process is, of course, far more complex and is not so easily conceptualized as a one to one competitive game plan.

Customers

There are two types of north of England males according to popular myth. There are those that go shopping in Marks & Spencer with their wife and those who wait outside the doors of Marks & Spencer for their wife to come out of the shop. In the US, customers may appear very different:

> What peaches and what penumbras! Whole families shopping at night! Aisles full of husbands! Wives in the avocados, babies in the tomatoes! – and you, Garcia Lorca, what were you doing down by the watermelons? (Ginsberg, 1956, p. 281)

Consumer tastes and behaviours vary considerably and for many reasons. Cultural influences will affect individuals attitudes to shopping and the products they purchase. Even within societies, marketers recognize a wide range of motivations and stimuli. In the international context an even wider variety of influences will mould behaviour patterns. It is not possible to explore those differences fully in this context, but it is worth noting certain fundamentals which are taken for granted in some societies but which are not seen as the norm in others.

It is a tenet, which modern retailing textbooks will expound, that prices are essentially fixed (Lewison, 1989, p. 4). Our northern male shopper who waits outside the store would no more enter the store than his compatriot who does venture into the store would ask for a discount. Marks & Spencer is renowned for the slogan, and its early success was based on the slogan, 'Don't Ask the Price its a Penny'. The prices are fixed. The early Marks & Spencer customer was drawn to the store because it provided a context of social assurance. Costs were not going to mount uncontrollably as purchases were totalled and potential embarrassment caused. In the retail context, into which the Penny Bazaar was introduced, the urbanized and industrialized Britain, the new working-class shoppers of the industrial town were attracted to the fixed price retailer as they sought to avoid the traditional middle-class shopping facilities.

The British are not a nation of negotiators in the retail outlet. Negotiation, as noted above, is often perceived as adversarial in the Anglo-Saxon context. The early development of chain stores in the UK is in part explained by customers willingness to accept fixed pricing and avoid negotiation. In the UK, car purchasers frequently complain of the negotiating process they have to become involved with when purchasing a car. In consequence, Asda, the UK hypermarket retailer, attempted to establish an operation called Asdadrive in 1986, to provide customers of their stores to buy cars at fixed prices an avoid the negotiation encountered at the traditional distributors' outlets. The scheme did not survive an initial roll out stage but the basis of the scheme remains relevant in the 1990s. Daewoo in their marketing have focused on such customer concerns. Indeed, Daewoo announced, in April 1996, that they were teaming up with Sainsbury to provide sales facilities outside Sainsbury's stores.

The Anglo-Saxon aversion to negotiation is not shared by other cultures. Walk into a small Italian store and you will be aware that 'un usconto e possibile'. Discounts – usconti – are a feature of some consumer cultures, this reflects the wider culture within which shopping habits develop. Marketing prides itself on being a management philosophy which ensures that products don't come back but customers do. Shopkeepers in many parts of world continue a tradition that has recognized that the price marked on the good is a starting point and that customers who are local and to whom a discount is given may very well come back.

The culture of service will also vary around the world. US service operatives are internationally known for the 'Have a Nice day' message. To outside observers, this may sound like the spontaneous offering of a culture oriented to service and customers' needs. Exposure to the reality to US retailing may, however, lead the observer to suggest that 'Have a Nice day' is a formalization and in itself does not reflect enthusiasm born or a service culture but management concern at poor service provision. Likewise, US service providers are far more tip (gratuity) oriented than unsuspecting visitors might expect. Tipping is something with which the British have a cultural problem. It is hardly surprising, therefore, that proposed legislation (1996), such as the Earl of Bradford's Restaurant (Service and Cover Charges) Bill, which would require charges in restaurants to be all inclusive, has been introduced in the UK Parliament. Extra tipping would therefore not be required.

Fundamentally, of course, it is also true that customer tastes vary considerably. Nevertheless, consumer tastes may not be as unusual as some early European visitors to Caribbean would suggest. Early visitors to the Caribbean were eager to describe cannibalistic behaviour amongst the local population.

> According to one (a Frenchman), the Caribs thought the French were delicious, the English so-so, the Dutch tasteless and the Spanish so tough as to be virtually inedible. (Tannahill, 1988, p. 212)

This description is informative of the way outsiders judge markets; the details may owe more to the observers own prejudices toward their own kind, and the facts may have little in common with the truth. Nevertheless, tastes do vary and even less dramatic examples of cultural peculiarity may engender strong reaction.

Vincent: . . . But you know what the funniest thing about Europe is?
Jules: What?
Vincent: It's the little differences. I mean, they got the same shit over there that we got here, but it's just, just, there it's a little different.
Jules: Example?
Vincent: Well, you can walk into a movie theater and buy a beer. And I don't mean just, like, in no paper cup. I'm talking about a glass of beer. And in Paris, you can buy a beer at McDonald's. And, you know what they call a Quarter-Pounder with Cheese in Paris?
Jules: They don't call it a Quarter-Pounder with Cheese?
Vincent: No, man, they got the metric system there, they wouldn't know what the fuck a Quarter-Pounder is.
Jules: What'd they call it?
Vincent: They call it a Royale with Cheese.
Jules: (*repeating*) Royale with Cheese.
Vincent: Yeah, that's right.
Jules: What'd they call a Big Mac?
Vincent: Well, Big Mac's a Big Mac, but they call it Le Big Mac.
Jules: Le Big Mac. What do they call a Whopper?
Vincent: I dunno, I didn't go into Burger King. But you know what they put on French fries in Holland instead of Ketchup?
Jules: What?
Vincent: Mayonnaise.
Jules: Goddamn!
Vincent: I seen 'em do it, man. They fuckin' drown 'em in that shit.
Jules: Yuck.

(Tarantino, 1994, pp. 14–6)

Measurement of difference

While anecdotal evidence may be immediately enlightening and insightful, there is the distinct danger that it may be countered by other anecdotal material or qualified into oblivion. Measurement of culture, nevertheless, is a difficult process. However, work has been carried out on this area, some of the most interesting and accessible of which is Hofstede's work within the organizational context (Hofstede, 1980, 1983a, 1983b).

Hofstede used four polarities to measure and discuss national culture. On the basis of his research, as long as we accept his findings, we are able to say that it is more than likely that Danes and Jamaicans working for Frenchmen will find them surprisingly dictatorial and disinclined to consider useful suggestions. Austrians and Israelis working for Indians will find the decision making processes of the senior manager wilful and arbitrary. Indians and Malayans working for Swedes will find them unwilling to take responsibility and will be confused by the suggestion that they should provide alternative options to managers who are, in their opinion, there to lead, while Austrian and Israeli co-workers will find the Swedes inclined to negotiate in circumstances where rules should be well-applied.

Hofstede's polarities are individualism against collectivism, large power distances against small power distances, strong uncertainty avoidance against weak uncertainty avoidance and masculinity against femininity. They are described in

Exhibit 12.4 Hofstede's individualism/collectivism and large/small power distance polarities

Individualism/collectivism
This polarity measures the relationship between the individual and the group in which the individual lives.

Individualism: here individuals consider that the ties they have with other members of their society are weak. They may have little respect for the notion of society and take full advantage of the freedom their 'society' or more suitably community, provides them. Self-interest is paramount and even the close family group may find their collective interests must be subordinate to the individual's self expression.

Collectivism: the word tribal is appropriate in this context. The tribe or 'ingroup' are important in determining the individual's views and behaviour. Individuals must contribute to the maintenance of the group. Family members must be considered and helped.

Large/small power distance
This polarity measures the individual's social environment in terms of the society's willingness to accept inequality.

Large power distance: here autocratic centralization is accepted. There are large distances between those who lead and those who follow. However, there remains a social contract, the system could not work without it, so that the led are happy to be managed in this way, without such leadership they feel lost.

Small power distance: here there is not a great social distance placed between the main body of individuals in the group and those doing the guiding, indeed, the guiders are at pains to involve their subordinates in the decision making. Again both groups feel comfortable with this arrangement.

Source: Hofstede, 1983a.

exhibit 12.4 and exhibit 12.5. Different national societies may be plotted against these polarities. When power distance were plotted by Hofstede against individualism, a large number of 'third world' countries were described as large power distant low individualistic societies, while North European and Anglo-Saxon societies were characterized by small power distance and high individualism. There was less correlation between other factors. Power distance and uncertainty avoidance produced a number of groupings, where, for example, Irish responses showed a society of weak uncertainty avoidance and small power distance, where an attitude of 'Don't tell me what to do, I'll take a risk if I want to' contrasted with a French response of large power distance and strong uncertainty avoidance which translates as 'I'm in charge and we will ensure no unnecessary risks are taken'.

When measures of masculinity were set against uncertainty avoidance, Japan and Greece were described as societies where strong avoidance of uncertainty combined with a high level masculinity in direct contrast to Sweden, where gender roles were not rigorously defined and there was weak uncertainty avoidance.

Overall four general approaches to social interaction emerged from Hofstede's research.

Village market: where negotiation between parties was seen as the best alternative.

Family: where the head of the establishment decides on the basis that suits him at that time.

Pyramid: where the head of the establishment decides on the basis of accepted principles.

Well oiled machine: where principles and teamwork regulate action.

Hofstede (1983a) notes that individualistic societies were certainly in the ascendent when compared with GNP in 1970; however, as he also noted those societies such as the Japanese where individualism was less well respected had been developing quickly in 20 years preceding his research. The individualism of Reganite and Thatcherite economics development were a celebration of individualism and a reassertion of some of the cultural elements to be found within the societies they represented.

CONCLUSION

We are all influenced by culture. We are all foreign to someone. Our cultural idiosyncrasies will be treated affectionately by some, derisively by many and considered blasphemous by others. All that matters is we are aware of the situations where such reactions will occur. International retailers operating in unfamiliar cultures face the prospect of trespassing on cultural values on a daily basis. In some cultures, international retailers will not be able to trade because they are who they are. If there is one golden rule, it is that no trader should be ignorant of their own cultural values and assume that they are universally acceptable.

Exhibit 12.5 Hofstede's strong/weak uncertainty avoidance and masculinity/femininity polarities

Strong/weak uncertainty avoidance

This polarity measures the acceptance within society of uncertainty and thus the willingness to accept risk.

Strong uncertainty avoidance: here individuals will exhibit signs of concern for the future and will seek to avoid risk and uncertainty through various mechanisms such as laws, institutions and religious adherence, whether in the theological or philosophical sense. The individual aggressively seeks truth, and is not prepared to tolerate that which challenges the accepted norm.

Weak uncertainty avoidance: here individuals learn to accept the problems that uncertainty brings. This acceptance of uncertainty will encourage members of the society to take risks. Such societies will be tolerant but will not encourage hard work.

Masculinity/femininity

This measures the apportioning of social roles between genders.

Masculinity: here the social gender based division of activities is maximized. Masculine behaviour which is in this context characterized by high visibility assertive behaviour is the norm. The Übermensch is lauded.

Femininity: here gender roles are not clearly demarcated and society is less inclined to raise one member of the group above others. The emphasis is on quality not quantity, preservation, and helping.

Source: Hofstede, 1983a.

This chapter has sought to raise questions concerning culture. Discussions on culture are always prone to reflect the author's perspective rather than any illusion of objective truth. In discussing culture, we are always in danger of revealing our own cultural perspectives whether we are testosterone enhanced, melamine deficient, Eurocentrics or not.

QUESTIONS – DISCUSSION POINTS

1   Is culture nothing more or less than 'collective mental programming' as Hofstede (1983a) suggests?

2　Does national culture exist, or is a 'national' culture merely the culture of the dominant subgroup in any society?

3　Is language the most important component of cultural identity?

4　Is social memory or written history the most important determinant of collective perceptions of the past?

5　Some retailers would claim to offer a standard and consistent service across national boundaries. Is this possible, even within apparently similar cultural contexts, or will retailers always compromise in some way?

6　With reference to exhibits 12.4 and 12.5, assess your own cultural preferences. Where would you place yourself against the various polarities?

REFERENCES

Alexander, N., (1990a) Retailers and International Markets: Motives for Expansion, *International Marketing Review*, Vol. 7, No. 4, pp. 75–85.

Alexander, N., (1990b) Retailing Post-1992, *Service Industries Journal*, Vol. 10, No. 2, pp. 172–87.

Boyd, W., (1984) *Stars and Bars*, Penguin, Harmondsworth, 1985 edition.

Brierly, W., (1993) The Business Culture in Italy, C. Randlesome (ed.) *Business Cultures in Europe*, Butterworth-Heinemann, Oxford, pp. 141–201.

Bruton, K., (1993) The Business Culture in Spain, C. Randlesome (ed.) *Business Cultures in Europe*, Butterworth-Heinemann, Oxford, pp. 265–321.

Chambers, J., and Trudgill, P., (1980) *Dialectology*, Cambridge University Press, Cambridge.

Cleese, J., and Booth, C., (1977) *The Complete Fawlty Towers*, Mandarin, London, 1989 edition.

Crystal, D., (1987) *The Cambridge Encyclopedia of Language*, University of Cambridge, Cambridge.

Davies, R., (1995) *The Revolt of Owain Glyn Dwr*, Oxford University Press, Oxford.

Eurobarometer, (1988) *Eurobarometer*, Commission of the European Communities, Brussels.

Garner, J., (1994) *Politically Correct Bedtime Stories*, Macmillan, New York.

Gellner, E., (1964) *Thought and Change*, London, Weidenfield & Nicolson.

Ginsberg, A., (1956) A Supermarket in California, in C. Ricks, W. Vance (eds) *The Faber Book of America*, Faber and Faber, London, 1994 edition, p. 281.

Gordon, C., (1993) The Business Culture in France, C. Randlesome (ed.) *Business Cultures in Europe*, Butterworth-Heinemann, Oxford, pp. 87–139.

Hartley, L., (1953) *The Go-Between*, Hamish Hamilton, London.

Hofstede, G., (1980) *Culture's Consequences: International Differences in Work-Related Values*, Sage Publications, London.

Hofstede, G., (1983a) The Cultural Relativity of Organizational Practices and Theories, *Journal of International Business Studies*, Vol. 14, No. 2, pp. 75–89.

Hofstede, G., (1983b) Dimensions of National Cultures in Fifty Countries and Three Regions, J. Deregowski, S. Dziurawiec, R. Annis (eds) *Expiscations in Cross-Cultural Psychology*, Sweets and Zeitlinger, Lisse – Netherlands.

King, P., (1993) The Business Culture in the Netherlands, C. Randlesome (ed.) *Business Cultures in Europe*, Butterworth-Heinemann, Oxford, pp. 323–64.

Larke, R., (1994) *Japanese Retailing*, Routledge, London.

Lewison, D., (1989) *Essentials of Retailing*, Merrill, Columbus Ohio.

Llewellyn, R., (1939) *How Green Was My Valley*, Michael Joseph, London.

MacCarthy, F., (1989) *Eric Gill*. Faber & Faber, London.

Mikes, G., (1962) *The Best of Mikes*, Pan, London.

Neitzsche, F., (1923) *Beyond Good and Evil*, Translated by Helen Zimmern, 1923 edition, pp. 8–9.

Ricks, C., and Vance, W., (eds) (1994) *The Faber Book of America*, Faber and Faber, London. p. 243.

Roussseau, J-J., (1772) *Contract Social*, Garnier Frères, Paris.

Saul, N., (1995) Bodiam Castle, *History Today*, Vol. 45, No. 1, pp. 16–21.

Shaw, B., (1914) *Pygmalion*, Penguin, London, 1982 edition.

Smith, A., (1993) *National Identity*, Penguin Books, London.

Tannahill, R., (1988) *Food in History*, Penguin, Harmondsworth.

Tarantino, Q., (1994) *Pulp Fiction*, Faber and Faber, London.

van de Krol, R., (1996) Teamsters Union in US paints Dutch as bad guys, *Financial Times*, London, 11 January.

Welford, R., and Prescott, K., (1994) *European Business*, 2nd edition, Pitman Publishing, London.

Wilson, C., (1985) *First with the News: The History of W. H. Smith 1792–1972*, London: Jonathan Cape.

Wood, J., and Colosi, R., (1996) It takes more than two to agree, *Mastering Management*, Part 10, Financial Times, London, 12 January.

Retail Structure

OUTLINE

▌OBJECTIVES ▌

This chapter considers retail structure. The retail structure which exists in any market is the product of regulation, economic activity, society and culture within that market. It is also a reflection of indigenous retailers' ability to create competitive retail forms. Retail structures vary considerably, both within and between markets.

INTRODUCTION

The retail structure of a market is essentially the product of the other factors discussed in part IV. The nature of the structure will depend on the ability of commercial enterprises in a market to meet the customers' needs which in turn are determined by social and economic conditions within a regulatory framework and cultural context. The retail structure will be indicative of development in the market. Developed markets will share similar characteristics.

Throughout this chapter, the retail structure of EU markets is a central theme. This is because EU markets provide a collection of comparative figures while also providing a relatively wide variety of retail structures. It is often very difficult to draw comparisons between markets where there is a fundamental difference in the distribution presumptions of the market. For example, when mobile retail enterprises or local markets are an important feature of retailing in a market, then the ratio of fixed shops to population figures are not indicative of the conditions in the market. Likewise, a comparison of the number of shops per inhabitant in East Europe and West Europe immediately after the revolutions of the late 1980s would provide figures which would suggest a sophisticated retail system in the East because of shop population ratios, but would in fact reflect the regimes of Eastern Europe's lack of economic policy emphasis on distribution and an emphasis on manufacture.

The EU also provides an opportunity for comparison of other global-regional retail structures. Thus the US, Japan and 'third world' markets are discussed with reference to the European figures. Europe in most respects has been the recipient of innovation from the US market, while Japan's retail structure is still undergoing fundamental development. Thus, in the period 1960–90 Europe's retail structure has developed with reference to the US but in advance of the Japan's retail structure. This provides opportunities for market comparison.

ENTERPRISE DENSITY

Enterprise density is an important measure of retail structure. International retailers may gain a useful picture of a non-domestic market relatively quickly with reference to reliable enterprise density figures.

A large share of retail activity in more economically developed markets is carried on by large retail operations. Large retail operations have the financial capacity to invest in large efficient premises and exploit the technology available to them. They are able to negotiate with suppliers on more favourable terms, and through the specialized management functions they are able to adopt, they can more successfully meet the needs of their customers. This has a measurable effect on the enterprise density of the markets in which they operate. Such retailers are also the product of economically developed markets.

At the beginning of the 1990s, Greece had a GDP per capita at purchasing power parities of 9,850 ECU, nearly half the European average of 17,857 ECU and well below the US figure of 24,000 ECU (Eurostat, 1993). There were 175,000 retail outlets in Greece, the equivalent of 174 outlets to every 10,000 inhabitants. In contrast, the Western German Lander had a GDP per capita at purchasing power parities of 21,131 ECU. In the West German Lander there were 439,000 retail outlets the equivalent of seventy retail outlets per 10,000 inhabitants. In Germany, the average turnover of retail business was 813,000 ECU, in Greece, the figure was 114,000 ECU. Thus the higher the level of economic development, the fewer the number of retail outlets and the higher the turnover of the average business.

International retailers will be able to make immediate assessments on the basis of such enterprise density figures. In a market with a low number of outlets per inhabitant, assumptions may be made about the overall condition of the retail structure. Low figures, such as those indicated above with reference to Germany, will suggest a market with a developed structure. This may prove advantageous to operations which require a developed infrastructure in which to operate. Distribution channels will be reasonably developed and will not require development or require the retailer to make adjustments to operational procedures. Such markets, however, may offer a level of sophisticated competition which an incoming retailer would not relish. In contrast, markets with a high number of outlets per inhabitant may offer considerable opportunities for retailers prepared to manage the problems of operating within a structure and distribution system which does not offer the familiar features found in the domestic market. As a reward for managing these problems, the international retailer will have the opportunity to establish operations in the undeveloped market and have the potential to gain substantial market share in the developing market.

This relationship between the number of retail enterprises per inhabitant and the purchasing power of the local market may be seen throughout the EU. However, the relationship between wealth within a market and enterprise density is not strict, so that while both the Netherlands and the UK (19,147 ECU and 19,726 ECU GDP per capita respectively), have a lower GDP per capita at purchasing power parities than Germany's Western Lander, the Netherlands and the UK have a lower number of outlets per 10,000 inhabitants, sixty-four and sixty-one outlets. Economics is not the only determinant of the retail structure; regulation, as discussed in chapter 7, may make an important difference.

While most of the EU countries with a high enterprise density, that is more than 100 retail outlets per 10,000 inhabitants, are the Mediterranean countries of Greece, Italy, Portugal and Spain, the list also includes Belgium which has 128 outlets per 10,000 inhabitants. As was noted in chapter 7, Belgium has had strict regulations concerning the development of large retail enterprises. Belgium's enterprise density has historically been much higher than its European neighbours. In 1955, while in Belgium there were 294 establishments per 10,000 inhabitants, there were 175 in France, 154 in the Netherlands, 119 in West Germany and 116 in the UK (Jefferys and Knee, 1962).

Belgium's retail enterprise density has remained high throughout the last four decades. Both Belgium and the Netherlands saw rapid and sustained economic growth in the early years of the European Community, in the 20 years from 1955 to 1974, and both countries have continued to develop at the centre of the EU, both in a metaphorical and geographical sense, yet the enterprise density in Belgium has remained high compared to that of the Netherlands. Relatively, the enterprise density of these markets has remained surprisingly constant. In 1990, in the

Netherlands the enterprise density was 42 per cent of 45 years earlier; in Belgium the figure was 44 per cent. Strong historical forces, represented by social, and hence public policy, assumptions will constrain the development of retail structures, despite those structures being subject to the same kinds of pressure experienced in other markets where development has been more rapid.

MARKET CONCENTRATION

Strongly linked to enterprise density are the concentration levels which exist in a market. Concentration calculations measure the share of the market held be one of a group of retail enterprises. Retail concentration and retail density are closely linked, so that, as retailers increase their market share and hence, as their competitiveness is felt in the market, they will have an impact on enterprise densities as less efficient retailers are forced out of the market. Concentration levels have increased and thus enterprise densities decreased through the growth of innovative retail forms, such as the cooperative, the department store, the variety store, the discount store and the multiple store operation. Today, many of these forms may sound outmoded but they have all played an important role in increasing concentration levels.

Some of these retail forms have had a greater impact in some markets than others. In the UK, the multiple organization established an important position in the retail structure. By 1960, 20.8 per cent of UK retail sales were accounted for by the multiple organizations, whereas in Italy only 0.1 per cent of sales went through such organizations (Jefferys and Knee, 1962). Multiple retailers or chain store organizations have characterized UK retailing. Jefferys' (1954) work on the development of chain stores in the UK from the mid nineteenth century illustrates the role of such organizations in the development of UK retailing.

In Germany, in contrast, specialized chain operations did not develop as quickly. Only in recent years have specialized chains built a significant market share from 2.0 per cent in 1980, to 14.0 per cent, projected for 1995 (Eurostat, 1993). Specialist chains remain weak in some subsectors, although they are developing market share. The electrical appliance sector has not been an area of strength for the specialist chains. In 1988, they held only 3.9 per cent of the market rising to 9.0 per cent in 1992. In the retail clothing subsector, however, the 4.3 per cent market share of 1988 had only risen to 5.0 per cent by 1992.

In Scandinavian countries, the cooperative was a particularly influential retail form, with 34.0% of Finland's retail sales being accounted for by such enterprises in 1960 (Jefferys and Knee, 1962). In the UK, 11 per cent of sales passed through the cooperatives, but this figure hides the fact that in some parts of the UK, such as Scotland and Wales, this figure would have been much greater on a local level. The cooperative store remains an important element in the retail structure of some European markets in the 1990s: in Denmark at the beginning of the decade of 1,036 supermarkets between 400 sq m and 2,499 sq m, 387 were run by cooperatives (Eurostat, 1993), but the system has evolved considerably from its initial roots.

Indeed, the cooperative store has come to resemble the chain store or department store operation but retained a social mission. This has hampered the cooperative movement's attempts at modernization.

The department store, while having an important place in the development of retailing in the early twentieth century, has lost market share in many developed markets. Even in Japan, where the department store has overwhelmingly dominated the large store sector of the retail system until relatively recently, other mass merchandisers are playing an increasingly important role in the market. In 1960, all of the ten largest retail organizations in Japan were department store groups; in 1990, the top four companies were general merchandise retailers (Larke, 1994). In Europe, in 1960, the department store groups were particularly strong in Belgium, Germany and the UK, controlling between 4.5 per cent and 5.5 per cent of retail sales. In other countries such as Denmark, France, Ireland, the Netherlands, Switzerland department store groups controlled between 3.5 per cent and 4.5 per cent of the market (Jefferys and Knee, 1962). In the mid 1990s, German department stores control around 5.5 per cent of the retail market, but this is a decrease on previous years. In 1980, German department stores held a 7.2 per cent market share (Eurostat, 1993).

Variety store operations have also had an important role in the development of European retail structures, commanding 4.8 per cent of the UK retail sector by 1960, and between 3 per cent and 4 per cent in Belgium, France and Sweden. However, like the department store, this retail form has either lost market share to other forms of retailing or evolved into something akin to, but essentially different from, the original concept. Thus in the UK, Marks & Spencer, a variety store operation in its earlier days and certainly still classified as such in some contexts, no longer strictly conforms to the variety store model. Today, the discount store owes a lot to the variety store concept.

Since the 1960s, the impact of the hypermarket and superstore format on European retailing has been considerable. In some markets, such as France, Western Germany and the UK, this format has reached a mature stage of development, whereas in other markets, such as Portugal and Italy, these formats have still some opportunity for growth. In Germany, hypermarkets hold a 17.5 per cent market share: this represents an increase from 11.9 per cent in 1980 (Eurostat, 1993). At the beginning of 1995, Leclerc and Carrefour both had more than a million square metres of selling space in France in the form of hypermarkets or Tres Grands Supermarches (LSA, 1995). In January 1995, Carrefour operated four hypermarkets of at least 20,000 sq m of selling space.

Mail order has also experienced different fortunes within the markets of the EU. Mail order has stimulated the growth of some very large businesses in Germany. Otto Versand, Karstadt, and Schikedanz are amongst the largest twenty EU retailers: they are all based in Germany and have mail order as a main activity. In Germany, mail order accounts for around 5.5 per cent of retail sales (Eurostat, 1993). In France, La Redoute and Trois Suisses International has also maintained an important position in the market. Mail order, however, has only achieved around 5 per cent of market share. Non-store retailing has long been heralded as the future of retailing. Even vending machines have been described as an important challenge to fixed store operations. In the 1990s, the non-store retail challenge comes from the teleshopping; however, again, the form has not lived up to early visions of it.

PRODUCT SECTOR

The structure of retailing within different product sectors is also indicative of the stage of retail structural development. In Portugal at the beginning of the 1990s there were 1.1 non-food retail outlets for every food outlet. In the Netherlands, there were 2.2 (Eurostat, 1993). Therefore, as enterprise density decreases, so the ratio of non-food to food retail outlets rises. This is in part a consequence of the swifter decline in food stores to non-food stores as retailing has become concentrated in the hands of large retail organizations and food retailers in particular have utilized innovative retail formats in which to market their merchandise, but it is also due to the changing nature of income disposal as markets experience economic development.

The share of household income spent on food declines as income rises. There will always be cultural differences which affect that calculation but the general trend follows that rule in any one society. Thus, there is a point where the number of non-food shops per 10,000 inhabitants will rise, unless a fundamental change occurs in the distribution of non-food items. In Italy, between 1982 and 1990, the number of outlets selling food, drink and tobacco fell from 341,150 to 301,528, while the number of outlets selling textiles, clothing, footwear and leather goods rose from 153,761 to 171,552 (Eurostat, 1993).

As the retailing of food products was radically changed by the introduction of techniques associated with the supermarket, so retailing of non-food items has fundamentally changed with the introduction of the variety store and non-food discounters. The superstore format has also been transferred to the non-food sector in the form of DIY outlets to considerable advantage of major retailers often food retailers. The UK operation Sainsbury's DIY store Homebase, a joint venture with GIB of Belgium, has allowed the company to develop superstore operations in this non-food sector. The company acquired, in 1995, the Texas DIY chain, thereby increasing its share of the UK DIY market. In the 1980s the Italian non-food sector saw a fundamental change with the development of large specialist operations such as Bricocenter developed by Rinascente in the DIY sector, Ikea in the furniture sector, Expert developed by Sogema in the electrical and household appliance sector and Centro auto developed by Auchen in the car accessories sector (Eurostat, 1993).

In more developed markets in Europe, large food retailers have come to dominate their sector and hence have become some of the largest retailers in the economy. Of the largest ten retailers in the EU at the beginning of the 1990s, all ten had a major interest in food retailing, and for nine of them, food could be considered the main activity (Eurostat, 1993). Increased concentration levels within the

13.1 China

It would be easy to make the assumption that retail operations are managed by retailers, or investors who have concentrated their interest on the retail sector. This is not always the case.

Charoen Pokphand is based in Thailand but it has considerable commercial interests around the world with eleven of its subsidiaries listed on seven stock markets around the world.

The company operates nearly 300 7-Eleven stores in Thailand, while a further 250 are run by independent traders who have acquired franchises from Charoen Pokphand. The operation has a market capitalization around US$400m.

The company also has substantial interests in China but these are very different from convenience retailing. The company is the largest foreign investor in China with over 100 factories, and operates in nearly all of the countries thirty regions. One of the company's largest concerns is Ek Chor, a motorcycle manufacturer. The company is also expanding into brewing and the supply of construction materials.

In some cases, retail interests are only part of a companies portfolio of international interests.

Source: Bardacke, 1996.

food sector and the saturation of certain formats has led food retailers to consider alternative growth strategies. This has led food retailers to diversify into non-food retailing, as well as encouraging some into the international arena.

INNOVATION

The US market has historically been viewed as a source of innovation. The innovative retail operations that have had their origins in the US market, while they may owe much to the individual enterprise of retailers, were brought into being through the regulatory, economic, social and cultural environment in which they developed. The second industrial revolution which occurred at the end of the nineteenth century saw major changes in the distribution system of industrialized countries. At that time, the rapidly growing industrial economy of the US provided the domestic consumer with a new and wider range of goods. Such operations as Frank Woolworth's variety stores responded to the consumers' desire for mass produced merchandise (Woolworth, 1954). In the US, such new forms of retail enterprise were relatively unencumbered by the old order of retail distribution and urban congestion.

The US saw the early development of retail forms that were to make major contributions to the development of other retail structures. The vibrant retail operations of the US, which were developed within the context of economic growth, were to be exported either directly or indirectly to other markets in Europe and elsewhere. This exchange of innovation between markets takes a recognizable form. Innovation moves from developed to less developed retail structures. Markets which do not develop sufficiently, markets which are constrained for one reason or another from developing, are vulnerable to international operations and operations replicating non-indigenous formats.

The arrival of European food discounters, such as Aldi and Netto, in the UK during the early 1990s is an example of a market which failed to sufficiently develop a vital sector which could challenge non-indigenous international operators. The UK grocery retailers had concentrated their efforts on superstore operations and, by and large, ignored the opportunities which existed.

Innovation will flow from one market to another market. Innovation will tend to flow to markets which are less advanced than the market which provides the innovation. Thus, the retail structure of a relatively less advanced market which is open to ideas, and operations, from a more advanced market will begin to take on the characteristics of the more advanced market. However, that is not to say that the secondary market will exactly replicate the developments in the primary market; regulatory, economic, social and existing structural conditions will shape structural developments.

EMPLOYMENT STRUCTURE

The nature of employment in a market reflects the structure of retailing within that market. In Greece, at the beginning of the 1990s, there were on average 1.9 persons employed in Greek retail enterprises. In the retail outlets of Germany's Western Lander, at the beginning of the 1990s, there were 5.4. The average number of employees in Dutch and British retail outlets is higher than in Germany at 6.7 and 8.7 respectively.

As the retail structure develops, the average number of employees in retail outlets increases, the size of the outlet increases and the use of employee's time is adjusted to suit the demands placed on the store by its customers. Flexible hours allow retailers to address the need for more staff at specific times during the day. In Greece only 3.3 per cent of employees were registered as part-time at the beginning of the 1990s; 40.7 per cent were registered as part-time in the UK (Eurostat, 1993).

In retail outlets in less developed markets, the employment structure is more difficult to describe through the use of official figures. One reason for this is that members of the immediate family will be involved in the running of the shop who are not accounted for in official figures. Even in more developed retail structures, small shopkeepers make extensive use of family labour which is not easily accounted for in official figures but in markets where the small retail operation is dominant, assessments of labour involvement becomes even more problematic. In less developed markets, peripatetic retailing is a common feature. Fixed shops are easy to quantify; mobile operations, apart from those contexts in which licensing is strictly observed are more problematic. Therefore, employment figures for such markets may be highly unreliable.

As large retail enterprises gain market share, so the number of independent businesses decreases, thus in turn, the number of self-employed workers in retailing falls as a proportion of the total. In Denmark, Germany, Luxembourg and the UK, over 80 per cent of those working in retailing are wage or salary earners; in Greece, the figure is less than 30 per cent (Eurostat, 1993). This may have an important effect on local trading patterns. Independent shopkeepers will need middle-men, and such retail suppliers will be based within relatively small distances from the independent store. Retail structures where the small owner-manager is still an important part of the retail scene, will tend to exhibit examples of extended distribution channels where there exist a number of levels between the producer and the customer. Therefore, large international retail operations who buy directly from suppliers will have a distinct advantage before any other competitive factors are accounted for, as they will be able to offer cheap products through the avoidance of the costs occurred in less efficient distribution systems.

The number of females employed in retailing also rises in proportion in more developed markets. This is a product not only of the need for a workforce which is willing to work flexible hours but also the social acceptability and desire for part-time work amongst women. While in less developed retail structures in Greece and Portugal females will account for over a third of the workforce, in the UK and Germany they will account for nearly two-thirds of employees (Eurostat, 1993). Female activity rates were discussed in chapter 11. It was noted that activity rates are high in environments where GDP per capita is relatively high and social assumptions facilitate female employment. It should, however, be noted that in areas where female activity rates are low, where retailing is still a small-scale activity and male employment is high, thereby may exist a large hidden female, and essentially family, contribution to the workforce.

MERGING STRUCTURES

Carrefour's expansion into Spain as part of the general interest shown by French hypermarket groups in Spain is an example of the merging of retail structures across national boundaries. By the end of 1985, Carrefour with its twenty stores, owned by different subsidiaries was the biggest hypermarket operator in Spain (Burt, 1986). Carrefour entered the Spanish market in 1978. Promodès had entered the market 2 years earlier and was, therefore, the first French hypermarket to operate in Spain. Other French hypermarket retailers subsequently moved into Spain: Auchen, Docks de France, Intermarché, and Leclerc. French retailers owned seventy-one hypermarkets in Spain by 1991 (CIG, 1991), by the first of January 1993, this figure

13.2 Breaking-up is Hard to Do

Coles Myer is one of the world's largest retail operations but it remains an essentially Australian operation, although, the company does have stores in New Zealand.

Coles Myer has achieved such an important presence in the Australian market that it is a victim of its own success. This has even led to discussions within the company concerning breaking up the company into independently listed operations. While this approach has been used in other sectors and may have something to recommend it, Coles Myer decided in March 1996 not to pursue the idea, despite the factor that the company had asked three advisors to consider the option: Smith Barney, Macquarie Bank and KPMG Corporate Finance.

The company instead decided that it would, in the words of Nobby Clark, the company chairman, concentrate on 'the current strategy of co-ordinating and integrating Coles Myer's core retail brands'. The company has been refocusing its brands and has attempted a better integration of company wide functions to avoid duplication.

The company has a lot of work to do, nonetheless. Within a week of its announcement not to seek separate listings Coles Myer announced a sharp decline in profits. The company announced interim profits of A$194.5m (ending 28 January 1996) against A$272.9m for the same 6 month period a year before. This was in the context of a 8.5 per cent rise in sales.

The Kmart operation, which in Australia is managed by Coles Myer, saw profits fall from A$93.2m to A$50.6m before interest charges. Alongside this the 'World 4 Kids' operation saw a loss of A$14.7m increase to A$20.1m. The chain was intended to compete with the US Toys R Us operation, but Peter Bartels, the chief executive of Coles Myer, suggested on the announcement of these figures that the company might consider the sale of the operation.

The picture was not, however, all doom and gloom. The supermarket and alcoholic drinks operations saw an increase in profits of 16.7 per cent to A$128.7 on the basis of an 11.1 per cent increase on comparable store sales. In particular Liquorland saw sales rise by 20 per cent and profits increase from A$13.8m to A$15.3m.

Bartels blamed the company's fortunes on the weak pre-Christmas trading period. One of the great weaknesses of a large retailer based exclusively in one market is that it particularly susceptible to downturns in that market.

Source: Tait, 1996a; Tait, 1996b.

had risen to eighty-eight, of which Carrefour alone was operating forty stores (LSA, 1992).

While it would be inappropriate to suggest that French and Spanish food retail structures have fully merged, the development of Spanish food retailing by French companies has created very strong cross-border links. The measurement of retail structural integration requires conceptual development but one measure of retail integration, that of isoagoras, has been proposed (Alexander, 1994). Essentially, isoagoras connect locations of equal development. The isoagoras are built up through the use of diasystems which identify differences between locations. Thus, the diasystems will separate two locations where differences occur, hence plot the course of isoagoras, and indicate those locations contained within an isoagora. For example, town A may differ from town B because town B does not possess hypermarket operations. Both A and B may possess superstore operations. Thus town A will be included within an isoagora which indicates towns with hypermarkets, town B will not. Both towns will be included within an isoagora which indicates superstore development. A number of isoagoras will build up into a picture of retail structure development and retail structural difference. Isoagoras may be used to measure a number of structural features.

Through such measurements, it is possible to identify the merging of retail structures on the basis of retail formats and retail operations. In relatively simplistic terms, a measure of operational integration may be measured through the identification of cross-border expansion. Thus, the fact that forty-one French retail operations were active in Belgium by 1994 is indicative of merging structures (CIG, 1994). However, other factors also need to be measured before a complete picture may be built up. Retail structures, even within one country, may still exhibit considerable variations, therefore, the structural differences noted in the sections above, all need to be considered before assumptions of structural integration are made. Very frequently, international retailers focus their activities on key cities or regions within a market, thus what pertains to one region may not be relevant to another. At its most developed, this situation may lead to considerable international structural relationships in key cities but little, or sporadic, integration in other regions. As Myers (1995) has noted, regional divisions will remain important to food retailers expanding in Europe irrespective of the integration of public policy at the trans-national level.

GLOBAL STRUCTURES

A global retail structure does not exist. Following a period of international activity in the 1980s, global-regional structures have begun to emerge, or further develop. In the 1990s, there are three core global-regional structures: North America, Europe, and Asia. Apart from these, there are other regions which either provide international expansion opportunities today or will increasingly do so in the future.

Core regions

North America

Retailing in North America is dominated by US retailers. While Canadian retailers have a role to play in the development of North American retailing, few have been able to compete with US retailers on their home territory, although examples of successful companies do exist (Lane and Hildebrand, 1990). With the development of the NAFTA, US retailers and those Canadian retailers capable of large scale development, have increased opportunities to develop a regional retail structure. Within the context of a strong retail structure in Mexico, indigenous retailers will have an opportunity to develop beyond the level they may otherwise have achieved.

European Union

With the expansion of the EU to include other European Economic Area (EEA) states such as Austria, a geographical area is defined in which a retail structure is fast developing. Cross-border mergers, acquisitions, joint-ventures, organic growth, franchising and the development strategic alliances is creating a structure with increasing interrelationships. As suppliers have come to plan on a pan-European basis, so retailers are planning on a European basis. Within the Community, retailers from certain retail structures are contributing to the cross-border growth. Dutch, French, German and British retailers have played an important role in the building of a European retail structure.

Southern European markets are the recipients of much international activity in Europe. Spain and Greece have been developed by French hypermarket groups. Italy, is of interest to European retailers, but this market has also shown itself capable of producing strong retail brands, such as Benetton. While the markets of southern Europe may be under considerable pressure from developing North European retailers, the developments and technology transfer that will result will create greater opportunities for the development of larger indigenous retail operations, just as the influence and technology transfer of earlier periods from the US into North European markets stimulated distribution channel development.

Asia

In contemporary business literature, Asian retailing and its internationalization is associated with Japan. Japanese retailers have made considerable strides in recent years in the international arena. The rapidly developing economies of the Far East and the liberalizing market of China provide Japanese retailers with considerable opportunities to develop a regional retail structure across the major centres within these markets. However, there remains considerable room for development, not least because of the structure of Japanese retailing itself. In this, retailers from outside the region, from North America and Europe, and from within the Asian Pacific region from such markets as Australia, will have a role to play in the development of improved distribution channels and retail facilities.

Australia, although not a large market in itself has seen the development of large retail enterprises such as Coles Myer. Australia and New Zealand, as part of the Pacific Rim have a retail structure which is sufficiently developed to play an important role in the development of the Asian market.

Asia is like the regional markets of North America and Europe, in that it possesses developed retail structures from which cross-border development may take place. It also resembles the less developed markets of the world, in that there are considerable opportunities for development in markets which must first undergo fundamental environmental changes before they become attractive investment opportunities.

Peripheral regions

East Europe
With the change of economic policy in the countries of East Europe, both European and US retailers have entered the market seeking opportunities. Some of the reasons for entering the market are associated with the problem of repatriation of funds from other business activity, some are motivated by the approach that early entrants will build market share and hence long term rewards while other retailers have only tentatively entered the market, learning and preparing for the time when the markets will prove more interesting, and in many cases, more stable marketing opportunities.

This region, which had a centrally planned market structure provides considerable opportunities for European retailers expanding into these less developed markets. Research in the food sector indicates that Western European food retailers see considerable opportunities in the more accessible markets of Eastern Europe (Myers and Alexander, 1994).

Describing Eastern Europe as a separate region may be to perpetuate an inappropriate myth. The Czech Republic, for example, could easily be considered on similar terms to the East German Lander. It is, therefore, worth considering the Eastern European region at least in part an extension of the Western European market, rather than as a separate market, although, as retailers will discover, as they move east, a natural boundary between the European retail structure to the west and the developing retail market structure to the east will soon become evident.

Latin America
This market has been the subject of interest of US and European retailers for many years. The involvement of European retailers has extended throughout the century. However, political circumstances and economic instability in the markets of Latin America has truncated and discouraged investment. The inclusion of Mexico in the NAFTA bears witness to the same type of logic that Western European retailers may wish to apply to Eastern Europe; that this is their backyard and therefore a logical expansion opportunity. To some extent, this logic is sound, but again the logic applied to Eastern Europe should also be applied in this context;

that is, the markets will often prove to be very different and demand to be treated on very different terms.

Latin America, like Eastern Europe, will not be the preserve of retailers from the proximate core region. The French retailer, Carrefour has already begun to exploit the food retail opportunities in South America. Carrefour began building a chain of hypermarkets in Brazil in 1975 and by the beginning of 1993 was operating twenty-seven hypermarkets in Brazil and six in Argentina (LSA, 1992). In Brazil, the store size varies from 8,000 sq m of selling space in Berueri to 18,000 sq m in Campinas.

Middle East

To a great extent, the Middle East could be described as a developing market, along with markets of Latin America (Samiee, 1990). The markets of the Middle East resemble in many respects the developing markets of the world, although there is, of course, one major difference. Through natural resources, oil, Middle Eastern markets have had made available to them a source of capital which has facilitate the development of sophisticated retail shopping environments supported by general economic growth.

Therefore, in some respects, states, such as Kuwait, resemble certain markets in Asia, such as Hong Kong and Singapore. However, the case of Kuwait serves to show how political uncertainty may cause considerable problems when operating in such markets.

In markets such as Kuwait, oil revenue and the consequent contact with life-styles outside the region has stimulated growth in the retail sector (Al-Otaibi, 1990). However, retailers from outside the region must be aware of the cultural realities of the Middle East. This, as Al-Otaibi suggests, has not always been the case in the planning of shopping centres where the importance of local market structures and functions have not been fully acknowledged.

> In Middle Eastern cities the Souk performs a number of functions, as a social gathering place for merchants and powerful entrepreneurs, as the institutional base for a collection of craft guilds, as a credit information system, a religious and recreational centre, and as a central business district. (Al-Otaibi, 1990, p. 116)

The wholesale importation of 'Western' concepts and designs will not necessarily succeed in such environments. Rapid development, which has been experienced in the Middle East, serves to show how the concepts which suit certain global regions do not suit others.

Developing markets

As has been noted, retailers favour expansion into markets which appear familiar as far as public policy, economic, society, culture and retail structures are concerned. Therefore, retailers have avoided certain markets, unless a cosmopolitan centre provides the type of opportunity that some specialized retailers are able to provide. It has been noted that:

> To the analyst more familiar with retailing in the economically advanced nations, the first encounter with retailing in less-developed countries is something of an academic shock. (Paddison et al., 1990, p. 3)

Retail structures similar to those with which international retailers are familiar have not appeared in these markets because of the lack of capital available and a fundamental lack of economic development. Retailers, however, should be aware that these markets may become of increasing significance but they may require different operational systems. These markets have not always been as isolated as they are now from European Retailing:

> Many retailers moved overseas when European trading companies set up their colonies in Asia and Africa during the eighteenth and nineteenth centuries. (Sternquist and Kacker, 1994, p. 151)

Decolonization and the political, social and economic turmoil in which it resulted, however, has isolated many of these markets from European retail development.

CONCLUSION

A number of measurements may be used to identify the retail structure within a market. Enterprise density and market concentration are both useful measures. Figures derived from such data may be used to infer conditions within a market. Developed retail structures exhibit common characteristics.

Where international retailers identify less developed retail structures but a high level of economic development, opportunities may exist for expansion. The retail structure may be seen to lag behind general economic development in such a context, thereby providing an opportunity for retailers from a more developed retail structure to take part in the development of retail provisions within the less developed structure. However, retailers may find that such opportunities only exist because of public policy in the market which appears to offer development opportunities. Japanese retailing, in the 1980s, appeared to offer expansion opportunities because of retail structural characteristics such as the profusion of small retailers. However, Japanese public policy, which effectively supported the small retailer, artificially controlled structural development.

The retail structure of a market is a product of public policy, economic development, social conditions and cultural assumptions in that market. Measurements of the retail structure are therefore representative of these factors. International retailers should, therefore, be aware that, while opportunities may exist in a market, careful consideration should be given to understanding the overall structural form which retailing takes within a market, since markets, to a considerable degree, have the structure they want, or for which they are prepared to pay.

QUESTIONS – DISCUSSION POINTS

1 What do enterprise density figures tell retailers about a market?

2 Would concentration within a retail structure be an advantage or a disadvantage to a retailer entering a market?

3 Why do innovations flow from a more advanced market to a less advanced market?

4 Does the retail employment structure within a market indicate structural conditions, and if so how?

5 Are retail structures within Europe merging?

6 Where are the core and peripheral markets around the world?

REFERENCES

Al-Otaibi, O., (1990) The Development of Planned Shopping Centres in Kuwait, in R. Paddison, A. Findlay, J. Dawson (eds) *Retailing Environments in Developing Countries*, Routledge, London, pp. 96–117.

Alexander, N., (1994) Isoagora: Retail Boundaries in Free Trade Areas, presented at *Retailing: Theories and Practices for Today and Tomorrow, The Fourth Triennial AMS/ACRA National Retailing Conference*, 22–4 October, Richmond, Virginia.

Bardacke, T., (1996) Thai group may float store unit, *Financial Times*, 7 March, p. 29.

Burt, S., (1986) The Carrefour Group – the first 25 years, *International Journal of Retailing*, Vol. 1, No. 3, pp. 54–78.

CIG, (1991) *Cross-Border Retailing in Europe*, The Corporate Intelligence Group, London.

CIG, (1994) *Cross-Border Retailing in Europe*, London: The Corporate Intelligence Group.

Eurostat, (1993) *Retailing in the Single European Market 1993*, Commission of the European Communities, Brussels.

Jefferys, J., (1954) *Retailing in Britain, 1850–1950*, Cambridge University Press, Cambridge.

Jefferys, J., and Knee, D., (1962) *Retailing in Europe: Present Structure and Future Trends*, Macmillan, London.

Lane, H., and Hildebrand, T., (1990) How to Survive in US Retail Markets, *Business Quarterly*, Vol. 54, No. 3, pp. 62–6.

Larke, R., (1994) *Japanese Retailing*, Routledge, London.

LSA, (1992) Hypers Français a L'Etranger, *LSA*, No. 1331, 17 December, pp. 230A–235A.

LSA, (1995) Les hypermarchés et les TGS marquent le pas, *LSA*, No. 1426, 5 January, pp. 38–41.

Myers, H., (1995) The Changing Process of Internationalisation in the European Union, *The Service Industries Journal*, Vol. 15, No. 4. pp. 42–56.

Myers, H., and Alexander, N., (1994) European Food Retailers' Direction of Growth, *Working Paper Series, Department of Management Studies, University of Surrey*, No. 6/94.

Paddison, R., Findlay, A., and Dawson, J., (eds) (1990) *Retailing Environments in Developing Countries*, Routledge, London.

Samiee, S., (1990) Impediments to Progress in Retailing in Developing Nations, in R. Paddison, A. Findlay, J. Dawson (eds) *Retailing Environments in Developing Countries*, Routledge, London, pp. 30–41.

Sternquist, B., and Kacker, M., (1994) *European Retailing's Vanishing Borders*, Quorum, Westport Connecticut.

Tait, N., (1996a) Coles Myer rejects break-up idea, *Financial Times*, 6 March, p. 26.

Tait, N., (1996b) Coles Myer posts sharp fall, *Financial Times*, 14 March, p. 33.

Woolworth, (1954) *Woolworth's First 75 Years: The Story of Everybody's Store*, New York, Woolworth.

PART
V

Operationalization

International Growth Strategies

▍ OBJECTIVES ▍

This chapter addresses issues raised by the different growth strategies used by international retail operations. Methods of market entry are described and discussed. Retailers use a wide variety of entry methods in the international environment; some are better suited than others to specific market objectives.

INTRODUCTION

International retailing is not simply an exercise in replicating a company's fascia in other markets. The internationalization of retailing concepts may occur through the transfer of knowledge rather than the expansion of companies. Internationalization of the company may take a number of forms.

This chapter considers those means by which retailers establish an operational presence in non-domestic markets. The order in which the different options are considered is a reflection of the level of investment and day to day operational control which is required to maintain a presence in a non-domestic market.

STAGES IN THE DEVELOPMENT OF INTERNATIONAL OPERATIONS

It would be an oversimplification to suggest that all firms pass through the same phases of international development in exactly the same manner (Turnbull, 1987; Buckley et al., 1979; Cannon and Willis, 1981; Reid, 1983, 1984, 1986). However, research in the manufacturing and service sectors suggest that certain stages of internationalization are common to many firms. This 'stages' approach to

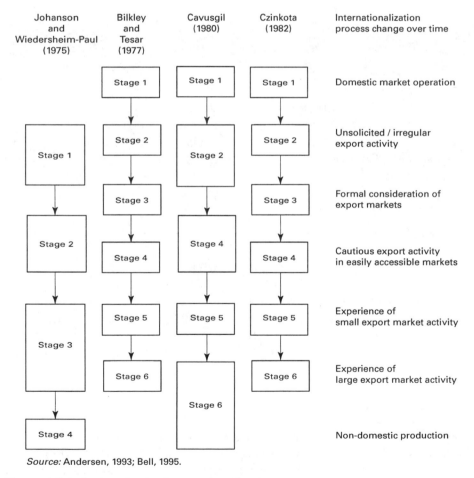

Source: Andersen, 1993; Bell, 1995.

Figure 14.1 Stages in the internationalization process

interpreting the internationalization process is well established in the literature: Johanson and Wiedersheim-Paul (1975), Bilkley and Tesar (1977), Cavusgil (1980) and Czinkota (1982). All these authors suggest that firms pass through stages of development, which range from domestic operations to a committed involvement with the internationalization process. Between these two extremes, companies pass through stages of increasing commitment to, and involvement with, the international market-place. While the different stages described by these authors differ, they agree on the general principles involved (Andersen, 1993). International firms become more committed to internationalization, less wary of it, and more confident within non-domestic markets (see figure 14.1).

Implicit within the stages approach to internationalization is the assumption that firms will become more confident in their interaction with non-domestic markets. This will encourage them to consider expansion in psychologically distant markets. This general process will also affect the entry strategies which firms adopt when considering international markets. Manufacturing firms may begin to consider manufacturing plants in non-domestic markets rather than straightforward export to those markets. Retailers will also adopt new approaches to international development as they become more aware of the international market place and the opportunities and threats which they encounter within it. The various options available to them require consideration.

EXPORT

Manufacturing companies are often encouraged to think about the international market-place as a result of the unsolicited orders they receive from non-domestic markets. Some retailers will also find themselves in this situation.

Where retailers have a distinct product profile, such as an own brand which is attractive to consumers in other markets, it is possible for retailers to begin to internationalize through the export of their merchandise. Marks & Spencer with its St Michael own brand label exported merchandise before it began to establish its international chain of stores.

Retailers will also be encouraged to expand internationally as a result of tourists or those on foreign business trips who visit retail outlets and are impressed by their offering. This has long been a feature of the internationalization of retailing and is closely associated with the international activity of luxury goods retailers. In recent years, the Body Shop has experienced this phenomenon. Potential customers and franchisees in the US inundated the company with requests for expansion in the US before the company was ready to enter that market (Roddick, 1991).

Where retail merchandise is exported to a market, and it is well received in that market this will be a useful indicator of the interest that a store may arouse in the non-domestic market. As, of course, is the interest shown by tourists visiting stores in the domestic market. However, such indicators are by no means guarantors of success but they are means by which certain types of retailer may explore and initially judge the option of internationalization.

14.1 Scenes from an Italian Restaurant

McDonalds has taken a pride in building its chain of fast food operations through organic and franchised growth. However, in March 1996, the company took the unusual step of announcing the acquisition of Burghy outlets in the Italian market.

Burghy was acquired by Cremonini, a privately owned catering and food group in 1985. It was originally established in the early 1980s by SME, the State-owned catering and food group. The chain was established in good locations and was unashamedly based on the McDonalds approach to fast food retailing.

McDonalds is accustomed to finding itself to be the leading fast food operation in markets around the world. In Italy, however, it languished far behind Burghy for many years. In early 1995, the McDonalds chain numbered only twenty-six outlets in the Italy, compared to over 500 in both Germany and the UK and more than 300 in France.

While the period 1995–6 saw a rapid increase in outlets to thirty-eight, the acquisition of Burghy has dramaticaly increased the McDonalds operation in Italy. Burghy's sales in 1995 were L200bn, an increase of 25 per cent on the previous year. The McDonalds chain achieved 28 per cent growth in the same period and sales of L107bn.

The eighty Burghy stores are a major acquisition in the market and they will allow McDonalds to achieve a greater market share and growth potential immediately. Such acquisition may also be seen as defensive, however, as both Quick the Belgian fast food retailer, and Burger King were reported to be interested in the Burghy chain which Cremonini were eager to sell to reduce debt.

Source: Hill and Tomkins, 1996.

The type of store that will be able to use these initial indications of non-domestic interest will possess a distinct image, have own brand products and, in the minds of the international market, will often possess a strong national image and association. Retailers such as Acquascutum, Burberry, Laura Ashley, Austin Reed and Marks & Spencer will convey a distinct cultural message to international consumers. Such retailers will be able to trade on their national associations, in the cases mentioned above their Britishness, whatever that may mean to American, Dutch or Japanese consumers.

This may prove an advantage in the short term but a controlling factor in the long term. While such associations may generate initial interest and sales, the company may wish to address a wider audience at it rolls out its retail operations in the new market. Marks & Spencer may appear to possess a distinctly British image in

Europe but the company will need to trade on something more substantial if it is to achieve the same market presence in the EU as it has in the UK.

The export arrangements entered into by the retailer may resemble the export activity of manufacturing companies who simply sell their product on to retailers who wish to stock their produce as part of their general merchandise range. The arrangements involved, however, may be developed on a more formal basis so that a licensing agreement is established. Licensing does not involve the retailer exporting the merchandise in capital investment in the new market but allows the exporting retailer to achieve a higher profile within the new market by providing the local retailer with the opportunity to strongly build sales on the basis of the exporting company's image. The J C Penney Collection outlets in the Middle East are an example of this type of arrangement, and may be considered by some to be the first stage in the internationalization of a company's retail operation (McGoldrick, 1995).

MANAGEMENT CONTRACTS

Retailers who are not associated with a distinct product range, but possess the necessary skills to provide them with a selling feature in the international arena, may consider management contracts as a means by which to achieve involvement with a non-domestic market. These contracts have not been widely exploited in the retail sector, although they have been used extensively in the hotel sector (Alexander and Lockwood, 1994). They provide retailers with an opportunity to experience the international environment without engaging in costly real estate purchases. In the hotel sector, the owner of a property will contract the management of their property to an operator. The owner of the property will receive a set fee. The incoming management operation brings skills to this particular task.

In retailing, this has not been a widely used means of operating in new markets or of less developed markets securing the techniques developed in more developed retail environments. However, Japanese retailers have exploited this option in the Taiwanese market (Cheng and Sternquist, 1994). The Today, Evergreen, Hsin-Hsin, Ming-Yao, Tonling, Hsin-Kuang and Far Eastern Department stores are all run on a management contract agreement by Seibu, Tokyo, Matsuya, Keio, Mitsukoshi or Ito-Yokado.

While it is the introduction of more advanced operational skills which provide the primary motivation behind such arrangements, there are also merchandise benefits. In terms of merchandise range development 'management contracts have provided Taiwan's department stores with additional foreign merchandise procurement sources' (Cheng and Sternquist, 1994, p. 63). This involvement with Japanese companies has given Taiwanese retail outlets access to Japan's idiosyncratic international sourcing operations which are strongly influenced by general trading companies or sogo sosha. These operations play an important role in the sourcing of goods internationally and have developed efficient trading systems which with the use of information technology has 'enabled them to pursue global sourcing

14.2 Starting Over

International growth may involve the acquisition of another retailer's international operations. Tesco did this in the Czech Republic, and Slovakia, when, in March 1996, it agreed to buy Kmart's stores in those markets.

The Kmart stores were acquired in 1992, as part of the country's privatization process. Since privatization, Kmart had invested heavily in the stores through refurbishment programmes. Kmart had spent $120m upgrading stores which it decided to sell to Tesco for $117.5m.

Kmart had been experiencing difficulties in its home market of the US where Wal-Mart and other discount operations were putting the company under pressure. The company has been forced to sell non-core assets as it struggles to stay afloat.

While the Czech and Slovak stores were expected to be well into profit by 1996, the sale, according to Floyd Hall, Kmart's chairman and chief executive:

> is in keeping with our determination to focus our energies and resources on our core operations in the US and North America.

Soon after the announcement of the sale of its Czech and Slovak operation to Tesco, Kmart announced poor quarterly results, but announced that the company's fortunes were on the turn. Fourth-quarter net losses were US$420m and full-year net losses US$571m for 1995.

Tesco had previously invested in retailing in Hungary and Poland, the Czech acquisition completed 'the geographic jigsaw for us in central Europe', as David Wild, Tesco's European corporate development director described it.

The acquisition, which gave Tesco six stores in the Czech Republic, and also gave the company seven in Slovakia. In total, the stores occupied around 1m sq ft of selling space and a turnover of £140m in 1995.

The merchandise mix of the stores was heavily weighted toward non-food under the Kmart operation. It is expected that Tesco will seek to increase the percentage of food sales but the stores will retain a stronger non-food element than the equivalent Tesco owned stores in the company's domestic, UK market.

Source: Boland and Tomkins, 1996; Tomkins, 1996.

strategies which assist them in outperforming their competitors' (Liu and McGoldrick, 1995, p. 109).

Management contracts offer distinct opportunities to retailers who do not possess a distinct own brand merchandise range but who do possess strong management skills. This method of international involvement holds particular opportunities for those retailers who recognize opportunities in less developed and less stable markets around the world. Their advanced systems approach to management and their distribution and sourcing experience would allow such retailers to operate in, but not be unduly financially exposed within, non-domestic markets.

CONCESSIONS

Certain benefits derived from management contracts are also derived from concessions and it could be argued that concessions are another form of management contract. They are also the next stage on from exporting or licensing. Here retailers operate an area of a store, such as a department store. The incoming retailer is responsible for merchandising. The concession is a shop within a shop. In this way, the retailer brings operational skills to the host store but the retailer also brings merchandise in a more overt manner than the management contract described above. The merchandise which the concession introduces is of primary concern and interest to the host store. The host store will build traffic if it attracts the right concessions.

Concessionary arrangements are another means by which retailers access non-domestic markets without making the financial and operational commitments which might otherwise be required. They provide retailers with an opportunity to access geographically and culturally distant retail markets. European companies have found concessions an attractive option in South East Asia and the Middle East. The UK electrical goods retailer, Thorn EMI entered the Indonesian market in 1993, and opened five concessions within a year. Dunhill operate small chains of stores in Malaysia, Singapore, Taiwan and Thailand. Dunhill also operates concessions in Kuwait and the United arab Emirates, the French fashion retailer Ted Lapidus has four concessions in Saudi Arabia (CIG, 1994).

Concessions are a useful means for retailers who focus on a market niche to access culturally and geographically distant markets. In Japan, European retailers have recognized the advantage of this system of market entry. The Spanish fashion retailer Sybilla has thirty outlets in Japan, while the French travel goods retailer Lancel operates sixteen concessions.

Concessions are not an option available to all types of retailer. They are useful to retailers with distinct product ranges and operating formats which may be contained within a restricted and limited square footage. They are not appropriate to retailers who lack own branded merchandise ranges or a strong internationally relevance. Concessions are an opportunity to test market opportunities but do not provide the retailer with the exposure which stand alone operations will achieve. However, they may be particularly useful to small firms with distinct merchandise and a niche strategy.

FRANCHISING

This market development strategy has led to the rapid expansion of a number of well-known global retailers. Properly managed, franchising provides concept retailers with the opportunity to build a global operation, in a way that organic growth or acquisition simply does not allow, within a short period of time and without putting considerable financial pressure on domestic retail operations.

This development strategy enables the incoming retailer to build a strong corporate identity in the new market, while also facilitating an input of local capital and local knowledge. The franchised operation is a means by which the concept retail operation is able to access local support and monitor local idiosyncrasies within the overall format and merchandise arrangement. Treadgold (1988) has described franchising as a low cost low control means by which to access international markets.

In markets which are distant from the retailer's country of origin and when the retailer has a distinct market position, franchising is a means by which rapid expansion may be achieved. In Hong Kong, fashion retailers, such as the Italian chains Benetton and Stefanel, operate franchises, alongside the French fashion outlets Cerruti 1881 and Ton Sur Ton (CIG, 1994). In other South East Asian markets, such names are present through the use of the franchise approach. Cerruti 1881 also operate franchises in China, Indonesia, Japan, Malaysia, Singapore, South Korea, Taiwan and Thailand (CIG, 1994). Cerruti offers fashion-conscious customers with up-market products in major centres around the world. For such an organization, access to wealthy customers with cosmopolitan tastes and life-styles means have to provide such customers with retail outlets in geographically distant and diverse markets. The company does not need to establish chains of stores in markets but provide products in key centres; for such an organization franchising is a viable option in a way organic growth could not be.

Franchising also offers retailers with ambitions to operate a chain of stores in an attractive but radically different market, the opportunity to avoid problems associated with management control carried out over considerable distances. The lucrative Japanese markets has attracted immense European attention in recent years; however, retailers have been aware of the problems of operating in a market which has developed retail and distribution structures in a different way from modern structures in Europe and the US. Retailers operate franchise stores in Japan in a remarkable number of different sectors. Specialist food retailers such as the French retailers Hediard and La Brioche Dorée franchise their operations in Japan, as does the furniture retailer Frette (Italy), the jewellery retailer Agatha (France), the department store operator Printemps (France), as do the maternity and childrens wear retailers Kid Cool UFC (Belgium), La Cicogna (Italy) and Mothercare (UK), the health and beauty stores The Body Shop (UK) and Yves Rocher (France) (CIG, 1994). In the fashion sector, the list is considerable, as is the size of some of the retail chains. Benetton (Italy) has over 400 franchised stores in Japan, while other fashion retailers have smaller but still sizeable chains: Agnes B thirty (France), Fil à Fill (France) twenty-five, Sonia Rykiel (France) twenty-four, Cerruti 1881 (France) twenty-two, Chantal Thomas (France) twenty (CIG, 1994).

Franchising may at times sound like the panacea to all international marketing problems; however, it also has its problems and disadvantages. Franchising involves legal agreements and this may lead to considerable problems of definition, control and rights. The nature of the agreement may involve franchisers ultimately in agreements which they would prefer to terminate but are unable to do so. Franchisers may also find that they have problems associated with the recruitment of suitable local managers (Dawson, 1994). While local management is an advantage as far as costs and local knowledge are concerned, local managers may not meet the educational, cultural and ethical requirements of the franchiser.

ACQUISITION AND MERGER

For many retailers, there is only one international retail strategic option available. Without a suitable concept to internationalize, many retailers are forced to consider acquisition rather than the internationalization of their domestic format.

They may acquire either a specific market-based operation or a retailer with already proven international appeal. A strong international brand will be particularly attractive to a far sighted acquiring organization. Renown's acquisition of Acquascutum (£74m in 1990) is an example of the acquisition of a strong international brand. Usually, however, retailers acquire an operation that is based in one market only. This reflects the general context in which internationalization occurs: only a relatively limited number of retailers in any one market have international operations and many retailers acquire operations as a means to access a market rather than as a means to acquire an intangible asset that has been proven already in the international market-place. This is likely to change, however, as retailers generally increase their international operations. Therefore, it will be more likely that when a company like Marks & Spencer purchase an operation in the US like Brookes Brothers, they will also acquire by virtue of such an acquisition operations in Japan as well.

International retailers will sometimes acquire a minor interest in a retail operation, in order to monitor the performance of that company. This was the case with Sainsbury with its acquisition of Shaws in New England. In 1983, Sainsbury acquired a 21 per cent share in the company for £13m. It was to be four years before Sainsbury announced a takeover of the company. During this intervening period Sainsbury had board representation.

Minority interests may lead to outright acquisition or they may simply be investments, or a means by which cooperation may be engendered. Strategic Retail Alliances may involve equity swops, as did the relationship established between Ahold (Netherlands), Casino (France) and Safeway (UK). Mitsukoshi the Japanese department store retailer acquired a minority holding in the Tiffany jewellery operation based in the US in 1993 (CIG, 1994). Tiffany has been involved with Mitsukoshi since 1990 when in a joint venture arrangement the Tiffany operation was introduced into the Japanese market. The Japanese retailer Aeon has also developed relationships with international retailers involving a share holding. In 1990, Aeon acquired 15 per cent of Laura Ashley. Two years previously Aeon acquired a majority holding in Talbots a women's wear retailer based in the US.

14.3 Baker Street

In a period when new international retail activity is commonplace, withdrawal from markets appears to be the exception rather than the rule. However, withdrawals from markets are not as unusual as they may at first appear.

Marks & Spencer has spent more than 20 years in Canada, but in 1996 it announced the sale of its second chain of retail outlets in that market. The company's history in the Canadian market has not been a happy one, but the company is prepared to admit its mistakes. As Sir Richard Greenbury the company chairman put it:

It would have been difficult to get it more wrong.

The company announced early in 1996 that it would be selling the D'Alliard store operation to Comark, the large Canadian speciality store operation. Comark is owned by the Brenninkmeyer family who own C&A, which is based in Europe.

Marks & Spencer had only comparatively recently sold the Peoples chain which it had operated in the Canadian market. This leaves the company with its own fascia, a chain of Marks & Spencer stores in the Canadian market after 20 years and a lot of experience in the market to contemplate.

Source: Oram, 1996.

Such relationships with Japanese retailers are often precursors to the introduction of the retail operation into the Japanese market. In 1990, the Talbot operation was introduced into Japan. This was the first international move that the Talbot operation had made, although, it was soon followed by expansion in Canada. Laura Ashley's Japanese operation is a joint venture with Aeon. Such relationships may also be precursors the acquisition of the retail operation by the Japanese company as the history of Ito Yokado shows. In 1973, Ito Yokado began franchising the US based 7-Eleven franchise in Japan. Today, the company has a majority stake in the 7-Eleven operation. Reciprocal internationalization (Sparks, 1995) is an interesting aspect of recent international developments.

Acquisition, while an attractive means to gain swift penetration of a non-domestic market is not free from problems. The acquired company may be available for acquisition because of fundamental problems in its management structure. Although the incoming retailer may believe it is capable of addressing such problems and introducing an new operating culture, such changes may take much longer to implement and come to fruition. Such changes are particularly difficult within an unfamiliar cultural environment. The acquired operation may also be in such financial difficulty that the acquiring company is burdened with debts which in the long-run damage the well-being of the international company. Acquisition is not, therefore, a strategy which companies should enter into lightly. A serious miscalculation may be very damaging to the acquirer. An error of choice may blunt the acquirer's international strategy, while divestment may send messages to the financial markets which the acquirer would not welcome.

Acquisition is a high-profile option and in consequence may result in high profile mistakes. Nevertheless, acquisition does offer swift market penetration, immediate positive cash flow, and the opportunity for subsequent organic growth on the basis of an established operational infrastructure.

JOINT VENTURES

Joint ventures have become an important aspect of international activity. Mostly, joint ventures involve one local and one incoming partner, however, there is no reason why two retailers should not form a joint company to enter a new market. The expansion of Toys R Us into Japan is an interesting example of how two US retailers established a joint venture in order to access the Japanese market. The partner in the arrangement, established in 1989, was McDonalds. Toys were to have an 80 per cent stake and McDonalds (Japan) Ltd 20 per cent (Mohnke, 1992). McDonalds were already operating in Japan and had, through their operations, acquired an awareness of the market that was considered beneficial to the incoming Toys operation.

Joint ventures provide the incoming retailer with an opportunity to learn about operations in a new market, while at the same time giving indigenous retailers the opportunity to learn from the international player. The relationship between the UK retailer Sainsbury and the Belgian retailer GIB is an example of this. Sainsbury plc were not familiar with the DIY sector, while to GIB, the UK market was an unfamiliar operating environment. The joint venture, of 1979, gave Sainsbury the majority 75 per cent holding. At this time, the DIY sector was developing rapidly in the UK and this joint venture gave Sainsbury the opportunity to diversify its interests away from the dynamic but limited food sector. By 1994, the company had opened seventy-six Homebase stores with a total sales area of 2.8 million sq ft, nearly 100,000 sq ft more than the sales area of the company's New England food operation Shaws (Sainbury, 1994).

Some retailers, while prepared to develop organically in markets which are geographically or culturally close, may consider joint ventures preferable in markets where they feel they have fewer cultural reference points. In some markets, planning controls may demand local input. Bureaucratic hold-ups may be avoided if partners are already aware, from operating in the market, of the problems that store developments are likely to cause. Although, it may be an unfortunate reality, local partners may appreciate who the local gatekeepers are and how they must be dealt with.

A major problem associated with joint ventures, however, is the incompatibility of trading partners. The fundamental premise which lies behind joint ventures, namely the differences which different partners bring to the relationship may undermine its long term survival. Joint ventures demand an ability to accommodate the needs of the other participant on a day to day basis. Organizational cultures may not be compatible. Joint ventures may save the internationalizing operation time and avoid problems in the new market but it will require an ability to share the benefits to be derived and an ability to accommodate other views.

ORGANIC GROWTH

Organic growth is defined as new store development within the existing or an integrated organizational framework. It is, therefore, a familiar growth strategy to most retail operations, a strategy which they have gained considerable experience of in the domestic market. It is, to use Dawson's (1994) phrase, internal expansion. Therefore, the replication of domestic operations abroad is an obvious strategic option which many retailers mistakenly take. However, to establish a distribution system and acquire sites before understanding the market may lead to a lack of initial success that will lead to withdrawal and a delay in further retail expansion. It is therefore worth noting the phrase McGoldrick (1995) uses to describe the process: namely, self-start entry. Organic growth demands a cold start in a new market, with all the potential problems associated with inexperience which this raises. Nevertheless, organic growth has proved a popular option amongst internationalizing retailers.

There are conditions in which organic growth will succeed. Where the internationalizing retailer is considering expansion in a geographically and culturally proximate market, organic expansion may be relatively painlessly achieved. Nevertheless, even in these circumstances, perhaps especially within these circumstances, care should be taken to understand those differences which do exist and of those, which will need particular consideration. That is, expansion into such markets must be treated as an international move and not merely an extension of the domestic operation. Canadian retailers have not been conspicuously successful in their expansion into the US market. It would certainly be very easy for a Canadian retailer to assume that the lucrative US market shared important characteristics with the Canadian market. However, this would be to ignore the important differences which exist between such markets. Such differences are a product of fundamental differences in the development of societies, even such apparently similar countries as Canada and the US (Burns and Rayman, 1995).

Organic development allows the retailer to maintain an identity and hence brand awareness which would be lost through other expansion strategies. Like franchising, the retailer's identity is retained but, unlike franchising, day to day management of sites is not handed over to local financial and operational partners. Therefore, changes may be introduced in-house, which some organizations would prefer. However, organic growth is an expensive exercise, particularly within the early stages, as sales are relatively small compared to overhead costs. Treadgold (1988) has described it as a high cost high control strategy. Organic growth may therefore limit the number of markets the retailer will be able to enter within any period of time.

Organic growth may be successfully undertaken where there is no strong brand identification in the new market. Operating efficiency may be seen by the company as the main reason for expanding a fascia across national boundaries. Organic growth is particularly appropriate where control may be exercised over comparatively small geographical distances. Belgium is an attractive market to Dutch, French, German and UK retailers alike; indeed, the country plays host to more international retail operations than any other major national market in Europe. While many of these international operations will involve franchise or joint venture arrangements, geographical proximity will readily allow expansion across national boundaries. By the mid 1990s, sixty-four retail operations based in France had expanded their operations into Belgium. French fashion retailer, C17, operates sixty in-house stores in Belgium along side smaller operations run by Agnes B, Chipie, Claverie and Naf Naf. Cultural connections between Paris and Brussels have facilitated international connections for a considerable period of time. This has not only been evident to French retailers. W. H. Smith opened a retail outlet in Paris in 1903, further expansion in 1920 occurred in Brussels at a time when 'Brussels and Ostend had seemed close to England' (Wilson, 1985, p. 430). The Brussels store was modelled on the Paris store.

Organic growth is an attractive means by which to establish international development. It allows the retailer to replicate its format in a non-domestic market as and how it wishes, within the regulatory framework of the new market. However, the temptation to assume the success of a tested format is considerable. Organic growth strategies may not be given sufficient management time as assumptions are inappropriately made. Organic growth has many advantages, but the greatest disadvantage is that the company concerned may not seek information on a wide enough basis.

CHOICE OF ENTRY METHOD

The choice of entry method will be influenced by three factors:

- the structure of retailing in the domestic market;

- the nature of the internationalizing retail operation;

- the structure of retailing in the non-domestic market.

Domestic market

Retail operations develop in the domestic market as a response to specific needs. These needs may also exist in other markets or the market-defined product may be attractive in another market because it originates in a specific market.

Retail operations develop within a competitive environment: that environment will help define the operations suitability to international expansion. Retailers who have reached a level of saturation in the domestic market may seek very different markets to those retailers who still have growth opportunities in the domestic market.

Retailers may find that they are constrained within the domestic market because of the political environment. Taxes may be high and the government's involvement in industry may limit growth opportunities. This may stimulate international activity.

These factors will help to determine the characteristics which the retail organization seeks in the international environment.

Retail operation

Retailers will have their different strengths and weaknesses in terms of operational assets and management expertise. Many retailers will assume that they are ready for internationalization when they have only recognized that they are reaching high market share levels in their domestic market.

The subsector in which retailers operate will in part determine their entry strategies. Retailers who operate non-food specialist operations will be able to develop international operations organically in a manner which food retailers will not be able to do. This will necessitate food retailers considering forms of market entry such as acquisition. To food retailers acquisition followed by organic growth would be a far more attractive operation in many cases than initial organic growth.

Retail managers' orientation to the international environment will be important in assessing certain opportunities. Managers, not least entrepreneurs and chief executives, will be culturally more inclined to some markets than others. Their language skills and cultural awareness will help to predetermine decisions.

Non-domestic market

Assessment of non-domestic markets should depend on key factors which the retailer considers fundamental to their success. Some of these factors will be common to all business and will concern such issues as political stability, economic conditions and regulatory constraints. Other factors will be more specific to retailing and the product sector in which the retailer operates.

The competitive environment in the market under consideration may offer greater opportunities for expansion. This may be the result of a developing market and/or the lack of indigenous retailers ready to fill the needs of consumers. The lack of indigenous retailers, however, may limit expansion. For example, food retailers wishing to expand into the US will have a range and type of acquisition target available to them which they would not have if they chose to enter to the Mexican market.

The market identified by retailers for international development may be developing in such a way as to offer considerable opportunities in the future and that early entry to the market will allow the retailer to build loyalty and market share. This, however, may demand certain strategies such as joint ventures so that the peculiarities of the market are properly accommodated.

The market may offer acquisition opportunities which would allow the retailer to engage in technology transfer from the new market to the old. The retail operation in the non-domestic market may not have recognized its appeal or fully exploit its management skills.

The non-domestic market should offer opportunities for foreign direct investment which are unavailable in other markets.

CONCLUSION

It would be a convenient fiction, as far as many large, publicly quoted retail operations were concerned, if it were assumed that extensive market entry analysis has occurred and continues to occur before market entry is considered. It would, however, remain little more than a convenient fiction. Retailers often follow border-hopping international development and an analogical route to international growth reminiscent of domestic market expansion without the levels of critical appraissal which would be appropriate in such circumstances.

Many international moves in retailing are determined on the basis of inappropriate factors. Retailers have not had the internal planning processes which have facilitated a thorough assessment of the market environment. Managers within operations successfully established in a domestic market environment have often responded to limited opportunities at home with what has amounted to desperate moves into non-domestic markets, in the hope that the domestic success achieved by the company will be replicated abroad. The marketing and operating implications of their market entry strategy has therefore not been fully explored.

Some retailers have found themselves pulled into markets because of the demand for their products from that market. Marks & Spencers' initial operation in France was a logical first step given the cross-channel demand for their goods, but operating in another market proved to be a very different experience from selling to tourists from that market. Likewise, assumptions about cultural affinity have also prompted inappropriate expansion strategies. Canadians spoke English as a first language, or at least some of them did, when Marks & Spencer went into Canada, but the operating environment was different to Luton.

With improved planning procedures in retail organizations and the development of marketing departments and research units retailers should seek to continually evaluate the regional or global environment. Likewise, retailers operating in non-domestic markets must continue to evaluate the conditions in that market. Market conditions will change considerably over time, and retailers should be aware of the relevance of their product to the market in which they are operating. This may require them to reassess their presence to the extent that they should withdraw from the market or that the format or merchandise lines used should be changed in response to new market conditions but it should also require them to reassess their market penetration strategies.

Many retailers are encouraged to expand internationally because they possess what they believe to be internationally appealing concepts and merchandise. They may indeed have such advantages which will be recognized on a global basis, however, many strengths may only be relevant to specific social and cultural contexts. Retailers may, therefore, have to recognize that if they wish to access certain markets, they will need to take a fundamentally different approach to meeting market needs and strategic development. This may involve the acquisition of an indigenous retailer where previously the company has only undertaken organic growth. Conversely, the retailer should be prepared to avoid certain markets, no matter how attractive they may appear, if the company is committed to a particular type of growth mechanism. In such circumstances, despite the positive attractions of the market, the retailer should seek to expand into other markets, if the international operation is committed to a global rather than a multinational strategy.

QUESTION – DISCUSSION POINTS

1   Do international retailers pass through recognizable stages of internationalization?

2   Select a number of retailers from different retail subsectors within the domestic market. Evaluate the appropriateness of different market entry strategies with reference to those retailers you have chosen.

3   How would your evaluations (see question 2) change in the context of different markets of destination?

4   What impact does the market of origin have on the entry strategies employed by retailers when they internationalize?

REFERENCES

Alexander, N., and Lockwood, A., (1994) Internationalisation: A Comparison of Growth Strategies in the Retail and Hotel Sectors, *Marketing: Unity in Diversity*, Proceedings of the 1994 Annual Marketing Education Group, Vol. 1, D. Carson, S. Brown (eds), pp. 32.

Anderson, O., (1993) On the internationalization process of firms: a critical analysis, *Journal of International Business Studies*, Vol. 24, No. 2, pp. 209–31.

Bilkley, W., and Tesar, G., (1977) The Export Behaviour of Smaller-sized Wisconsin Manufacturing Firms, *Journal of International Business Studies*, Vol. 8, pp. 93–8.

Boland, V., and Tomkins, R., (1996) Tesco to buy Kmart's Czech stores, *Financial Times*, 6 March, p. 19.

Buckley, P., Newbould, D., and Thurwell, J., (1979) Going International – the foreign direct investment decisions of smaller UK firms, *EIBA Proceedings*, Uppsala, pp. 72–87.

Burns, J., and Rayman, D., (1995) Retailing in Canada and the US: Historical Comparisons, *The Service Industries Journal*, Vol. 15, No. 4, pp. 164–76.

Cannon, T., and Willis, M., (1981) The Smaller Firm in International Trade, *European Small Business Journal*, Vol. 1, No. 3, pp. 45–55.

Cavusgil, S., (1980) On the Internationalisation Process of the Firm, *European Research*, Vol. 8, No. 6, pp. 273–81.

Cheng, L., and Sternquist, B., (1994) Product Procurement: A Comparison of Taiwanese and US Retail Companies, *The International Review of Retail, Distribution and Consumer Research*, Vol. 4, No. 1, pp. 61–82.

CIG, (1994), *Cross-Border Retailing in Europe*, London: The Corporate Intelligence Group.

Czinkota, M., (1982) *Export Development Strategies: US Promotion Policy*, Praeger, New York.

Dawson, J., (1994) Internationalisation of Retail Operations, *Journal of Marketing Management*, Vol. 10, pp. 267–82.

Hill, A., and Tomkins, R., (1996) McDonalds expands in Italy, *Financial Times*, 22 March, p. 19.

Johanson, J., and Wiedersheim-Paul, F., (1975) The Internationalization of the Firm – four Swedish case studies, *Journal of Management Studies*, Vol. 12, pp. 305–22.

Liu, H., and McGoldrick, P., (1995) International Sourcing: patterns and trends, *International Retailing: Trends and Strategies*, Pitman, London.

McGoldrick, P., (1995) Introduction to International Retailing, in P. McGoldrick and Davies, G., *International Retailing: Trends and Strategies*, Pitman, London, pp. 1–16.

Mohnke, M., (1992) Toys R Us, Inc., A. Hast, D. Pascal, P. Barbour, J. Griffin (eds) *International Directory of Company Histories*, Vol. V, St James Press, Detroit, pp. 203–6.

Oram, R., (1996) Marks & Spencer sells Canadian chain, *Financial Times*, 6 March, p. 20.

Reid, S., (1983) Firm Internationalization Transaction Costs and Strategic Choice, *International Marketing Review*, Vol. 1, No. 2, pp. 45–55.

Reid, S., (1984) Market Expansion and Firm Internationalization, in E. Kaynak (ed.) *International Marketing Management*, Praeger, New York, pp. 197–206.

Reid, S., (1986) Export Channel Choice and Export Performance: a contingency approach, in C. Tan, W. Lazer, V. Kirpalani (eds) *Emerging International Strategic Frontiers*, American Marketing Association, Singapore, pp. 260–4.

Roddick, A., (1991) *Body & Soul*, Ebury Press, London.

Sainsbury, (1994) *Annual Report and Accounts 1994*, Sainsbury, London.

Sparks, L., (1995) 'Reciprocal Retail Internationalisation: The Southland Corporation, Ito-Yokado and 7-Eleven Convenience Stores', *The Service Industries Journal*, Vol. 15, No. 4, pp. 57–96.

Tomkins, R., (1996) Dismal period for Kmart, *Financial Times*, 8 March, p. 31.

Treadgold, A., (1988) Retailing Without Frontiers, *Retail and Distribution Management*, Vol. 16, No. 6, pp. 8–12.

Turnbull, P., (1987) A Challenge to the Stages Theory of the Internationalisation Process, in P. Rosson, S. Reid (eds) *Managing Export Entry and Expansion*, Praeger, New York, pp. 21–40.

Wilson, C., (1985) *First with the News: The History of W. H. Smith 1792–1972*, Jonathan Cape, London.

International Retail Marketing

▌ OBJECTIVES ▌

This chapter addresses the issue of marketing in the international retail environment. Retailers who internationalize their operation may have to address issues they have not fully explored with respect to their domestic operation. Positioning a retail operation in a new market may prove to be a particularly daunting organizational experience.

INTRODUCTION

While there are many formal definitions of marketing, probably the most memorably is the simple statement that, marketing is selling products that don't come back to people who do. In the international retail environment, some retailers are very good at making people return to their stores, while many retailers, who have failed in the international environment, have been unable to persuade consumers to make even a first purchase. In part, this is a result of retailers failing to ask the fundamental question: what are we intending to achieve in international markets? All too frequently the answer will have reference to what has been accomplished in the domestic market. International markets are seen as an extension of the domestic market. This is evident in the growth of international retailers. Markets which are considered to be appropriate are entered in the belief that they will not provide undue challenges. Thus, there are groups of markets that appeal to retailers from certain markets of origin. UK retailers often seek initial expansion in Ireland, Canada and the US. French retailers may look to Belgium; Australian retailers to New Zealand; German retailers to Austria. However, the very act of choosing such markets may be an abrogation of responsibility as far as market planning is concerned. Whether the market is psychically close or not, retailers must analyse the non-domestic market on its own terms.

This chapter discusses the issues which retailers should address when considering the international market environment. Retail marketing is an area where considerable development has occurred in the recent decades. Not only have academics come to consider the problems associated with marketing in the retail environment in specific, and retailer oriented terms, but retailers themselves have also recognized the importance of market planning and formalized, integrated, marketing activities. This chapter does not attempt to provide a complete analysis of marketing theory and practice with respect to retailing; it aims to provide a consideration of the international retail marketing dimension.

MARKET RESEARCH

Successful marketing demands an understanding of the consumer. Why does the consumer use this product rather than another product, this store rather than its commercial rival? Retailers will often fall at this first hurdle in the international environment as they make all kinds of assumptions which are fundamentally flawed.

Market research should be carried out by any company entering a market. Ultimately, however, many retailers decide that only operational experience in a market will really tell them what they need to know. Hence retailers will enter a market through acquisition, small scale growth, joint-ventures, concessions or simply exports in order to test the market. Retailers are in a unique position to gather data on a market once they are operating in it. Through the use of point of sale data and hence electronic systems, they are able monitor their sales and adjust product ranges responsively. Benetton must be considered a prime example of a company capable of a flexible response to customer needs around the world, by virtue of its swift information systems and flexible suppliers. This should not however suggest that other methods of initial analysis should be ignored or underutilized.

Retailers should carry out initial market evaluations within the framework discussed in part IV. They should be aware of the regulatory, economic, social, cultural and competitive environment in which they will be operating. They will need to be aware of those factors which are crucial to the success of the type of retail outlets they propose operating in the new environment and the applicability of the merchandise range they intend to stock.

Where they are intending to introduce a fascia with an existing format and merchandise range they will have to consider if they are prepared to make adjustments to meet the needs of the new market. Retailers will, therefore, need to carry out detailed research on the competitive environment within the market in which they propose operating. The indigenous retailers within the market, along with those international retailers who have already entered the market, will have defined the competitive environment. Incoming retailers may identify a gap in the market which they are well suited to fill. Conversely, the position which the incoming retailer occupies in the domestic market may already be occupied by other retail operations. If the incoming retailer is able to bring competitive efficiency to the market, this may not persuade the retailer to stay at home but it would certainly help to determine the strategy the retailer would need to employ on entering the market.

There are certain key factors which retailers should be encouraged to consider when moving into a market. These factors may be considered suitable for initial market scans. Terpstra (1993) has suggested key factors, ranging from per capita GNP to constitutional status of governing regime, as worthy of initial consideration. Such factors are useful in creating checklists and may, as Dichtl and Koglmayr (1986) have suggested, be enhanced by the use of rating scales. Different markets may be compared on scales which recognize opportunities from very good to very poor. Such checklists provide an opportunity to create overall assessments but they do not necessarily provide an analysis of those critical factors which will facilitate successful expansion in a market. Care should also be taken with the checklist system of market analysis that it does reflect the important factors which are required for success. Scanning, an initial process of market assessment, should be used to exclude markets and not choose markets.

There will be some market characteristics, or factors, that are easily quantified there will be others which must be considered which demand qualitative assessment.

Quantifiable factors are:

- per capita GDP/GNP
- service sector contribution to GDP/GNP
- levels of international trade
- population size
- population growth
- life expectancy
- rail track density

- road density

- cars per 1,000 inhabitants

- urbanization

- number of urban centres over critical size

- number of households

- household size

- educational standards

- consumption patterns

Qualitative factors are:

- external political relations

- stability of political structure

- regulatory environment

- bureaucratic efficiency

- cultural introversion or extroversion

- labour relations

- attitudes to retail employment

- corporate ethical stance

Those factors which are quantifiable may then be rated according to their significance. Road density may be considered more importance and hence given more weight than rail track density. These may produce scores which may be totalled. Overall, however, it may be the qualitive factors which ultimately determine choice of markets. Evaluation is eventually needed; therefore, experienced international retailers will be in a position to make better market decisions than retailers developing their first international operations.

SEGMENTATION

When considering a non-domestic market, retailers should analyse the market and identify the key determinants of consumer preferences, so that they may better understand the different consumer groupings which exist in that market. The retailer will need to segment the market.

There are many means by which a market may be segmented as table 15.1 shows. The retailer must bear in mind that the factors used should be relevant to their offering, they should be identifiable and measurable. Although it may offer a sophisticated description of a market, psychographic profiling may not be the most practical method for the retailer to analyse a new market. Other, fundamental factors may be important and more readily identifiable determinants. Segmentation provides a means of measuring and hence building an understanding of the market and thereby facilitating the targeting of a consumer group and the subsequent positioning of the retailer with respect to the competition.

A hypothetical example will show the processes that a retailer entering a market should follow. In figure 15.1, a retail clothing market has been segmented on the

Table 15.1 Segmentation criteria

Geographic

Global region:	Asia, Europe, North America, South, America
Country size:	Under 10 million, 10–49 million, 50–99 million, 100 million plus
Country region:	Chubu, Hokkaido, Kantu, Kyushu, Shikoku, Tohoku
Urbanization:	Urban, suburban, rural
Climate:	Warm temperate, cold temperate, tropical

Demographic

Age:	0–4, 5–9, 10–14, 15–19, 20–24, 25–29, 30–34, 35–39, 40–44, 45–49, 50–54, 55–59, 60–64, 65–69, 70–74, 75–79, 80–84, 85+
Gender:	Female, male
Religion:	Bhuddist, Catholic, Episcopalian, Hindu, Jewish, Muslim, Protestant
Race:	Caucasian, Negro, Oriental
Nation:	Australian, French, Japanese, Malayan
Household size:	1, 2–3, 4–5, 5–7, 7+
Income:	Under DM 20,000, DM 20,000–39,000, DM 40,000–59,000, DM 60,000–89,000, DM 90,000–19,000, DM 120,000 plus
Disposable income:	Low, medium, high
Education:	Primary, secondary, tertiary
Social class:	Upper, upper-middle, middle-middle, lower-middle, upper-lower, lower-lower
Employment class:	A, B, C1, C2, D, E

Psychographic

Personality:	Extrovert, introvert
Benefit orientation:	quality, price, durability, fashionable

Behaviourial

User status:	Regular user, irregular user, first time user, potential user, ex-user, non-user
Usage:	Heavy, medium, light
Loyalty:	Very loyal, switcher, non-loyal
Occasions:	Birthdays, weddings, funerals

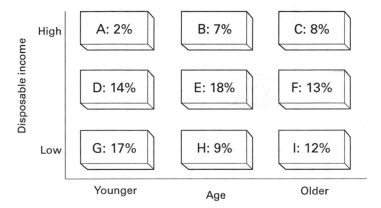

Figure 15.1 Segmentation

basis of disposable income and age. The retail operation appraising the market considers that this breakdown is the best available and that it accurately reflects the clothing market. Each segment is described in terms of the percentage of the population who fall into each segment. There are relatively few individuals in segment A as might be expected, although a large group of the population fall into segment E. Consumers in each segment will look for certain benefits on the basis of their age and disposable income. Consumers in segment C are prepared to pay relatively high prices for goods, although the goods must offer value for money and provide the consumer with an acceptable classic or traditional styling. In group D, consumers are fashion conscious but they are constrained as far as price is concerned. Most of these consumers do not have many commitments and many are earning full-time wages for the first time. They may share many of the fashion values of consumers in segment A, but they do not have the income to make purchases at the specialist high fashion shops that are favoured by members of their age group with high disposable incomes. This overall analysis may be very similar to the market encountered domestically by the retailer.

TARGETING

Having segmented a market, a retailer must decide which segment, or segments, it would be appropriate to target. Some retailers may wish to target all segments in the market. This might be achieved through offering a wide range of goods in different styles and at different price levels, or a middle market option which is acceptable to a majority of consumers at some time, especially in undifferentiated product areas. Otherwise, retailers might wish to target a number of segments. In figure 15.1, 38 per cent of the population fall into the low disposable income segments. This might encourage a retailer to offer a range of low price goods acceptable to a wide variety of age groups. More specifically, a retailer may prefer

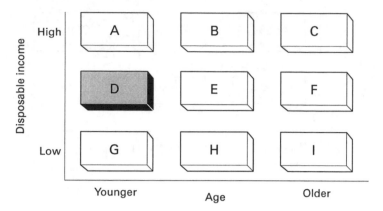

Figure 15.2 Targeting

to serve one segment with a distinct product range at a particular price level. The retailer may therefore opt for full market coverage, specialization, or concentration. There are examples of different strategies within international retailing. Some retailers, such as C&A, have positioned themselves in the middle of the market and therefore achieved a degree of full market coverage. However, many international retailers such as Benetton and The Gap have chosen a concentrated approach. Focusing on one segment has allowed some retailers to internationalize rapidly on the basis of a distinct image and narrow product range.

The choice of targeting strategy in the international environment will be strongly influenced by the operations of the company in the domestic or any existing non-domestic markets. In figure 15.2, segment D is highlighted. Developing the hypothetical example further, it is assumed that an incoming retail operation targets this segment in its domestic market. Its product range, price levels and other marketing mix elements are all focused on this market segment. The retailer hopes to transfer the domestic operation into the new market without undue alteration. The new market has similar social and economic characteristics to the retailer's domestic market, while cultural difference are not considered to be significant. This segment encompasses 14 per cent of customers in the new market, which is considered large enough to justify market entry. The retailer has experience offering reasonably priced merchandise in fashion conscious styles to this age group. Many of the company's products are commercial adaptations of more expensive designer clothes, which the company has shown itself capable of getting into its store quickly as a result of the close relationship the company has with its suppliers.

Retailer's targeting decisions should also take account of indigenous and international operators in the new market. If the segment which is attractive to the company is already served by a number of fascias, the company will either have to pay particular attention to certain marketing mix elements or, at the other extreme, avoid market entry altogether.

15.1 Colours

Price cutting is not the first message that customers receive when they think of Benetton, the Italian based but globally attractive clothing company. However, a 3 year price cutting exercise bore fruit for the company in 1996 when it announced an increase of profits for 1995.

The company's operating profit in 1995 was a healthy L444bn compared with L389bn in 1994. Profits had fallen as world wide demand had decreased. This saw the demise of some competitors but Benetton's price cutting exercise led to a 5.4 per cent increase in turnover to L2,940bn on consolidated sales and a 7.6 per cent increase of sales in the European and Asian market.

Source: Hill, 1996.

POSITIONING

Once the retailer has decided which segment or segments it wishes to target, it must communicate with the new market, informing consumers in that market what it stands for. As Kotler (1988, p. 308) has noted:

> Positioning is the act of designing the company's image and value offer so that the segment's customers understand and appreciate what the company stands for in relation to its competitors.

The incoming retailer must find a place in the minds of its potential customers, differentiating itself from its competitors. Some retailers may begin with an advantage that the market already accurately perceives what it represents. Benetton is a global brand. Its offering appeals to a global segment. On entering a new market, customers will be aware of what the company represents. In contrast, other stores may have less distinct images, or images which are easily misinterpreted. When Carrefour entered the UK market it did not have a distinct image other than it was a hypermarket operator. Hypermarkets were seen as challenging. The company therefore had to overcome negative perceptions associated with its format, as well as position itself in a market which was not familiar with the company's image. The company eventually sold its stores. Other retailers will find that they have an image that is different from their domestic image. The middle market Marks & Spencer operation in the UK has had a more up market image in European markets when it has opened stores. In Spain, the opening of the store was considered to be a fashion event.

Retailers will have difficulty positioning themselves in non-domestic operations if they fail to understand the nature of their operation. It is very easy for retailers that have operated for some time in their domestic market to become complaisant

15.2 Here, There and Everywhere

The Tengelmann group has achieved an impressive international standing. It was the largest retail enterprise in the EU in 1991–2, with a turnover of ECU22.8bn.

By 1991, 55.7 per cent of the group's turnover was from markets outside Germany. However, over the next two years this share declined, so that by 1993 only 50.3 per cent of turnover was non-domestic.

Operating in different markets has its advantages because the individual company may be protected from some of the ups and downs of individual markets. However, operating large chains of retail outlets may produce major headaches for those who must maintain a sound market position. One of the reasons that Tengelmann's international sales has fallen is the performance of the group's A&P operation in the US. A&P accounts for around 20 per cent of group turnover, but sales have not been as strong as they were previously. In February 1993, the company recorded a 9.5 per cent drop in sales. Annual turnover for 1992–3 stood at US$10.5bn.

A&P has, therefore, undergone a period of change. By the middle of 1993 the number of stores had been reduced to 1,193. The company has found it necessary to close fifty-six in the previous 12 months. This was against an opening programme of eleven stores and 102 refurbishments. These changes were also to have an impact on the number of people employed by A&P. The workforce was reduced by 4,600 to around 90,000. At the same time, the group strengthened its market presence in the Atlanta region with the acquisition of forty-eight Big Star outlets.

The company, however, has not lost confidence in the A&P name. In the Netherlands, it has decided to convert its Hermans operation to A&P, and is continuing to develop its A&P own brand products in the European market-place.

The company was also experiencing problems in Austria. Although sales had increased by 10 per cent in the year 1991–2, they rose by only 2.5 per cent in the following year. The company would like to expand its operation in the market but recent moves to acquire the Familia operation and approaches to Meinl were not successful.

Interestingly, the change in the balance of domestic and international turnover has also in part been the product of expansion opportunities in the old East Germany. Tengelmann, like other German retailers, suddenly found that there considerable marketing opportunities within their expanded home market.

Source: Euromonitor, 1996.

15.3 Africa

International retailers depend on international and domestic suppliers. Internationalization will only occur where supplies will be guaranteed. The importance of strong locally based suppliers is particularly important in fresh food retailing.

The recent expansion by the French company Danone, one of the largest food groups in the world, into the South African market is a further indicator of the restructuring which is occurring in that market and the distribution developments which are occurring.

Danone launched in 1996 a joint-venture with Clover, a local dairy operation. The joint-venture involves the acquisition by Danone of a 33 per cent share in Clover. As a result of the venture, Danone will produce value-added products which will be specifically targeted at higher income groups living in the metropolitan environment.

Danone sees Johannesburg as the ideal base from which to launch a drive into African markets. The African consumer, however, is very brand loyal and Clover, with a 33 per cent share of the dairy market in South Africa, is seen as a suitable vehicle for market penetration.

Danone already has experience of the Latin American market and will bring its experience to the South African market.

Source: Ashurst, 1996.

about their operation and its market positioning. Internationalization is often a shock to the collective company psyche. Non-domestic markets challenge assumptions built up in the domestic market. Therefore, it is often companies who have a focused strategy and which are of relatively recent origin who are most successful in internationalizing their operation. It is not surprising to find certain niche operations in Treadgold's (1988) world powers cluster, as McGoldrick and Ho (1992, p. 61) have noted:

> A major challenge for the 'cross-border' retailer is to identify and adopt the most appropriate positioning within other national markets. Some retail formats, especially in specialized niches, have been exported very successfully.

In the hypothetical example so far discussed in this chapter, the incoming retailer has decided to address a single market segment, which is large enough to support a chain of stores and which is not currently served by the existing operators in the market. However, after opening stores in the market, the retailer finds that it has not appropriately positioned its fascia (x) as far as the consumers in the market are concerned (see figure 15.3). While the retailer may have successfully positioned itself in its domestic market, in the non-domestic market the fascia is

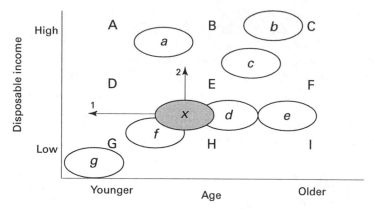

Figure 15.3 Positioning

perceived as appealing to an older age group, and slightly more down-market than it had intended. Its position in the new market also brings the incoming retailer into closer competition with two indigenous retailers (d and f). This retailer will there-fore have to reposition itself through communicating with its customer group. This will entail various adjustments in the marketing mix.

The original failure to position properly in the new market may be the result of company or market factors. The company may have failed operationally to distrib-ute its range of goods quickly enough in the new market, unfamiliar as it is with international operations. The market may also be particularly fashion oriented in a way that the domestic market is not, so that the company's product range may appear 'dowdy' to its target market and associated with an older age group.

Retailers must convey certain messages to the new market. They must educate the market in respect of the benefits that the operation brings. The benefit might be price, quality or style. The benefit may be relative to the benefits offered by existing retailers: lower price, higher quality, more style. In figure 15.3, the fascia represented by position x, will have to emphasize its relative fashion orientation relative to retailers d and f, its quality relative to retailer g, and its price conscious-ness relative to a.

A retailer that has not positioned itself properly may be guilty of one of three positioning mistakes. It may have underpositioned its fascia, by failing to commu-nicate with the market. This may be the result of too strong a belief in the retail brand image. The retailer may have overpositioned itself so that it is loosing potential sales in segments that it might be able to serve. The retailer might achieve confused positioning so that the operation is seen in one light by some consumers and in a very different light by others.

McGoldrick and Blair (1995) have shown that retail operations such as C&A and Marks & Spencer may be perceived very differently against the competition in markets such as Strasbourg (France), Chester (England) and Hong Kong. In Chester, Marks & Spencer's reputation for quality for fashion was good, in Hong

15.4 Running for the Red Light

While Meat Loaf might invite us to go South of the Border and get some Tequila, Mexican consumers are keen to go North of the Border and get some shopping done.

In Arizona, in towns such as Sierra Vista, which sits just North across the border from Mexico, cross-border traffic is an essential commercial reality for some stores. Mass-market retailers such as Wal-mart and Payless Shoes, rely heavily on cross-border traffic, to the extent that they would not be there if it was not for the Mexican consumer.

In Arizona, illegal immigration and the increasingly Spanish nature of every day life is of considerable concern to some sections of the community, who, during the 1996 Republican primaries, were attracted by the 'America first' sentiments of candidates such as Pat Buchanan. However, for many retail outlets the message is very different and they are still prepared to say 'welcome to the neighbourhood'.

Source: Waldmeir, 1996.

Kong its reputation for fashion was not as strong. In Strasbourg C&A was seen as offering cheaper merchandise, in Chester customer perceptions did not suggest such low prices.

THE MARKETING MIX

The question is almost standard in examinations, what are the marketing mix elements? The answer is equally standard, the 4Ps: Product, Price, Place, Promotion. This draws on McCarthy's (1964) work. However, marketing was developed in a context of large manufacturing operations and the marketing mix elements were well suited to that orientation. However, considerable work has been carried out on services marketing in recent years and this has suggested that a new set of mix elements need to be considered in the service context. For example, McGoldrick (1990) has suggested that seven elements need to be considered: product range, product image, consumer franchise, shelf price, distribution, shelving, advertising. Walters (1988) has suggested that the retail marketing mix should be discussed in terms of product characteristics, price considerations, customer service, store location, facilities, institutional profile/image, in-store ambience, design and visual merchandising, and consumer communication. Many of these elements may be considered within McCarthy's four elements although they highlight the need to stress certain aspects of the basic marketing mix configuration. The marketing mix elements discussed below are a recognition of the need to adapt the marketing mix to both the retail and international environment.

Image

One interpretation of retail internationalization, as Brown and Burt (1992, p. 81) have noted:

> is that based on the transfer of a retail brand, with its associated image for consumers, across national borders.

Image is crucial to the successful internationalization of a retail format. Many retailers have successfully built a consumer franchise by shifting loyalty away from manufacturer brands to retail stores. Such retailers have built up their own brand products as a rival to manufacturers products on the basis of both price and quality. In consequence, these retailers have also built product ranges which appeal to their customers and which provide them with the ability to convey a distinct message to the market in which they operate. The image they have thereby created has been an important tool in their international development.

The development of a strong image with international appeal may prove an important marketing advantage: however, many retailers have not shown themselves capable of developing such advantages. Some retailers are able to internationalize their domestic fascias, others are not. Where their existing fascia will not possess a distinct image in the international market retailers should consider either acquiring a local fascia or developing a new fascia for the international market. Boots, the UK based pharmaceuticles company and retailer has divested itself of its once extensive international operations. The Boots fascia did not posses a distinct image in the international market. However, the company also experimented with the Sephora chain in France which focused on a relatively narrow product range.

Product range

Product ranges will need to be adjusted slightly for any market. However, most retailers will seek to retain their merchandise range as much as possible. In 1988, a group of seventy-four of the largest UK retailers were asked if their European merchandise ranges would primarily be determined by local conditions only 33 per cent said that they would. Just over half (51 per cent) said that they would seek to retain at least a broadly similar merchandise offering to their UK operations (Alexander, 1989).

The domestic experience will be influential in determining the international product range. Nevertheless, retailers must remain flexible and sensitive to local needs. As retailers extend their operation into new markets, they will find that they have to adjust their ranges for many different reasons. They may find that the styles acceptable in some markets would not be acceptable elsewhere. Laura Ashley has built its international operation on that 'quintessentially English look' but the quaint floral pattern image of the 1970s has become less relevant in the company's domestic market where clothes product ranges were adapted in the 1980s to encompass a working woman theme. Elsewhere, however, the softer image of

15.5 Turning Japanese

With Brooks Brothers, that most American of menswear retailers, in British hands (Marks & Spencer) and the typically British Acquascutum, owned by the Japanese (Renown), consumers around the world may be buying national styles but ultimately they may not be buying from retailers from that market.

If there is one retail operation which summons up images of rural England, it must be Laura Ashley. Despite the fact that for many years much of the company's operation and production was based in Mid-Wales, the company sold its English image hard. The company built its success on the Englishness of its products and the marketable value of that image has taken the company into markets such as the US, where there are over 150 outlets, Japan, where there are more than thirty outlets and Australia where the company has over twenty outlets.

The company has, however, taken on a much more international air in recent years. In 1990, following years of rapid development, the company began to show the strains associated with growth, to the extent that 15 per cent of the business was sold to the Japanese retailer Aeon, who valued the strong market value of the product.

American ingenuity and management skill followed Japanese money, so that by April 1996, there was an American chief executive, Ann Iverson, who was appointed in 1995, and an American chairman John Thornton, appointed 1996. Thornton, co-head of investment banking for Goldman Sachs in Europe is also a Director of the Ford Motor Company, and you don't get much more quintessentially American than that.

Source: Hall, 1996; CIG, 1994.

country life and motherhood has allowed the company to retain an image and sell products that would be unacceptable to many domestic customers. In the US, the company generates valuable sales volume from its matching mother and child clothing, a concept that the domestic customer would not cherish. That which is fashionable in one market may not be fashionable in another market.

Format

As is the case with merchandise, so with format; retailers will seek to retain those forms with which they are familiar, when they internationalise. Only 27 per cent of large UK companies surveyed in the run up to the SEM said that they would be primarily influenced by local conditions when introducing their format into the European market. 57 per cent said they would retain their UK format to a considerable degree (Alexander, 1989).

15.6 Hong Kong Garden

It would be difficult to describe Dairy Farm International, the food retailing operation owned by Jardine Matheson, the Singapore-listed company, as anything other than a company with dispersed international retail interests.

By 1994, the company had built an impressive array of international operations in Australia, China, Hong Kong, New Zealand, Singapore, Spain, Taiwan, and the UK. The company has bought into some well known trading fascias. In Hong Kong, it operates around 300 7-Eleven convenience stores. In the UK, it has a stake in the Kwik Save discount operation, and in New Zealand it owns Woolworth stores.

However, global expansion will also produce considerable problems when consumer needs are not being met. Some analysts would say this is what has happened to Dairy Farm. In 1994, Dairy Farm International secured profits of US$213.8m but in 1995, the figure had fallen to $135.2m. In 1996, Kleinwort Benson estimated profits in 1997 would not rise above $190m.

Market share in Australia and Spain slipped, according to Schroder Securities Asia, as a result of major restructuring. Franklins, the Australian arm of the operation has undergone a restructuring which has placed a far greater emphasis on fresh produce. In Spain, the Simago operation increased its sales volume but has likewise been undergoing considerable restructuring and store refurbishment.

Capital expenditure has risen at Dairy Farm, as the company puts in place the systems which are needed in the competitive market-place of the late 1990s. The company is improving its information technology systems. Also, the company is developing new logistics and distribution systems, in order to supply new store formats with improved product ranges.

Dairy Farm is based in Hong Kong. Strategically well placed in the growing South East Asia market, the company is expanding the 7-Eleven operation in China, which it entered in 1992.

Source: Lucas, 1996; CIG, 1994.

The format that a company employs, and the operational advantage that it gives the company through the benefits it delivers to the consumer, may be the main determinant of international expansion. The internationalizing retailer may find that advantages which are derived from an innovative format may cause considerable problems when introducing a new format into the non-domestic market. In such circumstances, the retailer will have to be aware of the planning implications of introducing its store format and the possible opposition that will be generated in the new market. When Costco entered the UK in the early 1990s, the indigenous retailers took legal action to stop the company operating from locations from which they were not able to locate in and which offered a cost advantage to the Costco operation. The format that the company utilized was a major operational feature.

The format the retailer operates in the new market will require access to extraneous facilities. A box-unit operator in a mall will be surrounded by other facilities which will service customer needs and provide a framework of operations. Other operators who do not wish to be constrained or by virtue of their operation are not suited to such an environment will have to provide facilities to the customer. The facilities that the consumer considers basic will vary from market to market.

The in-store ambience and design of a store may be a distinguishing feature of the operation. The Gap maintains a distinct image through the display of merchandise items. Other operators, such as the Body Shop with their refill service, create an atmosphere which helps to build and maintain a customer franchise. The format and in-store layout will be interpreted in the mind of the consumer. In the international market, retailers must be aware of the associations customers have and hence the messages that format design will convey. Customers will not wish to be unduly challenged by the operating procedures and format in the store, although they will want to be interested and in some cases involved in the service provision.

The McDonalds format is very much on the edge of the retail and restaurant definitions. It is a place to consume food and in that sense is a restaurant but the retail-like qualities of the dispensing of the food items is an example of the regimentation of the service experience which customers seek in many retail encounters. The success of the Woolworth operation and its international appeal was in great part built on the lack of social challenge which operating procedures set customers. Prices were set at limited points and merchandise was openly displayed. This contrasted with the more traditional shop atmosphere into which the Woolworth variety store operation was introduced. In a similar fashion, McDonalds is built on retail, over the counter, formulaic exchange relationships, while providing a product which is usually associated with a more overt service provision, which is often associated with uncertainty of role playing. The McDonalds customer does not peruse a wine list evaluating the relative appropriateness of a white Burgundy or a red Bordeaux in the context of the social setting and culinary experience to follow. McDonalds provides a set of limited options, in a defined setting, where the host culture, for the most part, is left at the door and a limited range of responses are required from customers and staff alike. Luxury goods retailers may trade on the basis of greater customer service staff interaction, but as a basis for internationalization it may be limited to only a few markets, customer groups and, thus, sites within those markets.

Price

Descriptions of the internationalization process often concentrate on companies which expand as a result of the format, merchandise and strong image. Price is a factor which is often ignored in such descriptions. This is not because price is an unimportant element within the retail marketing mix but because it is not readily comparable on an international level.

A price conscious retailer may deliver distinct benefits in international markets. This may be achieved through a basic retail format, such as that offered by discounters and warehouse clubs; it may be through experience in sourcing on a large scale; it may be though the reduction of service levels which are not essential in merchandise display. By such methods, retailers are able to reduce their operating costs. If the same retailers are also prepared to accept low margins, because they a confident their low prices will build high consumer traffic, then they are capable of having a major impact on indigenous retailers. Recent developments in the Canadian markets have seen incoming retailers offering lower prices to customers because they have accepted lower margins and have built their operations on cost advantages (Jones et al., 1994).

US retailers internationalizing in the Canadian environment may be able to assume certain pricing structures and retain their domestic pricing structure to a considerable degree: however, internationalization within less culturally, economically and socially similar markets may demand a major reappraisal of pricing points and positioning. In an economically less advanced market the price conscious retailer's offering may seem more up-market than it would in the domestic market. Thus Littlewoods' (UK) operation in St Petersberg will not have the same price message as it will in Liverpool. Likewise, Kmart has opened stores in the Czech Republic and in Slovakia. While its cost-reducing format and operations, along with its cost conscious building of merchandise range may make such locations feasible, outlets will not give the same pricing message as they would give in more advanced retail structures and economies.

Some companies are considered to charge higher prices outside their domestic markets. Marks & Spencer has been described in this way (Buckley, 1994) although research has shown that at least in the French and Hong Kong markets perceptions of pricing levels are the same as in the domestic (UK) market (McGoldrick and Blair, 1995). Comparisons of pricing arrangements must always be carefully qualified. Price, along with quality, is one determinant of value and arbitrary evaluations of price are in danger of ignoring the context in which prices are charged. Simple exchange rate calculations may seem a satisfactory way for tourists to calculate their expenditure, but indigenous consumers, because of their standard of living, may make very different calculations.

Location

Both in the domestic as well as the international environment, location issues are crucial. Retailers entering a new market should be aware that the perceptions they have of their companies location needs may have to be altered in the new environment.

Marks & Spencer has been, and remains, predominately a high street operation in the UK. When the company moved into Canada, however, the high street, was not necessarily the best option. The climate of Canada and hence the shopping habits which this has created demands a more protected environment wherever possible. Marks & Spencer had to come to terms with this new reality.

Retailers have usually built up a wealth of information on the locations they use in their domestic market by the time they move into the international environment. However, in the new environment they will face the prospect of the need for a relatively rapid store development programme in a market with which they are unfamiliar. There is a considerable danger that they will acquire inappropriate properties in this initial development phase which lead to poor trading results, a loss of confidence, a reduction in the store development programme and often a growing disillusionment with internationalization.

There is much to be said for initial internationalization activity to be considered an opportunity to learn about operating conditions. Retailers who enter a market through organic growth will not be able to run at greatest efficiency with only a limited number of stores, but they will be able to avoid some of the pitfalls of poor location decisions. A gradual roll out of units will allow the retailer to compare the success of different locations and the respective problems encountered.

Nevertheless, it is possible for retailers to learn from the mistakes they made in their home market when they were developing a chain of outlets. The Habitat operation in France developed a far more space efficient property portfolio than it had achieved in the UK. In the UK the financial pressures of early development had forced the company to make location decisions which were not entirely appropriate to the developing merchandise lines of the company. In France, with its established merchandise range it was able to operate a balanced portfolio with, for example, larger merchandise items being located in its large out of town stores where square footage prices were lower, and retain in its town centre operations a range of less space hungry items.

Distribution

The problems associated with the movement of goods to a retail outlet in the international market has the potential to render the international operation ineffective and unsuccessful. The nature of the distribution will depend on the company, its level of vertical integration, and its product range. Grocery retailers are particularly prone to serious problems if the distribution system is not efficient. They depend on a very swift turn over of goods and cannot afford unnecessary delays in the system. Thus, grocery retailers are more likely than other retailers, such as clothing retailers, to acquire an operation in the international environment before growing organically.

This is not to say however that clothing retailers are not vulnerable to distribution problems. Laura Ashley encountered considerable distribution problems in the US at the end of the 1980s, when its autumn range arrived months late in the US outlets. As a result of such distribution problems, the company entered into a joint arrangement with Federal Express. Federal Express helped Laura Ashley develop an efficient distribution system based at Laura Ashley's centre in Newtown in Mid-Wales. On the other hand, much of Benetton's success is due to its ability to use its distribution system to react quickly to the needs of franchise stores as consumer demand dictates a reappraisal of styles and colours within the merchandise range.

Both Laura Ashley and Benetton are closely involved in the production of the goods which appear in their stores. Laura Ashley has produced more goods in-house than has Benetton, a company which depends on a system of subcontractors. Where such subcontactors are traditionally based in one market tensions may appear when the operation internationalizes. Marks & Spencer encountered problems in Canada when its suppliers in that market did not develop the same relationship with the company as its British suppliers.

Promotion

Retailers have available to them vast amounts of information and many opportunities to promote their store and merchandise. They may favour major television campaigns promoting the store or a bundle of goods under the store banner. Equally, they may favour the targeting of particular groups in the locality in which they have an outlet. They may achieve considerable recognition through their involvement with the local community and a vast amount of publicity which has the distinct advantage of being free. They are able to promote their product through the presence of their outlets in malls, on hight streets in out of town locations. They have the opportunity to promote products in store with special signage and service staff advice and recommendations. In the international environment they will have to reconsider tried and tested methods of successful promotion.

On entering a new market, a retailer will be faced with relative ignorance. Some stores may be greeted with a barrage of publicity, as The Body Shop was when it entered the US market. This may, as was the case with the Body Shop, mean that the store does not have to engage in crippling advertising costs. However, many retailers may have to begin promotional campaigns which they have not engaged in before. They will have to position themselves in the market and advertising is one means by which they may achieve this. If they do not communicate their message in store customers may misinterpret low prices as poor quality rather than good value.

CONCLUSION

In the non-domestic market, retailers will encounter a new set of competitors and usually new customers perceptions. On entering a market, retailers must be aware of the competitive advantage that they believe they have, but also as, the operation is established, the new perceptions of the operation, as far as the consumers within that market are concerned.

Many of the issues and problems discussed in this chapter imply that the internationalizing retailer has adopted a global approach to its product development. That is, the retailer is attempting to replicate the same formula in a number of markets. This is only one option available to the retailer. The retailer may wish to adopt a multinational approach. In such circumstances, where the retailer operates distinct fascias in different markets, a tailored stance will be possible in a way which the global approach does not permit. The multinational approach may have involved acquisition which in itself will mean that the existing operation already has a market position. The international operation may wish to reposition the operation but many of the start-up issues will have been avoided. The overall international strategy adopted by a retailer will therefore have major implications for its marketing activities in individual markets.

QUESTIONS – DISCUSSION POINTS

1   Are international retailers able to assume that the position they occupy in the domestic market will be the same position they will occupy in international markets?

2   What weight should be given to qualitative as opposed to quantitative factors when evaluating international markets?

3   How important are indigenous retailers to an incoming retailer when targeting is considered?

4   Are niche retailers more likely to be successful in international markets than retailers who target a broad range of consumers?

5   What impact is internationalization likely to have on the way in which retailers manage the marketing mix?

REFERENCES

Alexander, N., (1989) The Internal Market of 1992: Attitudes of Leading Retailers, *Retail and Distribution Management*, Vol. 17, No. 1, pp. 13–15.

Ashurst, M., (1996) Danone, *Investing in South Africa, Financial Times*, 28 March, p. VII.

Brown, S., and Burt, S., (1992) Conclusion – Retail Internationalisation: Past Imperfect, Future Imperative, *European Journal of Marketing*, Vol. 26, No. 8/9, pp. 80–4.

Buckley, N., (1994) Food for thought, *Financial Times*, 10 November.

CIG, (1994) *Cross-Border Retailing in Europe*, Corporate Intelligence Group, London.

Dichtl, E., and Koglmayr, H., (1986) Country Risk Ratings, *Management International Review*, Vol. 26, No. 4.

Euromonitor, (1996) Tengelmann Group, *Retail Euromonitor International*, London, January.

Hall, W., (1996) Thornton to chair Laura Ashley, *Financial Times*, 22 March, p. 13.

Hill, A., (1996) Benetton benefits from price cuts, *Financial Times*, 29 March, p. 28.

Jones, K., Evans, W., and Smith C., (1994) *New Formats in the Canadian Retail Economy*, Centre for the Study of Commercial Activity, Ryerson Polytechnic University, Toronto.

Kotler, P., (1988) *Marketing Management*, 6th edition, Prentice-Hall, Englewood Cliffs, NJ.

Lucas, L., (1996) Dairy Farm International hit by competition, *Financial Times*, 28 March, p. 30.

McCarthy, E., (1964) *Basic Marketing: A Managerial Approach*, Homewood, Ill, Irwin.

McGoldrick, P., (1990) *Retail Marketing*, McGraw-Hill, London.

McGoldrick, P., and Ho, S., (1992) International Positioning: Japanese Department Stores in Hong Kong, *European Journal of Marketing*, Vol. 26, No. 8/9, pp. 61–73.

McGoldrick, P., and Blair, D., (1995) International Market Appraisal and Positioning, *International Retailing: Trends and Strategy*, Pitman, London, pp. 168–190.

Terpstra, V., (1993) *Comparative Analysis for International Marketing*, Allyn & Bacon, Boston, p. 146.

Treadgold, A., (1988) Retailing Without Frontiers, *Retail and Distribution Management*, Vol. 16, No. 6, pp. 8–12.

Waldmeir, P., (1996) Immigration becomes hot election issue, *Financial Times*, 28 February, p. 5.

Walters, D., (1988) *Strategic Retail Management*, Prentice Hall, Hemel Hempstead.

Conclusion

Conclusion

▌ OBJECTIVES ▌

This chapter provides some concluding remarks on retail internationalization.

INTRODUCTION

International retailing has developed rapidly in recent years. The study of international retailing has developed in its wake. By the late 1990s, international retailing had become an important strategic option for the world's leading, largest and most innovative retailers. In the academic environment, it has become a well-established aspect of retail management studies. The process of internationalization has however been under way for some time but is, in great part, still only at a relatively early stage of its latest cycle of development. Academic study had started to provide some frameworks for further study but there is much work to be carried out.

DISCUSSION

International retail activity is a rapidly developing aspect of the global economy. Statements made about international retailing today will have to be qualified remarkably quickly. Nevertheless, there are certain fundamentals which may be recognized.

In the chapters above, the work of a large number of academics and commentators is described and discussed. Some of the work described has already stood the test of time and remains a valid contribution to this area of study. Hollander's (1970) work stands out as an example of such a valuable contribution. Many of the other contributions referred to here have been the product of the relatively recent past. Work carried out in the years after 1985 are particularly prominent in this book. The last dozen years has seen an explosion of research, comment and debate. In time, these contributions will be refined, refuted or even rejected; few will be accepted in their entirety in the new contexts in which international retailing is analysed.

One of the attractions yet, in counter balance, one of the frustrations of addressing the issue of retailing in the late 1990s, is the knowledge that very much is likely to change, both in terms of the activity itself but also in terms of a general understanding of the activity. It is a subject area which requires constant reassessment.

That having been said, it is also true to say that the study of retailing has reached a stage in its development where certain fundamentals have been established, or at the very least exposed, as issues worthy of further consideration. This book has discussed these themes such as the direction of international growth, the motivations which stimulate international activity, operationalization issues of strategy and marketing and the market characteristics which retailers encounter. These themes reflect those issues considered worthy of detailed consideration by academics working in this area in Asia, Australasia, Europe and North America. They reflect also the experience of international retailers and their current concerns.

In the opening decade of the twenty-first century, these themes will be supplemented by other themes which will either grow out of those already partially explored or develop from original perspectives. Again, this will reflect the concerns and activities of international retailers. At the end of the twentieth century, information and the communication of information through new technology is a live issue. Claims are made that international communication computer to computer will revolutionize retailing. A company based in Tokyo will be able to supply a customer based in Rome on the basis of an order initiated at a computer terminal, where a global mall of stores is represented. This, some would argue, will add a totally new dimension to international retail operations. If this were to occur on any scale the answer would be, in some senses yes, in other senses no. Yes, the method of ordering might be new, but, no, the system is an old one. Orders still have to be physically delivered no matter how the ordering occurs, and Hollander (1970) as was noted in chapter 3, shows that direct selling has been used in global markets for many years.

CONCLUSION

While it may appear a little prosaic to conclude with a warning that there is nothing new under the sun, it is also worth bearing in mind that international retailers have often fallen foul of a belief in innovation where it does not exist. The international process has for many retailers shown them, amongst other things, that they are often underaware of the problems and strengths they possess in the domestic market. Internationalization, to the aware retailer, should be neither an escape from the constraints of the domestic market nor a reluctant exercise to be undertaken when all else has been explored in the domestic market. Internationalization should occur where a retailer has real benefits, whether merchandise or operationally based, to offer a new market. Retailers are better placed to do that when they appreciate what they have done, and are capable of doing, in the markets with which they are familiar. It is often the relatively new retailers who are capable of taking up the international challenge because they have recently had to address their fundamental strengths and weaknesses; it is the older, more well established operations, who face the greatest challenge, because it is those operations who have for too long taken for granted their place in their domestic market. For the older, larger operations, within which strategic vision and direction is lacking, the internationalization of the retail environment is the greatest challenge and threat. The autochthonic dinosaurs of retailing will increasingly have to face the proactive innovators of the global market-place.

REVIEW QUESTIONS – CONCLUDING DISCUSSION POINTS

1   Are international retailers the most dynamic force within retailing today, or will small retailers, who emerge from markets around the world always prove to be the most innovative force in retailing?

2   Will electronic trading on such systems as the internet develop international retailing in a new and dynamic way?

3   Will international retailers increasingly address the needs of less developed countries in the future?

4   Are Pacific Rim retailers likely to be the dominant international retail force in the first decade of the twenty-first century? Will the Pacific Rim prove to be the most attractive market?

REFERENCE

Hollander, S., (1970) *Multinational Retailing*, Michigan State University, East Lancing, MI.

Glossary

ambitious international retailer A retailer who aggressively addresses opportunities in non-domestic markets. Such retailers are already experienced international operators.

autochthonic retailer A retailer who has limited international appeal and has growth opportunities in the domestic market.

border-hopping The process by which retailers expand into geographically close markets.

buying alliance *see* strategic retail alliance.

cautious international retailer A retail company with some international exposure but is not yet an experienced international operator.

cross-border expansion This term is often used to describe an international move: it is, however, usually used in a context of geographically proximate markets.

cultural proximity The relationship between two markets which have a high level of cultural similarity.

expansive retailer A retailer who has international appeal and has exhausted growth opportunities in the domestic market.

global retailer This term has different meanings, depending on how and when it is used. (1) When a retailer has a spread of operations in markets around the world. (2) When a retailer does not modify, in any significant manner, its operations in the global market-place.

globalization This term may refer to retail structure, where there is considered to be the development of a global retail structure. This term may also refer to a retailer who is achieving, rather than has achieved, a considerable international presence, since the phrase implies a process.

host market The market into which a retailer expands. Host markets may also be the domestic market of other international operations: however, many markets with less developed retail structures are primarily host markets.

internationalization The process by which international retailing occurs (see chapter 2).

isoagora Lines on a map which join points of equal retail structural development.

market of destination The market into which a retailer expands. Markets of destination may also be the domestic market of other international operations, however, many markets with less developed retail structures are primarily markets of destination.

market of origin The market out of which a retailer expands. Markets of origin may also be the market of destination for other international operations. Markets of origin may appeal to retailers who are attracted by developed markets which provide an operational infrastructure.

multinational retailer This term should be used carefully. It has different meanings, depending on how it is used. (1) When the retailer has operations in a few international markets. (2) When a retailer operates differently in each or a group of international markets.

proactive internationalization This is the process whereby a retailer actively seeks opportunities in the international market-place primarily as the result of the identification of opportunities in non-domestic markets. Here pull rather than push factors are more important (*see* reactive internationalization; pull factors; push factors).

proactive retailer A retailer who has international appeal and has growth opportunities in the domestic market.

psychological proximity The relationship between two markets, where there is a high level of psychological similarity. This may be the product of cultural proximity, a phrase which is often considered to be synonymous, but does not imply the same variety of factors as the phrase psychological proximity.

pull factors Those influences which encourage a retailer to operate in a non-domestic market.

push factors Those influences which encourage a retailer to move out from the domestic market into the international market place.

reactive internationalization The process whereby a retailer is forced into the international market-place through the lack of opportunity in the domestic market. Here push rather than pull factors are more important (*see* proactive internationalization; pull factors; push factors).

reactive retailer A retailer who has limited international appeal and has exhausted growth opportunities in the domestic market.

reluctant international retailer A retailer who is fundamentally a national operator and who becomes involved with international expansion in the absence of opportunities in the domestic market.

regionalization   The development of a retail structure within a global region such as Europe.

retail structure   The aggregate form retailing takes within a defined market.

saturation   A state of development whereby there is the lack of growth opportunities in a market. This may be the product of regulation or competition.

strategic retail alliance   Retailers in different markets may come together to form an alliance. This is often described as a buying alliance, and joint purchasing activity may be an element of the relationship. However, such relations may be better seen as a forum for the exchange of information, or a defensive response to the development of international operations.

transnational retailer   A retailer who attempts to reconcile the organizational advantages of adopting a global (*see* global retailer, definition (2)) approach to operations, while remaining responsive to local needs.

Boxed Illustrations – Title References

Message in a Bottle – Police, A & M, 1979

Promises – Paris Red, Colombia, 1993

Papa Don't Preach – Madonna, Sire, 1986

What in the World's Come Over You? – Scott, J., Top Rank, 1960

Norwegian Wood – Beatles, Northern Songs Ltd, 1965

Young Americans – Bowie, D., RCA, 1975

Handyman – James, J., MGM, 1960

All Around the World – Jam, Polydor, 1977

Waking Up the Neighbours – Adams, B., A & M, 1991

American Pie – McClean, D., United Artists, 1972

I'm a Tiger – Lulu, Colombia, 1968

High Hopes – Sinatra, F., Capitol, 1959

Identity – X-Ray Spex, EMI, 1978

Taxman – Beatles, Northern Songs Ltd, 1966

Deutscher Girls – Ant, A., Ego, 1982

Champagne Supernova – Oasis, Creation Records, 1995

Telling Tales – Lightening Seeds, Epic, 1994

China – Amos, T., East West, 1992

Breaking-up is Hard to Do – Sedaka, N., RCA, 1962

Scenes from an Italian Restaurant – Joel, B., CBS, 1977

Starting Over – Lennon, J., Geffen, 1980

Baker Street – Rafferty, G., United Artists, 1978

Colours – Donovan, Pye, 1965

Here, There and Everywhere – Harris, E., Reprise, 1976

Africa – Toto, CBS, 1983

Running for the Red Light – Loaf, M., Virgin, 1995

Turning Japanese – Vapors, United Artists, 1980

Hong Kong Garden – Siouxsie and the Banshees, Polydor, 1978

Index